# A Wilderness of Words

For Jerry,
    perceptive poet,
    talented teacher,
    fantastic friend,
        with very best wishes,

                Ted

# A Wilderness
## of
## Words

Closure and Disclosure
in Conrad's Short Fiction

Ted Billy

Texas Tech University Press

This book was set in Humanist BT and President and printed on acid-free paper that meets the guidelines for permanence and durability of the Committee on Production Guidelines for Book Longevity of the Council on Library Resources. ∞

Design by Rob Neatherlin


Printed and manufactured in the United States


Library of Congress Cataloging-in-Publication Data
     Billy, Theodore.
          A wildernesss of words : closure and disclosure in Conrad's
     short fiction / Ted Billy.
               p.   cm.
          Includes bibliographical references (p.      ) and index.
          ISBN 0-89672-389-5 (cloth : alk. paper)
          1. Conrad, Joseph, 1857–1924—Criticism and interpretation.
     2. Conrad, Joseph, 1857–1924—Technique.  3. Closure (Rhetoric)
     4. Short story.  I. Title.
     PR6005.04Z5629   1997
     823'.912—dc21                                    97-24388
                                                      CIP


          97 98 99 00 01 02 03 04 05 / 9 8 7 6 5 4 3 2 1



Texas Tech University Press
Box 41037
Lubbock, Texas 79409-1037 USA
800-832-4042
ttup@ttu.edu

To my sister, Esther,

and

to the memory of

William Bysshe Stein

There never had been such a wonderful man as Mr. Stein.

—*Lord Jim*

Worthy of my undying regard.

—*The Shadow Line*

# Contents

# Acknowledgments

I am indebted to the University of Delaware for giving me a research grant that allowed me to begin this study several years ago. I am also grateful to Saint Mary's College, which provided me with a sabbatical leave that enabled me to complete this work. Three valuable editorial assistants helped me at critical stages of this project: Dorita Forehand, who tirelessly accumulated much of the source material noted in my list of works cited; David Connolly, whose perspicacity in evaluating Conrad's fiction and Conradian criticism often put my own insights to shame; and Cora Sandberg, whose painstaking work was invaluable in putting this book into its final form. I am also thankful to David Leon Higdon, Zack Bowen, Leonard Orr, Lisa and Daniel Fraustino, and Milena and Richard Davison for their constant support of my Conradian endeavors. In addition, I am grateful for the wise counsel generously provided by Arnold Davidson, Brian Shaffer, and Ray Stevens. John Nizalowski helped me considerably with perceptive commentary on the early versions of many of the chapters that follow. Judith Keeling and Fran Kennedy, my editors at Texas Tech University Press, provided me with sound advice and staunch support. I also received judicious counsel from the anonymous outside readers, to whom I am endebted. But my greatest debt of gratitude is to the late William Bysshe Stein, "quite an original genius," as Melville would say, who inspired this study and whose uncompromising spirit continues to inspire me in my pedagogical and scholarly enterprises.

# Abbreviations

All parenthetical page references to Conrad's works (excepting *Heart of Darkness, Lord Jim,* and *The Nigger of the "Narcissus"*) pertain to the Canterbury Edition of *The Complete Works of Joseph Conrad* (Garden City, N.Y.: Doubleday, Page, 1924). For convenience, I have abbreviated the titles as follows:

| | |
|---|---|
| C | *Chance* |
| HD | *Heart of Darkness,* ed. Robert Kimbrough, 3d ed., Norton Critical Edition (New York: Norton, 1988). |
| I | *The Inheritors* (Conrad and Ford) |
| LJ | *Lord Jim,* ed. Thomas C. Moser, Norton Critical Edition (New York: Norton, 1968). |
| NLL | *Notes on Life and Letters* |
| NN | *The Nigger of the "Narcissus,"* ed. Robert Kimbrough, Norton Critical Edition (New York: Norton, 1979). |
| OI | *An Outcast of the Islands* |
| PR | *A Personal Record* |
| SA | *The Secret Agent* |
| SL | *The Shadow Line* |
| SS | *A Set of Six* |
| T | *Typhoon and Other Stories* |
| TH | *Tales of Hearsay* |
| TLS | *'Twixt Land and Sea* |
| TU | *Tales of Unrest* |
| UWE | *Under Western Eyes* |
| V | *Victory* |
| WT | *Within the Tides* |
| Y | *Youth—A Narrative; and Two Other Stories* |

I have also abbreviated the titles of the following frequently cited texts:

| | |
|---|---|
| BCM | Bernard C. Meyer, *Joseph Conrad: A Psychoanalytical Biography* (Princeton, N.J.: Princeton University Press, 1970). |
| CL | Frederick R. Karl and Laurence Davies, eds., *The Collected Letters of Joseph Conrad,* 4 vols. (Cambridge: Cambridge University Press, 1983–90). |
| FRK | Frederick R. Karl, *Joseph Conrad: The Three Lives* (New York: Farrar, Straus and Giroux, 1979). |

*IW*   Ian Watt, *Conrad in the Nineteenth Century* (Berkeley and Los
      Angeles: University of California Press, 1979).
*LG*   Lawrence Graver, *Conrad's Short Fiction* (Berkeley and Los
      Angeles: University of California Press, 1969).
*WWB*  William W. Bonney, *Thorns and Arabesques: Contexts for
      Conrad's Fiction* (Baltimore: Johns Hopkins University Press,
      1980).
*ZN*   Zdzisław Najder, *Joseph Conrad: A Chronicle* (New Brunswick,
      N.J.: Rutgers University Press, 1983).

# Prelude
## The Language of Fiction
## and the Fiction of Language

One does one's work first and theorises about it afterwards. It is a very amusing and egotistical occupation of no use whatever to any one and just as likely as not to lead to false conclusions.
—Conrad, author's note to *Tales of Unrest*

Joseph Conrad, perhaps the last Victorian and the first modernist, approached the art of fiction from the unique perspective of a multilingual cosmopolitan who had become acquainted with English only in his adulthood. He began writing fiction with an awareness of the insubstantiality of language, yet from the outset of his artistic apprenticeship to the twilight of his literary career, Conrad maintained his linguistic skepticism together with an abiding fascination for the enchantment of words.[1] Frequently, he seemed as suspicious of the capacity of language to encompass experience as he was doubtful of his own imaginative productivity.[2] As a creative writer, he relied extensively on the mental recreation of memories gleaned from his seafaring experiences to succeed in his second profession.[3] Nevertheless, he often disdained the notion that words can capture or denote reality, for Conrad recognized too well the gulf separating word from thing to place his wholehearted trust in arbitrary and provisional verbal counters, the word-glorifying preface to *The Nigger of the "Narcissus"* notwithstanding.[4] This may explain, in part, his penchant for superlative negations (e.g., *unspeakable, unfathomable, imponderable, impenetrable*), which prompted F. R. Leavis to fitful gusts of exasperation. Viewing language as a pseudo-reality, an irresistibly ensnaring illusion that dictates rather than interprets human action, Conrad depicts Western culture as goal- and word-oriented, and betrayed by both.[5] Using words to emphasize the duplicities of language, he seems to engage in what postmodern critics might call a deconstruction of the art of fiction.

Conrad's ambivalent attitude toward language originated during his formative years in his partitioned homeland.[6] Poland in the mid-nineteenth century was an ethnic composite of speakers of Ukrainian, Byelorussian, Lithuanian, Latvian, Yiddish, and Polish (*ZN*, 3). Conrad's father, Apollo Korzeniowski, was not only a revolutionary but also an adept translator of Shakespeare, Dickens, Hugo, and other authors, for he had mastered English, French, German, and Russian (*ZN*, 5).[7] Apollo taught his son to speak French and to read Shakespeare in translation. In his excellent biography, Zdzisław Najder notes that Conrad left Poland as a young man with a fluent command of French, a good working knowledge of Latin and German, and perhaps a bit of Greek (*ZN*, 38).[8] Conrad learned English by necessity when he signed on with his first British vessel. Mastering English became a high priority for him because he needed to pass a written examination in seamanship to become an officer in the British merchant marine (*ZN*, 66). The letters he wrote in English while at sea suggest, in their syntax and phraseology, that Conrad's thoughts originated in Polish and then were translated into an English prose that seems stiff and artificial (*ZN*, 86). Moreover, Conrad's voyages brought him into contact with many foreign cultures and languages, particularly in India, Malaysia, and the China Seas. He became a global villager, a wanderer akin to his fictive counterpart Marlow.

Given his extensive background in various languages, we must still ask why Conrad began to write fiction. While many sailors like to spin yarns, Conrad may have instinctively viewed himself as following in his father's footsteps when he wrote his stories—translating not from one language to another but from life to literature, from experience to words. Why, then, did Conrad choose to write in English rather than Polish or French? The reason for this is far more difficult to ascertain. Although in his later years Conrad remarked that he would never have become a creative writer if not for the enchantment of the English language, we cannot take this statement at face value, any more than we can Ford Madox Ford's counterassertion that Conrad abhorred the English language because of its indefiniteness (*Joseph Conrad*, 214–15). He had ample reasons for writing in French, for Flaubert and Maupassant were among his favorite authors and he corresponded with Marguerite Poradowska, who also wrote novels in French. Although Conrad expressed dislike for the French people, he still tried to have his works translated into French after he had attained critical acceptance in England. Perhaps the most persuasive argument for his selection of English lies in the political situation of the 1880s, when Conrad began to write fiction. At that time Great Britain not only ruled the waves but world commerce as well. Self-exiled from a divided country with a string of failures and a bungled suicide attempt behind him, Conrad may have been attracted to the power and triumph of the British Empire, even though he chronicles the excesses of imperialism in his fiction.⁹ Moreover, England had a rich literary tradition and a large reading public, and above all, Conrad desired to be read by the masses.¹⁰

Conrad's positive attitude toward language is perhaps most evident in his preface to *The Nigger of the "Narcissus,"* in which Conrad praises the power of words "to make [the reader] see" (*NN,* xiv). But even in this aesthetic manifesto he distinguishes between creative and mundane expression, claiming that the imaginative artist strives so "that the light of magic suggestiveness may be brought to play for an evanescent instant over the commonplace surface of words: of the old, old words, worn thin, defaced by ages of careless usage" (*NN,* xiii).¹¹ One might even place this statement in the context of Flaubert's *le mot juste,* to which Conrad frequently assented.¹² Through language one can create the illusion of the past recaptured, and although illusion may have a negative denotation, it does have a function to a novelist who admired the Spanish saying *la vita es sueño* (life is a dream). At times he verges on sarcasm in evaluating the potency of language, as the logo-skeptical Marlow comments in *Lord Jim:* "There is a weird power in a spoken word. And why the devil not?" (*LJ,* 174). Later in the novel, Marlow adds that "words also belong to the sheltering conception of light and order which is our refuge" (*LJ,* 313). Conrad acknowledges the capacity of language to offer consolation to us as we confront the darkness of existential uncertainty. As the language teacher remarks in *Under Western Eyes,* "There must be a wonderful soothing power in mere words since so many men have used them for self-communion. . . . [W]hat all men are really after is some form or perhaps only some formula of peace" (*UWE,* 5). In a letter to Sir Hugh Clifford (9 October 1899), Conrad exalts the connotative power of language as part of his apotheosis of literary art:

> [W]ords, groups of words, words standing alone, are symbols of life, have the power in their sound or in their aspect to present the very thing you wish to hold up before the mental vision of your readers. The things "as they are" exist in words; therefore words should be handled with care lest the picture, the image of truth abiding in facts, should become distorted—or blurred. (*CL,* 2:200)

Along similar lines, at the outset of "A Familiar Preface" to *A Personal Record,* Conrad affirms the persuasive force of language, wryly adding that "the power of sound has always been greater than the power of sense" (*PR,* xiii). He even makes an Archimedean boast

concerning the wizardry of printed matter: "Give me the right word
and the right accent and I will move the world" (PR, xiv). In the
author's note to the same volume, written in 1919, Conrad speaks of
being adopted by the genius of English, which influenced his temperament and character (PR, 7).[13]

Contemporary critics, however, have challenged this glowing assertion. Martin S. Ray, for instance, contends that Conrad did not view
words as "transparent symbols" but as immovable weights that had to
be laboriously manipulated by the artist's imagination ("Gift of Tongues,"
86). Ray notes that with his multilingual background Conrad could not
have had a naive confidence in the efficacy of words: "[W]hat is
pertinent is that Conrad was not a born writer *in the English language*,
and his consequent detachment from words gives rise to a healthy
skepticism and distrust about the medium of his art" (92). Ray also
disputes Ford's claim that his occasional collaborator disliked English
because of its inexactness. He even surmises that Conrad may have
been attracted to English because these features of the language gave
him stylistic freedom (93).[14] In *Conrad's Narrative Voice*, Werner Senn
maintains that the Polish expatriate adhered to the conviction that
language could provide a glimpse at the truth behind the visible
world, despite the impossibility of apprehending the nature of reality
through language (9). Conrad attempts to communicate truth by
exploiting the "alleged shortcomings of the English language" (17).
Senn thus reverses the notion that Conrad complained about the
imprecision of English, claiming that "Conrad relied for his effects
precisely on words with 'blurred edges,'" so as to arouse a "momen-
tary uncertainty as to the meaning intended" (17, 19).[15]

Conrad's faith in the power of the written word undoubtedly
contributed to his frequent affirmations of the value of the craft of
fiction. He endorsed the role of a creative writer not only in his celebrated preface to *The Nigger of the "Narcissus"* but also in other authorial
statements, particularly "A Familiar Preface" to *A Personal Record*:

> I know that a novelist lives in his work. He stands there, the only reality
> in an invented world, among imaginary things, happenings, and people.
> Writing about them, he is only writing about himself. But the disclosure
> is not complete. He remains, to a certain extent, a figure behind the
> veil; a suspected rather than a seen presence—a movement and a voice
> behind the draperies of fiction. (PR, xv)

Later in the same volume Conrad declares that a novel has the
capacity to confirm the existence of an imaginary character with far

more "verisimilitude" than any "documentary history" (PR, 15).[16] And yet, despite such virtual equations of literature and life, Conrad often repudiated the idea that language can encompass the truth of experience.[17] In particular, he bemoaned the vagueness of terms that lack a practical, concrete denotation. As Ray observes: "[T]echnical words enjoy a direct correspondence with the objects which they describe; they are like counters, and in the process of communication the hearer simply exchanges the word for the thing. Such efficient and economical adjustment of the word to its meaning is, Conrad laments, precisely what is lacking in literary language" ("Language and Silence," 29). Thus, we have one possible explanation for Conrad's ambivalence toward the written word. Out of this paradox emerge Singleton, the laconic exponent of careful steering, and Marlow, the pontificating yarn-spinner who insists that every generalization requires infinite qualification, both of whom embody Conrad's dichotomous linguistic perspective.

On many occasions Conrad graphically described the pernicious snares of language. In an essay on Maupassant, he praises the French author for not being "a dealer in words" while casting a suspicious glance at the magic incantations of language: "Words alone strung upon a convention have fascinated us as worthless glass beads strung on a thread have charmed at all times our brothers the unsophisticated savages of the islands" (NLL, 27–28). In the opening of "A Familiar Preface" (PR), Conrad mocks the specious power of language: "You perceive the force of a word. He who wants to persuade should put his trust not in the right argument, but in the right word. The power of sound has always been greater than the power of sense. . . . [Y]ou cannot fail to see the power of mere words; such words as Glory, for instance, or Pity" (xiii). By capitalizing the above abstractions, Conrad pays an ironic tribute to the emotive force of words that have no fixed meanings.[18] His pleas for "the right word" and "the right accent" mock the capacity of language to serve as a sort of Archimedean lever, for the movement words create is illusory (PR, xiv).

One can easily find abundant evidence concerning Conrad's distrust of language in his fiction and correspondence. His letters, in particular, demonstrate that despite his commitment to the art of fiction he recognized how language frequently interferes with meaning rather than aiding its expression.[19] Time and again in his personal correspondence, Conrad reveals his mistrust of language, his awareness of the treacheries of the word. One of his most impassioned outbursts of linguistic skepticism occurs in a letter (14 January 1898) to R. B. Cunninghame Graham:

> Life knows us not and we do not know life—we don't even know our own thoughts. Half the words we use have no meaning whatever and of the other half each man understands each word after the fashion of his own folly and conceit. Faith is a myth and beliefs shift like mists on the shore: thoughts vanish: words, once pronounced, die: and the memory of yesterday is as shadowy as the hope of to-morrow,—only the string of my platitudes seems to have no end. (CL, 2:17)

The self-directed irony of the final clause is the signature of a skeptic who apprehends the pomposity underlying philosophical utterances. Aware of the insubstantiality of verbal signs and symbols, he doubts the capacity of words to convey the truth of human existence. This linguistic skepticism also pervades his fiction, both early and late. In "An Outpost of Progress," Conrad emphasizes the radical disjunction between word and thing: "Everybody shows a respectful deference to certain sounds that he and his fellows can make. But . . . we know nothing real beyond the words" (TU, 105). To Conrad, words are beguiling snares that entrap those who feverishly seek order and meaning in a bewildering universe. Language functions as a magical enchantment, operating to inspire or delude individuals.[20] Conrad could never forget that every language is an arbitrary symbol system and thus, at bottom, a useful illusion that can be carried to dangerous extremes.[21] Conrad also recognizes that words may transcend rationality, yet without diminishing their force. In Lord Jim Marlow remarks that "the power of sentences has nothing to do with their sense or the logic of their construction" (75). He also compares words to bullets in assessing their destructive potential (LJ, 174). Furthermore, one need only consider the various verbal labels attached to Kurtz throughout Heart of Darkness to discern Conrad's distaste for linguistic tags and epithets.[22]

One of the most emphatic expressions of linguistic skepticism in Conrad's fiction appears on the first page of Under Western Eyes. It begins with the narrator's complaint that his imagination has been

> smothered out of existence a long time ago under a wilderness of words. Words, as is well known, are the great foes of reality. I have been for many years a teacher of languages. It is an occupation which at length becomes fatal to whatever share of imagination, observation, and insight an ordinary person may be heir to. To a teacher of languages there comes a time when the world is but a place of many words and man

appears a mere talking animal not much more wonderful than a parrot. (*UWE*, 3)

The narrator's profession is particularly apt because through him Conrad not only expatiates on "the imperfection of language" but also dramatizes the inadequacies of translation from one language to another. He resorts to what he calls an "old saying" to articulate a paradoxical view of the value of words, affirming that "speech has been given to us for the purpose of concealing our thoughts" (*UWE*, 261). In his later novels, Conrad's mistrust of language frequently bursts forth in declamations of contempt, as when Marlow, as the interior narrator of *Chance*, calls into question the validity of abstractions: "You know the power of words. We pass through periods dominated by this or that word—it may be development, or it may be competition, or education, or purity, or efficiency, or even sanctity. It is the word of the time" (*C*, 74). Marlow views language as a wind instrument with the capacity to inspire and deflate the human spirit: "See the might of suggestion? We live at the mercy of a malevolent word. A sound, a mere disturbance of the air, sinks into our very soul sometimes" (*C*, 264). As "the expert in the psychological wilderness" (*C*, 311), Marlow recognizes the deleterious effects of abstract words and preconceived ideas in the attempt to deal with things as they are. In *Victory* Conrad adopts a similar perspective in addressing the inadequacy of relying on words to determine the meaning of experience, especially with regard to the elder Heyst, whose pessimistic philosophy develops as an outgrowth of his discovery that "fine words" are really "counterfeit" currency (*V*, 195, 196).[23]

Conrad's skeptical attitude toward verbal meaning carries over into his iconoclastic outlook on the nature of meaning itself and the capacity of fiction to serve as a conveyor of truth. The illusory quality of fiction is an insistent leitmotif throughout Conrad's correspondence. Very late in his career, in a letter to George T. Keating (14 December 1922), he wrote with humorous self-deprecation: "It's the concoction of artistic lies that is my strong point, as twenty-four volumes of pure fiction testify."[24] More than two decades earlier, in a letter to E. L Sanderson (12 October 1899), Conrad mocks himself for choosing the "fool's business" of writing "fiction for a living" before launching his most sarcastic invective at his second career:

The unreality of it seems to enter one's real life, penetrate into the bones, make the very heart beats pulsate illusions through the arteries. One's will becomes the slave of hallucinations, responds only to shadowy impulses, waits on imagination alone. A strange state, a trying experience, a kind of fiery trial of untruthfulness. And one goes through with it with an exaltation as false as all the rest of it. One goes through it—and there's nothing to show at the end. Nothing! Nothing Nothing [sic]. (CL, 2:205)

Conrad's reference to waiting on his imagination may tempt us to suspect that he may have depended too much on memory and not enough on his creativity in the "concoction" of his artistic lies, but once again we must recall his ambivalent attitude toward the power of words, which colors his view of the fiction-making process.[25] Further-more, Conrad frequently alluded to the illusory quality of existence itself, as when he wrote to Edward Garnett (23–24 March 1896) that "one's own personality is only a ridiculous and aimless masquerade of something hopelessly unknown" (CL, 1:267). In a letter to Marguerite Poradowska (29 March or 5 April 1894), Conrad links the unrealities of life and fiction when he emphasizes the insubstantiality of his artistic creations and his hope that as a result of the ordeal of writing perhaps something can be born from "the collision of indistinct ideas" (CL, 1:151). Suspicious of the power of language to transmit truth, skeptical of the value of fiction as a mirror of existence, and doubtful that life could ever be fathomed by the human mind, what other kind of fiction could Conrad create but narratives of indeterminacy?[26]

Conrad was far from the only late-nineteenth-century author who found himself in this predicament. For in his essay "On Truth and Lie in an Extra-Moral Sense" Nietzsche radically challenged the custom-ary notion of human understanding.[27] Insisting upon the arbitrariness of the human intellect, he contends that knowledge serves as a deceptive shroud that prevents us from comprehending the essence of external reality. According to Nietzsche, the mind thrives on simu-lations of what lies beyond our subjective consciousness; thus, we "are immersed in illusions and dream images," and our eyes merely glide over "the surface of things" (43). And because we are confined within our spellbound consciousness, we take pride in assuming that deceptions are actually truths, whereas the truth remains mysterious. Nietzsche extends his critique of the human psyche to mankind's sociolinguistic dependencies, for in order to take the first step toward living in "herd-fashion" we must have verbal agreement among our neighbors about what words mean. Therefore, "a regularly valid and obligatory designation of things is invented, and this linguistic legisla-tion also furnishes the first laws of truth" (44). Nietzsche's theoretical study of philology gave him the same understanding that Conrad had acquired from his practical mastery of several different tongues. Both would come to doubt that the verbal designations of things really coincide with the things themselves. As Nietzsche skeptically inquires, "Is language the adequate expression of all realities?" (45). Conrad would join his German contemporary in an everlasting no. Furthermore, Nietzsche affirms that every word has become a concept , thus losing its uniqueness and establishing a general category rather than an individualized case. Hence, "[e]very concept originates through our equating what is unequal" (46). Although we like to think of our words as revealing, rather than concealing, reality, language is ultimately metaphorical, even though the meanings of words "after long use seem firm, canonical, and obligatory to a people: truths are illusions about which one has forgotten that this is what they are" (47). Thus, herdlike, we feel the obligation to cling to deceptions according to the "fixed convention" of the language that dictates our thought processes.

Nietzsche's perspective on language and knowledge parallels Conrad's own outlook at the turn of the century. But one of the earliest and most profound literary influences on Conrad, Guy de Maupassant, helped to shape his view of fiction as the art of illusion-making. Both in his critical remarks and creative works, Maupassant emphasizes that truth remains evasive because life is too complex, contradictory, and amorphous. He contends that literary artists cannot hope to do anything more than convey their own illusion of reality. Because of the inherent subjectivity of human understanding, Maupassant affirms that artists must be free to select their own unique methods of presentation in order to convey their sense of the world as they see it. He most clearly brings this out in "The Novel," the famous preface to *Pierre and Jean,* which influenced Conrad's own preface to *The Nigger of the "Narcissus."*[28] Working from the premise that existence is asymmetrical, and thus the antithesis of a well-constructed story, Maupassant insists that the realism typical of mid-nineteenth-century fiction fails to express the essence of life as we experience it. The realist of true genius, he contends, is someone who reproduces illusions: "[E]ach of us creates for himself an illusion of the world. . . . And the writer has no other mission than to reproduce this illusion faithfully with all the artistic techniques he has learned and can bring to bear" (27–28). Believing that talent depends on unhabitual thinking and perceiving, he argues that authors must trust in their own originality and disregard the conventional expectations of readers. Their success depends on how well they structure the elements that contribute to their vision of the world. Conrad follows Maupassant almost to the letter in his declared mission to make the reader see what he himself sees.

Another significant influence on Conrad's fictive strategies is the expatriate novelist he addressed as *"Cher Maître."* Conrad's indebtedness to Henry James's experimental techniques hardly requires documentation,[29] and in "Henry James: An Appreciation" (1905) he praises the boundless versatility in his American contemporary's fiction: "[T]here is no suggestion of finality, nowhere a hint of surrender, or even of probability of surrender, to his own victorious achievement in that field where he is a master. Happily, he will never be able to claim completeness; . . . otherwise than by the brutality of our common fate whose finality is meaningless—" (*NLL,* 12). Here Conrad refers to mortality as life's ultimate closure, and these remarks, given his admiration of James's versatility, may help to explain Conrad's refusal to provide conventional endings in his own fiction. At the end of this same essay, Conrad makes this point explicit in his commentary on the renunciations of James's fictive characters. After noting that James's practice of ending a novel or tale with a renunciation is not satisfactory to readers who hunger for a sense of finality, Conrad affirms: "One is never set at rest by Mr. Henry James's novels. His books end as an episode in life ends. You remain with the sense of the life still going on; and even the subtle presence of the dead is felt in that silence that comes upon the artist-creation when the last word has been read. It is eminently satisfying, but it is not final" (*NLL,* 18–19).[30] It is scarcely surprising that Conrad associates James's conclusions with the way unpatterned human existence terminates, rather than with the conventional endings desired by much of the reading public, for in the final pages of his fictions, James employs tactics that may have influenced Conrad's complicated schemes of closure.[31]

Whereas Conrad viewed James as his master in the art of fiction, he was at least on an equal basis with his younger American contemporary, Stephen Crane, whose fiction also offers a revealing analogue to Conrad's own shorter works. In a letter to Edward Garnett (5 December 1897), Conrad links himself to Crane as a "slippery" artist who manipulates readers throughout a narrative only to release them abruptly at the end:

> He is the master of his reader to the very last line—then—apparently for no reason at all—he seems to let go his hold. It is as if he had gripped you with greased fingers. His grip is strong but while you feel the pressure on your flesh you slip out from his hand—much to your own surprise. That is my stupid impression and I give it to you in confidence. It just

occurs to me that it is perhaps my own self that is slippery. I don't know. (*CL*, 1:416).

Or perhaps the still-developing literary artist in this early letter was criticizing a trait in Crane's fiction and his own that he would later consider a strength when he reached his artistic maturity. Certainly the endings of Crane's impressionistic short stories have affinities with Conrad's endgame strategies, for they resist univocal interpretation through their multiple ironies.[32]

Conrad would find irony and indeterminacy most congenial to his temperament because of his conviction that existence is enigmatic, and therefore one can draw no firm conclusions from the fleeting phenomena of our daily lives. Moreover, he hints at the inscrutable quality of the end of an individual life in a letter to Arthur Symons (29 August 1908) in which he asserts that life is "a mystery play, childish and poignant, ridiculous and awful enough" (*CL*, 4:113). Conrad goes on to say that he writes "for the sake of the spectacle, the play with an obscure beginning and an unfathomable denouement" (*CL*, 4:114). And because the end of human life is unfathomable, it would be presumptuous and artificial to end the story of a fictional life on a definitive note. Conrad affirmed this point of view late in his artistic career, in a letter to Barrett H. Clark (4 May 1918), when he declared himself "no slave to prejudices and formulas" (Jean-Aubry, *Joseph Conrad*, 2:204).[33] The author maintains that he is always striving for freedom within his artistic limits and states his conviction that "a work of art is very seldom limited to one exclusive meaning and not necessarily tending to a definite conclusion" (2:205). In a letter to Richard Curle written in the year before his death (14 July 1923), Conrad designates fluidity, rather than finality, as the basis of his art (2:317). He ruminates that critics have had difficulty in classifying his fiction because of his commitment to "giving varied effects of perspective" (2:317). Surely multiple points of view and scrambled chronologies undermine the notion of a definitive conclusion in a work of fiction.[34] Furthermore, in the letter to Barrett H. Clark (4 May 1918) cited above, Conrad adds a surprising declaration when he maintains that it is the critic's task to determine an author's "final effect." He also cautions critics not to become "trammeled by superficial formulas" (2:205). It is significant that Conrad clings to the notion of artistic freedom while warning against the tendency of critics to apply superficial formulas to his "final effects." Conrad's best fiction displays a dynamic sense of an ending that resists attempts to apply Procrustean schemes of formulation.[35] No theoretical system can encompass the diversification of the literary artist at work.

In my analysis of the endings in Conrad's short fiction, I have been influenced by two theoretical perspectives that deserve mention. Although Barbara Hernstein Smith concentrates on poetry rather than prose in her study *Poetic Closure,* she does provide some useful guidelines for evaluating the concept in relation to fiction.[36] Smith defines closure as "[t]he sense of stable conclusiveness, finality, or 'clinch' which we experience" at the end of a literary work (2). She attributes to closure the functions of establishing a sense of order, gratifying expectations, and resolving or releasing heightened tensions that have been built up during the work (3). Although the sense of an ending depends on the cultural response to the efficacy of language, closure historically has signified "stability, resolution, or equilibrium" (36).[37] Historically, novelists and dramatists have "typically exploited the natural or traditional stopping places of life to secure closure" (118), but this is no longer true of literature, for fiction, like poetry, seems to have abandoned the strong sense of an ending as an outmoded device. Traditional literature had operated on the basis of a secure certainty; readers consider the end point appropriate and not arbitrary and are convinced that they know everything necessary (120). The sense of an ending may also convey a "sense of the structure of a work" (152). When this is in effect, the reader experiences *"validity,* a quality that leaves him with the feeling that what has just been said has the 'conclusiveness,' the settled finality of apparently self-evident truth" (152). She also notes that a *"tone of authority"* may convey the sense of validity, even if the unqualified assertion contradicts our expectations (157).[38]

Borrowing a term from the nomenclature of music, Smith identifies a poetic coda as a closural device that is separate from the thematic structure of the rest of the work and makes "a generalized or in some way stable comment upon it from the 'outside'" (188). Smith also speaks of a "cultural lag" that occurs when an author uses an outmoded convention which seems inappropriate to a new style of writing (229). Such a device creates an incongruent sense of an ending and tends to undermine the authoritative conclusiveness of the closure (232). The author may or may not be conscious of this effect. When the author deliberately creates a weak ending, the result is an "open-ended or anti-closural conclusion [which] will convey doubt, tentativeness, an inability or refusal to make absolute and unqualified assertions. It will affirm its own irresolution and compel the reader to participate in it"

(233). Anti-closures "may imply moral and epistemological attitudes" transcending the specific work: "They ask, 'What do we know? How can we be sure we know it?' They question the validity and even the possibility of unassailable virtue, the moral or intellectual legitimacy of final words" (233–34). Smith views anti-closure as a "recognizable impulse in all contemporary art," testifying to a lack of faith in causal certitudes (237). She relates this "anti-teleological character of contemporary art" to the pervasive skepticism of modern life (239).[39]

Marianna Torgovnick also provides a cogent discussion of the topic of endings in her study *Closure in the Novel*.[40] She begins from the premise that endings function to determine the form and meaning of fiction. Serving as a kind of final judgment on the action, "endings create the illusion of life halted and poised for analysis" (5). Admitting that endings remain open to charges of falsifying and distorting human experience, Torgovnick also insists upon the significance of an ending as a frozen moment in time, a photograph of arrested motion; it may be artificial, but it provides an insightful glimpse "in a way that defamiliarizes and makes us feel anew the artfulness of a fictional structure, the essence of some human experience or both" (209). An ending, of course, is only part of the artistic whole, but Torgovnick argues that endings provide a sense of coherent structure, and therefore seemingly petty details may gain in importance (7).

Torgovnick goes a long way toward developing such a vocabulary without introducing ideological jargon. She accepts Boris Eikhenbaum's definition of epilogue as an ending that alters perspective by a shift in the time-frame and provides an "after-history" for the principal characters (11).[41] But Torgovnick notes that epilogues often feature scenic elements, so the mere labeling of endings will not explain the workings of closure. She also points out that circularity may control closure "when the ending of a novel clearly recalls the beginning in language, in situation, in the grouping of characters, or in several of these ways, . . . a familiar and obvious kind of circularity is the 'frame' technique common in narratives. When language, situation, or the grouping of characters refers not just to the beginning of the work but to a series of points in the text, we may speak of *parallelism* as the novel's closural pattern" (13).[42] In addition, Torgovnick defines another functional term when she notes that an incomplete closure may suggest either circularity or parallelism but lacks a required element to achieve this (13). An epilogue often features an overview, which provides "a clear view of the novel's major action, one that immediately makes sense to the reader. In an overview ending, the author's or narrator's

understanding . . . is often superior to that of the characters" (15). A
"close-up" is the opposite of an epilogue: no time passes between
episodes at the end of a narrative (15). Naturally, since overviews and
epilogues have much in common, scenic endings, like those in James's
fiction, frequently employ the close-up, usually to convey an author's
point indirectly and without obvious intrusion (16). In defining the
confrontational ending, Torgovnick comes close to formulating the
strategy Conrad employs in many of his ironic endgames: instead of
attempting to create a sense of congruence between author and reader,
the author confronts readers with an ending that thwarts their expectations in order to achieve artistic or philosophical objectives (18).
Confrontational endings, Torgovnick contends, stem from an artistic
rebellion against fixed forms—an urge to exaggerate or demolish existing
conventions which began in the 1840s, continued through early
modernists such as James, and ended about 1920, when audiences
emerged from the cultural trauma of the shock of the new and were
prepared to read Faulkner and Woolf with an open mind (201).[43]

   Although I employ Smith's and Torgovnick's terms in my study of
the endings of Conrad's short fiction, I am nevertheless wary of the
categorizing imperative of criticism, which, ultimately, cannot withstand the charge of subjectivity. I agree with Arnold E. Davidson
(1984), who maintains that the sense of closure in Conrad's fiction
cannot be objectively reduced to the convenient dichotomy of open
and closed form. True, some of Conrad's best tales conclude on an
ambivalent note that seems consonant with what has become known
as the open form of modern literature, but many of his other significant stories close with a scene or a summary statement that seems to
clash with the various strands of the narrative. It often seems as if
Conrad were supplying a formulaic conclusion for the sake of the
average Victorian or Edwardian reader and at the same time creating
a problematical literary mosaic for his more careful readers. And he
does this too often to dismiss this tactic as merely a sign that the
pressures of publishing deadlines forced him into compromising his
initial artistic vision. Perhaps this is why Conrad's endings seem so
slippery even today. Moreover, as Davidson notes, "the ending cannot be evaluated by itself, but must be weighed in relationship to the
whole work, which necessarily means evaluating the whole work" (1).
In the chapters that follow, I am concerned, first and last, with how
Conrad's endings harmonize or clash with the other narrative elements in nineteen of his short novels and tales.

   Despite the hundreds, if not thousands, of studies of *Heart of Darkness* and scores of critiques of "Youth," *The Shadow Line,* "Typhoon," and "The Secret Sharer," Conrad's short fiction has had few full-scale treatments. Edward Said did a fine job of relating the short stories to Conrad's life in *Joseph Conrad and the Fiction of Autobiography* (1966), and Lawrence Graver's study of *Conrad's Short Fiction* (1969) was a good general, albeit discursive, examination of all of his shorter works, but over the last quarter century book-length evaluations of Conrad's fiction have concentrated almost exclusively on the major novels.[45] In the present study, I have defined Conrad's short fiction as those narratives that are briefer than *The Nigger of the "Narcissus,"* and I have selected from among these works the texts that seem to feature problematical endings that call into question any attempt at a univocal interpretation. Because the plots of several of these stories may be dimly recollected by even the most veteran Conradian, I have summarized the action of those texts in order to put Conrad's conclusions in context. To some readers, it may seem that I am putting formalistic methods to deconstructive ends. Perhaps so, but I hope to illuminate the endgame strategies of a literary artist who presents knowledge of the world as fundamentally illusory and derides our goal-oriented fixations in fictions that speak to our late-twentieth-century sensibilities even more dramatically than they spoke to his own contemporaries.

It is only with the denouement constantly in view that we can give a plot its indispensable air of consequence, or causation, by making incidents, and especially the tone at all points, tend to the development of the intention.
—Poe, "The Philosophy of Composition"

The smallest hope, a bare continuing to exist is enough for the anti-hero's future; leave him, says our age, leave him where mankind is in its history, at a crossroads, in a dilemma, with all to lose and only more of the same to win; let him survive, but give him no direction, no reward; because we too are waiting, in our solitary rooms where the telephone never rings, waiting for this girl, this truth, this crystal of humanity, this reality lost through imagination, to return, and to say she returns is a lie.

But the maze has no center. An ending is no more than a point in sequence, a snip of the cutting shears.
—John Fowles, *The Magus*

[T]here is no classification of the universe that is not arbitrary and conjectural. The reason is very simple: we do not know what the universe is. . . . We must go even further; we must suspect that there is no universe in the organic, unifying sense inherent in that ambitious word. If there is, we must conjecture its purpose; we must conjecture the words, the definitions, the etymologies, the synonymies of God's secret dictionary.
—Borges, "The Analytical Language of John Wilkins"

# 1
## First Command

Although Conrad is popularly recognized as the Polish expatriate who became an English sea captain before turning to fiction, he actually spent only a little more than one year as a captain (not counting his steamboat experience in the Congo) in a maritime career that spanned almost two decades (*ZN*, 162). It is scarcely surprising, therefore, that his sea tales should emphasize the illusions of anticipation and the disillusionments of accomplishment. "The Secret Sharer," "Falk," and *The Shadow Line* chronicle how unfounded hopes dissipate in the trials of a first command. Moreover, they dramatize an incomplete initiation as each narrator attempts to reconstitute his sense of self following his encounter with confounding human experiences. In general, the reason Conrad's characters seldom make progress in their lives is that they are victims of the linguistic illusions endemic to goal-oriented existence. In Conrad's fiction, goal orientation leads to a counterproductive, grail-hungry fixation that isolates the protagonist in a state of anticipation, and thus he makes the least of the present moment. The closing scene of these stories of a first command compromises the narrator's efforts to embrace triumph in a world where duplicity and emptiness reign supreme. Thus, Conrad encourages his escape-oriented readers to grasp at the falling straws of victory while he pulls the rug out from under them.

## "The Secret Sharer"

The psychological dimensions of "The Secret Sharer" have established it as one of Conrad's most frequently anthologized short stories and have inspired extensive critical controversy.[1] Contemporary criticism of "The Secret Sharer" has polarized into mutually exclusive viewpoints, with many commentators seeing Leggatt, "the secret self," as an agent of the narrator's initiation into the rites of passage of mature self-command,[2] and other critics stressing the narrator's delusive egoism, which prompts him to risk the welfare of his ship to insure Legatt's safe departure.[3] Although this long-running debate has not overshadowed the significance of the closing scene, with its enigmatic focus on the narrator's hat floating on the sea, it has partly obscured the integrity of Conrad's artistic vision and his emphasis on the self as an unknown and unknowable phenomenon, as objectified in the image of the disembodied hat.[4] Conrad's original title, "The Secret Self," offers a more helpful hint for comprehending his psychological perspective in this story—a perspective that is consistent with the theme of the unfathomability of human existence, which pervades much of his fiction. Conrad, by seeming to split selfhood into conscious (i.e., the narrator) and unconscious (i.e., Leggatt) exponents, associates the Western psyche with a polarized personal identity.[5] The narrator becomes fixated on determining whether Leggatt is his higher, moral self or his lower, amoral self. Many critics share this fixation, but Conrad does not. Instead, he establishes the unfathomability of human identity and derides our convenient compartmentalization of the will into conscious and unconscious impulses.

Conrad's plot is too familiar to need recapitulation here, but I want to underscore the mirroring effect of the opening and closing scenes, which gives his ending a subtle sense of circularity, to use Turgovnick's term.[6] The narrative begins with a view of a barren landscape suggestive of the isolation and estrangement of the narrator-captain's heightened self-consciousness. Prone to egoistic self-absorption, he views his first command as an opportunity to define his own identity by discovering his hidden potential. But the unexpected arrival of Leggatt initiates a crisis of self-command. In the closing scene, after the narrator sees his own floppy hat upon the water, he is once again alone with his ship, this time apparently in "perfect communion" with his first command. Yet his attention continues to dwell on the image of the floating hat and the unknown destiny that awaits Leggatt, now alone with his freedom. Hence the narrator remains divided, even at the end, when he speculates about his alter ego's eventual fate, as he had earlier wondered about his own.

Conrad's scenario should be viewed in the context of the late-Victorian preoccupation with "the true self," "the better self," or "the higher self." Although Freud and Jung had made psychoanalysis an important concept by the time Conrad wrote "The Secret Sharer" in 1909, Western psychology had long been promulgating "the war in the members," assisted by literary precursors such as *Doctor Jekyll and Mr. Hyde;* that is, they had polarized the individual personality into sharply defined dualisms: good versus evil, head versus heart, conscious will versus sub- or unconscious drives. Conrad exploits this dichotomizing tendency to full advantage, though he does offer significant hints of an opposing viewpoint when he strategically places two obtrusive references to a great Buddhist pagoda in his narrative. He juxtaposes the first reference with a view of "barren islets, suggesting ruins of stone walls, towers, and blockhouses," that dominates the opening lines of the story (*TLS,* 91). The narrator surveys

> lines of fishing-stakes resembling a mysterious system of half-submerged bamboo fences, incomprehensible in its division of the domain of tropical fishes, and crazy of aspect as if abandoned forever by some nomad tribe of fishermen now gone to the other end of the ocean; for there was no sign of human habitation as far as the eye could reach. (*TLS,* 91)

This vista, so suggestive of disorder and abandonment, and perhaps foreshadowing Fitzgerald's "valley of ashes" in *The Great Gatsby,* reinforces the protagonist's sense of estrangement. Yet one detail stands out as the most imposing feature towering above the wasteland: "[A] larger and loftier mass, the grove surrounding the great Paknam pagoda, was the only thing on which the eye could rest from the vain task of exploring the monotonous sweep of the horizon" (*TLS,* 91–92). *Vain* is the key word in this description, for Conrad implies both vanity and futility. Conrad recognized that Western explorations of the East resulted in conquests testifying to the triumph of imperialistic vanity. He makes this apparent at the close of the first paragraph, as the narrator's "roving eye" (perhaps a pun on "I," the narrator) follows the smoke of the tugboat that had left his ship safely anchored, until he loses it "behind the mitre-shaped hill of the great pagoda. And then I was left alone with my ship" (*TLS,* 92). The multiple denotations

of "mitre" illuminate Conrad's subtle juxtaposition of Eastern and Western cultures. A mitre (or miter) is a ceremonial headpiece worn by
bishops of the Western Church. However, it also signifies a ritualistic
headdress formerly worn by Asiatics. The narrator, of course, is expe-
riencing his first command as captain (captain is derived from the
Latin caput, "head"). And, appropriately enough, he first views his
secret self as a "headless corpse!" (TLS, 97).[7]

Conrad's second reference to the Paknam pagoda occurs midway
through the second part of the story, when the narrator asks the mate
"to take a compass bearing of the Pagoda" (TLS, 125). At this point,
the protagonist feels inadequate to command the ship because his
mind oscillates between the duties of navigation and thoughts of "the
secret sharer" in his cabin. Here, the narrator's sense of a divided self
conflicts with the representational aspects of the pagoda, objectifying
Buddhist self-denial (especially the doctrine of anatta, the nonexistence of the self).[8] Conrad's capitalization of "Pagoda" calls attention
to the religious monument as a navigational cynosure, the spiritual
significance of which is lost on a narrator who embodies the opposite
of selfless devotion, for even his compassionate treatment of Leggatt
has traces of self-congratulation. Moreover, the captain unconsciously
reveals his obsession with externalizing selfhood early in the tale,
while the first reference to the pagoda still lingers in our minds: "In
this breathless pause at the threshold of a long passage we seemed to
be measuring our fitness for a long and arduous enterprise, the
appointed task of both our existences to be carried out, far from all
human eyes, with only sky and sea for spectators and for judges" (TLS,
92). The narrator's "we," in this case, refers to his ship and himself,
indirectly excluding the crew from any noteworthy part in his "enterprise." Covertly, Conrad exposes the essential nullity of the protagonist's vision of his responsibilities, indicating that the captain allows his
vocation to define the meaning of life, and, in the process, to separate
his fate from that of the crew. This egocentric impulse later manifests
itself in his reckless navigation of the ship, which almost amounts to a
suicidal urge, as he shaves close to the land in order to liberate his
"double." If the Buddhist references serve as an interpretive rubric,
they unveil the captain's moral dereliction, his arrogant belief that he
can sail the course of life under the pragmatic sanctions of his personal
craving for success. Consequently, his psychological ordeal unfolds as
a sham initiation into maturity, despite the positive rhetoric at the end
of the story.

As in "The End of the Tether," Conrad's manipulation of topographical features contributes to the moral tension of the narrative. In the closing scene, the "towering shadow of Koh-ring" replaces the great Paknam pagoda as the dominant image (*TLS,* 141). Koh-ring, a fictive island, objectifies the mystery of the narrator's "secret self," the enigmatic fugitive who is preparing to swim away as silently as he had arrived. From another vantage point, Koh-ring suggests an overwhelming oblivion, an external void: "[T]he black southern hill of Koh-ring seemed to hang right over the ship like a towering fragment of the everlasting night. On that enormous mass of blackness there was not a gleam to be seen, not a sound to be heard" (*TLS,* 139). As in *The Shadow Line,* the ship's motionlessness and the eerie presence of Koh-ring unite to create an eerie sense of nothingness. Moreover, Conrad compares the vessel to "a bark of the dead floating in slowly under the very gate of Erebus" (*TLS,* 140). Erebus, the nether region of darkness and damnation, seems an appropriate destination for a divided captain and his perplexed crew, as Conrad again defines Koh-ring in negative terms as "the great shadow gliding closer, towering higher, without a light, without a sound" (*TLS,* 140). Yet, as soon as the narrator speculates that Leggatt may have already departed, the ominous shadow begins to veer away from its near collision, and now that the brooding black mass no longer threatens catastrophe he forgets Leggatt as he recalls that he is a stranger to his own ship (*TLS,* 141). Conrad associates Koh-ring, the unknown island, with the nameless ship, with Leggatt (the "secret self"), and with the captain, who had earlier confessed to estrangement as he wondered if he would actually measure up to his "ideal conception" of himself (*TLS,* 94). Here Conrad compounds the sense of mystery with the risk of imminent catastrophe: the ship is threatened by "the black mass of Koh-ring like the gate of the everlasting night towering over her taffrail" (*TLS,* 142). In this context, the Koh-ring reference suggests oblivion once again. Yet Conrad links the threat of oblivion and its prevention once more to the secret sharer, albeit indirectly, when the narrator discovers his own white hat, now forsaken or lost by Leggatt. The hat becomes the "saving mark" for the captain, for "it was saving the ship, by serving me for a mark to help out the ignorance of my strangeness" (*TLS,* 142).[9] His "ignorance," of course, refers to his confusion over how to prevent the ship from running aground. But, in a wider sense, the narrator's ignorance about his true priorities has been apparent throughout the tale. Neither Koh-ring nor the pagoda nor the mysterious felon hiding in his cabin can distract him from his naive egoism. Only the imminent possibility of annihilation, perhaps suggesting loss of self-esteem, rouses him to action. And even then, the captain only gives orders while "standing still like a statue" (*TLS*, 142). He speaks the proper commands and then sees his white hat marking the spot where his secret sharer had plunged into the water. Ironically, Conrad presents the fugitive's freedom as Leggatt's "punishment"—an intriguing displacement of the guilt the captain should be feeling for his reckless conduct as master of the ship.

True to the circular pattern of the narrative, Leggatt first appears by arising from the sea and departs by plunging into the sea. As the captain's secret self, he stands for the unknown self hidden inside every individual behind the thin veneer of civilized self-consciousness. The white hat that floats on the sea of consciousness, like the tip of an iceberg, represents only a small fraction of total identity. Unknown and unknowable, the self seems, like the menace of Koh-ring and the selfless sublimity of the pagoda, an awesome and even terrifying prospect. The narrator's hat covers the secret self for a short time only. It is more than an emblem of a secret partnership between the captain and Leggatt, for it comes to objectify the futile attempt to comprehend the unknowable in rational terms. Early on, the narrator labels the fugitive a "mystery," for Leggatt seems to have arisen from the bottom of the sea of the unconscious. The narrator learns precious little from the fugitive. More often than not, he must fill in the important blanks in Leggatt's account. In structuring his narration, Conrad shows that he is not primarily interested in the power of blackness (evil) but in the power of blankness (the void, both inner and outer). The captain's psychological ordeal takes him to "the very gateway of Erebus," a land of nether darkness leading to Hades, to assume command of his first ship (*TLS*, 143). Conrad views the undiscovered self as a darkness lying beneath the surface of consciousness and defying all attempts at exploration. The captain, who converses with the secret self at such length, imagines his double departing as "a free man, a proud swimmer striking out for a new destiny" (*TLS*, 143). But such an optimistic view only reflects his own incorrigible egoism, a stubborn and unfounded sense of pride in his own dreams of accomplishment. The captain, who hopes he can fulfill his ideal conception of himself at the outset of the tale, still engages in wishful thinking at the close, after he has irresponsibly endangered his crew to fulfill his fantasy.

Conrad's captain, like Lord Jim and the narrator of *The Shadow Line*, lives vicariously in his speculations on whether he can measure up to his ideal self-image. In this connection, Leggatt represents neither a higher, ideal self nor a lower, instinctive self, but rather an unknown self, whose nature may or may not ultimately manifest itself. Among the other parallels between "The Secret Sharer" and *Lord Jim* is the similarity of a small detail in Conrad's novel and a dominant emblem in his short story.[10] For at the climactic moment of Jim's indecisiveness aboard the beleaguered *Patna*, he loses his hat to the gale force of the wind and, shortly thereafter, in a kind of mental fog, jumps into the lifeboat (*LJ*, 110).[11] Conrad employs this minor detail to signify that Jim's "cowardice" is an unpremeditated act, a deed accomplished without rational deliberation. Jim consistently tells Marlow that he was not aware of his decision to jump. Throughout the novel, Jim has trouble justifying his act because his cowardice undermines his heroic self-image. But Marlow perceives that the impetus to desert the *Patna* came from Jim's unknown self, the enigmatic phenomenon that lies beneath Jim's ideal self-concept. This is why Jim's plight so intrigues Marlow (and Conrad), for Marlow recognizes Jim's heart of darkness, the unknown or true self, as the mystery within every individual. Conrad conveys this idea more overtly in "The Secret Sharer." Just when the captain wonders whether his inner self will prove compatible with his ideal self-image, the secret self emerges from the dark water, looking like "a headless corpse!" (*TLS*, 97). From this point on, until the captain sights his own hat floating on the sea, he acts unreasonably, recklessly endangering his ship and crew in an irrational and unlawful attempt to shelter and eventually liberate a fugitive stranger he thinks of as his secret self. The narrator's act of crowning Leggatt's head with his own captain's hat prior to the fugitive's departure climaxes his irrational abdication of power and authority. Only when the narrator sees his disembodied hat on the sea, and he no longer holds parlance with an imaginary or real double, does he make the proper decisions for his ship. Just as Jim loses his hat (i.e., his head) in his act of cowardice, and just as Leggatt is struck by "a bit of the forecastle head" as he grapples with an obstreperous crewman on board the *Sephora*—"a crash as if the sky had fallen on my head" (*TLS*, 102)—so, too, the narrator parts with his hat (his head, or rational self) prior to regaining command of the situation.[12] But he never regains the hat itself, which floats on the ever-shifting surface of the sea, representing the protean flux of existence.

The narrator's fortuitous sighting of his floppy hat saves the ship from wrecking and at the same time saves him from the incipient madness that hovers over him during his stay on board the ship. Even at the outset, the captain's sense of being a stranger to his vessel and to himself appears quasi-pathological. Conrad emphasizes the narrator's estrangement, which makes the novice captain feel "unrelated" to everything else. Leggatt's arrival signals the presence of a nightmarish doppelgänger, the "grey ghost" (*TLS*, 103) who haunts the narrator's consciousness, arousing both curiosity and insecurity in long fits of intense introspection. After deciding to shelter Leggatt covertly in his own L-shaped cabin, the captain becomes aware of an embryonic psychological division: "I sat there . . . trying to clear my mind of the confused sensation of being in two places at once" (*TLS*, 111). And shortly thereafter he says: "I was doubly vexed. Indeed, I felt more dual than ever" (*TLS*, 112). The comic yet eerie feeling of being beside himself leads the narrator into a conspiratorial arrangement with his alter ego: "The Sunday quietness of the ship was against us; the stillness of air and water around her was against us; the elements, the men were against us—everything was against us in our secret partnership; time itself—for this could not go on forever" (*TLS*, 123). Soon the narrator's paranoia about his secret partnership gives rise to an outright absurdity, his feeling that the crewmen (who still obey their captain and have no knowledge of Leggatt) oppose his command. Again and again, his divided consciousness prevents him from fully concentrating on his duties:

> I was not wholly alone with my command; for there was that stranger in my cabin. Or rather, I was not completely and wholly with her. Part of me was absent. That mental feeling of being in two places at once affected me physically as if the mood of secrecy had penetrated my very soul. . . . I felt that I was appearing an irresolute commander to those people who were watching me more or less critically. (*TLS*, 125–26)

The unnerved captain, haunted by the ghostlike presence of Leggatt, even wonders whether he alone can see the secret sharer: "I think I had come creeping quietly as near insanity as any man who has not actually gone over the border" (*TLS*, 130). At this point, the narrator's rhetoric recalls Marlow's assessment of his vicarious role in Kurtz's tragedy. Like Marlow on the Congo river voyage, the narrator fears he may "go irretrievably to pieces" (*TLS*, 135). But once he gives Leggatt his own hat and the final scene commences, all references to madness cease, for the menace of Koh-ring has now replaced Leggatt's situation as his primary concern. The captain saves the ship, to be sure, but from a peril created by his own self-division.

While "The Secret Sharer" does unfold as a symbolic descent into the self, Conrad ironically alludes to the seductive and sedative illusions of Western civilization, which support the myth of attaining self-knowledge and self-command. He stresses words such as *inscrutable, wonder, mystery, enigma, incomprehensible, strange, shadowy, illusion, uncertain, elusive,* and *darkness,* for his aim is to make the reader see the unfathomability of human identity, which resists distillation into linguistic formulations. "The Secret Sharer" ends ambiguously. Like Marlow bidding farewell to the enigmatic personality of Jim, who is both hero and coward, Conrad's narrator never fully comprehends the secret self who seeks immersion in the destructive element of the sea. The narrator may believe he has achieved a kind of reintegration of the self as a result of Leggatt's plunge, but this cannot be synonymous with authentic maturity. In a story that features imposing psychological details such as the Buddhist pagoda and the towering mass of Koh-ring and emphasizes the motif of the double, Conrad forces us to confront the void, within and without. In the search for final answers to the questions of human existence, the answers are only provisional. Like Poe, whose narratives often terminate in an apocalypse of nothing, Conrad lures us to a door that remains closed, even to the most ingenious penetration, and despite the triumphant note at the end leaves us grappling with a mystery rather than revelation.

## "Falk"

Despite Conrad's lifelong enthusiasm for "Falk," the least impressive of his tales of first command, many commentators either ignore it completely or dispute its value.[13] However, a number of critics have advanced favorable analyses of the tale.[14] Generally, these interpretations emphasize Conrad's contrast of Hermann's civilized order and Falk's atavism.[15] They emphasize that the narrator, who serves as mediator of the conflict, ultimately switches his allegiance from the corrupt Hermann to the primitive Falk, whom he views as the embodiment of the "will to live."[16] Yet Conrad should not be confused with the narrator, who compromises his integrity to attain his personal objectives. Despite the glowing final scene promising matrimonial unity, Conrad does not share the narrator's myopic, idyllic view of Falk's courtship of Hermann's niece as an arcadian romance. Rather, he translates their affair into an ironic commercial transaction in which each partner obtains a satisfactory financial settlement. Ultimately, the tale's ending takes us back to the beginning, for a second reading of the narrative reveals neither a glorification of the outdated myth of "the noble savage" nor an endorsement of Schopenhauer's "will to live" but a depiction of decadent capitalistic commerce based on self-delusion.[17]

"Falk" is certainly one of Conrad's most involuted scenarios, and thus worth a bit of recapitulation here. Subtitled "A Reminiscence," the story opens with an elaborate frame that calls to mind the beginning of *Heart of Darkness*. Dining on ancient food and favored with a good view of "Lower Hope Reach," several men of the sea exchange "artless tales of experience" (*T*, 146). A passing German tugboat escorting a Norwegian ship reminds one of the veteran seafarers of an "absurd" episode from his past. The old captain proceeds to narrate the story of his first command, which he received at age thirty in an unnamed Eastern port, which unfolds as follows. While preparing for departure, the captain (the narrator) relaxes by periodically visiting Hermann and his family aboard their ship, the *Diana,* where he notices that Hermann's robust niece has attracted the attention of Falk, who commands the only tugboat in the seaport. Falk refuses to move the captain's ship, thinking he has competition for the niece's affection. He even makes off with the *Diana,* much to Hermann's chagrin. At Schomberg's hotel, behind the camouflage of a make-believe card game, the captain reassures Falk that he has no designs on the niece and agrees to act as an intermediary. But later Falk nearly ruins the captain's "diplomacy" by coarsely announcing that he once had to resort to cannibalism in order to survive at sea. Hermann balks at the prospect of bestowing his niece on a cannibal, but he finally acquiesces, not because he arrives at a higher judgment but because he can save money on the return voyage to Europe without his niece tagging along. By placating Falk and compromising Hermann, the captain also attains his goal: an expedient departure for his ship.

Conrad saves his most subtle irony for the ostensibly affirmative conclusion. The narrator's idyllic last glimpse of Falk and Hermann's niece places them in a mythological context: "They were a complete couple. In her gray frock, palpitating with life, generous of form, olympian and simple, she was indeed the siren to fascinate that dark navigator, this ruthless lover of the five senses" (*T,* 239). This dramatic depiction differs radically from the mundane description of husband and wife aboard the German tug at the outset of the tale: "[A] woman in a red hood, quite alone with the man at the wheel, paced the length of the poop back and forth, with the gray wool of some knitting work in her hands" (*T*, 146). Not only does the color gray link the woman to Falk's beloved, but the casual reference to knitting signals also the characteristic activity of Hermann's wife and niece throughout the story, and the two characters in the vignette thus prefigure the eventual matrimonial situation of Falk and his Olympian siren. Moreover, the knitting reference recalls the somber women knitting wool in the sepulchral city prior to Marlow's African voyage in *Heart of Darkness*. In both instances, Conrad suggests the mysterious operations of fate. If the married couple at the beginning of the story corresponds to the eventual fate of the Falks, then the red hood that shrouds the woman's features as she paces on the tug corresponds to the diminished passion of Hermann's niece after her marriage.

In a more obviously ironic juxtaposition, Conrad combines romantic rhetoric with the tawdry reality of everyday life. First, he emphasizes the animal magnetism of Falk and his beloved: "It seemed to me they had come together as if attracted, drawn and guided to each other by a mysterious influence. . . . From afar I seemed to feel the masculine strength with which he grasped those hands she had extended him with a womanly swiftness" (*T*, 239). But Conrad then travesties the poignancy of this scene when one of Hermann's children gravitates toward Falk: "Lena, a little pale, nursing her beloved lump of dirty rags, ran toward her big friend" (*T*, 239). Lena recoils at Hermann's sharp command, but Conrad has made his point, degrading the mutual attraction of Falk and the niece by linking their relationship to the child's infatuation with a rag doll. Conrad's romance of old clothes receives another turn of the screw when he juxtaposes the happy couple with a mundane activity that mocks their idyllic romance. A mere three feet away from where they stand, a seaman dips his fingers in a "tar-pot, as if utterly unaware of their existence" (*T*, 239). The oblivious sailor, in such close proximity to the couple, is sufficiently arresting, but Conrad may be engaging in word play as well. As a former sea captain, Conrad would certainly be familiar with the slang word *tar*, meaning sailor. He might also be conversant with the kindred expression *tar-fingers*, signifying a petty pilferer, a usage that dates back to the early nineteenth century.[18] Falk's acquisition of Hermann's niece amounts to little more than petty larceny, if viewed in the context of competitive business ethics. Conrad's final irony, decidedly more conspicuous, concerns the narrator's return to the seaport five years later, when he discovers that the couple has fled, probably to avoid Schomberg's scandalmongering, and finds amusement in the lingering rumor that Falk "had won his

wife at cards from the captain of an English ship" (*T*, 240). This misinfor-
mation ironically punctuates the tale, for Falk had earlier confessed
his ignorance of card games and the narrator had only pantomimed
the motions of playing cards during their interview as a smokescreen
to keep Schomberg and other eavesdroppers at a distance.

Throughout the tale, Conrad conveys his mercenary or mercantile
motif via the interaction of the three major characters: Falk, Hermann, and the narrator. Although Hermann's rage for order seems to
put him in opposition with Falk's atavism, all three characters display
corrupt tendencies, even the silver-tongued narrator. But Conrad
initially draws our attention to the overt tendencies of the title character, for, driven by primitive impulses, Falk is one of Conrad's most
rapacious characters, albeit childlike in his stubborn willfulness. Conrad transforms Falk, a "bloated monopolist," into a modern centaur, a
"man-boat" driven by physical passion. Cupidity, not Cupid, animates
Conrad's absurd comedy. Even Falk's most expressive gesture becomes a stale cliché through tedious repetition: "Sprawling there in
the chair, he would, now and again, draw the palms of both his hands
down his face, giving at the same time a slight, almost imperceptible,
shudder" (*T*, 163). This melodramatic example of Falk's habit undermines the categorization of Falk as a "noble savage" or idealized
exponent of Schopenhauer's "will to live."

No matter how much the narrator tries to rehabilitate the tugboat
skipper's reputation, he still views Falk as a "member of a herd"
whose main concern is self-preservation. Falk's herculean physique
and coarse physiognomy, suggesting jungle undergrowth, exemplify a
man "possessed" by carnal "desire." Falk is a "strange beast" in search
of respectability, who lacks the ability to express his desire. The
narrator interprets Falk's bewildered babble as "the absolute truth of
primitive passion" (*T*, 223). To the narrator, the linguistically defunct
Falk embodies Schopenhauer's archetypal will:

> He wanted to live. He had always wanted to live. So we all do—but in
> us the instinct serves a complex conception, and in him this instinct
> existed alone. There is in such simple development a gigantic force, and
> like the pathos of a child's naive and uncontrolled desire. He wanted
> that girl, and the utmost that can be said for him was that he wanted
> that particular girl alone. . . . He was hungry for the girl, terribly hungry,
> as he had been terribly hungry for food. (*T*, 223–24)

Falk's carnal appetite functions merely as another dimension of the
need to consume, a perennial Western preoccupation. Suffering from

the pangs of a hungry heart is as close as Falk ever comes to real love. After the admission of cannibalism, when Falk despairs of satisfying his sexual desire, the narrator marvels at how Falk's impassive countenance seems unable to display emotion (*T*, 225). While recapitulating Falk's version of the cannibalism episode, the narrator defines Falk's role in the crisis as befitting "all the qualities of classic heroism": "pitiless resolution, endurance, cunning, and courage" (*T*, 234). Yet classical heroes are generally more than merely instinctive survivors, and they usually face death bravely with more at stake than sheer self-preservation. Thus Falk falls short of the mark. To the narrator, he may exemplify the will power of mythical heroes of the golden age, but Conrad subtly distances himself from such a misguided view. Although the hyperbolic narrator links Falk to centaurs, Hercules, and "the fable of the *Flying Dutchman*" (*T*, 235), Conrad ironically names him "Christian," in contrast to his pagan attributes, and never names the woman who becomes Mrs. Falk, who seems a refugee from Wagner's Valkeries. In sum, Falk represents natural man in a Neanderthal state. Like the falcon (an association suggested by his name), he embodies the predatory impulse that lies beneath the thin veneer of civilization.

Civilized decadence seems to be the hallmark of Hermann, who in the closing scene only smokes while sitting in his shirtsleeves, with a leisurely arm draped over the back of his chair. To a great extent, his role in Conrad's endgame has been taken over by Mrs. Hermann, who embodies domesticity on the *Diana* and seems to bless the marriage of Falk and her niece. Superficially, Hermann seems the complete antithesis of the primeval Falk, for Conrad caricatures him as a "shopkeeper" monotonously toiling in the "German comic papers." Yet the ship Hermann commands seems more suitable to Falk. The *Diana* presents an image of "primitive solidity," and its chief distinguishing feature relates to a domestic ritual that converts the ship into a "multi-colored grotesque riot":

> The afternoon breeze would incite to a weird and flabby activity all that crowded mass of clothing, with its vague suggestions of drowned, mutilated, and flattened humanity. Trunks without heads waved at you without hands; legs without feet kicked fantastically with collapsible flourishes; and there were long white garments, that taking the wind fairly through their neck openings edged with lace, became for a moment violently distended as by the passage of obese and invisible bodies. (*T*, 148–49)

Conrad's fanciful description of the hanging clothes billowing in the breeze amplifies his ironic presentation of Hermann as *Herr Mann*, an example of the "snivelized" humanity produced by a decadent civilization. Understandably, the narrator finds the name *Diana* "ridiculously unsuitable" for a ship beset by "a gang of four children" (*T*, 149), but Conrad strategically capitalizes on Diana's dual role as goddess of the hunt and personification of chastity, for the vessel serves as the meeting place for the hungry hunter and the chaste voluptuary, Falk and Hermann's niece. Conrad may also be playing verbal games with Falk's first name, Christian, when he distinguishes the *Diana* of Bremen from the Diana of Ephesus. Although Ephesus was the site of the celebrated sanctuary of Artemis, one of the Seven Wonders of the Ancient World, it is also famous in Christian tradition as the city addressed in one of Saint Paul's epistles. Superficially, Conrad may be contrasting pagan and Christian traits, but on another level he alludes to conventional Christianity as a more sophisticated, hypocritical form of self-preservation.

In contrast to his benevolent image at the end of the story, Hermann actually worships the god of mammon. Even before Hermann learns of Falk's interest in his niece, he complains of how much it will cost him to take his family back to Europe. His pecuniary mentality overrides his ethical principles and his sense of familial obligations. When the narrator relays Falk's proposal, Hermann immediately launches a tirade against Falk's "cupidity" and "stupidity," but his own cupidity compels him to relent, especially since his niece has been of relatively little value to him since she met Falk. Later, when confronted with the confession of cannibalism, Hermann calls Falk a "beast." Yet he seems shocked not by the fact of cannibalism but by Falk's audacity in confessing the act. True to the hypocritical code of Western civilization, Hermann wishes that Falk had suppressed the truth, for he wants to preserve his own respectability. Falk, on the other hand, wishes to regain the respectability he thinks he lost when he had to resort to cannibalism. Ultimately, Hermann's shopkeeper's morality overwhelms his professed aversion to cannibalism, and he yields his niece to Falk in order to book only one cabin for the long voyage home. His bourgeois materialism is only a cultivated form of Falk's basic instinct of self-preservation.

The narrator, who diplomatically performs as matchmaker in the final scene, is the most problematical business partner in Conrad's absurd transaction.[19] Like the narrators of "The Secret Sharer" and *The Shadow Line*, though not as overtly, the young captain dwells on his dreams of personal accomplishment. Conrad employs two narcissistic references that underscore the narrator's foolish self-glorification. In the first instance, the narrator nearly falls into a trance when he gazes into a mirror as he brushes his hair, "looking at myself in the glass" (*T*, 169). Then, after meditating on the floundering fates of other mortals, he overhears news of Falk's abduction of the *Diana* while he is "in the very act of smiling at myself in the glass" (*T*, 169). Falk's "infernal trick" interrupts his narcissistic primping in the mirror, and he quickly dubs the towing operation the "rape" of the *Diana*. Yet he soon forgets his own agitation as he belittles Hermann's anxiety: "[A]s Hermann's excitement increased it made me comfortingly aware of my own calmness and superiority" (*T*, 182). Like his counterpart in *The* Shadow Line, the young captain uses the royal "we" in addressing himself during introspective moments, though he resorts to a more egocentric pronoun to express his overactive subjectivity: "For my further action, my youth, my inexperience, my very real concern for the health of my crew must be my excuse" (*T*, 195).

Taking pride in his presence of mind, the narrator refrains from making an "idle" judgment of Falk during their conversation at Schomberg's hotel. At this point, Conrad accents the captain's eagerness to play a machiavellian "game" to earn "success" on his first command. Deciding to fight duplicity with duplicity, he avows the triumph of "my diplomacy" repeatedly throughout his account of their discussion. To the narrator, "diplomacy" is sagacious duplicity: "By pretending hard enough we come to believe anything—anything to our advantage. And I had been pretending very hard, because I meant yet to be towed safely down the river" (*T*, 205). Willing to use pretense to attain his own goals, the narrator does not care what Falk has done in the past; he only worries about what complications may ensue from Falk's confidential testimony. He prefers not to hear any of Falk's confidences, for this might interfere with his "assumed role of matchmaker" and prevent him from arguing against Hermann's repugnance (*T*, 206–7). The narrator concludes that the most expedient solution is the path of duplicity, that is, playing the role of matchmaker and rationalizing away Hermann's protest.

But Conrad's irony is sharpest when the narrator sums up the colloquy to himself: "The game was won and the honour was safe" (*T*, 207). Congratulating himself on the preliminary success of his diplomacy, he begins rehearsing for his performance as the sham ambassador of love: "It was time for me to assume the character of an ambassador, and the negotiation would not be difficult except in the matter of keeping my countenance. It was all too extravagantly non-sensical, and I conceived that it would be best to compose for myself a grave demeanour" (*T*, 210). The narrator succeeds in his attempts at manipulation, until Falk's confession renders Hermann temporarily implacable. In response to Hermann's rage, he does not fabricate a reason for Falk's repugnant act; instead, he merely qualifies the offense by saying that all the circumstances have not been brought to light. Later, the narrator actually manufactures a relativistic truth for Hermann, one that expresses everything and nothing: "It is true just as much as you are able to make it; and exactly in the way you like to make it. For my part, when I hear you clamouring about it, I don't believe it is true at all" (*T*, 223). Questioning the pragmatic value of truth, the narrator seems to operate as if belief is merely a consoling fiction, limited by the bounds of the imagination. Therefore, Hermann imagines cannibalism as a heinous crime, whereas the captain interprets it as an uncommon fact of life.

As the narrator asks Falk about the cannibalism episode, he feels that, as with Hermann, his mind is "full of preconceived notions" concerning the topic. Conrad insists that we are too preconditioned to appreciate phenomena at first hand. Like Captain MacWhirr, who must retire to his ship's library to learn how to prepare for the onset of a typhoon, we cannot liberate ourselves from enslavement to the language habit, with its convenient but petrifying system of categories and references. *Cannibalism* is a loaded word, burdened with preconceived notions that screen the phenomenon from human apprehension. Preconceived ideas never apply to the particular, and thus they impede authentic perception. The only way the narrator can transcend these notions is by attaching himself to the idea of getting his ship safely out of port. To do this he must endorse Falk and convince Hermann to sanction the marriage. The extent of the narrator's complicity becomes most apparent when Hermann elicits his opinion on the day after Falk's confession: "'In all these tales,' I observed, 'there is always a good deal of exaggeration'" (*T*, 237). Instead of informing Hermann of the evidence of Falk's own testimony, the narrator continues to minimize the seriousness of the incident. Choosing to conceal rather than reveal the truth about Falk's cannibalism, he endorses duplicity, not honesty, as the most expedient policy.

Because Conrad's text undermines the validity of his narrative voice, the hyperbolic descriptions of the *Diana's* pristine innocence and the idyllic romance of Falk and Hermann's niece disintegrate into romantic verbiage. For example, the narrator uses a fairy-tale vocabulary to depict the *Diana* as an "innocent" refuge from the "wicked" sea and the "corrupt world." Yet, ironically, this utopian ship's captain is the easily corruptible Hermann, and its chief visitors are the predatory Falk and the duplicitous narrator. Thus, the *Diana* represents a serene "sanctuary" only in the narrator's overheated imagination, which envisions the ship as a "patriarchal old tub," innocent of life's iniquities as if it were "some saintly retreat" (*T*, 156). Like a modern day Noah's Ark, aloof from the bitter realm of human experience, the *Diana's* purity evokes "images of guileless peace, of arcadian felicity" (*T*, 158). But into this hermetically sealed paradise comes the strong, elemental Falk, empowered by a simple desire. The narrator brands Falk's crude confession of cannibalism a "ruthless disclosure," but he eventually sides with the "elemental man," not out of a Rousseau-like reverence for the power of nature but because he recognizes that Falk will hold his ship hostage until Hermann surrenders his niece.

As Joel R. Kehler (1974) has suggested, the narrator experiences a vicarious thrill in romanticizing the animal magnetism of Falk and Hermann's niece.[20] Speaking of what the girl must mean to Falk, he enthusiastically strains for unwarranted superlatives: "[T]he figure of Hermann's niece appeared before my mind's eye, with the wealth of the opulent form, her rich youth, her lavish strength. With that powerful and immaculate vitality, her girlish form must have shouted aloud of life to that man" (*T*, 206). It is the narrator, and not Falk, who envisions her as Diana the huntress standing upon the ugly, uninspiring ship, the *Diana* of Bremen. Conrad's explicit contrast of the majestic goddess and the shopkeeper's vessel leads to the more generalized contrast of the real and the ideal in romance, as reified in the opening and closing glimpses of the Olympian couple. Characteristically, Conrad scrambles his chronological structure so that only a second reading of the story reveals the specious quality of the happy ending.

Dramatizing love as a sort of lie that blinds, Conrad mocks the pretensions and conventions of archetypal passion. Though Falk and the niece never exchange a word throughout their courtship, the young captain interprets their eye contact as a "solemn declaration" of love. Perhaps unspoken as well is the narrator's vicarious lust for Hermann's niece, for after he is deprived of her life-enhancing presence, he resorts to the pathetic fallacy as he surveys the barrenness of a "desolate arena":

> The rocky islets lay on the sea like the heaps of a cyclopean ruin on a plain; the centipedes and scorpions lurked under the stones; there was not a single blade of grass in sight anywhere, not a single lizard sunning

himself on a boulder by the shore. When I looked again at Hermann's
ship the girl had disappeared. I could not detect the smallest dot of a
bird on the immense sky, and the flatness of the land continued the
flatness of the sea to the naked line of the horizon. (T, 209)

On more than one occasion the narrator gazes spellbound at the
niece, but he either deceives himself or his audience by claiming that
she represents "the eternal truth of an unerring principle" (T, 236).
Apparently, the siren's "profusion of sensuous charms" has "bewitched"
the narrator as well as the covetous Falk (T, 236). Yet when he speaks
to Hermann about Falk's proposal, he refers to the niece as if she were
a commodity, a piece of merchandise to be sold at a substantial profit.
Moreover, all along the narrator has been referring to her in the
possessive form as "Hermann's niece," never bothering to name this
enchanting creature. Covertly, Conrad demonstrates that the young
captain shares Hermann's mercantile sensibility as well as the cupidity
of Falk's hungry heart, yet this aspect of the narrator's mercenary
matchmaking remains obscured due to pervasive romantic glossing.
    Conrad also interlards his romantic-mythical scenario with religious
references that offer an ironic counterpoint to the materialistic attitudes and actions in the story and subvert the reconciliation of opposites at the end. Falk's first name, Christian, and his murder of a carpenter
in self-defense, during the cannibalism incident, may obliquely allude to
the betrayal of the Gospel of Christ in the dog-eat-dog world of
Western capitalism. More overtly, Conrad strategically employs five
references to a Buddhist pagoda to provide an ironic commentary on
the events, much as he does in "The Secret Sharer."[21] I only want to
single out for brief commentary Conrad's first reference to the pagoda, which occurs as Hermann and the narrator pursue a petty thief
in vain: "The Chinaman fled silent like a rapid shadow on the dust of
an extremely oriental road. . . . A long way in the rear my mate
whooped like a savage. A young moon threw a bashful light on a plain
like a monstrous waste ground: the architectural mass of a Buddhist
temple far away projected itself in dead black on the sky" (T, 158).
The physically dominant pagoda dwarfs the petty preoccupation of
Westerners savagely and vainly pursuing stolen property in the heart
of a vast wasteland. But Conrad also castigates modern Far Eastern
culture in the flight of the Chinese thief, whose petty larceny contradicts its perennial philosophy. In much the same way, Falk, Hermann,
and the narrator betray Christian ideals by bargaining and scheming
for the disposition of a young woman whom they view solely in
materialistic terms.

In his 1919 author's note, Conrad asserted that the heart of his story concerns not the events themselves but "their effect upon persons in the tale. . . . If we go by mere facts then the subject is Falk's attempt to get married; in which the narrator of the tale finds himself unexpectedly involved both on its ruthless and its delicate side" (*T,* ix–x). Of course, subject matter should not be confused with theme. Conrad's theme, always a slippery element, concerns the narrator's "delicate and ruthless" maneuvers with regard to the corrupt Hermann and the atavistic Falk. In the process he identifies intermittently with the petit bourgeois in Hermann and the animalistic predator in Falk. Conrad presents civilization as a refinement of primal savagery, capitalism as an evolutionary phase of the struggle for existence, and institutional religion as a haven for hypocrites. Moreover, by making animal magnetism the basis of a capitalistic transaction, Conrad posits self-interest, enlightened or otherwise, as our fundamental heart of darkness. The presiding muse of inspiration in this story may not be Rousseau or Schopenhauer but rather Marx. Living on dreams and delusions, Conrad's characters define existence in terms of cannibalistic competition and survival—whether in the jungle, on the high seas, or in the "monstrous" cities of Europe. Rejecting human solidarity to glorify personal ambition and achievement, they project the illusion of life as perpetual conflict.

## The Shadow Line

Encouraged by Conrad's prefatory remark that he aimed to dramatize "the change from youth, care-free and fervent, to the more self-conscious and more poignant period of maturer life" (*SL,* viii), critics have institutionalized *The Shadow Line* as a tale of initiation in the manner of "Youth" and "The Secret Sharer." Conrad's subtitle ("A Confession") and his original title ("First Command") offer additional support for a reading of the story as a kind of bildungsroman in miniature. Scholars have interpreted *The Shadow Line* as a seriocomic account of the young narrator's conflicting drives toward egotism and altruism, which culminate in his passage from self-absorption to "awareness of his place" in the world (*LG,* 92).[22] But *The Shadow Line* resembles *Heart of Darkness* as well as calling to mind the less intricate tapestry of "Youth." Conrad fashions not only an incomplete initiation story but also a confrontation with nothingness in telling the story of a young captain who assumes his first command in relative tranquillity only to experience a physical and psychological ordeal on his first voyage.[23] In addition to objectifying the narrator's steps toward self-command, *The Shadow Line* dramatizes a gradual reduction of the modern individual as he is divested of all symbols of authority and certainty. Without appeal to anyone or anything external, whether transcendent or immanent, the individual must adhere, like Marlow in the heart of Africa, to the practical matters of existence to forestall disintegration.

As Conrad's scenario opens, a nameless narrator gives up his comfortable duties aboard a ship for no particular reason and decides to return to Europe. While staying at the Sailor's Home in preparation for his voyage home, he learns via the irritating promptings of Captain Giles that the steward has kept secret from him an invitation to assume command of a vessel. The narrator receives his command from Captain Ellis, the harbor master, and thanks Captain Giles for goading him on. Prior to sailing, the narrator must tolerate the nearly insane ravings of Burns, the chief mate, who expresses his preternatural fear of their former captain, who was buried at sea. As if in keeping with Burns's spectral outbursts, the ship halts in a prolonged calm at the point where the corpse was heaved overboard. During the calm, the narrator battles a new outbreak of fever that leaves only the cook, Ransome, and himself fit to run the ship. When the narrator discovers that his precious quinine is actually sugar, he begins to put credence in Mr. Burns's superstition. For eighteen days the ship remains situated over the former captain's watery grave. Then a fierce storm breaks out and nearly wrecks the vessel before it reaches the safety of a port.

In a concluding scene that undermines the narrator's sense of accomplishment, Ransome, the "consummate seaman," requests permission to collect his wages and go ashore, intending to give up sea duty permanently. The narrator expresses surprise at seeing him leave, even though he knows that Ransome has a dangerous heart condition. He fails to locate Captain Ellis, who has retired and returned to Europe, but he does encounter Captain Giles, who advises him "that one must not make too much of anything in life" (*SL*, 131). Following this philosophical pep talk, the narrator bids farewell to Ransome, who departs "like a man listening for a warning call" (*SL*, 133), as if aware of the burden of mortality. On this ominous note Conrad's novella closes, but its anticlimactic denouement subverts the notion of the narrator's passage from youth to maturity, from self-indulgence to self-possession. Actually, the narrator passes from enthusiasm to emptiness, crossing "the shadow line" that divides illusion from contingency in the struggle to exist. At the conclusion of the tale, the

narrator, divested of the symbols and attributes of control which he
has acquired from institutionalized authorities, recovers from his dark
night of the soul with a new awareness of the proximity of the abyss.
But this harrowing vision of the void soon dissipates as he rejoins the
hectic pace of civilized life. Though Conrad dedicated *The Shadow
Line* to his son Boris and others fighting in World War I, the narrator's
ordeal reflects the fate of the late-Victorian sensibility passing through
phases of dependence on divine authority, reliance on the illusion of
progress, and faith in secular humanism. Feeling betrayed by God,
science, and humanity, the narrator has no recourse but to cultivate
his delusion that the role of being a captain confers meaning upon his
life. Like Marlow in the heart of the Congo, he copes with the
disillusionments of experience by projecting onto it his own illusion of
the meaning of existence.

Ransome's decision to leave the ship at the end of the tale parallels
the narrator's choice to disembark at the outset. By abandoning the
relative complacency of his snug berth, the narrator forsakes the first
of three deific authorities who dominate the wondrous and enchanted atmosphere of the early chapters of the novella.[24] Conrad
depicts the owner of the ship as an Arab wielding "occult power"
among his people: "an old, dark, little man blind in one eye, in a
snowy robe and yellow slippers. He was having his hand severely
kissed by a crowd of Malay Pilgrims" (*SL*, 4–5). An absurd conflation
of Odin, Jehovah, and Allah, the Eastern owner of a Scottish ship
expresses his mock-divinity in a display of almighty almsgiving. Despite his decision to leave, the narrator professes absolute delight with
his work: "I could not have been happier if I had had the life and the
men made to my order by a benevolent Enchanter" (*SL*, 5). The
adjective "benevolent" and the capitalizing of "Enchanter" set the
stage for the narrator's farcical encounter with two other deific characters representing figures from pagan mythology and Christian tradition. As a fully integrated work of art, *The Shadow Line*, with its
movement from enchantment and illusion to emptiness and contingency, seems to be a fictive elaboration of Conrad's quarrel with God.

Captain Ellis, "the supreme authority" of the harbor, functions as
Conrad's second divinity figure. When the narrator visits his office,
Ellis's underlings speak of him reverently, and Conrad capitalizes the
pronouns "Him" and "He" in their dialogue. Ellis is the object of
servile devotion and the subject of preposterous self-worship: "Captain Ellis looked upon himself as a sort of divine (pagan) emanation,
the deputy-Neptune for the circumambient seas. If he did not actually

rule the waves, he pretended to rule the fate of the mortals whose lives were cast upon the waters" (*SL*, 29–30). Although the narrator views him as a bureaucrat whose greatness lies only in "unwarrantable assumptions" based on the "uplifting illusion" of control, Ellis's authoritarian pretense infects the young man's sensibility. Captain Ellis personifies the mythologizing mania of the "Rule Britannia" jingoism that licensed global imperialism throughout Conrad's lifetime. In a comic metamorphosis, Conrad substitutes an "official pen" for "Neptune's trident," the classical emblem of sea power. The narrator's contractual agreement to command the ship dazzles him with its majestic symbolism, for he considers his commission an extraordinarily potent gift that makes his head swim (*SL*, 32). In the narrator's mind, his first command is an affirmation of manhood and an endorsement by higher powers. Ellis personifies that lordly hegemony, speaking in a "loud, authoritative voice, the voice of our deputy-Neptune" (*SL*, 33). Like Kafka's land surveyor K. contemplating the monolithic castle, the narrator views the bureaucrat who bestows his commission in political-religious terms. He sees himself as a mere ghost in contrast to the titanic individual inside "the consecrated walls" of the harbor office. Yet this bureaucratic Ancient of Days becomes the *deus absconditus* of Conrad's closing scene, retiring with all his "artificial superiority" to some Olympian home for abstract authorities. Ellis consecrates the narrator's temporal ambitions and then vanishes into the woodwork, leaving the narrator to make his own accommodation with chaos.

Captain Giles, Conrad's third divinity figure, also plays on the narrator's conceit, both before and after the ill-fated voyage. Conrad emphasizes the Captain's expertise in "intricate navigation," noting that his mind is a "perfect warehouse" full of geographical knowledge (*SL*, 12). He personifies the Western intellectual tradition with his cartographic consciousness that segments the seamless web of organic life into linguistic categories and stereotypes. Conrad satirically implies Giles's divinity by persistently labeling him as "perfect" and "benevolent." Yet the narrator comes to distrust the captain's irritating air of "perfect" complacency, regarding the old man's benevolence as simply the positive side of "the most dull, unimaginative man I had ever met" (*SL*, 15). Giles's "immense sagacity" and "perfect stupidity" combine to form an oxymoronic image of the traditional Christian deity; he's a pipe-smoking Jehovah who looks "so guileless, dense, and commonplace, that it seemed hardly worth while to puzzle him either with truth or sarcasm" (*SL*, 18). Conrad's pun on *guile* makes sport of the captain's deistic image as an anthropomorphic God who knows all the answers but cannot set things aright. As the narrator struggles to comprehend the drift of Giles's promptings, he considers the old man either insane or "the most tactless idiot on earth" (SL 22).

Conrad continues to heap redundant superlatives on the Captain throughout the comic encounters preceding the narrator's first command. To the younger man, Giles is "indescribable" and "incomprehensible." The Captain's "smouldering black pipe," emblematic of the old man's mental machinations, serves as a beacon of enlightenment for the narrator, who belatedly acknowledges "the commonplace solidity of his wisdom" (SL, 37). Of course, the narrator's newfound admiration for Captain Giles directly stems from his egoistic dreams of reward and personal fulfillment, now apparently substantiated by the prospect of a first command. The Captain's sublime superiority increases in direct proportion to the growing likelihood of the younger man's commission. Furthermore, Giles's complacency contributes to the narrator's illusion of his own manifest destiny, a dream that Conrad shatters dramatically during the circuitous course of the voyage. The narrator's goal orientation launches him into the world of action where, according to Western tradition, one may attain self-knowledge. However, even prior to the disastrous ordeal, the novice begins to suspect a malevolent ulterior motive in the Captain's good deed. Here Conrad conjures up the image of a trickster-God as delineated in Descartes' *Meditations*.

Like Descartes, the narrator abandons his conception of a divine deceiver only after he convinces himself that salvation is certain. His egoism and his faith in a providential scheme of things go hand in hand throughout the tale. For example, Conrad emphasizes the transcendental appearance of the narrator's appointment, for the young captain begins to imagine himself as "specially destined" for his new command by a higher power beyond his comprehension. This sense of exultation blinds the narrator to "prosaic" reality and propels his egocentric imagination into a wonderland of shadowy illusions, which limit his ability to control his situation, as Conrad intimates in the narrator's farcical interjection "'Let us be calm,' I said to myself" (SL, 36). Conrad develops this embarrassing lapse into the royal "we" in a comic allegory of the divine right of captaincy:

> I was already the man in command. My sensations could not be like those of any other man on board. In that community I stood, like a king in his country, in a class all by myself. I mean an hereditary king, not a mere elected head of a state. I was brought there to rule by an agency

as remote from the people and as inscrutable almost to them as the
Grace of God. (*SL*, 62)

The narrator naively assumes that his sailors stand in awe of him, just
as he reveres Captain Giles, but Conrad's regal similes expose the
naiveté of the narrator's self-absorption. Therefore, the novice is both
the agent and victim of his romantic preconceptions. In Conrad's
exposition of the illusions and disillusionments inherent in human
experience, the subject of the narrator's ordeal at sea is not courage
or duty but rather the maintenance of a culturally conditioned identity
in the face of an existential crisis. Conrad again resorts to the Cartesian
image of a trickster-God (*Dieu trompeur*) as the traumatized narrator
contemplates "the formidable Work of the Seven Days, into which
mankind seems to have blundered unbidden. Or else decoyed. Even
as I have been decoyed into this awful, this death-haunted command" (*SL*, 97–98). Giles, the purveyor of the "awful" command,
serves as a divine decoy. His "benevolence" evolves into malevolence,
his "sagacity" into satanic wisdom, his superiority into an infinite and
inscrutable aloofness. Yet as soon as the crisis ends, the narrator
suddenly reaffirms his unshakable faith: "We were now in the hands
of a kind and energetic Providence" (*SL*, 125). Thus, the narrator's
crisis of faith, in God or in Giles, or both, has but a superficial veneer
of optimism.

   I have dwelt at some length on the characterization of Captain
Giles because he plays the major role in the anticlimactic denouement. Apparently, Conrad compressed the narrator's last conversation
with Ransome, for in a letter to Sidney Colvin (27 February 1917) he
admitted that his "last scene with Ransome is only indicated" (Jean-
Aubrey, *Joseph Conrad,* 2:182). This foreshortening of Ransome's
departure permits the conversation between Giles and the narrator to
assume greater importance at the close of the novella. In sum, their
colloquy is an exchange of bromides, platitudes, and catch phrases, a
litany of specious insights into human existence. Echoing Hamlet's
rhetoric, as he does throughout the narrative, Conrad presents a
simplistic stoicism through the voice of Captain Giles, which is amplified by the narrator:

   "The truth is that one must not make too much of anything in life,
good or bad."
   "Live at half-speed," I murmured perversely. "Not everybody can do
that." (*SL*, 131)

As aphorisms, these epigrammatic statements by Giles and the narrator have some appeal, but as a resolution of the conflict or as an interpretation of the action they fall short of the mark. Conrad views existence as fundamentally mysterious, having no fixed boundaries. His "shadow line" is the only line of demarcation applicable to life, and that line, or lie, is one that we subjectively impose on the seamless web of creation.[25] The narrator survives his ordeal because of his capacity to make "too much" of his status and duties as captain. Yet Ransome, who *must* "live at half-speed" because of his weak heart, resigns his post at the earliest opportunity.

Conrad continues his undermining of the illusion of progress when Captain Giles retorts that success lies in pressing forward, no matter what, and then proceeds to lecture the narrator on the necessity of struggle in character development. In so doing, Giles once again asserts his role as the "exemplary" navigator, representing the Western mind upholding its precious ideal of human progress. Conrad, writing against the prevailing belief in scientism, which still held fast in wartime Europe, calls into question this maritime metaphor, and with it modern civilization's guiding spirit of optimism. The navigational metaphor promotes the illusion that by understanding the ordering formulas of the external world one can achieve temporal bliss. Thus, Conrad ridicules Giles's notion that success and self-realization depend on adherence to the empirical doctrines of Western thought. In contrast to the Eastern emphasis on selfless action, the West glorifies self-affirming activity.

When the narrator remarks that he will have little rest while commanding his vessel in the Indian Ocean, Giles undergoes a subtle transformation while making his final response: "'Yes, that's what it amounts to,' he said in a musing tone. It was as if a ponderous curtain had rolled up disclosing an unexpected Captain Giles. But it was only for a moment, merely the time to let him add: 'Precious little rest in life for anybody. *Better not think of it*'" (*SL*, 132; emphasis added). Although Giles gives lip service to the narrator's urge to sail as soon as possible, the resignation implicit in his final words offers a new glimpse into this deific personality. By introducing "an unexpected Captain Giles" so late in the novella, Conrad undermines what Giles has represented throughout, subverting the narrator's romantic impulses even further. The Captain's fatalistic revelation negates the novice's juvenile adventurism in a solemn, almost elegiac moment. Giles, the benevolent divinity, the exemplary navigator, ultimately

admits his own existential mystification. The West's faith in providence, science, and progress seems unverifiable.

In the narrator's last conversation with Ransome, which ends the
anticlimactic closing scene, Conrad presents further evidence of the
illusory power of abstract authority. Throughout the text, Ransome
serves as a model seaman, utterly self-sacrificing in his devotion to
duty. But his reliability obscures his hidden weakness, for, recognizing
the enemy within him, Ransome has developed a "systematic control"
of his actions (SL, 68). Like the narrator, Ransome has rationalized his
role on the ship, deciding to make the best of his limitations. The
narrator marvels at Ransome's graceful efficiency in spite of the
knowledge of his vulnerability. Almost a deific figure himself, Ransome assumes the "silent" and "serene" attitude of a mystic throughout his arduous toils, prompting the narrator to express a nearly
religious reverence during one of their encounters: "He possessed an
unimpaired physical solidity which was manifest to me at the contact.
He was leaning against the quarter-deck capstan and kept silent. It
was like a revelation. He was the collapsed figure sobbing for breath I
had noticed before we went on the poop" (SL, 110). Ransome's
"serene temperament," systematized rather than natural, seems immune to the fever that immobilizes the rest of the crew. Yet the
narrator cannot trust Ransome sufficiently to ask him to take the
wheel, the symbol of authority. At the end of the ordeal Ransome and
the narrator work side by side, and the young captain views him as
risking his life in order to live up to "some distinct ideal" (SL, 126).

At the close of the novella, however, the "consummate seaman"
working for some distinct ideal takes leave of the narrator.[26] The bond
of brotherhood snaps as Ransome announces that he wants to go
wherever it is quiet. Ransome's request harmonizes with Captain
Giles's fatalistic revelation. Both comprehend the futility of grandiose
aspirations and the inherent emptiness of human accomplishments.
Moreover, Ransome's abrupt departure recalls the narrator's unexpected leave-taking at the opening of the novella. Thus, The Shadow
Line comes almost full circle, projecting the disturbing image of life as
a blind transit. Unlike the euphoric narrator at the outset, Ransome
arrives at his pragmatic decision with an attitude of profound disenchantment: "He gasped and a look of almost savage determination
passed over his face. For an instant he was another being. And I saw
under the worth and comeliness of the man the humble reality of
things. Life was a boon to him—this precarious hard life—and he was
thoroughly alarmed about himself" (SL, 129). This new view of Ran-

some as someone striving merely to survive conflicts with the narrator's earlier description of a heroic figure romantically guided by a "distinct ideal." Ransome, like Giles, sees through the thin veneer of idealism to the actual world of risk and hazard. He knows the nether side of life, the external world that refuses to conform to human dreams of triumph.[27] Ransome's final appearance underscores Conrad's emphasis on existential contingency:

> He was like a man listening for a warning call. . . .
> . . . I listened to him going up the companion stairs cautiously, step by step, in mortal fear of starting into sudden anger our common enemy it was his hard fate to carry consciously within his faithful breast. (*SL*, 133)

Ominously yet also anticlimactically, Conrad concludes the novella by linking Ransome to the narrator one final time. Life is indeed a boon, but its ransom is the constant awareness of mortality, "our common enemy." Conrad's ironic ending subverts any estimate of the narrator as a successful "man who has come through," in the Lawrencian sense.[28] In the loss of youthful ideals and romantic attitudes, the narrator has become more experienced, but he has not yet attained maturity.

Conrad's solemn denouement contrasts to the comic euphoria of the opening chapters, for the narrator's passage from enchantment to emptiness begins on an artificial emotional plateau.[29] He depicts young manhood as a second edenic paradise, an enchanted garden glowing with the promise of achievement. Although the experience may be universal, the narrator's expectations seem peculiar, especially in view of his Pateresque vocabulary. Conrad enhances the enchanted aura surrounding the spellbound narrator by converting the maritime commission into a mythical mantra: "[W]ith the magic word 'Command' in my head I found myself suddenly on the quay as if transported there in the twinkling of an eye, before a portal of dressed white stone above a flight of shallow white steps. . . . Command is a strong magic" (*SL*, 28–29). Conrad's imagery situates the narrator's appointment in a bureaucratic heaven where legerdemain prevails. The narrator receives his commission as if in a trance—"dealing with mere dream-stuff "—and then takes flight in the pride of his new-found dignity: "It seemed as if all of a sudden a pair of wings had grown on my shoulders. I merely skimmed along the polished floors" (*SL*, 33). Like Icarus and Phaethon, he indulges in self-congratulation while floating on a cloud of unknowing, above the external world that he views as simply the arena of his future exploits: "It was only another miraculous manifestation of that day of miracles. . . . I floated down the staircase. I floated out of the official and imposing portal. I went on floating along" (*SL,* 35). The subtle evocation of Alice falling down the rabbit hole is only one of Conrad's many allusions to the works of Lewis Carroll in his fabulation of a South Seas Wonderland.[30]

Conrad underscores the narrator's euphoria to dramatize how the newly appointed captain has myopically embraced his authority as if it were an absolute abstraction that will shield him from the vicissitudes of existence. As if engrossed in the most recondite "abstraction," the narrator displays an absolute detachment from the world. He foolishly translates his ego-inflated exuberance into mythical terms, affirming that his first command has come "as if by enchantment. I ought to have been lost in astonishment. But I wasn't. I was very much like people in fairy tales. Nothing ever astonishes them. When a fully appointed gala coach is produced out of a pumpkin to take her to a ball Cinderella does not exclaim. She gets in quietly and drives away to her high fortune" (*SL,* 39–40). The narrator's elation depends on the promise of good fortune and on the talismanic quality of the abstract idea inherent in the word *command.* His allegiance to Western activism—the deceitful mystique of power, wealth, and social status—dictates his secular aspirations. Hoping for instant success as he imposes formulas of meaning upon his experiences, the narrator deludes himself into believing he can chart his voyage according to his personal cravings.

Even before his portents of fortune metamorphose into omens of misfortune, the narrator begins questioning the value of "experience," an advantageous commodity that sometimes entails disagreeable complications, "as opposed to the charm and innocence of illusions" (*SL,* 65). Leaving the Prospero-like divinities Giles and Ellis far behind, he confesses to a feeling of disillusionment upon setting sail, which is a direct consequence of his unfounded, grandiose anticipations. But as the narrator's ship increases its distance from the security of the harbor, and as fever gradually depletes his crew, he begins to worship a new idol, putting his trust in the contents of the medicine chest: "[T]here was the quinine against the fever. . . . I opened it full of faith as a man opens a miraculous shrine" (*SL,* 79). Thus, the narrator pays homage at a new altar, believing totally in the shore doctor's admonition to put his trust in the quinine. Making a sudden transition from providential pilgrim to superstitious disciple, the beleaguered novice embraces the wonderful benefits of medical science:

I fully believed that quinine was of very great use indeed.

I believed in it. I pinned my faith to it. It would save the men, the ship, break the spell by its medicinal virtue, . . . and, like a magic powder working against mysterious malefices, secure the first passage of my first command against the evil powers of calm and pestilence. (*SL*, 88)

As in much of Henry James's fiction, Conrad employs the rhetoric of salvation in a comic vein, focusing here on personal salvation: the narrator's inflated ego is threatened. But the ultimate confrontation with nothingness coincides with his sudden realization that the "un-failing panacea" is bogus (*SL*, 88). This "appalling discovery" prompts him to let each bottle smash on the floor as a semiconscious gesture of dismay.

The dramatic impact of this discovery is underscored by the nu-merous echoes of *Hamlet* throughout Conrad's novella. The narrator's discovery of the quinine fraud has an effect similar to the disclosure of the murder of Hamlet's father. Throughout the narrative, but espe-cially after this discovery, the narrator affects the melancholy idioms of Hamlet (e.g., "this stale, unprofitable world" [*SL*, 28]; "the seething cauldron of my brain" [*SL*, 34]; "a mere passing show" [*SL*, 50]; "unknown powers that shape our destinies" [*SL*, 62]; and "[h]aving thrown off the mortal coil" [*SL*, 73]). Conrad's allusions accentuate the aesthetic distance between the self-dramatizing narrator and the de-tached author. By casting Hamlet's inky cloak over the narrator's shoulders, Conrad satirizes the romantic posturings of the young captain and dismantles the emotional foundation of his ego-identity to expose, in another allusion to Shakespeare, "the stuff dreams are made of" (*SL*, 50). The narrator's capacity for dreaming is one of his most distinguishing traits. While the calm lingers and the fever rages, confronting the void without and sensing the void within, the narrator only sustains himself by investing his status as captain with the abstract value of absolute authority. This idea becomes his saving delusion.

Conrad stages the narrator's confrontation with finitude after the novice captain loses confidence in the restorative powers of the pseudo-quinine and the demigod-like authority of Giles and Ellis. But he foreshadows the narrator's encounter with emptiness in an earlier scene dominated by a mood of enigmatic tranquillity:

I came out on deck again to meet only a still void. The thin, featureless crust of the coast could not be distinguished. The darkness had risen around the ship like a mysterious emanation from the dumb and lonely waters. I leaned on the rail and turned my ear to the shadows of the night.

> Not a sound. My command might have been a planet flying vertiginously
> on its appointed path in a space of infinite silence. I clung to the rail as
> if my sense of balance were leaving me for good. How absurd. (SL, 73–74)

In this passage Conrad abandons Byronic irony for the pathetic absurdity of existential angst. By defamiliarizing the contours of the
external world, he paints an ambiguous picture of the outer void.
Estranged from habitual points of reference and infinitely remote from
the deific authorities who nurtured his youthful vanity, the narrator
commences his dark night of the soul. However, in Conrad's fiction,
soul is merely another abstract idea lacking substantiation. As a matter
of self-preservation, the narrator associates every sign of nothingness
with the diabolical forces working against him night and day: "I faced
an empty world, steeped in an infinity of silence, through which the
sunshine poured and flowed for some mysterious purpose" (SL, 91).
The silence of the sea coincides with the soundless enemy assailing
the fever-stricken crew in the ship's hold, and the sea stretches out on
the horizon as a barren, hopeless, monotonous mirror of "the empty
curve of the sky" (SL, 91). Against this bleak backdrop reminiscent of
Crane's blank seascape in "The Open Boat," the narrator adopts a
skeptical philosophy, concluding that "[n]othing should ever be taken
for granted" (SL, 95).

Conrad gradually eclipses the narrator's inflated self-image by shifting the sense of the void from the external world to the novice's
troubled consciousness. Sighting only a few black islets, the narrator
expresses his remorse in a withering sequence of negations that again
recall Crane's bleak universe in "The Open Boat": "[T]here was no
speck on the sky, no speck on the water, no shape of vapour, no wisp
of smoke, no sail, no boat, no stir of humanity, no sign of life,
nothing!" (SL, 96). Denied any semblance of a conventional frame of
reference, the narrator loses his psychological bearings, internalizing
the featureless, shapeless, outer world and becoming paralyzed by his
awareness of existential contingency. Like Marlow on his voyage to
Kurtz's Inner Station, the narrator has a naked encounter with incertitude and isolation. Conrad links the narrator's temporary inability to
act to his intense preoccupation with his inner worth and its attendant
insecurities. The narrator wages war against his "sense of unworthi-
ness," yet he actually struggles against a conviction of his idealized self
that exists only in his imagination.

Ironically counterpointing the narrator's immature preconceptions
and overactive imagination, the chief mate Burns personifies an outlook contrary to romantic idealism, sometimes playing Sancho Panza

to the narrator's Don Quixote, but more often these roles are reversed. Conrad gives Burns a limited role in the final scene, in part because the transformed Giles and Ransome assume his function at the end.[31] As the narrator prepares to disembark, he takes a last look at the weird Mr. Burns, who now resembles a frightful scarecrow (*SL*, 130). Burns, who occasionally calls to mind Kurtz's appearance and attitude, personifies the immanence of mortality on the Coleridge-like Life-in-Death ship. His skeletal anatomy and moribund countenance constantly remind the narrator that providential designs have no jurisdiction over the harrowing life on the sea. A character of "enigmatic moods," Burns acts as though all visible phenomena were preposterous "make-believe," causing the narrator to reassess his own self-satisfaction: "I became aware of what I had already left behind me—my youth. And that was indeed poor comfort. Youth is a fine thing, a mighty power—as long as one does not think of it. I felt I was becoming self-conscious" (*SL*, 55). Self-consciousness implies self-examination, and self-examination should lead to self-knowledge. But as the narrator's faith in abstract authority fades, his consciousness of cosmic absurdity increases. His common sense, threatened by Burns's insane delusions, stands in need of a fixed idea that is compelling enough to provide stability. The encroachments of madness become so menacing, in fact, that he begins to admire Burns's "preternatural" self-possession, whereas he is beset by tumultuous thoughts and feels reluctant to confront the hellish situation. Ironically, the predicament calls for Rabelaisian laughter instead of logic or self-pity.[32] To combat Burns's infernal lunacy, the narrator merely substitutes superstition for the supernatural in an attempt to liberate himself from a chain of causation that he fails to comprehend. Yet freedom does not come to one who avoids confronting the essential facts of life by blaming black magic and praising providential schemes promoting his own self-aggrandizement.

It is appropriate that Burns, who like Ransome personifies the immanence of mortality and the negation of youthful idealism, should play a pivotal role in the climactic scene. When Burns's bizarre laughter precedes the sudden gust of wind that carries the ship across the shadow line, the narrator again resorts to the rhetoric of popular superstition: "By the exorcising virtue of Mr. Burns's awful laugh, the malicious spectre had been laid, the evil spell broken, the curse removed. We were now in the hands of a kind and energetic Providence" (*SL*, 125). Whether the narrator really believes in spirits is not at issue. What does matter is the way the narrator couches his account in supernatural and superstitious rhetoric, revealing that throughout the whole novella he is unable or unwilling to accept nature as an indifferent force in his anthropomorphic universe.

Conrad's main target in *The Shadow Line*, the human fabrication of a moral order in the universe despite evidence of cosmic apathy, implies our creation, or re-creation, of God in our own image. Psychologically ill-equipped to deal with chaos, the narrator fashions his own system of convenient rationalizations to cope with his unnerving experience. He clings to the abstract authority inherent in the title *captain* in a desperate attempt to salvage his beleaguered self-image. Furthermore, Conrad persistently undermines the narrator's tendency to view the ship and its voyage as mere extensions of his possessive ego, the cultural inheritance of the Western mind: "My ship! She was mine, more absolutely mine for possession and care than anything in the world; an object of responsibility and devotion. She was there waiting for me, spellbound, unable to move, to live, to get out into the world (till I came), like an enchanted princess" (*SL*, 40).

The vessel becomes the arena for the playing out of the narrator's brash ambition. He views his first command as a long-awaited opportunity to reach his "heart's desire," a presumption that quickly proves unwarranted. But prior to his nightmarish voyage, he indulges his naive pride in fanciful self-glorification, walking the deck "in anxious, deadened abstraction, [his thoughts] a commingling of romantic reverie with a very practical survey of my qualifications. For the time was approaching for me to behold my command and to prove my worth in the ultimate test of my profession" (*SL*, 48). The narrator's proclaimed absorption in the professional challenge he faces glosses over the fact that he had earlier decided to abandon his sea career until lured back by the promise of a captaincy. Even though he asserts that the sight of the ship provokes "an unselfish delight," the narrator contradicts this when he confesses to a feeling of deep satisfaction while standing on deck (*SL*, 50). He romanticizes his role as captain in his frequent use of unrealistic superlatives:

> Nothing could equal the fullness of that moment, the ideal completeness of that emotional experience which had come to me without the preliminary toil and disenchantments of an obscure career.
> My rapid glance ran over her, enveloped, appropriated the form concreting the abstract sentiment of my command. (*SL*, 50)

Speaking like a lover who is visually appraising the charms of his beloved, the narrator reveals his cupidity in the detailed admiration of his ship. In his desire for intense experiences, he considers his youthful enthusiasm a sign of his uniqueness. And when his naive elation evaporates in the midst of crisis, the narrator clings precariously to the idea of his invested authority, for the power to give commands helps to steady him. Unlike Marlow, who survives his African ordeal through pragmatic diligence, the narrator of *The Shadow Line* endures because of his faith in his role as commander of the ship. Spiritually blinded by his exalted expectations, he refuses to face the appalling vision of universal nothingness and clings to any belief that might offer a prop for his ego. Although his endurance does contribute to the "tempering and maturing" of his character, the narrator associates his survival with his unshakable belief in the magic powers inherent in a captaincy, and he responds with muted disenchantment to Ransome's decision not to sail again on the next voyage. Thus, Conrad's anticlimactic final scene subverts the narrator's triumphant sense of selfhood.[33]

Conrad presents his strongest image of the aimlessness of human experience in describing the captain's job during the tense but monotonous days and nights of unrelieved calm. The image of the wheel not only links nautical navigation and psychological navigation, but it also expands into cosmic significance, as in the following extract from the narrator's notebook:

> [T]he nights and the days wheel over us in succession, whether long or short, who can say? All sense of time is lost in the monotony of expectation, of hope, and of desire—which is only one: Get the ship to the southward! Get the ship to the southward! The effect is curiously mechanical; the sun climbs and descends, the night swings over our heads as if somebody below the horizon were turning a crank. It is the pettiest, the most aimless! . . . and all through that miserable performance I go on, tramping, tramping the deck. How many miles I have walked on the poop of that ship! A stubborn pilgrimage of sheer restlessness. (*SL,* 97; Conrad's ellipsis)

The passage evokes the cosmic wheel of *samsara*—the endless cycle of birth and death enslaving restless pilgrims who are attached to egoistic expectations, hopes, and desires. Conrad's narrator is not the captain of his fate but the master of his own misfortune. His obsessive drive to determine his own destiny only brings consternation during his aimless pilgrimage in calm waters. More dramatically than in "Youth" or perhaps even in *Lord Jim,* Conrad derides naive romantic enthusiasms, which remain insubstantial until tested by experience. *The Shadow Line* discloses more than Conrad's quarrel with God; it also unveils the sacred rights of human pride as the narrator confers divinity upon himself in the misguided conviction that he is fortune's favorite.[34]

Conrad, looking back after three decades on the travails and misperceptions of his first command, has created a divine comedy replete with ironic hindsight. Throughout the novella, Conrad and his fictive surrogate remain distinctly apart, separated by a shadow line marking the boundary between enlightened self-awareness and deluded self-indulgence. Most of Conrad's characters rarely get anywhere because they become victims of delusions of how their lives will attain completion. In *The Shadow Line,* stagnation rules and the narrator winds up where he began, without an authentic sense of accomplishment or completion.[35] Furthermore, as Conrad learned from reading Maupassant and from his own experiences, the transiency of life compromises all temporal successes, so that egoistic vanity can never be permanently satisfied. *The Shadow Line* discloses the external void, just as *Heart of Darkness* reveals the internal void, for the abyss is both within us and around us.

# 2
## The Clash of Nebulous Ideas

Like the works discussed in the previous chapter, "Youth," "An Outpost of Progress," and *Heart of Darkness* could be considered stories of a first command, and each is an initiation story in which the reader's expectations are subverted in the concluding scene. In all three cases, anticipated revelation gives way to mystification, as Conrad refuses to endorse the notion that language can serve as a vehicle for the unmediated apprehension of reality. At the close of "Youth" he offers a transcendent vision, but one that lies outside the world of words, defying Western culture's insistence that language can control or encapsulate human experience. The concluding scene in *Heart of Darkness* suggests the darkness behind the affirmation of human existence, as Marlow bestows the fatal yet reassuring lie upon Kurtz's Intended and his listeners on board the *Nellie* either confront or evade his withering vision of the essential hollowness of the self. The circular ending of "An Outpost of Progress" dramatizes the regressive tendencies of modern civilization, whose mechanized members use words as a substitute for feelings. Ultimately, *progress* becomes synonymous with *rubbish* as two pieces of human "litter" exterminate themselves by doing nothing, far from the reaches of institutional hierarchies. Thus, rather than finding a meaning for their lives that redeems their passage from innocence to experience, the protagonists in these tales must bear witness to an anticlimax, as each journey documents the perennially frustrated search for meaning in a world of uncertainty.

When writing about *Heart of Darkness* and "An Outpost of Progress" in his letters, Conrad shed some light on his approach to narrative endings. He speaks of how the final scene in both stories locks in the meaning of the whole fiction, but he also insists that the endings transcend their specific contexts. Therefore, Marlow's lie to the Intended has a universality that goes far beyond Kurtz's breakdown in the wilderness, and the obscene tongue that the Managing Director encounters in "An Outpost of Progress" is far more than a personal affront to an absentee despot. Likewise, the nostalgia expressed by Marlow and implicitly affirmed by his sympathetic auditors at the end of "Youth" becomes an ephemeral daydream when held up against the timeless wisdom of the East. Each locking scene functions as an agon between conflicting attitudes or ideas, and the nebulous fusion that results must stand as Conrad's closest approximation to the truth of human experience. If the self and the world are illusory, then what is the point of self-consciousness and self-realization?

## "Youth"

Most frequently interpreted as an initiation story dramatizing the passage from innocence to experience, "Youth" seems perfectly balanced between a wistful nostalgia for the lost idealism and vitality of youth and a mature judgment that perceives young enthusiasms as necessary illusions. Most of the critical controversy surrounding the tale centers on whether the young Marlow truly matures during his initial voyage to the East.[1] However, Conrad transcends the narrow scope of this critical debate by refuting the stereotypical opposites of youth and maturity. The notion of coming of age, or crossing "the shadow line," serves mainly as a fictional prop for Conrad because in his view the Western sensibility is not moving on an ascending path of growth but stuck in a futile cycle of desire and frustration.[2] Young Marlow's brash egoism has its counterpart in Captain Beard's obsession to reach his projected destination and his attachment to materialistic goals. At the conclusion, Conrad contrasts the Western lust for action and success with the serene silence of the East. Finally, he caps the story with a brief closing scene, described by the external narrator, that reveals the middle-aged Marlow and his mature listeners as incorrigibly seeking personal fulfillment. Culturally conditioned victims of the fallacies of hope, they have become jaded cynics mourning their lost vitality and bitter regrets, only partially understanding the wellspring of their discontent. Rather than a spiritual journey from youth to maturity, "Youth" chronicles the Western psyche's enslavement to egoistic action and the "romance of illusions."

Subtitling his story "A Narrative," Conrad accentuates Marlow's retelling of the hazardous episodes, not the episodes per se. The seriocomic abandonment of the *Judea* provides the occasion for Marlow's first command, yet he disobeys the order to keep the boats together, refuses to hail a nearby ship because it might take him in the opposite direction, and generally converts a practical rescue operation into a long distance race to port. Marlow's first glimpse of the East is tainted by a volley of verbal abuse, in English, spewed out by the captain of the ironically named *Celestial*, who mistakes Marlow's craft for a shore boat. The brusque, demanding voice reflects the Western sensibility, thoroughly self-absorbed and vexed by mundane desires. Thus, young Marlow's thwarted sense of triumph dissolves into middle-aged Marlow's eloquent regret for the evanescence of youth.

Presenting this narrative as a sea yarn spun out by Marlow for four cronies, Conrad includes representatives of diverse professions who, in their youth, once shared "the fellowship of the craft" (Y, 3). Marlow's auditors appear to be the same characters who listen to his narrative in *Heart of Darkness*: a director of companies, a lawyer, an accountant, and an unnamed external narrator, who seems at least partially sensitive to the drift of Marlow's words. In a final paragraph crowning the conclusion, Conrad again mentions their vocations, perhaps to underscore their materialistic attachments. Although they seem to regard Marlow as one of them, they do not respond to his narrative with animation, even though Marlow has prefaced his tale by claiming that his first voyage to the East might symbolize human existence (Y, 4). When Marlow finally concludes his yarn, his audience once again comes into focus:

> And we all nodded at him: the man of finance, the man of accounts, the man of law, we all nodded at him over the polished table that like a still sheet of brown water reflected our faces, lined, wrinkled; our faces marked by toil, by deceptions, by success, by love; our weary eyes looking still, looking always, looking anxiously for something out of life, that while it is expected is already gone—passed unseen, in a sigh, in a flash—together with the youth, with the strength, with the romance of illusions. (Y, 42)

The repetition of the phrase "we all nodded at him" may indicate agreement with Marlow or merely appeasement on the part of his auditors. The issue remains in doubt because they offer no verbal reply. Apparently puppets of fortune and misfortune, they follow Marlow's train of thought without endorsing his summation. The lines of their wrinkled faces testify to countless involvements in the deceptions of life, yet their weary eyes show that they remain Western seekers, looking for purpose and significance in their lives. They cannot heartily support Marlow's conclusion that existence, except for a brief span of youth, has nothing to offer but bitterness and futility. Living under the dominance of unwarranted expectations, they share a kinship with young Marlow and Captain Beard, whose fixation on the dream of a destination subverts the practical concerns of life. Only the external narrator seems partially aware that youth and maturity are mythic phases of an absurd continuum in the perennial Western romance with illusions.

The wrinkled faces of Marlow's cronies recall Mrs. Beard's incongruous appearance. Her wrinkled face contrasts with her girlish figure, just as the weary eyes of the auditors beam with unwarranted anticipation. Such incongruity is not found in Conrad's description of the wisdom of the East, as articulated by Marlow. The East represents the antithesis of the dreams and illusions endemic to Western culture. To Marlow, the East signifies the romance of youth, but it really signifies the abandonment of his naive joys and aspirations. He views the East as silent and serene; its inhabitants are content to look on and make no sound. Immersed in the stream of eternity, the philosophical Orient remains untainted by temporal obsessions and egoistic passions. Marlow's yarn unfolds by progression and digression, until his arrival in the East, where a tranquil stasis takes over. The narrative dissolves, rather than halting abruptly, as Conrad fashions a bifocal closure. The final pages delineate Marlow's pyrrhic victory against a background of inscrutable Eastern silence and confounding Western verbalizations, and the last paragraph offers a poignant yet pathetic tableau—the dumb acquiescence of Marlow's auditors, who mechanically concur with him, even though they remain in bondage to illusions of the future and ineradicable memories of frustrated desires. Within this framework, therefore, maturity functions as a cardinal Western myth, a small consolation for the burden of remorse, which is inseparable from modern existence.

Conrad's ironic surrogate, the middle-aged Marlow, stands midway between the follies of his younger self and the dotage of Captain Beard. Although his words and deeds display unmistakable signs of egoistic euphoria, young Marlow occasionally surpasses his elder comrades in matters of practical seamanship. Nevertheless, his identification with the hopelessly heroic motto "Do or die" reveals his melodramatic tendencies, which surface during the long delay for repairs, when impatience prompts him to frivolous actions. While Beard wonders whether the ship will float, Marlow loses himself in the prospect of his destination: "To Bankok! Magic name, blessed name. . . . [T]he East was waiting for me" (Y, 15). Marlow's youthful dreams are a compound of "ignorance and hope," based on a desire to embody the "mature" code of conduct of a sea captain that the middle-aged Marlow and his auditors would affirm. Young Marlow consistently transmutes the voyage into a test of manhood, as when he disregards the failures of others following the explosion and goes below to battle the fire, only to be overcome by smoke and dragged back on deck. Yet by the time Marlow brings his ship and crew to Java, he has reversed roles with his superior, presumptuously cautioning an exhausted and perhaps slightly demented Captain Beard to beware of the end of a jetty as he brings his boat into port. Age is apparently no guarantee of wisdom.

Conrad's chief authority figures, Beard and Mann, fail to demonstrate the sagacity their names seem to imply. Though more than sixty years old, Beard is undertaking his first command on the ancient *Judea*. His attachment to the ship's prescribed destination in the Far East seems as tenacious as Marlow's infatuation with the blessed name "Bankok." Even as fire gradually consumes the ship, Beard insists that the goal can be attained, and he remains focused on getting his ship to Bankok with a single-minded intensity. Young Marlow and old Captain Beard share the same *idée fixe*, the same "placid ignorance" of the welfare of others, and each terminates his first command in the inscrutable East—Beard in abject defeat and Marlow in empty triumph. The image of Beard shaking "his fist at the sky" (Y, 27) comically suggests the foolishness of the Western psyche's unfounded dreams of destiny.[4] Beard's fragile sense of selfhood does not depend on inner confidence but rather on the accumulation of fragments of authority. Although the sailors honor the captain's request to salvage as much of the ship's gear as possible, they covertly dump much of Beard's memorabilia into the sea: "One would have thought the old man wanted to take as much as he could of his first command with him" (Y, 30). Ironically, after he declines in authority and must be awakened by Marlow to abandon ship, Beard reverts to his traditional role, ordering, "Youngest first." Even after reaching port, Beard instructs Marlow to learn whether a nearby steamer is English, so they may be conveyed to another destination, even though their cargo has been lost. At Java, Beard sits mutely, "a broken figure at the stern, wet with dew, his hands clasped in his lap. His men were asleep already" (Y, 38). Here Conrad transforms the Eastern port into a garden of Gethsemane where the Western psyche confronts a disintegration of values, the inevitable consequence of delusive dreaming.

To Marlow, sea voyaging means heroic adventuring; hence his distaste for the mundane Beard, who falls short of the type of colossus Marlow would prefer to see in command. For in the process of mythologizing the grandeur of youth, Marlow converts Beard's decrepit vessel into a vehicle of his own egoistic fancy: "Oh youth! the strength of it, the faith of it, the imagination of it! To me she was not an old rattletrap carting about the world a lot of coal for a freight—to me she was the endeavor, the test, the trial of life" (Y, 12). Marlow views the voyage as a test he must pass; dissatisfied with his humdrum tasks, he yearns for a mission. Youth, then, is a time for yearning, for dreaming, for hoping—and for living in ignorance. And because the "glamour of youth" insists on achievement *in time*, the nullification of youthful dynamism occurs when determined dreamers fully realize that they are running out of time. Conrad employs the image of the slowly burning ship to signify time passing; appropriately, the vessel itself never reaches the fabled East, a realm of timeless serenity which marks the end of Marlow's youthful abandon. In an elegy lamenting the loss of his personal sense of immortality, Marlow defines self-realization as the grand illusion in the prison house of linear time:

> I remember . . . the feeling that will never come back any more—the feeling that I could last for ever, outlast the sea, the earth, and all men; the deceitful feeling that lures us on to joys, to perils, to love, to vain effort—to death; the triumphant conviction of strength, the heat of life in the handful of dust, the glow in the heart that with every year grows dim, grows cold, grows small, and expires—and expires too soon, too soon—before life itself. (Y, 36–37)

Long before T. S. Eliot, Conrad showed us "fear in a handful of dust." This summation of the deceptive lures of youth and the vain efforts of life, echoed by the external narrator in the final paragraph, immediately precedes Marlow's arrival in the East, where the illusions plaguing the Western psyche have no hold on consciousness. Conrad juxtaposes the middle-aged Marlow's claim that he has learned the secret of the East with young Marlow's myopic first glimpse of the mysterious shore. Far from attaining enlightenment, Marlow remains rooted in mystery, as he admitted earlier in the narrative: "I knew very little then, and I know not much more now" (Y, 6). What he does know is that he and his auditors have shared the delusions of youth as well as the fellowship of the sea. Their mute agreement implies only a partial understanding, for the somber note of futility and frustration in Marlow's narrative stifles any verbal assent at the conclusion.

From the outset of his retrospective, Marlow underscores the futility of human endeavors. As the narrative continues and he physically progresses from West to East, he appears to move from an occidental to an oriental viewpoint, stressing more and more emphatically the ephemeral nature of life: "youth, strength, genius, thought, achievements, simple hearts—all die. . . . No matter" (Y, 7; Conrad's ellipsis). Conrad's subtle wordplay ("No matter") derides the Western fetish for material acquisition. By separating the world into component parts, the occidental mind engages in metaphysical dissection. Images of fragmentation abound in Marlow's description of the sailors' dogged efforts to save the ship while it is obviously falling apart. Yet Conrad most fully communicates his entropic vision of nothingness in the bleak sequences of negations that punctuate the narrative.

Early in the tale, Conrad defines by negating in his description of a terrifying storm that threatens to shatter the vessel: "[T]here was not a break in the clouds, no—not the size of man's hand—no, not for so much as ten seconds. There was for us no sky, there were for us no stars, no sun, no universe—nothing but angry clouds and an infuriated sea" (Y, 11). This passage calls to mind the beginning of Crane's "The Open Boat" and illustrates, in part, Conrad's tactical use of indefinite superlatives, a rhetorical gambit he perfected in Heart of Darkness and continued to employ throughout his career. But he is also the artist of suggestiveness, and the excerpt above offers one of many depictions of the void in his fiction. By negating the concept of form, Conrad compels us to envision nothingness. The unknown paralyzes our faculties of perception because it resists categorizing and stereotyping. An excursion into chaos cannot have genuine maturation as its end product. If the ship's voyage has symbolic value at all, it resides in the dramatic transformation of the Judea, which objectifies the young Marlow's foolhardy aspirations and perhaps the rickety structure of the Judeo-Christian tradition as well.[5] As the ship deteriorates on its eastward course, it gradually loses layers of culturally enforced meaning and finally consumes itself: "[T]he paint had gone, had cracked, had peeled off, and there were no letters, there was no word, no stubborn device that was like her soul, to flash at the rising sun her creed and her name" (Y, 35). Here Conrad completely effaces the mercantile vessel, implying the stripping away of the thin veneer of Western optimism. Marlow himself undergoes a similar alteration when he recovers from the impact of the explosion: "I did not know that I had no hair, no eyebrows, no eyelashes, that my young mustache was burnt off, that my face was black, . . . I had lost my cap, one of my slippers, and my shirt was torn to rags. Of all this I was not aware" (Y, 23–24). The explosion reconstitutes Marlow in its own image, making him a human counterpart of the "wilderness of smashed timber" that once was a seafaring craft. In keeping with the imagery of disintegration, as Marlow approaches the East, his disenchantment with Western dreams of success is gradually transformed into a confirmed pessimism. Yet his ultimate disillusionment is intertwined with the most enigmatic vision of nothingness—the silent watchfulness of "an Eastern crowd" as his boat reaches port: "And all these beings stared without a murmur, without a sigh, without a movement. They stared down at the boats, at the sleeping men who at night had come to them from the sea. Nothing moved. The fronds of palms stood still against the sky. Not a branch stirred along the shore . . ." (Y, 40–41). Conrad's emphasis on Eastern perception and attention deftly counterpoints the image of slumbering Europeans, who have arrived in darkness and do not see the light of day. Marlow and his comrades, lacking the intuitive wisdom of the rats that fled the ship, become objects of curiosity under the scrutinizing gaze of the East.[6]

Conrad's ending juxtaposes the baffling silence of the East with the voiceless assent of Marlow's cohorts. The auditors, like their loquacious comrade, regret squandered opportunities and the passage of time.[7] Conditioned to think dualistically in terms of past and future, they share a legacy of unrealized dreams and vague hopes. In the closing scene, Conrad contrasts Eastern and Western ways of "looking." Eastern observers remain detached from the deceptions of temporality and do not become fixated on egoistic desires; Western seekers crave "something out of life" to provide them with the gratifying illusion that they have fulfilled themselves. Although Conrad's scenario affirms the need to attend to the present moment, the main characters have escapist tendencies. Beard constantly adheres to an unattainable destination; young Marlow lives vicariously in his romantic fantasies; the middle-aged Marlow, soured by pessimism, dwells nostalgically on an embellished version of the past;[8] and the auditors (mute phantoms of the past rather than living embodiments of the present) regret the past, dread the future, and cling anxiously to unfounded hopes. Conrad, detached from his deluded audience, brings his seriocomic sea yarn to a close by effacing "the shadow line" between youth and maturity. Despite his voyage to the East, Marlow has learned little about the root cause of Western discontent, and what separates him from his younger self is not "maturity" but the burden of years.[9] Incorrigibly attached to the fascinations of past and future, he and his comrades continue to indulge themselves in the supreme Western preoccupation—killing time.

Before moving on to a discussion of Conrad's time killers par excellence, Kayerts and Carlier in "An Outpost of Progress," I want to examine how the ending of "Youth" casts light on Conrad's artistic strategy in the closing scene of Lord Jim. At one time, Conrad intended to publish "Youth," Heart of Darkness, and Lord Jim in a single volume of short fiction, but the expansion of Jim to novel length forced him to insert "The End of the Tether" instead. Had Conrad been able to publish the volume as he originally planned, it would have been a kind of Marlovian mini-trilogy, for Marlow serves as narrator for all three works, which reflect three distinct aspects of Conrad's philosophical outlook. Yet young Marlow's first glimpse of the East at the end of "Youth" has more in common with Jim's melodramatic death than we might imagine. In both works Conrad associates Easterners with silence and immobility (e.g., Doramin has to be helped to his feet to shoot Jim, which he does without uttering a word), and he links Westerners to frantic and ultimately futile activity. Furthermore, in "Youth" Marlow and his auditors seem fixated on the abstraction of lost time and lost youth; Jim, along similar lines, has willfully divorced himself from life by his marriage to an abstraction: "He goes away from a living woman to celebrate his pitiless wedding with a shadowy ideal of conduct" (LJ, 253). The external narrator of "Youth" admits that Marlow's auditors are "looking always, looking anxiously for something out of life, that while it is expected is already gone—has passed unseen . . ." (Y, 42). Similarly, Jim, despite being shot through the chest,

> sent right and left at all those faces a proud and unflinching glance. . . . Not in the wildest days of his boyish visions could he have seen the alluring shape of such an extraordinary success! For it may very well be that in the short moment of his last proud and unflinching glance, he had beheld the face of that opportunity which, like an Eastern bride, had come veiled to his side. (LJ, 253)

From one perspective, Jim's life can be judged as successful, for he dies at the peak of his youthful "romance of illusions" (Y, 42) and never admits the folly of his "excessively romantic" and "exalted egoism" (LJ, 253). Yet note the key word veiled in the above passage and the kindred words associated with Jim in the final paragraphs of the novel: "He passes away under a cloud, inscrutable at heart, . . . an obscure conqueror of fame, . . . like a disembodied spirit astray . . . ready to surrender himself faithfully to the claim of his own world of shades" (LJ, 253). If Jim is representative of the Western psyche, as the egoistic young Marlow certainly is, then the older Marlow who narrates the novel seems justified in viewing himself as another disembodied spirit: "He is one of us—and have I not stood up once, like an evoked ghost, to answer for his eternal constancy?" (LJ, 253).

In vivid contrast to young Marlow's enchantment with the East near the end of "Youth," Conrad ends Lord Jim on a poignant note of disenchantment—not for Jim but for Jewel and Stein: "[T]he poor girl is leading a sort of a soundless, inert life in Stein's house. Stein has aged greatly of late. He feels it himself, and says often that he is 'preparing to leave all this; preparing to leave . . .' while he waves his hand sadly at his butterflies" (LJ, 253; Conrad's ellipsis). Jewel's mute, devitalized existence following the loss of her lover scarcely requires commentary, but the transformation of Jim's mentor in the novel's final paragraph corresponds to Conrad's depiction of the world-weary faces of Marlow's auditors in "Youth": "lined, wrinkled, our faces marked by toil, by deceptions, by success, by love; our weary eyes looking still . . ." (Y, 42). It is tempting to read "weary eyes" as weary Is in this context, for although Conrad identifies each auditor with a profession, Marlow elicits silent confirmation from them that they regret the lost glamour of their youth. Likewise, Stein's rapid aging documents his morose reaction to Jim's death and Jewel's bereavement, but it also provides Conrad with a way of bringing Jim back to life metaphorically as an inveterate, aging escapist who can only wave feebly at his butterflies, organic symbols of transformation and transcendence, for the net in which he might trap these fleeting creatures is either lost or beyond his power to grasp. The last glimpse of Stein is reminiscent of Flaubert's poignant last glimpse of the mournful Charles Bovary, whose final days are devoted to a futile worship of his dead wife's romantic excesses.

In Lord Jim, Conrad puts on display a young, a middle-aged, and an elderly egoist. Jim, Marlow, and Stein all fail to attain the objects of their respective quests: Jim only atones for his previous failure to be heroic through his self-destructive victory; Marlow, despite his insistence that Jim is "one of us," ultimately brands him "inscrutable at heart" twice in the novel's last three paragraphs; and Stein never recovers from the shock of becoming a failed puppet master, even though he encouraged Jim to immerse himself in the destructive elements of life. The flitting butterflies associated with Stein at the end of *Lord Jim* suggest the illusions and deceptions that pervade the ending of "Youth." Unlike the butterfly, which truly transforms itself as it grows, Conrad implies that we may grow older but we never grow up.

## *"An Outpost of Progress"*

Often considered a companion piece to *Heart of Darkness*, Conrad's first African tale has been viewed by critics as a one-dimensional story of how civilized individuals can go to pieces while in isolation. Yet "An Outpost of Progress" has as much in common with Flaubert's *Bouvard et Pecuchet* as it does with *Heart of Darkness*.[10] Like Flaubert's savage attack on bourgeois stupidity, Conrad's tale satirizes the dull, mechanical sensibilities conditioned by Western culture's mania for organization and regimentation. Conrad's robot-like drones function only within the confines of their routines, and once removed from their habitual frame of reference they begin to disintegrate.[11] But a culture that thrives by exploiting the stupidity and indolence of its masses eventually will be undermined by these same qualities. Ultimately, Conrad's main target is the hierarchical authority of Western civilization, not its mindless automatons.[12]

Conrad weaves his web around the inane predicament of two simpletons, Kayerts and Carlier, who command a trading post in a remote part of Africa. With caustic wit, Conrad details their absurd incompetence at an outpost where "progress" means ivory and "civilization," extermination. They understand nothing and do nothing, except to straighten the large cross marking the grave of the first chief, who built the station, and to protest feebly before finally acquiescing when they learn that Makola, their native assistant, has sold their workers and some villagers into slavery in return for ivory. Emotionally overwrought by prolonged isolation, Kayerts accidentally shoots Carlier in a squabble over sugar rationing. Hearing the whistle of the approaching company steamer, Kayerts reacts insanely by killing himself. His body hangs from the cross until the Managing Director sees it and orders it cut down.

The arrival of the "Managing Director of the Great Civilizing Company" (*TU*, 116) brings the narrative full circle structurally, since the opening pages deal with the establishment of Kayerts and Carlier at the post and the departure of the Director in the steamer.[13] Conrad's exaggerated capitalizing of the Director's title flaunts his contempt for the philanthropic pretense of colonial enterprise.[14] As the fog dissipates, the apprehensive Director makes out the form of Kayerts hanging from the cross like a suspended puppet: "[H]e seemed to be standing rigidly at attention, but with one purple cheek playfully posed on the shoulder. And, irreverently, he was putting out a swollen tongue at his Managing Director" (*TU*, 117). In a letter to E. L. Sanderson (21 November 1896), Conrad indicates his dramatic emphasis on this grotesque final image by protesting against the division of the tale into two parts for serialization. He argued that "the thing halved would be as inneffective [sic] as a dead scorpion. There will be a part without a sting,—and the part with a sting,—and being separated they will be both harmless and disgusting" (*CL*, 1:320). In a follow-up letter to Sanderson (27 January 1897), Conrad expanded on this point: "The sting of the thing is in its tail—so that the first installment, by itself will appear utterly meaningless—and by the time the second number comes out people would have forgotten all about it and would wonder at my sudden ferocity" (*CL* 1:335). The "sting" refers, literally as well as figuratively, to the gallows humor of the ending, as the dead Kayerts irreverently sticks his tongue out at his superior.[15] For Conrad, this obscene gesture expresses the total import of the story. He suggested as much to Edward Garnett in a letter (14 August 1896), asking if "the last few pages save the thing from being utterly contemptible" (*CL*, 1:300). In a letter to Cunninghame Graham (14 January 1898), Conrad amplified his intentions:

> "Put the tongue out" why not? One ought to really. And the machine will run on all the same. The question is, whether the fatigue of the muscular exertion is worth the transient pleasure of indulged scorn. On the other hand one may ask whether scorn, love, or hate are justified in the face of such shadowy illusions. The machine is thinner than air and as evanescent as a flash of lightning. The attitude of cold unconcern is the only reasonable one. Of course reason is hateful—but why? Because it demonstrates (to those who have the courage) that we, living, are out of life—utterly out of it. (*CL*, 2:16)

Conrad portrays modern individuals as ephemeral victims who have no assertive power except to indulge their scorn. Here we might recall the image of Dostoyevsky's Underground Man sticking out his tongue at the Crystal Palace, the mid-nineteenth-century icon of materialistic progress. At the close of "An Outpost of Progress," Conrad heaps his scorn on the "machine," a metaphorical word that appears twice in the above passage and many times in the tale itself. Kayerts and Carlier have been mechanized by the "progressive" force of civilization and must play their assigned role in the African wilderness. They emerge from the womb of Western society "incapable of independent thought" or of departing from the routine: "They could only live on condition of being machines" (*TU*, 91). Even their most nostalgic moments at the outpost consist of longing for the monotony of their former roles in Europe. Like Bouvard and Pecuchet, Conrad's caricatures of Western selfhood only come to life in reflexive response to the romantic books they read.[16] Discussing characters in Dumas, Cooper, and Balzac as if they were "living friends," they drown their feeble sensibilities in an emotional steambath and never genuinely engage life. Neither has an original thought until Kayerts sits entranced before Carlier's corpse. But by this time Kayerts' new ideas merely indicate the breakdown of his conditioned ego. Moreover, at this point Kayerts has abandoned the forms of the European world. He is momentarily free, but only to destroy himself when he hears the whistle signaling the Managing Director's return. Conrad's closing scene underscores that these two mediocrities cannot function except as sluggish machines. At the end both are dead, and Kayerts' defiant gesture seems a morbid but natural consequence of death by hanging.

Although nothing in this closing scene refutes the mechanistic conditioning of Kayerts and Carlier, Conrad does employ a provocative phrase in the final paragraph that broadens the scope of his satire. In a radical departure from the rhetoric of a documentary denouement, Conrad calls attention to one of Kayerts' cheeks "playfully posed on the shoulder" (*TU*, 117). This comment evokes a theatricality that has been implied throughout the tale but never overtly expressed. Histrionics play a major role in the melodramatic conclusion and are also evident, to one degree or another, in every episode of the narrative.

Conrad employs this theatrical tone to dramatize the hypocrisy and duplicity of the colonial enterprise. The "Managing Director" assembles his "Company" of actors, who play the roles he assigns them. He initially expresses confidence in his agents, even though he privately considers them "imbeciles." His colleague, the "old stager," tells the Director, "They [Kayerts and Carlier] will form themselves there" (*TU*, 88). But instead of forming their characters in Africa, isolation only makes their hollowness more conspicuous, and they disintegrate in idleness. Kayerts and Carlier, bit players on the imperialistic stage, see their role as tragic; however, for Conrad the whole play is a farce. They are descendants of Lewis Carroll's Tweedledee and Tweedledum and precursors of Beckett's Estragon and Vladimir in *Waiting for*

*Godot*. They never act without the prompting of a script, as when
Carlier, impressed with his own role after reading propaganda about
the sacred civilizing mission of "Colonial Expansion," rushes out to
replant the cross more firmly. Conrad's comic dupes also foreshadow
the existential nullity of Stoppard's inept Rosencrantz and Guilden-
stern. Desensitized by the machinery of civilization and then stripped
of all security and certainty in Africa, they degenerate and then
blunder into self-destruction.

In the closing scene, Conrad subtly thwarts our expectations. We
might anticipate the death of Kayerts and his discovery by the Managing Director. Yet Conrad surprises us by presenting the Director as a
victim, of apprehension, surprise, and shock. Earlier, the Managing
Director predicted that "nothing will be done" by the "two imbeciles"
(*TU*, 88). And nothing is done by them; they accomplish nothing
but their own extermination. They had conceived of progress as
being able to remain idle while "savages" brought them ivory.
Kayerts and Carlier pontificate on illusory civilized virtues while they
make a "fellowship of their stupidity and laziness. Together they did
nothing, absolutely nothing, and enjoyed the sense of idleness for
which they were paid" (*TU*, 92). Yet they cannot even succeed at
idleness. As machines they are hopelessly inefficient. As actors, they
play cameo roles without a trace of talent. Habituated to the received
ideas of their culture, they suddenly find themselves isolated from
everyone else in the world. In the wilderness, the paper-thin veneer
of civilization vanishes, and they confront their own incapacity and
insignificance. Lacking the palpable reinforcement of their previous
conditioning, their fragile confidence falls victim to "the negation of
the habitual":

> Few men realize that their life, the very essence of their character, their
> capabilities and their audacities, are only the expression of their belief

in the safety of their surroundings. The courage, the composure, the confidence; the emotions and principles; every great and every insignificant thought belongs not to the individual but to the crowd: to the crowd that believes blindly in the irresistible force of its institutions and of its morals, in the power of its police and of its opinion. (TU, 89)[17]

Kayerts and Carlier, remote from the comfort and security of the source of their herd mentality, resemble puppets gradually coming unstrung. They have no inner principles to guide their conduct in the face of the mysterious and incomprehensible.

But Conrad turns the tables in the closing scene when he depicts the Managing Director in the same fashion. Earlier in the narrative, Conrad presented the Director of the "Great Trading Company" as a ruthless but efficient authority figure arriving in a steamer resembling "an enormous sardine box." The Director merely goes through the motions of a change of command, planting the cross on the gravesite and placing Kayerts in charge, before delivering a specious oration revealing merely his "grim humour." However, as the final scene begins, Conrad uses his own grim humor to turn the Director's character inside out, depicting him as a disoriented, impetuous scout who "incontinently lost sight of the steamer" (TU, 116). The dense fog shrouding the riverbank and the unceasing sound of the station's bell give the impression of a man departing a life of regimentation and entering the realm of chaos. Using the rhetoric of melodrama, Conrad ridicules the Managing Director, describing his frantic actions from the perspective of the sailors following him:

> Suddenly they saw him start forward, calling to them over his shoulder: "Run! Run to the house! I've found one of them. Run, look for the other!"
>
> He had found one of them! And even he, the man of varied and startling experience, was somewhat discomposed by the manner of this finding. He stood and fumbled in his pockets (for a knife) while he faced Kayerts, who was hanging by a leather strap from the cross. (TU, 117)

Conrad's odd mixture of hyperbole and understatement, the way exclamatory sentences bracket the phrase "somewhat discomposed," makes the tone of this passage difficult to fathom. Moreover, the shock value of the final scene upstages Conrad's more subtle ironies. The Director, who planted the cross on the first chief's grave, also cuts down the second chief, Kayerts, from the cross that has become a scaffold. The mock crucifixion implies the perversion of the tree of life into an instrument of destruction. Conrad views institutional Christianity as a

facade for ignorance, just as he considers civilization a pretense for
compulsive conditioning, and colonization an excuse for genocide.
All characters identified with the cross (the first chief who lies under it;
the Director who plants it; Carlier, who replants it more firmly; and
Kayerts, who hangs himself on its arm) ultimately plunge into absurdity. None of them sacrifices himself to an ideal. Instead, they squander
their lives away. Conrad subverts their unfounded beliefs as early as
the first paragraph, when he devotes equal attention to "a tall cross
much out of the perpendicular" and to Makola's faith in "the Evil
Spirit that rules the lands under the equator" (*TU*, 87).

Throughout the tale, Conrad makes sport of the frivolous preoccupations of Kayerts and Carlier. But in the conclusion he shifts his focus
to the Managing Director and the hypocritical society he represents.
For all its lofty illusions of virtue, progress, and humanitarianism,
modern society is like a "rubbish heap" where the reigning passion is
the rapid acquisition of wealth. The idiotic agents, who bring their
"litter" of belongings to the great unknown, spring from that hypocritical culture but utterly fail to understand it. Conrad's conclusion shows
us the Managing Director in travail; he is a puppet-master whose
wind-up dolls no longer function, except to childishly mock his former
mastery. The final scene unfolds as a kind of dumbshow, almost a
late-nineteenth-century foreshadowing of Beckett's *Act without Words*, a
pantomime dramatizing the emptiness of civilized values. Conrad
recognizes that modern society conditions the behavior of its members with hollow words and seductive illusions. Ultimately, individuals
lose the ability to discriminate between pragmatic facts and specious
rhetoric, between words and what words represent. Desensitized
individuals respond like robots to mere words, rather than embracing
and understanding genuine ideas or emotions, as when Kayerts and
Carlier pay lip service to the evil of slavery:

> *They believed their words.* Everybody shows a respectful deference to
> certain sounds that he and his fellows can make. But about feelings
> people really know nothing. We talk with indignation or enthusiasm;
> we talk about oppression, cruelty, crime, devotion, self-sacrifice, virtue,
> and *we know nothing real beyond the words*. Nobody knows what
> suffering or sacrifice mean—except, perhaps the victims of the myste-
> rious purpose of these illusions. (*TU*, 105–6; emphasis added)

Conrad's dupes, psychologically enslaved to the autocratic dictates
of Western culture, earn little sympathy in their final pratfall. The
projected titles for the story—"A Victim of Progress," "Two Victims of

Progress" (Hobson, "A Textual History," 151)—suggest Conrad's original focus on the agents' lack of self-reliance. Yet the final title and the shift in focus (but not in tone) in the final scene show that Conrad's dark comedy of errors indicts Western culture's fixation on organization and control, which is assisted by illusions provided by language. Beginning with a farcical scrutiny of two pieces of human "litter," Conrad ends his absurd tale by relegating institutional authority to the dustbin of progress.

## Heart of Darkness

> [W]e really ought to free ourselves from the seduction of words.
> — Nietzsche, *Beyond Good and Evil*

Conrad drew attention to the last pages of *Heart of Darkness* in his letter of 31 May 1902 to William Blackwood, in which he says that "the interview of the man and the girl *locks in*—as it were—the whole 30000 words of narrative description into one suggestive view of a whole phase of life, and makes of that story something quite on another plane than an anecdote of a man who went mad in the Centre of Africa" (*CL*, 2:417; emphasis added).[18] Instead of concluding in the heart of the Congo, the tale comes full circle to its point of origin, the Thames, by way of Marlow's return to the sepulchral city and subsequent encounter with Kurtz's Intended.[19]

Conrad's impressionistic depiction of Brussels, both early and late in the narrative, externalizes the sham and hypocrisy he sees at the heart of Western civilization. On the second visit, Marlow takes offense at the "irritating pretense" of perfect security reflected in the faces of the insignificant citizens. Yet here, in the heart of the city of untruth, Marlow lies to conceal the horror of Kurtz's degradation and, apparently, to reinforce the Intended's "saving illusion." True, Marlow does admit his contempt for lies early in the narrative, but his African nightmare transcends conventional polarities such as truth and falsehood, good and evil, appearance and reality. He finally recognizes truths as convenient fictions, useful in matters of survival, but totally invalid in terms of understanding the nature of life. Marlow lies (at least, so he tells us) to preserve the Intended's opportunity for affirmation and survival. He also lies because he perceives something of Kurtz in himself as well as in the Intended. The melodramatic interview ends with Marlow bowing before the inscrutable enigma of existence. Conrad insinuates throughout this crucial locking, or summarizing, scene that in order to sustain life one must project one's own illusions for living. Self-deception, the essential condition for happiness, becomes a kind of existential higher understanding, and thus Conrad invalidates all conventional truths and moralities in his iconoclastic narrative of the truth of fiction and the fiction of truth.[20]

Conrad's critical attitude toward verbal expressions of truth in *Heart of Darkness* closely parallels Nietzsche's skeptical outlook. As critics have noted, Conrad and Nietzsche adopted similar attitudes toward language.[21] Conrad views language as an imprecise—if not deceptive—means of communication, as does Nietzsche in his essays "On Truth and Lie in an Extra-Moral Sense" and "On the Prejudices of Philosophers." In the former essay, Nietzsche argues that the mind is an arbitrary instrument of knowledge more concerned with flattering deceptions than with perceiving the truth beyond appearances. Defining man as an assemblage of masks, roles, poses, and postures, he sees the vanity of the human race as dependent on the capacity for self-deceit. External reality mystifies the modern individual, who remains imprisoned within a self-deceiving consciousness that decrees, in accordance with "linguistic legislation," that truth must be always agreeable and never damaging to the ego: "And, moreover, what about these conventions of language? Are they really the products of knowledge, of the sense of truth? Do the designations and the things coincide? Is language the adequate expression of all realities?" (Nietzsche 1968, 45). Language is general and conceptual, but each experience is particular and unique, and therefore words fail to communicate without equivocation: "[T]ruths are illusions about which one has forgotten that this is what they are; metaphors which are worn out and without sensuous power; coins which have lost their pictures and now matter only as metal, no longer as coins" (47). Truth, debased and defrauded into surface truths, no longer functions as anything but an agent for conditioning and conformity: "[T]o be truthful means using the customary metaphors—in moral terms: the obligation to lie according to fixed convention, to lie herd-like in a style obligatory for all" (47).

In his essay "On the Prejudices of Philosophers," he further contends that since reality is unknowable through conventional means, primarily logic and language, existence would be impossible without a consistent falsification of the world as it is. Recognizing "untruth as a condition of life," one can no longer seriously entertain questions of truth or falsehood; instead, what really matters is the affirmation or denial of life.[22] If illusions are necessary to preserve and promote life, Nietzsche maintains, the human ego will abandon the search for true judgments and explanations of existence in favor of conventional fictions, that is, the specious consolations of language, logic, and other formulaic systems of reference.

Although I am not arguing that Nietzsche's linguistic skepticism directly influenced Conrad,[23] some of Nietzsche's works may have been available to Conrad before he began writing *Heart of Darkness* (see Whitehead, "The Active Voice," 121–35). But what Nietzsche was propounding in theoretical terms Conrad expressed in the fabric of his fiction, becoming one of the first major twentieth-century authors to challenge the efficacy of language as a vehicle for transmitting meaningful communication.[24] More specifically, Conrad targets the deleterious effects of the labeling function of language. Words and things are not synonymous. Or, as Djuna Barnes puts it, writing almost four decades after the publication of *Heart of Darkness*: "Life is not to be told, call it as loud as you like, it will not tell itself. . . . There is no truth, . . . you have been unwise enough to make a formula; you have dressed the unknowable in the garments of the known."[25]

Yet Conrad's ending involves more than Marlow's lie and its motivation. In particular, Marlow's saving falsehood gains new significance in light of the intricate series of corresponding words and phrases that pervade the final pages of the novella. These correspondences are sometimes superficial, as when Marlow compares Kurtz's "ebbing" life to the swiftly running "brown current." In the last paragraph, Conrad's narrator reports the Director's announcement "We have lost the first of the ebb," and states that "the tranquil waterway . . . seemed to lead into the heart of an immense darkness" (*HD*, 76). This takes us back to the opening of the narrative, when the *Nellie* waits "for the turn of the tide" at "the beginning of an interminable waterway" (*HD*, 7). Conrad's nautical imagery suggests that Marlow and his auditors must share Kurtz's fate, an implication that seems substantiated by the name of their cruising yawl, the *Nellie,* perhaps a comic diminutive of death k<u>nell</u>, as the geographical reference to "Gravesend" may corroborate. Employing death as a metaphor for disillusionment, or spiritual extinction, Conrad chronicles the failure of human intentions and lofty aspirations. At the heart of darkness, Marlow, who has been linked to Kurtz as one of the new breed of agents, finds himself "numbered with the dead" (*HD*, 67). Conrad again identifies Marlow with Kurtz in the final scene when Marlow rationalizes his visit to the Intended as an attempt to give up everything that remains of Kurtz. But the meeting does not unfold as Marlow imagines, and he finally accepts the burden of insight as a

permanent part of his psyche. Marlow must live with the memory of
Kurtz's horror for the rest of his life.

Kurtz dies before the locking scene begins, but he reappears as a
phantom to haunt Marlow in the sepulchral city, speaking through the
mouthpiece of the Intended to dumbfound him once again. Conrad
hints at the correspondence of Kurtz and the Intended by punning on
the word *expression*. In Marlow's estimation, Kurtz's greatest attribute
is his "gift of noble and lofty expression" (*HD*, 67), and while admiring
the Intended's portrait, Marlow remarks that "she had a beautiful
expression" (*HD*, 76). Kurtz's eloquent rhetoric corresponds to the
beauty of his fiancée's countenance. But we must also keep in mind
that Marlow interprets Kurtz's cry "The horror" as "the expression of
some sort of belief; it had candour, it had conviction, it had the
appalling face of a glimpsed truth" (*HD*, 69). Much earlier, Marlow
had digressed to discuss the "flavour of mortality in lies" (*HD*, 29);
however, Conrad asserts that truth can also be appalling, as in Kurtz's
shock of recognition ("The horror!") preceding his death.[26] The "flavour of mortality" also becomes manifest in the final scene, when
Marlow begins a sentence and the Intended finishes it, substituting
her own words and feelings for Marlow's:

> Then before the appealing fixity of her gaze that seemed to watch for
> more words on my lips I went on, "It was impossible not to . . ."
>
> "Love him," she finished eagerly, silencing me into an appalled
> dumbness. "How true! How true!" (*HD*, 73)

Truth can be appalling more often than appealing whenever it
negates life. The example of misunderstanding above suggests that
knowing the truth about Kurtz might destroy the Intended's sentimental cocoon.[27] Marlow seems no more capable of enlightening her than
he was with Kurtz when he attempted to speak common sense to him
at the Inner Station. Conrad's linking of Marlow with Kurtz and Kurtz
with the Intended implies that we are prisoners of our own preconceptions about life. Truth and falsehood have little to do with the
affirmations and negations that render existence purposeful or pointless.

Conrad also links Kurtz to the Intended by emphasizing their mutual
capacity for belief. In Europe, a journalist tells Marlow that Kurtz "had
the faith. He could get himself to believe anything—anything" (*HD*,
71). Marlow echoes this assessment in much the same language when
he describes the Intended: "She had a mature capacity for fidelity, for
belief, for suffering. The room seemed to have grown darker as if all
the sad light of the cloudy evening had taken refuge on her forehead"

(*HD*, 73). Here, light and darkness do not correspond to truth and falsehood. Rather, the "sad light" represents a diminishing beacon of faith in a devouring chaos of darkness. Moreover, Conrad often calls attention to the Intended's "ashy halo" (an arresting oxymoron) in this scene: "[W]ith every word spoken the room was growing darker, and only her forehead, smooth and white, remained illumined by the unextinguishable light of belief and love" (*HD*, 73). Fidelity, whether well-founded or unfounded, seems the sole alternative to the psychological paralysis of unmitigated despair. Conrad transmutes the metaphysics of despair into a poetics of immobility and blindness when he immerses Kurtz in "impenetrable darkness" on his deathbed to contemplate the harrowing thought of his own emptiness. In similar fashion, Conrad stages the interview with the Intended in a room that gradually succumbs to dusk and darkness. As the room grows darker, Marlow realizes he must keep secret Kurtz's withering words: "The dusk was repeating them in a persistent whisper all around us, in a whisper that seemed to swell menacingly like the first whisper of a rising wind. 'The horror! The horror!'" (*HD*, 75). By lying, Marlow does not give Kurtz the justice he had requested: "I could not tell her. It would have been too dark—too dark altogether . . ." (*HD*, 76; Conrad's ellipsis). Yet, by attempting to save the Intended from the despair that consumed Kurtz, Marlow affirms Kurtz's original intentions, rather than the actual consequences of those intentions. Marlow keeps the darkness within himself, refusing to extinguish the Intended's dim light of belief. His lie functions as a surface truth that preserves life at the price of deceit.

There is also the question of how Marlow can be convinced that he knows the truth about Kurtz.[28] The Intended asks for Kurtz's last words, but Marlow was dining in the mess room at the time of his death. It is possible that in his delirium Kurtz could have spoken almost anything without being overheard. Marlow cannot be sure that Kurtz's *last* words were "The horror! The horror!" And even if they were, what do they really mean?[29] The secret lies with Kurtz, not with Marlow, who expatiates on the topic ad nauseum without providing a clear-cut explanation. Does Kurtz's cry "The horror!" signify his recognition of the abominable evil he has committed? Or is it an acknowledgment of his inner emptiness?[30] Like Ahab's doubloon in *Moby-Dick*, Kurtz's outburst has as many meanings as interpreters. Ultimately, the meaning of this stirring exclamation must be determined subjectively, and individually, by each reader and on each reading of the novella.

Throughout the locking scene, the Intended represents the image of light threatened by darkness, of order besieged by chaos. In the dusk, her "pale head" seems to float toward Marlow, as if disembodied from her black garments. Conrad calls attention to "the last gleams of twilight," the "glitter of her eyes," and the "glimmer of gold" hair that "seemed to catch all the remaining light" (HD, 74). When the Intended assumes a posture of supplication that reminds Marlow of Kurtz's other woman, his native mistress of inextinguishable faith, he describes her as "stretching bare brown arms over the glitter of the infernal stream, the stream of darkness" (HD, 75). Conrad's light and darkness correspond to affirmation and negation, not to truth and falsehood, for Heart of Darkness unfolds as a journey to the brink of cosmic nihilism and back again to a broken world of dim beliefs.[31] Marlow ultimately views the Intended's delusion as a sanctuary from the snares of experience, as he finds himself "bowing my head before the faith that was in her, before that great and saving illusion that shone with an unearthly glow in the darkness, in the triumphant darkness from which I could not have defended her—from which I could not even defend myself" (HD, 74). His lie forges a solidarity of belief among himself, Kurtz, and the Intended. Marlow's compassionate act may serve as a temporary triumph for life set against the backdrop of the inevitable triumph of darkness. A case can even be made for the view that Marlow's real lie is his attempt to rid himself of the burden of Kurtz at the Intended's doorstep. Marlow realizes that he cannot dispose of the memory so easily, and he departs with the "truth" and the trauma still within him. He confesses to a "feeling of infinite pity" for the woman who had more faith in Kurtz than Kurtz had in himself. Given a "choice of nightmares," Marlow ultimately selects the lesser of two negations—the appalling "lie" instead of the annihilating "truth."

Conrad presents Marlow's visit to the Intended as a ghostly reunion with Kurtz; every detail gives the impression of a posthumous existence. Even her street resembles a "well-kept alley in a cemetery" (HD, 72). Unable to cast off his memories, Marlow envisions Kurtz "on the stretcher opening his mouth voraciously as if to devour all the earth with all its mankind" (HD, 72). The voice that Conrad accentuates throughout the tale intimidates Marlow even long after Kurtz's death. Marlow imagines Kurtz staring at him from the panel of the door "with that wide and immense stare embracing, condemning, loathing all the universe" (HD, 72). The white and black piano keys suggest the disparity of Kurtz's idealistic rhetoric and his rapacious lust for ivory.

But Conrad also employs more subtle tactics in this scene. The Intended suddenly materializes, dressed in black, as if Kurtz had died only the day before. Catching sight of her, Marlow also feels that time has stopped since the death of Kurtz:

> I saw her and him in the same instant of time—his death and her sorrow—I saw her sorrow in the very moment of his death. Do you understand? I saw them together—I heard them together. She had said with a deep catch of the breath, "I have survived"—while my strained ears seemed to hear distinctly, mingled with her tone of despairing regret, the summing-up whisper of his eternal condemnation. (*HD*, 73)

Beneath the rhetoric of late-Victorian melodrama, Conrad implies that the Intended embodies Kurtz's short-lived intentions as an apostle of idealism and that the phantom whisper represents Kurtz's well-deserved damnation, his total psychological inversion in the heart of Africa.[32] Marlow apprehends this duality as the general condition of mankind, not as an isolated eccentricity of human nature.[33] Earlier, he had remarked that the human mind is capable of anything. Marlow even perceives this duality within his own identity, when he faces the failure of his misguided mission as an emissary of light and realizes that company officials have lumped him with Kurtz as practitioners of advanced methods of colonialism. But Marlow most distinctly hears this judgment against the hollowness of humanity in the disconsolate words of the Intended: "[T]he sound of her low voice seemed to have the accompaniment of all the other sounds full of mystery, desolation, and sorrow I had ever heard . . . the faint ring of incomprehensible words cried from afar, the whisper of a voice speaking from beyond the threshold of an eternal darkness" (*HD*, 74). Seeing Kurtz in the glowing face of the ever-faithful Intended, hearing Kurtz's insane whisper in her trembling voice, Marlow recognizes once again the inescapable phantom he had earlier called the "initiated wraith from the back of Nowhere" (*HD*, 50). It dwells within him, within all humankind. Kurtz literally is the nowhere man; his ancestry stems from all over Europe, and his corpse lies *somewhere* in a muddy hole.[34] His shade is everyone's shadow. Marlow understands this implicitly and realizes the futility of all ego-oriented actions.[35] His lie temporarily preserves his integrity and the Intended's illusion, but like the "life-lie" in Ibsen's *The Wild Duck* the deception does not ensure salvation but merely survival.[36]

Marlow does survive. He survives what Kurtz failed to endure in the heart of the wilderness. Marlow affirms that like ancient explorers in the great age of navigation modern individuals must learn "to live in the midst of the incomprehensible which is also detestable" (HD, 10). The language of Heart of Darkness amplifies "the incomprehensible" with acute exaggerations of Conrad's own account of his journey to the inner recesses of Africa.[37] Conrad's rhetoric, with its preponderance of superlative and indefinite abstractions, consistently dramatizes the gulf between human experiences and the imprecise linguistic representations of those events.[38] Heart of Darkness unfolds as an excursion into the absurd, a penetrating scrutiny of nothingness, and a dramatic example of Conrad's evolving articulation of humanity's perennially frustrated search for meaning. The very novella itself, according to Peter Brooks, calls into question the "epistemology of narrative" and demonstrates "the inadequacy of the inherited orders of meaning" (238).[39] Truth remains elusive, and any effort to package it in linguistic wrapping seems doomed to failure. So why speak at all?[40]

In the final paragraph, Marlow returns to his original posture, silent and detached "in the pose of a meditating Buddha" (HD, 76). This ultimate parallel, Marlow as Buddha, actually conceals Marlow's role as mediator between the benevolence of Buddha and the rapacity of Kurtz. Marlow plays the part of the man of action who turns to a life of contemplation, even though, paradoxically, he "still followed the sea" (HD, 9). The external narrator's reference to Marlow's "pose" as Buddha may suggest that he is mocking Marlow's pontificating wisdom, yet Conrad's unnamed external narrator does conclude the story with the image of the Thames, the civilized counterpart of the primeval Congo, leading to "the heart of an immense darkness" (HD, 76). If the external narrator has any awareness of Marlow's grim revelation, then he is certainly unique, for the other auditors never respond to Marlow's interpretation of his experience, except by way of petty objections or stupefied silence. Enveloped in their own little word-worlds, invisible cocoons of catch phrases and slogans, they consider Marlow's "inconclusive" narration a usurpation of their right to fritter away the hours playing dominoes.[41] They function, in the more sophisticated "jungle" of progressive London, as counterparts to the worthless pilgrims who litter the deck of Marlow's steamboat in the Congo. Like Kurtz, they exist on the fringe of egomania, fitting inheritors of Kurtz's I-me-mine sensibility: "My Intended, my station, my career, my ideas—these were the subjects for the occasional utterances of elevated sentiments" (HD, 67). The Managing Director's utterance in the last paragraph—"We have lost the first of the ebb" (HD, 76)—rings with the same hollowness. Even the Intended's turn-of-the-century sentimentality is expressed in reflexive language. Each character speaks in the idiom of his or her cultural conditioning, from the minor figures to the Intended, Kurtz, and Marlow himself. None of them breaks down the barriers prohibiting authentic communication.

By happenstance or design, Conrad has fashioned in *Heart of Darkness* a logomachy, or battle of words. On one level, he constructs a semiotic framework whereby concrete signs stand for abstract symbols (e.g., the river is the inexorable stream of time; the wilderness, the irrationality of life; and the darkness, the vacuous heart of mankind). In juxtaposition to this scheme, he establishes a semantic pattern that undermines much of the particularity of the narrative. For example, most of the characters either have no name, like the external narrator and Kurtz's African mistress, or are identified only by occupation: the Director of Companies, the Lawyer, the Accountant, the manager, the brickmaker, and so on. Or else Conrad links the character to a verbal tag, as in the case of the Intended, the Harlequin, and Marlow's pose as a modern European Buddha. Conrad's rhetoric, replete with superlatives and indefinite abstractions, consistently dramatizes the gulf between human experiences and the imprecise linguistic formulations that allegedly correspond to them. Conrad's verbal tactics tend to render the whole narrative of Marlow's journey as an amorphous cloud of moon-mist and to alchemize abstractions such as "immense," "unspeakable," and "unknowable" into concrete form.[42] The great fecundity of scholarly commentaries on *Heart of Darkness* testifies to Conrad's genius in crafting such a multifaceted jewel for meticulous appraisal. Critics, like early explorers, must write "in the midst of the incomprehensible" (*HD*, 10). And every attempt at a definitive interpretation of the narrative ultimately falls short of a full disclosure.[43] By taking us to the heart of darkness, Conrad paradoxically uses words to demonstrate the inability of language to encompass the unfathomability of human existence.

# 3

## Homo Ludicrous

The endings of "A Smile of Fortune" and "Typhoon" underscore Conrad's caustic assessment of human nature as doomed to being duped by illusions. Viewing modern existence as pathetic rather than tragic, he catalogues the many ways in which we make ourselves ridiculous. In "A Smile of Fortune," Conrad juxtaposes romance and commerce to dramatize the acquisitive mania that typifies Western culture. He also plays off the narrator's positive self-concept against the selfishness that dictates his compromising actions throughout the novella. Ultimately, the narrator is revealed as a shallow individual who loathes himself and yet cannot break free from the cultural pressures that prompt him to value his social status over his personal conscience. Our craving for fortune, in whatever form, is our common misfortune.

"Typhoon," another tale in the comic mode, offers an even more disturbing profile of human behavior. Conrad's conclusion invites us to take a stand for or against Captain MacWhirr, whose heroism and inadequacy have both been analyzed by critics. But, ultimately, we must go beyond evaluating the Captain's psychological make-up to examine Conrad's strategy of using three different letters to present diverse interpretations of the crisis he faces at sea. By calling into question our ability to make judgments about others objectively through the medium of language, Conrad seems to undermine authority while testifying to our need to believe in some kind of authority, even if we have no authentic reason for placing our trust in anyone or anything outside ourselves. MacWhirr is a nautical ignoramus, yet he pilots his vessel safely into port and resolves the problem of the coolies' money in perhaps the only way possible without further upheaval. In a sense, the Captain succeeds despite himself. But Conrad never lets us forget that chaos is always closing in, regardless of our reliance on logic and language as the most useful tools by which we hope to control the external world.

## "A Smile of Fortune"

Like Poe, Conrad has rarely been credited with a sense of humor.[1] His reported bafflement in reaction to Shaw's bantering insults on their first meeting has reinforced the impression of him as a humorless author.[2] Thus, it is not surprising that critics have found ways to avoid addressing Conrad's antic spirit when dealing with the seriocomic "A Smile of Fortune." Commentators generally eschew the humorous content and focus on other aspects. They have analyzed the story as a dramatization of Maupassantian moral solitude,[3] as a psychodrama pitting the commercial self against the noncommercial self,[4] as a treatment of the betrayal of love and of the maritime code,[5] as a psychological critique of the confusion of romantic and business conventions (WWB, 71–77), and as a cynical assessment of sexuality that leads to "unintentional and almost ruinous comedy" (LG, 158–63).

Yet Conrad has comedy very much in mind throughout "A Smile of Fortune." He sets his mock-romance in the context of a mock-commercial cruise and plays one off against the other with absurd results. His narrator (ostensibly the same captain as in The Shadow Line, older but apparently no wiser) blunders into a preposterous cast of characters and faces a sequence of events that defies belief. The surname shared by three of these caricatures, Jacobus, may offer a clue to Conrad's artistic strategy in this story. Conrad was greatly amused by the comic sea tales of W. W. Jacobs, perhaps best known as the author of "The Monkey's Paw." In A Personal Record, Conrad praises "the inspired talent of Mr. Jacobs for poking endless fun at poor, innocent sailors in a prose which, however extravagant in its felicitous invention, is always artistically adjusted to observed truth . . ." (PR, 136–37).[6] In the manner of Jacobs, Conrad exposes his embarrassingly innocent narrator to ridicule from all sides, on ship and on shore, but most especially in the enchanted garden of love.[7] Conrad, not guilty here of the excesses of incorrigible romanticism as some critics suppose, employs exaggerations ironically to convert finance into farce, romance into voyeurism, and a tale of initiation into a tale of disillusionment.

Conrad's story opens with the narrator's rapturous description of Mauritius, the "Pearl of the Ocean," a fertile island where he hopes to acquire a large cargo of sugar. He is unexpectedly treated to a lavish breakfast by Alfred Jacobus, an opportunistic ship's chandler whom the narrator mistakes for his brother Ernest, an important merchant. Once he discovers his error, he ignores the chandler's importunities, yet he frequently defends the man's questionable morality. Alfred tries to convince the narrator to buy a shipment of potatoes, even enticing him to visit his walled garden where his seventeen-year-old daughter, Alice, passes time. Her father eventually lures the young captain to his house so he can obtain quarter-bags necessary for the sugar cargo. Upon meeting Alice, who behaves like a reclusive "wild animal," the narrator becomes obsessed with her and proceeds to haunt her garden daily. Before leaving port, he finally makes a romantic overture on one of his visits and follows this up with a kiss on the forehead. After Alice pushes the narrator away and runs to her room, her father suddenly arrives on the scene. Never mentioning the indiscretion, Jacobus successfully maneuvers the young captain into trading all his money for the potatoes he wants to sell. In the narrator's last meeting with Alice, a scene of melancholy disenchantment, his muted passion resurfaces as if for a somber curtain call. He departs furtively in the night and seeks forgetfulness at sea. But the omnipresent smell of potatoes reminds him of his romantic failure throughout the voyage.

Throughout the final pages, Conrad emphasizes the "commercial" aspects of the offensive cargo. To chief mate Burns, the potatoes represent the young captain's excessive good will. But the narrator views his entrapment into making a "bargain" with Jacobus as a sign of his defunct social status: "My reputation had suffered. I knew I was the object of unkind and sarcastic comments" (*TLS,* 81). When it turns out that there is a great market for potatoes at the next port of call, the narrator becomes financially successful, but his self-esteem continues to decline and he resigns his command rather than return to the "Pearl." The young captain who had sought material success at the outset finally becomes a disillusioned pessimist who cannot shake his guilty conscience. The accounting of profit and loss pervades Conrad's ending, as the narrator regains his money several times over and rids his ship of an apparently useless burden. However, he fails to experience the balm of forgetfulness that usually accompanies life at sea. Without this blessing, he remains haunted by memories of Alice: "I was for ever questioning myself as to the nature of facts and sensations connected with her person and with my conduct" (*TLS*, 82). Shortly after losing his easy conscience, he gives up the ship he loves and the pride of his first command. In Conrad's ridiculous mockery of the "tragic" fall, Alice and the young captain play the roles of the first man and woman in the "garden of flowers and scents" (*TLS*, 82). A "satanic" irony, absurdly objectified in the stench of decaying potatoes, arises from "corruption" engendered by supposedly innocent human beings. Jacobus could be interpreted as the snake in the garden, but Conrad assigns him a rather subsidiary role and emphasizes instead the endless *mea culpas* of the narrator.

Throughout the voyage, the narrator wishes he could close the lid on the cargo permanently and erase the memory of his "commercial venture" and all its romantic associations.[8] Burns, who undermines the captain's naive enthusiasms at the outset, prevents the narrator from evading his memories at the close by carefully preserving the potatoes, even though the "horrid" smell threatens to flavor the cargo of sugar that, in the tale's opening paragraphs, Conrad had linked to the narrator's dreams of success. Frustrated in the midst of an "unprecedented and comic situation," the narrator remains preoccupied with thoughts of Alice in her lush garden wonderland.

The narrator's second contact with land, at a colony thousands of miles from Pearl, sets the stage for the closing scene of Conrad's capitalistic farce. Here, Conrad converts the narrator's naive hope for good fortune into an obsession to sell his potatoes at a substantial profit. Upon learning of a scarcity of potatoes in the colony, he zealously begins to recoup his financial losses: "I felt plunged into corruption up to my neck. . . . The spirit of covetousness woke up in me. . . . That night I dreamt of a pile of gold in the form of a grave in which a girl was buried, and woke up callous with greed" (*TLS*, 84). The burial motif has intriguing Freudian connotations, but surely Conrad overloads this passage with too much melodrama to take seriously. He rehearses the myth of the fall only to plunge the narrator deeper into pathos. The cargo of decaying potatoes, sole produce of a postlapsarian pseudo-paradise, constantly reminds the narrator of his bungled romance with Alice, and he attempts to transform his loss (financial as well as psychological) into a considerable gain. But although he sells at higher and higher prices, his profit is merely monetary; psychologically, he remains at a loss: "I didn't want to see a potato as long as I lived; but the demon of lucre had taken possession of me" (*TLS*, 85). Conrad adds insult to idiocy by contrasting the narrator's lachrymose moanings with Burns's triumphant exultations

at the unexpected success of the "commercial venture." Burns has no
idea that his captain's mind persistently returns to "dreams concerned
with castaways starving on a desert island covered with flowers" (*TLS*,
85). Conrad's absurd image crowns the narrator's comic dementia, as
the author embellishes the genial humor of W. W. Jacobs with his
own characteristic concerns: solitude, obsessions, unfulfilled dreams,
wasted potentialities, and melodramatic disillusionment.

The narrator's resignation immediately follows his futile attempt to
persuade the ship's owners to give up the sugar trade, and visits to
Pearl, so he may chart a new commercial course. He puts his letter of
resignation in his "pocket—against [his] heart" (*TLS*, 86). On Pearl, his
need for "pockets" or quarter-bags led to intimate acquaintance with
Jacobus and his daughter. Conrad links passion and business by
stressing the captain's placement of the letter, a sign of his dual
romantic failure—concerning Alice and the ship he professes to love.
The narrator's walk to post the letter becomes a symbolic march of
defeat and degradation. Conrad never reveals why the captain resigns
his command, though one may speculate that it is due to his fear of
scandal or genuine intimacy or the prospect of marriage or the sight of
Jacobus, or several of these apprehensions in combination.[9] In any case,
fortune seems to smile on Burns as the chosen successor but frowns
on the narrator's hopes for future success: "I sat heavy-hearted at that
parting, seeing all my plans destroyed, my modest future endangered—for this command was like a foot in the stirrup for a young
man" (*TLS*, 88). But what has he really lost as a result of this self-
unhorsing? Nothing but the dream of an illusion, a petty disenchantment that Conrad depicts with ludicrous overtones.

Conrad converts nearly everything he establishes at the outset into
its opposite by the end of the story. These drastic inversions reflect the
narrator's topsy-turvy life as the events unfold. Conrad sets the stage
for these transformations by naming the island "Pearl," thus making it
an emblem of organic metamorphosis. Even the story's title undergoes
a subtle alteration. At the opening, it refers to the narrator's optimism
as he anticipates a successful voyage. But at the end, after *fortuna
tranquilla* becomes *fortuna mala*, fate seems to smile not on him but
on Burns, despite the acquisition of a tidy financial profit. The narrator's wish for good fortune has been granted in the form of a small
fortune, yet he feels compelled to resign his command and renounce
his ship. He first glimpses Pearl as "the astral body of an island risen to
greet me from afar" (*TLS*, 3). When quarter-bags are in short supply,
he reverses his bucolic impression of the island and echoes another

captain in calling Pearl an "infernal hole of a port!" (*TLS,* 42). Near the end of the story, the narrator muses that the Pearl had "grown odious." Conrad's last line ironically echoes his opening paragraphs as the fortunate Burns, not the jaded captain, exults in newfound opportunities.

Another radical transformation pertains to the narrator's frequent professions of "commercial innocence" early in the tale. Conrad interrupts the captain's reverie with a mundane digression recalling the purpose of the voyage: "[H]orrid thoughts of business interfered with my enjoyment of an accomplished passage. I was anxious for success and I wished, too, to do justice to the flattering latitude of my owner's instructions" (*TLS,* 3–4). Shortly thereafter, the narrator wonders why the sea must be used for selfish commercial purposes. However, Conrad undermines the nobility of the captain's professed aversion to trade almost immediately when the narrator rationalizes his opportunism: "But, living in a world more or less homicidal and desperately mercantile, it was plainly my duty to make the best of its opportunities" (*TLS,* 6). The rest of the tale dramatizes the farcical events that follow the captain's voluntary abandonment of the ethic of human solidarity to pursue "selfish aims of no great importance." His final disclaimer of community occurs while he is attending the funeral of the child of another sea captain when he violates the solemnity of the occasion by allowing thoughts of commerce and success to dominate his mind. "Time's money," he muses, echoing the business ethics of Franklin's *Autobiography.* He also avoids taking blame for his increasing preoccupation with commercial affairs, noting, "[T]hese thoughts . . . pursued me" (*TLS,* 16).

Conrad emphasizes compulsive activities throughout "A Smile of Fortune," especially with regard to the narrator's business dealings and mock-romance with Alice. The narrator admits his attachment to Alice stems from an "irrealizable desire" that prevents him from seeing his own folly while in her presence: "It was like being the slave of some depraved habit" (*TLS,* 59). He becomes dependent on simply seeing her: "It was what I was coming for daily; troubled, ashamed, eager; finding in my nearness to her a unique sensation which I indulged with dread, self-contempt, and deep pleasure, as if it were a secret vice bound to end in my undoing, like the habit of some drug or other which ruins and degrades its slave" (*TLS,* 62). The narrator's absurd enslavement to voyeuristic pleasure unfolds as a mockery of the eye-romance, one of the crucial elements of the courtly love tradition. But Alice is no regal damsel, though she casts a spell on the captain: "[W]hen she passed near me I felt with tenfold force the charm of the peculiar, promising sensation I had formed the habit to seek near her" (*TLS*, 65). Alice is "the fascinating object" he must keep before his eyes at all cost. Even when compromised by Jacobus, after the passionate wrestling match with the animalistic girl, he despairs at the thought of breaking his romantic routine: "I wanted to stay for one more experience of that strange provoking sensation and of indefinite desire, the habit of which had made me . . . dread the prospect of going to sea" (*TLS*, 73).

Conrad portrays the narrator's comic reenactment of the fall from innocence to experience by evoking the image of the garden, which also undergoes a transformation mirroring the captain's descent into corruption and cowardice. The first glimpse of Alice's garden recalls his description of the beautiful, solitary island: "It was really a magnificent garden: smooth green lawns and a gorgeous maze of flower beds in the foreground, displayed around a basin of dark water framed in a marble rim, and in the distance the massed foliage of varied trees concealing the roofs of other houses. . . . It was a brilliantly coloured solitude, drowsing in a warm, voluptuous silence" (*TLS*, 42–43). Initially, this sensuous labyrinth seems a perfect setting for a love tryst. But when the narrator's visits become habitual and his obsession with Alice intensifies in response to her stubbornness and petulance, Conrad converts the place of assignation into a funereal landscape: "The garden was one mass of gloom, like a cemetery of flowers buried in the darkness, and she, in the chair, seemed to muse mournfully over the extinction of light and colour. Only whiffs of heavy scents passed like wandering, fragrant souls of that departed multitude of blossoms" (*TLS*, 53).

This denatured setting foreshadows the chilling of the narrator's hothouse passion, which follows the surprise intrusion of Jacobus and the agreement to purchase the cargo of potatoes. Once more, Conrad indulges in melodramatic rhetoric as he burlesques the tawdry encounter of man and woman:

> The shadows lengthened, deepened, mingled together into a pool of twilight in which the flower-beds glowed like coloured embers; whiffs of heavy scent came to me as if the dusk of this hemisphere were but the dimness of a temple and the garden an enormous censer swinging before the altar of the stars. The colours of the blossoms deepened, losing their glow one by one. (*TLS*, 76)

What separates this purple passage from kindred poetic expressions, such as Keats's "Ode to a Nightingale" and "Ode on a Grecian Urn," is the inappropriateness of its garish imagery when viewed in the context of the whole story. Conrad's tone oscillates from whimsicality to grave earnestness in the manner of W. W. Jacobs.[10] When the narrator finally realizes the failure of his relationship with Alice, he absconds like a thief making off with ill-gotten booty, leaving her alone. The narrator does not return to the image of Alice's incarceration until the end, when, prior to the rash of potato dealings, a pilot mentions the word *garden* casually, and the captain has "a vision of gorgeous colour, of sweet scents, of a girlish figure crouching in a chair" (TLS, 84). The memory of "sweet scents" contrasts with the rotting potatoes in the mind of the transformed narrator, who is compromised, if not quite thoroughly corrupted, by his need to preserve his social status.

The narrator also wants to preserve his romantic perspective on the isolation of Alice and her father, a tendency that serves as a parodic element. Undoubtedly, they are social outcasts, but the captain celebrates their solitude in rhetorical reveries that even he cannot take seriously:

> I had a conception of Jacobus and his daughter existing, a lonely pair of castaways, on a desert island; the girl sheltering in the house as if it were a cavern in a cliff, and Jacobus going out to pick up a living for both on the beach—exactly like two shipwrecked people who always hope for some rescuer to bring them back at least into touch with the rest of mankind.
>
> But Jacobus's bodily reality did not fit in with this romantic view. (TLS, 39)

Despite the narrator's awareness of his proclivity for exaggeration, he continues to view Alice as a damsel in distress awaiting rescue by a shining knight. Conrad's allusion to Cinderella's glass slipper later in the tale also contributes to the fairy-tale quality of his scenario. As the captain's visits to Alice's garden become a daily ritual, he begins to sound like the wretched knight in Keats's "La Belle Dame sans Merci": "[I]n the scent of the massed flowers I seemed to breathe her special and inexplicable charm, the heady perfume of the everlastingly irritated captive of the garden" (TLS, 62). He not only romanticizes Alice and her father, and the sultry garden worthy of Rappaccini's daughter, but also projects the whole world as a global steambath of passion and fear. Such language befits potboiler fiction, but beneath the surface of excessive verbalizing Conrad does dramatize the narrator's transition from naive dreamer to confirmed pessimist, one who awakens to see "the lost illusion of vague desires" disappear from sight.

Conrad consistently parodies romantic sensuousness, particularly by presenting Alice as a "tragic" heroine out of a sentimental novel. Immobilized by reverie, she lapses into trances that exaggerate the artificiality of the tableaux: "[S]he did not stir, staring straight before her as if watching the vision of some pageant passing through the garden in the deep, rich glow of light and the splendour of flowers" (*TLS*, 43). Her "black, lustrous locks" give the "impression of magnificently cynical untidiness" (*TLS*, 44), as if Ligeia's lush mane had suddenly sprouted Medusa's serpentine split ends. Crouching as if ready to spring into action—her characteristic posture—she is like a noble savage in corset. On occasion, however, this feline creature adopts the posture of Rodin's *Thinker*.[11]

Like Melville's Bartleby, Conrad's Alice prefers not to heed prevailing social conventions: "[T]he girl by means of repeated 'Won't!' 'Shan't!' and 'Don't care!' . . . conveyed and affirmed her intention not to come to the table, not to have any dinner, not to move from the verandah" (*TLS*, 49). In addition to portraying her as a human negation, Conrad depicts Alice as an absurd combination of Aphrodite and Buddhist monk:

> I loved to watch her slow changes of pose, to look at her long immobilities composed in the graceful lines of her body, to observe the mysterious narrow stare of her splendid black eyes, somewhat long in shape, half closed, contemplating the void. She was like a spellbound creature with the forehead of a goddess crowned by the disheveled magnificent hair of a gipsy tramp. (*TLS*, 58–59)

Alice's statuary poses make her seem a goddess in marble, but more often they suggest the rigidity of a corpse. The narrator acts as Pygmalion to her Galatea, but Conrad aborts the mythic scenario to dramatize the failure of communication in the modern world. Even the captain's promise not to harm her when he takes her into his arms prompts another exaggerated transformation: "To watch the change in the girl was like watching a miracle . . . That black, fixed stare into which I had read a tragic meaning more than once, in which I had found a sombre seduction, was perfectly empty now, void of all consciousness whatever, and not even aware any longer of my presence" (*TLS*, 68). But when Alice breaks away from the narrator's embrace, he immediately brands her a "mortal enemy," a "serpentine" enchantress who has transformed the edenic garden into a psychological inferno. From this point on, Alice lingers in his memory only as a shadowy figure representing failure: his foiled attempt to

rescue her by passion. He abandons Alice to her darkening garden as
she stares with "empty eyes" (like Fitzgerald's Dr. T. J. Eckleberg) at
nothing at all.

Conrad's seriocomic romance ends on a sour note of futility, with
both potential lovers voicing pessimistic attitudes. Alice's nihilism
results from her ingrained conditioning. Her habitual reading of crime
reports in sensationalist newspapers gives her a grisly, one-dimensional view of life: "[S]he had formed for herself a notion of the
civilised world as a scene of murders, abductions, burglaries, stabbing
affrays, and every form of desperate violence. England and France,
Paris and London . . . appeared to her sinks of abomination, reeking
with blood, in contrast to her little island where petty larceny was
about the standard of current misdeeds" (TLS, 60–61).[12] Alice's perverse, pervasive "love of nothing" arises out of the stagnation of
prolonged isolation and is reinforced by the chronic nay-saying of her
governess and the unethical predisposition of her father.

But the narrator's pessimism, which echoes the girl's petulant
negations, has no such natural point of origin. Instead, his cynicism
grows out of egoistic frustration, his persistent failure to make the
world conform to his own views. Conrad first indicates the narrator's
evolution toward discontent at the funeral service the young captain
attends solely out of a sense of obligation. His "critical detachment"
from the ceremony stems not only from his feeling that the ritualistic
language is empty rhetoric but also from his unwillingness to think
about the dead child he has never known. Instead, the narrator's
thoughts gravitate to business matters, specifically his ambition to achieve
personal success. His cynicism diminishes thereafter and does not resur-
face until his infatuation with the socially taboo Alice. The captain uses
the royal "we" as a rhetorical defense mechanism and then proceeds to
place full blame on the girl who has captivated his interest:

> How weak, irrational, and absurd we are! How easily carried away
> whenever our awakened imagination brings us the irritating hint of a desire!
> I cared for the girl in a particular way, seduced by the moody expression
> of her face, by her obstinate silences, her rare, scornful words; by the
> perpetual pout of her closed lips, the black depths of her fixed gaze
> turned slowly upon me as if in contemptuous provocation, only to be
> averted next moment with an exasperated indifference. (TLS, 56–57)

So long as the absurd romance continues, the Werther-like narrator
takes refuge in his illusion of her total responsibility for his obsession.
But in his final farewell to Alice, he begins to internalize her version of

the abyss. He meditates on the blankness of her stark denial of life: "I heard in her sullen tone the faint echo of that resentfully tragic note which I had found once so provoking. But it left me unmoved except for a sudden and weary conviction of the emptiness of all things under Heaven" (TLS, 78–79). The narrator's Weltschmerz has a specific cause: his failure to reanimate the tragic and provocative girl who has become his idée fixe.

Fueling the narrator's cynicism, the sense of unrealized potential plays a central role in Conrad's tragic farce. The lamenting of lost opportunities intrudes frequently, as in the early funeral scene, when the narrator notices a sentimental "old sea-dog" shedding tears for the dead child, though he had no wife or children of his own. The captain speculates that the sailor's grief stems from his memories of squandered chances. He feels ashamed of his own callous nature, for he cannot weep. The elegiac celebration of life in a funeral setting foreshadows the narrator's rejection of Alice during his last visit to the garden. After he has agreed to buy the cargo of potatoes, he lingers after the chandler's departure to try to see Alice one more time. He calls her name, only once, and then sinks into melodramatic dejection when she fails to appear. Yet he discounts the fact that she eventually does return to him: "I received the impression that she had come too late. She ought to have appeared at my call. She ought to have . . . It was as if a supreme opportunity had been missed" (TLS, 77; Conrad's ellipsis). Conrad never discloses what sort of "supreme opportunity" has been wasted, but he does undermine the narrator's integrity with the repetition of the word ought, which implies a moral imperative, an obligation or responsibility. The narrator views Alice as a beautiful commodity on display for purchase from her father, yet he ends up buying a load of potatoes instead.

Conrad accentuates the materialistic side of culture by presenting Alfred Jacobus, a procurer of goods and services, as an exploiter who operates on the basis of double-entendre. His sycophantic business procedures include courting the captain's favors (as though wooing a blushing maiden) and using his daughter Alice as bait. Jacobus's offer to procure a new female figurehead foreshadows his pandering his seventeen-year-old daughter. The image of Alfred Jacobus as a "figurehead-procuring bloodsucker" seems ludicrous at first, but it becomes ironically apropos at the story's end. To Jacobus, life is a series of commercial transactions, carried out amicably whenever possible. He even converts his residence into a place of sale when he asks the narrator to make himself at home and then departs after introducing

his daughter. Jacobus gives his benign approval to the captain's frequent visits, and Conrad insinuates that they share more than merely
a polite partnership: "A sort of shady, intimate understanding seemed
to have been established between us" (TLS, 51). The narrator begins
to suspect that Jacobus sanctions his attentions to Alice because he
wants to dispose of her conveniently as unwanted property. He complains of a sense of "moral discomfort" about the chandler, as if they
had made a secret pact between them. When Jacobus suddenly
interrupts the aborted love scene between Alice and the narrator, his
subtle blackmailing scheme reveals his true nature as a merciless
exploiter: "He thought it over, his calculating gaze lost in mine, for
quite a long time before he came out in a thoughtful tone with the
rapacious suggestion" (TLS, 74). Conrad adds another irony in the final
pages when the narrator discovers that the chandler's worthless cargo
of potatoes can actually be sold for a considerable profit at the next
port of call. Thus, the character who has been fleeced by the financial
bloodsucker becomes comparatively wealthy at the end, due to an
irrational smile of fortune.

As previously suggested, the word *fortune* suggests two related
concepts: luck and wealth.[13] At the outset, the captain apparently
hopes for nothing more than a successful voyage. But Conrad hints at
his latent greed throughout the tale. Even in the opening paragraphs,
he strongly emphasizes the captain's profit motive, specifically per-
taining to the potentially large cargo of sugar. Conrad associates the
narrator's anxiety for success with his desire to please *his* owners, not
the *ship's* owners, in Conrad's phraseology. When Jacobus boards his
ship before breakfast, the narrator wonders whether Pearl is an "enchanted nook" where "wealthy merchants rush" to ships as soon as
they enter the harbor. When the captain learns that he has been
talking to the wrong Jacobus, he still respects the chandler because
"[h]e had told me many useful things—and besides he was the brother
of that wealthy merchant" (TLS, 13). He even implies a willingness to
compromise his ethics when speaking of the need to adapt to new
circumstances. When the narrator actually encounters a compromising
situation—his need for 1,100 quarter-bags, which are in short supply
on the island—he is willing to try any means to obtain them, for he is
focused solely on making a quick round trip. Missing a dinner engage-
ment to talk to Jacobus about obtaining the quarter-bags, the narrator
dismisses the prior obligation in favor of his greater priority: "[I]t had
procured me a more amusing evening. And besides . . . [t]he sacred
business" demanded his attention (TLS, 50). "The sacred business"

even extends to his romance with Alice. In response to her cynicism and indifference, he reacts as though he has been fleeced in a commercial transaction: "I felt as though I had been cheated in some rather complicated deal into which I had entered against my better judgment. Yes, cheated without any regard for, at least, the forms of decency" (*TLS*, 68). The narrator feels doubly cheated when Jacobus blackmails him into buying the potatoes. It scarcely matters that the humiliating cargo proves so marketable, since he has been hoodwinked by the "rapacious" chandler. Overreacting to his shameful failure, the captain resigns his command and returns to Europe, in a self-imposed exile from his ship that is not so much tragic as pathetic.

The narrator's fear of a scandal may also play a part in his melancholy abdication. As chapter 4 opens, he expresses surprise that the public is "scandalised" not by Ernest Jacobus's brutal treatment of his mulatto assistant but by his own abruptness in terminating their conversation. Shortly thereafter, he learns of Alfred Jacobus's "perfectly scandalous" love affair with the circus rider, which resulted in the birth of Alice. Her presence serves to perpetuate the notoriety of the scandal on the island (*TLS*, 37). Only the urgent need for quarter-bags prompts the narrator to enter the chandler's scandal-ridden house. However, recognizing the capricious wheel of fortune that desolated the chandler does not prevent the narrator from yielding to the same fate. For he allows his sentimentality to overwhelm his rational judgment in viewing Alice as "condemned to moral solitude by the verdict of a respectable community" (*TLS*, 64). However, he changes his tune after Alice breaks away from his embrace and Jacobus, holding his daughter's abandoned shoe in his hands for psychological leverage, extracts all his money for a cargo of potatoes:

> I did not want an open scandal, but I thought that outward decency may be bought too dearly at times. I included Jacobus, myself, the whole population of the island in the same contemptuous disgust as though we had been partners in an ignoble transaction. . . . Was this the fortune the vapours and fair apparition had held for me in its hard heart, hidden within the shape as of fair dreams and mist? Was this my luck? (*TLS*, 74)

Pearl is indeed an island of ironic transformations, for Conrad converts the narrator's naive optimism into cynical self-loathing, his romantic infatuation into monetary lust, and his inexperience with trade into an indoctrination in unscrupulous business practices.

"A Smile of Fortune," though far from a masterpiece, resists scholarly attempts at classification, and for good reason. The tale is part tragedy and part farce, part self-dramatization and part self-parody, part realism and part *reductio ad absurdum*. Poe would have called such a story an arabesque, and its incongruities seem to point in that direction. But Conrad scorned all literary schools, systems, and categories. He reveals little about the story in his author's note except to state that, despite its "autobiographical form," the tale does not derive from "the record of personal experience" (*TLS*, ix). Whether Conrad is being candid or merely camouflaging potentially embarrassing facts remains an open question. Yet the text must stand on its own merits.[14] Throughout this ambiguous and incongruous tale, Conrad demonstrates the shallowness of both romantic yearnings and materialistic cravings. The grip of passion can be as destructive as the frantic pursuit of wealth. Whether through timidity or disillusioning self-knowledge, the narrator retreats from his entanglements in the romantic and financial playgrounds of the acquisitive ego. Like Axel Heyst in *Victory*, but unlike Kurtz and Falk, he does not blindly follow the dictates of his hungry heart to the end. At last, he gains a glimpse of the folly and frivolity behind the blissful vision of the smile of fortune.

## "Typhoon"

In 1969 critic Lawrence Graver could feel justified in calling "Typhoon" a "masterpiece of clarity and good sense. Unlike most of Conrad's best stories, it is without mystifying elements and has never provoked the kind of interpretive arguments that have characterized critical discussions of *Lord Jim* or even *The Secret Agent*" (*LG*, 94–95).[15] This comforting opinion hinges, however, on the assumption of Captain MacWhirr's unqualified heroism and sound judgment in dealing with the hurricane and the unruly Chinese coolies below deck. For a time such an assumption was accepted almost without question.[16] But just as Conrad's title metamorphosed from "Equitable Division" to "Skittish Cargo" to "Typhoon" (see *CL*, 2:169, 237), so, too, has the estimate of MacWhirr undergone a transformation upon closer critical scrutiny.[17] Conrad's protagonist can no longer be seen as the ideal model of a sea captain, but neither can he be dubbed a "caricature" of "a simple sea captain" (*BCM*, 163), for MacWhirr's personality contains too many incongruities and outright contradictions to be easily reconciled with the image of sound, practical seamanship that Conrad espouses in his essays, letters, and other stories (*WWB*, 33–36). Seen in the light of more intensive critical evaluation, MacWhirr still seems a simple, unimaginative, literalistic character, but we must now acknowledge that Conrad's treatment of his experience is more complex, ambiguous, and paradoxical than Graver and others had once assumed.[18] Moreover, MacWhirr's complex characterization calls into question the overall meaning of "Typhoon."[19] If the steady perseverance of the Captain is thoroughly compromised, then what lies at the heart of the novella?

An examination of the plot structure shows that MacWhirr does teach a lesson in human endurance to Jukes, the fanciful and loquacious chief mate. Conrad's story opens as the *Nan-Shan* steams toward Fu-Chau carrying some cargo and two hundred Chinese coolies. When a falling barometer alerts the crew to expect a siege of stormy weather, MacWhirr retires to the chart room to consult nautical books on how to deal with severe storms at sea. But to the exasperation of Jukes, the Captain dismisses the cautious advice he finds in the volumes. During the long ordeal, the second mate goes mad and Jukes gives way to despair, but MacWhirr continues to give orders in an authoritative voice. When the Captain learns that the Chinese are fighting among themselves over money scattered by the lurching of the ship, he sends Jukes and several crewmen to confiscate all the money and restore order. Conrad then takes a chronological leap forward to the sunny day when the battered ship reaches Fu-Chau. Almost immediately, he shifts the scene to the drawing room of the Captain's house, where his apathetic wife "thoughtlessly" reads his letter describing the ordeal. Another scene shift takes us to the home of Mrs. Rout, who reads a letter written by her husband, Solomon, chief engineer of the *Nan-Shan*. He writes simply that the Captain has done something very clever, but he never specifies the deed. Finally, Conrad discloses what happened during the last stages of the voyage in yet another letter, written by Jukes to a friend on an ocean liner. Jukes claims that the insensitive Captain disregarded his suggestion to keep the coolies imprisoned below deck until the ship reached a safe harbor. Instead, MacWhirr released them and measured out an equal share of the confiscated Chinese money to each coolie. Jukes concludes that the Captain succeeded in spite of innate stupidity and entreats his correspondent to write his own opinion of what he has read.[20]

Conrad's invitation extends to us as well, especially in view of the indirect mode of his final disclosures. The letters written by MacWhirr, Rout, and Jukes present three different perspectives on the outcome of the voyage.[21] Conrad cues the attentive reader to interpret these missives by discussing the peculiar writing habits of the three epistolary characters at the story's outset. To a certain degree, MacWhirr,

Rout, and Jukes collaborate in putting the finishing touch on Conrad's narrative of human nature in crisis. But their letters project their distinctive personalities rather than presenting an objective view of the events. For example, as a youth, the unimaginative MacWhirr mailed letters home to his parents that read like catalogues:

> The old people ultimately became acquainted with a good many names of ships, and with the names of the skippers who commanded them—with the names of Scots and English shipowners—with the names of seas, oceans, straits, promontories—with outlandish names of lumber-ports, of rice-ports, of cotton-ports—with the names of islands—with the name of their son's young woman. She was called Lucy. It did not suggest itself to him to mention whether he thought the name pretty. (*T*, 5–6)

In addition to establishing MacWhirr's mental enslavement to dull factuality, Conrad's emphasis on proper names and place names suggests the Captain's foolish belief in a name-bound, word-bound reality. MacWhirr's obtuse mind functions by organizing experience solely in terms of names and forms, what Indian sages and Benjamin Lee Whorf have called the fallacy of *Nāma-Rūpa*. By confusing names with the forms they represent, the Captain lives in a simplistically formulated world of his own and avoids any authentic encounter with experience.[22] Conrad directly alludes to the confusion of name and form in the names he bestows on the Captain and his ship.[23] *MacWhirr*, literally "son of Whirr," evokes the word *whir*, meaning to move about quickly with a buzzing sound. But this dynamic denotation seems completely unbefitting of MacWhirr's stolid disposition (unless perhaps the mechanical buzzing sound stands for his methodical mental processes). Early in the first paragraph, Conrad accentuates the Captain's blandness, asserting that his "physiognomy . . . was the exact counterpart of his mind: it presented no marked characteristics of firmness or stupidity; it had no pronounced characteristics whatever; it was simply ordinary, irresponsive, and unruffled" (*T*, 3). Not only is the Captain's name, which implies turmoil or frantic activity, ill-suited to his nature, but his ship, the *Nan-Shan*, meaning "southern mountain," also seems ill-named, considering its final condition as a battered hulk when it eventually reaches harbor.

Conrad supplements his paradoxical name ploys by providing incongruous details in his portrait of Captain MacWhirr, whose self-assurance springs from his lack of imagination.[24] His idiosyncratic harbor attire marks him as "uncouth," for, despite his bravado in facing a hurricane, he always takes an "elegant umbrella" clutched in "his powerful hairy fist" whenever he goes ashore. MacWhirr's habitual carrying of an umbrella might seem to suggest always being prepared, but this is not the case. Rather, the umbrella indicates his fixation on the *appearance* of being prepared. In harmony with MacWhirr's placidity, the *Nan-Shan* has the reputation of being "an exceptionally steady ship," a trait more attributable to fair weather rather than the Captain's knowledge of nautical procedures. In fact, the Captain does not even remember any of his answers to "simple questions" concerning circular storms posed to him by the commission that certified him as fit to command. Although he is too old and unimaginative to be identified with Conrad's insecure narrators in the tales of first command, he is nonetheless a genuine novice in the world of experience: "MacWhirr had sailed over the surface of the oceans as some men go skimming over the years of existence to sink gently into a placid grave, ignorant of life to the last, without ever having been made to see all it may contain of perfidy, of violence, and of terror" (*T*, 19). Why, then, does the Captain deserve superior status? Because the ship's owners prefer a functionary with tunnel vision who will guide the vessel (and its precious cargo) with care and without imagination, and because Conrad, like Dostoyevsky's Underground Man, views civilization as a sophisticated "ant-heap" where the specious promises of fate lure the human ego, "setting the unconscious faces of the multitude towards inconceivable goals and in undreamt-of directions" (*T*, 5). Conrad envisions life as a seriocomic puppet show in which the driving forces of existence remain outside our word-bound comprehension.

MacWhirr's letters to his "pretentious" wife, like his earlier letters to his parents, seem factual to the point of exasperation. Small wonder she reads them in a state of ennui while reclining in a plush hammock-chair. The monotony of the Captain's correspondence documents his psychological stagnation as he makes a transition from "Ordinary Seaman" to commander of the *Nan-Shan*. MacWhirr writes home with tedious regularity, asking to be "remembered to the children," but his daughter Lydia is ashamed of him, his son is indifferent, and his wife's main concern is that MacWhirr may decide to return home permanently. Thus, Conrad employs double-edged irony when the dreary MacWhirr signs his letters "'Your loving husband,' as calmly as if the words so long used by so many men were, apart from their shape, worn-out things, and of a faded meaning" (*T*, 15). MacWhirr's habitual inscription is not only a mindless cliché but also an indication of the one-sided nature of his family ties. Rather than expressing genuine love, his inscription suggests blind commitment to labels and names and testifies to his submissiveness to the sterile institutionality of marriage. By giving love a societal stamp, Conrad undermines the authenticity of the feeling, as shown by the MacWhirrs' indifference to each other. The only time they acknowledge one another is when civilized convention dictates—MacWhirr in his letters and his wife when conversing with her friend. The monotonous accuracy of the Captain's letters testifies to the sterile complacency of his routinized life.

Conrad returns to this trite marital melodrama when he places MacWhirr's letter first in the sequence of three missives that closes the narrative. The Captain's written description of the typhoon crisis inspires the steward to read it surreptitiously with "absorbing interest," but MacWhirr's wife, the letter's intended reader, scans the lines with obvious disinterest: "Mrs. MacWhirr, in the drawing-room of the forty-pound house, stifled a yawn—perhaps out of self-respect—for she was alone" (T, 93). Her artificial gesture of boredom reveals her predisposition to posing and posturing. She also shows a cool hypocrisy when she prattles words of endearment about her husband in the company of friends and neighbors. In a sense, Conrad matches husband and wife well; MacWhirr writes methodical letters and his wife reads them "perfunctorilly." Yet Conrad elicits sympathy for the dull Captain in the description of the lavish decor of Mrs. MacWhirr's surroundings: "She reclined in a plush-bottomed and gilt hammock-chair near a tiled fireplace, with Japanese fans on the mantel and a glow of coals in the grate. Lifting her hands, she glanced wearily here and there into the many pages" (T, 93). She is too blasé to notice her husband's rare "disclosure" that between four and six o'clock on Christmas morning he lapsed into despondency, believing he would never see his family again. Conrad not only exposes Mrs. MacWhirr's insensitivity to her husband's feelings in this passage but also deftly implies that the typhoon occurs on the eve and morning of the anniversary of the birth of Christ. Curiously, except for this isolated reference, no one even casually acknowledges this fact before, during, or after the crisis.

Mrs. MacWhirr seems oblivious to the exploitation of her husband's dogged industriousness, as a "black marble clock" with a "discreet stealthy tick" marks the time of his absence from their spiritually defunct marital union (T, 94). Both mother and daughter react to his letter with indifference, rewarding themselves with a shopping spree to rid their minds of the latest communication from the absent head of their family. They step into a street that Conrad depicts as a funereal panorama of middle-class hedonism:

> Mrs. MacWhirr smiled upon a woman in a black mantle of generous proportions armoured in jet and crowned with flowers blooming falsely above a bilious matronly countenance. They broke into a swift little babble of greetings and exclamations both together, very hurried, as if the street were ready to yawn open and swallow all that pleasure before it could be expressed. (*T*, 95)

In this scene, Conrad accentuates the idleness and hypocrisy of social discourse—in vivid contrast to the comment of the laconic MacWhirr, who tells Jukes that he cannot comprehend humanity's love of conversation. Conrad's digression evokes sympathy for the Captain, who has steadfastly endured an intense trial while his wife lounges in leisure and chatters insincerely. Such sympathy not only obscures the Captain's confession of despair but serves to counter the charge of stupidity leveled against MacWhirr in Jukes's letter.[25]

Conrad associates the second letter, written by Solomon Rout, with a funereal atmosphere as well. Rout's wife reads the letter aloud to her husband's elderly mother, who sits in an armchair seemingly "lost in watching the last flickers of life" (*T*, 96). Caring for Rout's mother, who has trouble recalling her youngest and only surviving child, prevents his wife from joining her husband in the South Pacific. In his letter, Rout provides little information about the typhoon; instead, he deals with the outcome of his harrowing experience: his intensified loneliness and longing for his wife. Conrad's depiction of the Rout family inverts the apathetic relationship of the MacWhirrs. In this more appealing household we hear Rout's assertion that the Captain has managed to do something very clever, despite his innate simplicity, though this only confirms what he had written earlier about MacWhirr in a "jocular and convivial letter": "Give me the dullest ass for a skipper before a rogue" (*T*, 16). If Conrad is counting on us to accept the wisdom of Solomon (Rout), then we have some evidence of the Captain's diligence, but Conrad qualifies this endorsement with a left-handed compliment, noting that the "airy generalization" stems from MacWhirr's "honesty, which, in itself had the heavy obviousness of a lump of clay" (*T*, 16). Once again, Conrad brings the matter of the Captain's dense mind to the forefront.

The third letter, which Conrad cites verbatim, contains the most damaging charge against MacWhirr, save for the unnamed narrator's criticism of the Captain. Jukes, like Solomon Rout, never changes his

written opinion of the Captain from first to last,[26] though he himself
may change in the course of the story.[27] In his letter, Jukes conceals
his inadequacies behind a facade of fortitude, describing how he
restored order among the coolies in phrases "calculated" to make him
seem indomitably resolute. His "animated and very full" account of
the storm brands the Captain as having the sensitivity of a "bedpost"
(T, 97, 98). What has inspired this criticism is the Captain's rejection
of Jukes's scheme to lock up the coolies and throw their money down
into the hold to create a diversion for their anger. MacWhirr certainly
resolves the problem without violence or scandal, but it would be
erroneous to view his artful dodging of the problem as ingenious or to
consider the Captain as a humanitarian in his dealings with the
coolies.[28] Ultimately, the Chinese agree to his terms for redistributing
the confiscated money because they fear losing everything to their
own corrupt officials. Yet the battered coolies display respect for the
Captain as he doles out each man's share. Their cautious respect far
exceeds Jukes's minimal approval of MacWhirr's policies.

If Conrad's story primarily concerns the stubborn perseverance of
Captain MacWhirr throughout the typhoon's assault, then it is very
surprising that the final chapter does not depict the triumphant moment of survival, namely, the release of the ship from the threat of
disaster. Conrad omits any mention of the crew's exultation and does
not call attention to the Captain's well-deserved respite from his round-
the-clock activities. Instead, Conrad closes with Jukes's long account
of how MacWhirr dealt with the Chinese and their money, which
seems anticlimactic at best. Even more importantly, Conrad does not
describe the second onslaught of the storm, even though he has
provided ample foreshadowings of its inevitability.[29] To gain a greater
appreciation of Conrad's literary endgame, we must carefully consider the narrative as an experience, conveyed through the imprecise
medium of language, that raises significant epistemological questions.[30]

One of Conrad's telling, but apparently inconsequential, details is
obscured in the closing scene in which Jukes praises MacWhirr's
judicious handling of the Chinese money. In a casual comment about
the sanitary operations on the ship after the coolies have been ap-
peased, Jukes describes how the sailors went below to clean up the
mess and "shovelled out on deck heaps of wet rags, *all sorts of
fragments of things without shape, and that you couldn't give a name
to,* and let them settle the ownership themselves" (T, 102; emphasis
added). The chaotic aftermath of the storm mirrors the power of
natural forces to disintegrate the artificial constructs of civilization.[31]

Throughout "Typhoon," Conrad dramatizes the fragmentation of human order brought about by the formless manifestations of nature. He insists that these dynamic phenomena transcend mortal comprehension and mock our sense of control, which depends so much on verbal constructs.

Human understanding depends on the illusion of security, and just prior to the storm Conrad calls attention to the image of a misty "halo of the sun," which seems to betoken a providential order. But this sign of salvation begins to fade when MacWhirr attempts to see clearly in the darkness: "[A] few amazing stars drooped, dim and fitful, above an immense waste of broken seas, as if seen through a mad drift of smoke" (T, 37). Previously, the Captain had rested in the comfortable supposition that the China seas are merely "tangled facts that nevertheless speak to a seaman in clear and definite language" (T, 15). But now the ocean becomes as indistinct to MacWhirr as the sailors who toil in expiring light: "Suddenly darkness closed upon one pane, then on another. The voices of the lost group reached him after the manner of men's voices in a gale, in shreds and fragments of forlorn shouting snatched past the ear" (T, 37). Conrad associates the storm's disruption of the sailor's unity and cooperation with the essential human predicament, as the chaotic wind strips away the fabric of language. He also fragments the verbal exchange between MacWhirr and Jukes, underscoring the problem of communication in a world that resists linguistic categorizing, for Conrad's typhoon fragments mind as well as matter: "It seemed to explode all around the ship with an overpowering concussion and a rush of great waters, as if an immense dam had been blown up to windward. In an instant the men lost touch of each other. This is the disintegrating power of a great wind: it isolates one from one's kind" (T, 40). The word *concussion* links the destructive power of nature to the precarious vulnerability of the human psyche.[32] Conrad depicts the ship's travail as emblematic of our perennially frustrated quest for meaning in a world of uncertainty, ambiguity, and (as he seems to imply here) emptiness: "The motion of the ship was extravagant. Her lurches had an appalling helplessness: she pitched as if taking a header into a void, and seemed to find a wall to hit every time" (T, 42–43). The ship's plunge into the abyss, like Marlow's voyage to Kurtz's Inner Station in *Heart of Darkness,* ushers us into a world of indecipherable sounds and blurred outlines. Like Poe's "The Fall of the House of Usher," Conrad's "Typhoon" begins with a sense of order that gradually dissipates into chaotic disorder and then reconstitutes itself as a unified entity once more.

Throughout the crisis, Conrad stresses the storm's fragmentation of the vessel, which evolves into "ruins" created by the deafening wind and crushing "masses of foam." Facing this oceanic nightmare, MacWhirr and Jukes have no other choice but to grasp hold of each other; once they separate in the darkness, the Captain seems to no longer exist for Jukes. Chaos also reigns within the ship's hold where two hundred "Celestials" become a "mound of writhing bodies" struggling for space and for lost money. In fragmentary sentences, MacWhirr orders Jukes to quell the disturbance, an absurd command that the mate nevertheless executes successfully. Conrad depicts the Chinese brawl as a dark vision of fragmentation, a confusing clash of dismembered body parts: "Jukes saw a head bang the deck violently, two thick calves waving on high, muscular arms twined round a naked body, a yellow-face, open-mouthed and with a set wild stare, look up and slide away" (T, 62). In this passage Conrad not only extends the fragmentation motif but reveals Jukes's view of the Chinese men as a threat to the order of the ship. The confusion among the coolies is a microcosm of the chaos engulfing the vessel: "[I]t seemed that an eddy of the hurricane, stealing through the iron sides of the ship, had set all these bodies whirling like dust: there came to them a confused uproar, a tempestuous tumult, a fierce mutter, gusts of screams dying away, and the trampling of feet mingling with the blows of the sea" (T, 77). When Jukes disappears in the "struggling mass of Chinamen," the sailors attempt to rescue him by force:

> They charged in, stamping on breasts, on fingers, on faces, catching their feet in heaps of clothing, kicking broken wood; . . . Jukes emerged waist deep in a multitude of clawing hands. In the instant he had been lost to view, all the buttons of his jacket had gone, its back had got split up to the collar, his waistcoat had been torn open. (T, 77)

Jukes's violent divestment turns the sailors into savage brutes, who restore order by pushing back the coolies into a "compact scrimmage" and then organize them into rows. They become paranoid passengers as the ship enters the eye of the hurricane.

Conrad accentuates the pervasive fragmentation of the ship, sailors, and passengers to dramatize the limitations of all human systems based on verbal constructs. Unlike many of Conrad's protagonists, MacWhirr is not a myopic egoist deluded by dreams of future accomplishment. In fact, he is quite the opposite, for the Captain has no capacity to project himself into the future. MacWhirr seems admirable to some critics for his perseverance and tenacity. But Conrad's fragmentation motif mocks the Captain's simplistic endeavors to achieve a sense of command and personal salvation through artificial means. MacWhirr endures and survives, but he does not really prevail. He never prevails because he remains attached to names and labels in the belief that he is mastering reality; he never perceives the actual world of organic transformations and shifting perspectives.[33]

Conrad exposes the Captain's inadequacies in diverse ways. Although MacWhirr is not a prisoner of the past or the dupe of an imaginary future, he sees only the externals of the present moment, and never visualizes a "distant eventuality." When Jukes objects to the "ridiculous Noah's Ark elephant" on the ship's new flag symbolizing the transfer of the *Nan-Shan* to Siamese registry, MacWhirr rushes to the chart room to consult his "International Signal Code Book" so he can compare "the real thing" to the ensign on the flagstaff. The Captain's reference to the colored drawing in the book, rather than the actual flag, as the real thing testifies to his hidebound literalism. MacWhirr insists at length that the elephant, after the fashion of the Union Jack in the British flag, must stand for something. Jukes, the Captain's opposite in nearly every sense, simply considers his commanding officer a jackass.

The literal MacWhirr seems as ignorant of similes as he is of life. Reacting to Jukes's fanciful vocabulary, he expostulates against using figures of speech in matter-of-fact conversations. But Conrad derides the Captain's maxims only a few paragraphs later by having the impersonal narrator describe a sunset in the most fanciful language imaginable:

> At its setting the sun had a diminished diameter and an expiring brown, rayless glow, as if millions of centuries elapsing since the morning had brought it near its end. A dense bank of cloud became visible to the northward; it had a sinister dark-olive tint, and lay low and motionless upon the sea, resembling a solid obstacle in the path of the ship. She went floundering towards it like an exhausted creature driven to its death. The coppery twilight retired slowly, and the darkness brought out overhead a swarm of unsteady, big stars, that, as if blown upon, flickered exceedingly, and seemed to hang very near the earth. (*T*, 26)

This welter of metaphorical imagery not only contrasts with MacWhirr's fondness for direct, denotative language but also ominously foreshadows the crisis that he blunders into as a result of his literalistic thinking.

Conrad cleverly dramatizes the Captain's dangerous foibles in the scene in which Jukes enters the chart room to warn his superior of the coming storm. In a humorous tableau, MacWhirr stands next to a

bookcase while reading a volume on "storm strategy." Surprised to see
Jukes, he releases his grip on the bookshelf and falls onto the couch in a
comic collapse. He regains his composure by getting up quickly, but
"[h]e had not dropped the book, and he had not lost his place" (*T,* 31).
Underlying the slapstick of this scene is the absurdity of a sea captain
resorting to a book for advice on dealing with an approaching storm.
Obviously, MacWhirr's fair-weather sailing has not equipped him
with the necessary wisdom to deal with the anticipated crisis.

　　Yet Conrad compounds the irony of this situation when MacWhirr
launches a tirade against the very advice that is the object of his
search. Actually, MacWhirr does not disagree with the advice so much as
he is totally confounded by the manner in which the information is
communicated:

> [H]e had waded with a conscious effort into the terminology of the subject.
> He lost himself amongst advancing semicircles, left- and right-hand quad-
> rants, the curves of the tracks, the probable bearing of the center, the shifts
> of wind and the readings of barometer. He tried to bring all these things
> into a definite relation to himself, and ended by becoming contemptu-
> ously angry with such a lot of words and with so much advice, all
> head-work and supposition, without a glimmer of certitude. (*T,* 32–33)

MacWhirr's infatuation with factuality leads him to consult an authoritative text, but his feeble intellect wades into technical verbiage that is
too deep for him to fathom. He fails to make a connection between
the cartographical rhetoric and his own pragmatic problem. Befud-
dled in his rage for order, frantic for an easy solution, he wants to see
the world as structured as the arbitrary and illusory geographical
demarcations segmenting the globe.[34] Finding no comforting certainty, the Captain makes an attitudinal about-face and declares that
one does not find everything in books (*T,* 34). This assertion becomes
an ironic refrain throughout the tale, testifying to his ignorance of
navigation. MacWhirr ridicules the notion that he "should be getting
out of the way of that dirt" (*T,* 32), citing financial reasons for not
adding another three hundred miles to the ship's course in order to
avoid the storm. The simple-minded Captain suffers from an absurd
case of goal-orientation: "All these rules for dodging breezes and
circumventing the winds of heaven, Mr. Jukes, seem to me the
maddest thing, when you come to look at it sensibly" (*T,* 34). Hence,
MacWhirr initially exposes his ignorance by consulting Captain Wilson's "Storm Strategy," and then he demonstrates his stupidity by
substituting his naive preconceptions for the written advice, which he

rejects as overly cautious. Small wonder that Jukes looks at his superior officer "dubiously."

Conrad mocks MacWhirr's self-professed authority throughout the tale, exposing him as a marionette hamstrung by his own foolhardy words. The Captain asserts his simplistic philosophy that "[a] gale is a gale" and calls the book's advice "the greatest nonsense" spouted by a "crazy man" (*T*, 34–35). Frustrated in his attempt to find advice that reinforces his own ideas, MacWhirr lapses into brain-fatigue: "He was tired, and he experienced that state of mental vacuity which comes at the end of an exhaustive discussion that has liberated some belief matured in the course of meditative years. He had indeed been making his confession of faith" (*T*, 35). A strange confession, to be sure, issuing from a character unused to meditating on either past or future. The Captain even has trouble dressing himself as the drafts turn the chart room into a wind tunnel: "The shoes he had flung off were scurrying from end to end of the cabin, gamboling playfully over each other like puppies. As soon as he stood up he kicked at them viciously, but without effect" (*T*, 36).[35] Emerging from his "personal scuffle" with the wind in such ludicrous fashion, the Captain comes on deck and attempts to see into the gale with "a blind man's helplessness": "The strong wind swept at him out of a vast obscurity; he felt under his feet the uneasiness of his ship, and he could not even discern the shadow of her shape" (*T*, 40). Reality, in Conrad's fiction, always lies beyond human perception and comprehension. Only the shadow of what is real can be observed. But MacWhirr cannot discern even this much.

At the point when MacWhirr begins to take charge of a seemingly impossible situation, Conrad temporarily abandons his lampoon of the Captain to emphasize the indomitable voice of command that seems to "withstand the power of a storm" (*T*, 48). While the fanciful and imaginative Jukes surrenders to despair and negation, MacWhirr is unable to see the extremity of their predicament. Conrad concentrates on the Captain's methodical voice, which counterpoints the shrill screaming of the winds. To Jukes, MacWhirr's plodding efforts to save the ship are merely a "blind and pernicious folly," yet chance, or fate, determines that the Captain's voice "would not be silenced." Nevertheless, from time to time, Conrad inserts reminders of MacWhirr's stupidity, which led to the crisis in the first place. As the ship enters the eye of the hurricane, the Captain tells Jukes, "According to the books the worst is not over yet." But immediately afterward he parrots his skeptical platitude once more: "You don't find every-thing in books" (T, 81).

MacWhirr, the literalist who is the butt of Conrad's humor, makes a comic spectacle of himself while staring at the low reading of the barometer like a "misshapen pagan" before a shrine. Yet Conrad does hint at a change in the Captain's obtuse world-view. Like "Hard-Facts Heyst," MacWhirr unwittingly entertains emissaries of chaos from the world outside his rigid mental framework. The wind and waves trans-form his Panglossian conception of bad weather and prompt him to expect the worst. His chart room, the sanctuary of rational decorum and hard facts, has been invaded by the spirit of disorder. MacWhirr's neatly arranged rulers, pencils, and inkstand "—all the things that had their safe appointed places— . . . were gone, as if a mischievous hand had plucked them out one by one and flung them on the wet floor. The hurricane had broken in upon the orderly arrangements of his privacy" (T, 85). MacWhirr's response to this chaos is a reflexive reaction: he lights a match, an action symbolizing the petty habits that shackle humanity to a monotonous existence. Conrad depicts the Captain as a prisoner in Plato's cave who cannot even perceive his own captivity: "He sat unseen, apart from the sea, from his ship, isolated, as if withdrawn from the very current of his own existence, . . . surren-dering to a strange sensation of weariness he was not enlightened enough to recognize for the fatigue of mental stress" (T, 86). Indeed, an isolation as intense as this provides an unlikely context for heroism.

Yet MacWhirr recovers from his dark night of the soul to emerge as a seemingly different personality, one that combines Jukes's fanciful-ness and loquacity with his own methodical deliberation. He surpris-ingly acquires the gift of a prophetic imagination: "'It will come very sudden,' said Captain MacWhirr, 'and from over there, I fancy, God only knows though. These books are only good to muddle your head and make you jumpy. It will be bad and there's an end'" (T, 87). Conrad inverts his stereotypical portrait of MacWhirr by giving the Captain a measure of fanciful speculation. Like Kurtz, MacWhirr be-comes only a voice, but a voice that confronts and withstands the impersonal onslaught of the cosmos. The Captain's most succinct advice to Jukes affirms the value of unflinching tenacity despite the appalling limitations of human nature: "Facing it—always facing it—that's the way to get through. You are a young sailor. Face it. That's enough for any man. Keep a cool head" (T, 89). What MacWhirr never faces, however, is his own culpability for putting the ship in danger by heading toward the typhoon. By neglecting to point out

MacWhirr's confusion of "facing it" with taking an unnecessary risk, Conrad lures us into wholehearted approval of the Captain's heroic capabilities. But MacWhirr's heroism seems indistinguishable from his foolhardy inflexibility. By presenting the physical unity of Jukes and the Captain so often during the crisis, Conrad displays his disdain for heroic individualism and shows his admiration for human solidarity. This pairing also seems to suggests that if MacWhirr had possessed Jukes's imagination, he would not have blundered into the storm; and if Jukes had possessed MacWhirr's single-minded fortitude, he would not have plunged into despair.

Conrad's closing scene stresses the Captain's judicious redistribution of money among the coolies. Wealth is a quantifiable commodity that MacWhirr can calculate without having to consider humanistic values. But Conrad also tallies the spoils that the Captain fails to quantify and redistribute. These entail (according to Jukes's letter) odds and ends left from the battle with "dirty" weather: "heaps of wet rags, all sorts of fragments of things without shape, and *that you couldn't give a name to*, and [we] let them settle the ownership themselves" (*T*, 102; emphasis added). Naming implies ownership, as when MacWhirr objects to Jukes calling the Chinese "passengers," for passengers own themselves and pay their own passage, whereas coolies serve owners, who pay for their shipment. At the outset, Conrad refers to the Chinese as "Celestials," who carry everything they own with them: "bits of *nameless* rubbish of conventional value, and a small hoard of silver dollars, . . . amassed patiently, guarded with care, cherished fiercely" (*T*, 7). What cannot be named cannot have value in conventional Western terms. But the silver dollars speak eloquently to Celestials and occidentals alike. With subversive irony, Conrad glorifies Captain MacWhirr's equitable economic judgment and covertly reveals his flagrant disregard of nautical wisdom that nearly sends the vessel to a watery grave.

# 4

## On the Brink of a Disclosure

The stories I have selected for discussion in this chapter all deal with the theme of betrayal, yet ultimately they reflect Conrad's transcendence of the conventions of fiction writing and his distrust of the efficacy of language. In "The Informer," Conrad juxtaposes anarchism and aestheticism to reveal the moral bankruptcy of any movement based on self-indulgence. The puppets in this absurd passion play move not in response to genuine feelings but because they have become habituated to the stimulus of revolutionary rhetoric. This world (like that of *The Secret Agent*) is a realm of highly wrought artifice, which only thinly disguises the shallow egoism and materialism at the core of each character. The story within the story of "Karain: A Memory" concerns the title character's guilt over the murder of his friend Matara, but Karain's treachery and guilt play no part in Conrad's complex final scene set in the heart of London, far removed from the South Pacific locale of the rest of the tale. Moreover, the closing conversation between Jackson and the narrator provides no univocal moral judgment on the action. Instead, Conrad abandons his focus on the contrast of civilized Westerners and superstitious natives to present a disturbing anatomy of modern urban culture. His closing scene suggests that the Westerners are as culturally conditioned as Karain, but in a more sophisticated way. Hypocritical materialists, they dwell nostalgically on the past or on fantasies of wishful thinking about the future, unable to perceive the fleeting moment for what it is. Conrad also implies that the language of fiction is yet another conditioning influence on modern consciousness, as he speculates in a conspicuous authorial intrusion on how the reader has been manipulated via the words of his narrative.

Like "The Informer" and "Karain," "The Partner" features a story within a story that centers on betrayal and ends with an inconclusive conclusion worthy of Charlie Marlow. In this ending Conrad crowns a strategy he employs throughout the work, in which he violates the traditional partnership between author and reader and affirms that fiction is a contrived tapestry of lies. Scorning both the gullible reader of conventional magazine fiction and the received ideas underlying formulaic romances, he questions the ideal of artistic integrity based on symmetrical patterns and underscores the essentially patternless nature of existence. His inconclusive ending makes sport of the reader's craving for a definitive interpretation of the action.

Another celebration of fiction as a tapestry of illusions, "The Inn of the Two Witches," may seem an unlikely choice to include in a study of the sense of an ending in Conrad's best or most problematical shorter works. To be sure, the derivative tale has few critical supporters, yet both its eccentric ending and its mock-editorial introductory section transcend the limitations of its cliché-ridden gothic plot. Not only does the epilogue have the faint smell of a red herring but the frame-story narrator's preposterous account of his discovery of the interior story can only be an outrageous fabrication. By deliberately confusing factuality and fictionality, Conrad implies that truth lies outside the net of words. Conrad abruptly terminates his melodramatic rehashing of supernatural skullduggery in an ironic coda that conceals more than it reveals. The real "witches" of the story are the words that haunt the protagonist until he is fortunate enough to lose consciousness and thereby inadvertently transcends the realm of rhetoric.

## "The Informer"

Linking the revolutionary politics of Peter Kropotkin and the "art for art's sake" credo of Walter Pater, presiding spirit of the British aesthetic movement, "The Informer" (originally entitled "Gestures") fuses the bombastic pronouncements of Nietzsche and the artistic extravagances of Whistler, Wilde, and Beardsley. Taking his hint from Henry James, Conrad establishes a dual frame of reference in the tale, overtly burlesquing the anarchist movement but also satirizing the shallow affectations of the aesthetic movement in the late nineteenth century. By employing the vocabulary of aestheticism in dramatizing a farcical story of anarchist insurgence, he underscores the histrionics of terrorism and the vacuous pretensions of its deluded practitioners. Simultaneously, Conrad also exposes the calculated artifice of the British dandies who made a religion of Pater's hyperbolic musings. Writing in 1905, Conrad would likely have been aware of George Du Maurier's caricatures of mumming aesthetes in *Punch* magazine and he was familiar with James's seriocomic portraits of late-nineteenth-century writers and artists. With these as models, or at least probable influences, Conrad infuses his potboiler plot with inside jokes and frivolous puns aimed at the fopperies and decadence of the fin-de-siècle cult of self-indulgence. Ultimately, he implies that the amoral wit and satanic wisdom of the aesthetic movement masks a narcissistic conceit.

Conrad's story within a story, with its complex point of view, verges on the absurd. One critic has even called the tale a self-parody.[1] Subtitled "An Ironic Tale," "The Informer" opens in a Jamesian manner with the introduction of a squeamish narrator who relates his encounter with an anarchist known as Mr. X. The two characters meet at the behest of an absent third party, a friend who shares their passion for collecting curiosities. At dinner, the fastidious narrator learns that the anarchist, despite his commitment to ultraviolence, has a taste for luxury. When the narrator comments on this incongruity, Mr. X relates a lengthy anecdote to prove that the idle rich have fostered the revolutionary cause without fully realizing its implications. His example concerns a young Englishwoman he calls the Lady Amateur, who offers her house on Hermione Street as headquarters for anarchist activity. Her romantic poses and gestures attract the attention of Sevrin, one of the anarchists who is also a secret informer for the police. Sevrin and the Lady Amateur conduct a "politico-amorous" relationship that quickly disintegrates when Mr. X and his cohorts raid the headquarters disguised as London policemen. During the fracas, Sevrin reveals his true colors in an effort to save Lady Amateur. Stunned by the revelation of Sevrin's treachery, she rebuffs him and he commits suicide. After reading the love rhapsodies in his diary, she retires to a Florentine convent. Mr. X concludes his anecdote by launching a tirade on the "mere gestures" of the privileged class.

This cynical outburst undermines the melodramatic action of the interior story, but, more importantly, it lays the foundation for the enigmatic closing that calls everything in the tale into question. The narrator never sees Mr. X again, but he does meet their mutual friend, the collector of personalities, who is anxious to learn what effect "this rare item of his collection" had on the narrator (*SS*, 101). Their babble of adjectival superlatives ranges from the friend's "unique, amazing, absolutely terrific" to the narrator's "abominable," a word repeated enthusiastically by the narrator's friend, who adds confidentially, "And then, you know, he likes to have his little joke sometimes" (*SS*, 102). This remark strikes the narrator as incomprehensible, and in the final paragraph he maintains that he still fails to understand it, having been unable to determine the meaning of the joke.

Perhaps the "little joke" derives from the dull-witted narrator's use of the word *abominable* in the verbal by-play that closes the tale. Earlier, in Mr. X's narrative, Conrad puns on the word *bomb* when he establishes the geographical details of the anecdote. He mentions a "fellow called Bomm" who runs an "agency for performers in inferior music-halls" (*SS*, 82). Conrad plays on the word again as the obtuse narrator remarks on the *"bombe glacée"* which Mr. X impassively attacks (*SS*, 82). In a variation of the culinary motif, Mr. X discusses the anarchist's appropriation of "Stone's Dried Soup," which provides a conveniently innocuous container for the export of blasting powder. While Mr. X indulges in his preposterous vaporings, the narrator watches what is left of the *bombe* gradually melt. This ludicrously deteriorating image gives way to another absurd image—soup cases stuffed with "revolutionary literature of the most inflammatory kind" (*SS*, 83). Conrad's culinary images shift the philosophy of bomb-throwing from the streets of London to the gourmet's kitchen, where dried soups and melting desserts have the same weight as terrorist activities. In these cases, Conrad's wordplay seems obvious, but in other instances his puns evince a more subtle irony. For example, the building that houses the anarchists stands on Hermione Street. The mythical Hermione was also called Harmonia; thus, the anarchists situate their base of disorder in the heart of harmony. But far more significantly, Conrad's language consistently evokes the pontifications of the aesthetic movement—the etherealized raptures of Pater, the droll witticisms of Whistler, and the Nietzschean paradoxes of Wilde—all slavishly mimicked by would-be sophisticates who idolize eccentricity for its own sake. Mr. X's "little joke" becomes part of Conrad's larger sociopsychological joke. Anarchists and aesthetes are extremists redeemed from their outcast state by vapid connoisseurs of novelty, as a superficial civilization turns to cheap tricks for its perpetual amusement. Conrad's "inside story" reveals that the great passion of the public is a pretense, the vicarious thrill of living on the fringe of society as an outsider. Conrad, himself a genuine outsider, recognized the charade.

From beginning to end, Conrad exploits his "little joke" by making anarchism a metaphor for the bohemian life of the aesthete, or rather, the aesthete *manqué*. Horne, the "guiding spirit" of the Hermione Street insurgents, "was an engraver and etcher of genius. . . . He began by being revolutionary in his art and ended by becoming a revolutionist" (*SS*, 83). One naturally thinks of Rossetti or William Morris, and Conrad's physical description of Horne as tall, gaunt, and swarthy confirms the plausibility of this connection. Bothered by just a slight case of insanity, he remains an artist appreciated by a "small group of connoisseurs." Even more provocative, the portrait of the Professor (who also appears in *The Secret Agent*) suggests another failed artist. A kind of Nietzschean nihilist, he spends his time perfecting new detonators. Mr. X dubs him "The Perfect Anarchist," a martyr to mediocrity: "His was the true spirit of an extreme revolutionist. Explosives were his faith, his hope, his weapon, and his shield. He perished a couple of years afterwards in a secret laboratory through the premature explosion of one of his improved detonators" (*SS*, 88). The Professor, an anthropomorphic *bombe glacée*, embodies the quintessence of terrorism: he has the mechanical capacity to profess ideas out of touch with critical reasoning and the single-minded desire to demolish all that exists.[2]

The cream of Conrad's jest, however, lies in his handling of the bathetic love affair of Sevrin and the Lady Amateur, both branded by Mr. X as "amateurs of emotion." The Lady Amateur deserves extensive scrutiny, not only because of her pivotal role in Mr. X's "inside story," but also because she seems partially modeled on the title character in James's *The Princess Casamassima,* an 1886 novel that details the misery of London workers and their embryonic revolutionary impulses.[3] Like James's princess, Conrad's Lady Amateur feels drawn to the radical cause in large part because of the men involved and because it offers a welcome relief from boredom. Both women indirectly lead their lovers (Hyacinth Robinson and Sevrin) to self-destruction, and both view radical enterprises as a novel sort of game. Mr. X describes the Lady Amateur as a gifted poseur who projects "the seductive appearance of enthusiasm" (*SS*, 80). But Conrad demonstrates that she is the seduced as well as the seducer. She seduces Sevrin almost unconsciously through her melodramatic gestures, but she has been ravished by the magical potency of abstract words, the language of revolutionary fervor. Like James's princess, the Lady Amateur offers her house for the use of the radicals, and Mr. X depicts her as a bit-player in a drama she can never understand: "She had

acquired all the appropriate gestures of revolutionary convictions—
the gestures of pity, of anger, of indignation against the antihumani-
tarian vices of the social class to which she belonged herself. All this
sat on her striking personality as well as her slightly original costumes.
Very slightly original" (*SS*, 81). Mr. X condemns her enslavement to
fashion and her addiction to the fad of social revolt. Indirectly he is
complaining that the privileged class not only continues to repress the
working class but also adopts the attributes and appurtenances of
sociopolitical rebellion.

Conrad's target, however, is more psychological than sociological,
for he mocks the mechanical habits of thought and behavior that
regiment human lives. The "gestures" of the aesthetes are simply
learned responses that signal conventional meanings. Lady Amateur's
gestures have no original content or spontaneous vitality because they
have been endlessly rehearsed. Conrad's point is that conventions in
themselves have no ultimate justification, and therefore Lady Amateur's gestures are fraudulent "informers." Thus Mr. X denigrates her
as a mindless robot useful only in parlor games. Conrad, himself, may
have more regard for her humanity, but he maintains his authorial
distance behind the cloak of Mr. X's cynicism.

Lady Amateur exhibits symptoms of the disease of "severe enthusiasm," displaying "all the gestures and grimaces of deadly earnestness"
(*SS*, 84). The etymologies of *gesture* (conduct or bearing) and *grimace*
(fear, panic, fright) suggest that she has been frightened into the
anarchist cause by messianic rhetoric. Lady Amateur is the puppet of
words, just as Sevrin is the plaything of her reflexive gestures of
humanitarian outrage and pity. The macabre adjective *deadly* implies
that her peculiar affliction, a faddish enthusiasm for revolution, is a
sickness unto death. This spiritual lifelessness carries over to her
dangerous liaisons with Sevrin: "It was the attitude of love-making,
serious, intense, as if on the brink of the grave. I suppose she found it
necessary to round and complete her assumption of advanced ideas,
of revolutionary lawlessness, by making believe to be in love with an
anarchist" (*SS*, 85). Mr. X stereotypes Lady Amateur as a willful child
who is completely oblivious to the falseness of her postures. Her
revolutionary ardor for reform is only inspired attitudinizing. Naturally
artificial, she is a sentimentalist who deludes herself into blind aspirations: "She interpreted her conception of what that precise sort of
love-making should be with consummate art. And so far, she, too, no
doubt, was in earnest. Gestures—but so perfect!" (*SS*, 85).

Like Emma Bovary, Lady Amateur is a gullible victim of the romantic-aesthetic sensibility cultivated by those who "knew little of anything except of words" (SS, 86). She never understands the shadow that falls between word and deed, intention and achievement, illusion and actuality. What she does know of life she has acquired from received ideas, fossilized fragments of knowledge that cannot be assimilated into a comprehensive vision. Mr. X speculates that she "had never known in her life a single genuine thought; I mean a single thought detached from small human vanities, or whose source was not in some conventional perception" (SS, 92). In this respect, she calls to mind Kayerts and Carlier, the doomed ivory agents in "An Outpost of Progress." One might say that her grammar of motives is an English translation of Flaubert's *Dictionary of Received Ideas*. She is a second cousin to Bouvard and Pecuchet, a female exponent of refined ignorance.

In Conrad's farce, Lady Amateur plays the role of an "unconscious comedian," unwittingly leading Sevrin to blind self-destruction. When she learns of her lover's role as the informer, she assumes a silent rigidity entirely without gesture, yet her immobile face still projects "an illusion of placidity." An attitude of stupid dismay replaces her postures and gestures of revolutionary indignation. When Sevrin stoops "to touch the hem of her garment," she melodramatically repudiates any further efforts to communicate: "And then the appropriate gesture came. She snatched her skirt away from his polluting contact and averted her head with an upward tilt. It was magnificently done, this gesture of conventionally unstained honour, of an unblemished high-minded amateur" (SS, 98). She reacts as if programmed to spurn her lover in a scene excerpted from romantic fiction that she has rehearsed on countless occasions. Her apparently spontaneous recoil is merely a reflex action prefiguring the deflation of her revolutionary enthusiasm. She undergoes a sudden metamorphosis, which Mr. X describes in conspicuously negative terms: she clings to Mr. X's arm and drags herself along like an old woman or else a "besotted reveller" (SS, 98). Like the naive narrator who fails to comprehend Mr. X's "little joke," she cannot understand Sevrin's last words, "from conviction."[4] Small wonder! Lady Amateur knows only poses, gestures, and attitudes—the fads and fashions of an imitative culture that worships its own extravagance. Her retreat to an Italian convent (the perfect abode for a lady "of conventionally unstained honour") has pathetic, rather than tragic, implications.

If Conrad presents Lady Amateur as a mediocre actress, he portrays Sevrin as a star-crossed lover who takes his lover's play-acting seriously and totally enters into the theatrics of romance with "the air of a taciturn actor or of a fanatical priest" (SS, 85). Conrad compares Sevrin's fanaticism, his intense dedication as a double agent, to that of a "converted atheist." Like Hyacinth Robinson in *The Princess Casamassima,* he completely recants his revolutionary views but does not abandon his radical devotion to the idea of a personal crusade. Lumping anarchists, priests, and actors into a common category, Conrad posits heightened emotionalism as their raison d'être. During the sham police raid, Sevrin's "shaven actor's face" shows a wary puzzlement, as if "he had seen through the game" (SS, 91). Yet the involvement of Lady Amateur turns Sevrin's "solidly fastened mask" into an imbecile's countenance. The "genius amongst betrayers" suddenly forgets his lines, falls out of character, and now experiences the stage fright of a novice thespian: "He was accustomed to arrange the last scene of his betrayals with a deep, subtle art which left his revolutionist reputation untouched" (SS, 93).

This unbearable situation becomes the final scene of Sevrin's life as well as the final expression of his art. Panic compels him to doff his mask before the footlights. Despite his travail, Sevrin attempts to resume his former role: "His sides worked visibly, and his nostrils expanded and collapsed in weird contrast with his sombre aspect of a fanatical monk in a meditative attitude, but with something, too, in his face of an actor intent upon the terrible exigencies of his part" (SS, 96). Once again, Conrad joins acting and preaching, adding that "Horne declaimed, haggard and bearded, like an inspired denunciatory prophet from a wilderness" (SS, 96). Horne, arch anarchist and arch aesthete, also plays the dual role of actor and priest. Likewise, Mr. X values fanaticism (or, in his words, "optimism") above all else. Accordingly, Sevrin's charade collapses once his fanaticism waivers. His demise is caused by semiotic misapprehension: "[H]e must have believed in the absolute value of conventional signs" (SS, 93). Misinterpreting Lady Amateur's conventional gestures as tokens of authentic affection, he grants her the status of playwright of their farcical romance: "Sevrin, the anti-anarchist, captivated and spellbound by the consummate and hereditary grimaces that in a certain sphere of life take the place of feelings with an excellent effect" (SS, 99). Victimized by Lady Amateur's grimaces and gestures, her substitutes for feeling, Sevrin serves as her ironic opposite. He masks his internal sentimentality with an impassive facade; she hides her inner blankness by projecting a superficial sentimentality.

Sevrin's role as a pathetic puppet calls to mind the reference to *"les petites marionettes"* in the epigraph to *A Set of Six*. Moreover, in a letter to Cunninghame Graham (6 December 1897), Conrad admits that although he rarely attends the theater

> I love a marionette show. Marionettes are beautiful,— . . . Their impassability in love in crime, in mirth, in sorrow,—is heroic, superhuman, fascinating. Their rigid violence when they fall upon one another to embrace or to fight is simply a joy to behold. I never listen to the text mouthed somewhere out of sight by invisible men who are here today and rotten tomorrow. I love the marionettes that are without life, that come so near to being immortal! (*CL,* 1:419)

The quasi-immortality of Sevrin and Lady Amateur lies in their puppet sensibilities: their capacity to pose, be exposed, and fall quickly out of fashion.

Conrad's interior story reverberates with insinuations of duplicity and histrionics. Mr. X calls his ruse a "theatrical expedient," and his "sham police" conduct themselves so as to produce "a really convincing effect" of verisimilitude (*SS,* 86, 87): "The man who personated the inspector (he was no stranger to the part) was speaking harshly, and giving bogus orders to his bogus subordinates" (*SS,* 88). When one of the surprised anarchists swallows a scrap of paper to keep the information from the sham police, Mr. X confesses that he felt "amused at that perfectly uncalled for performance" (*SS,* 89). With no small measure of pride, he labels his clandestine deception a "theatrical coup." But when the narrator derides the whole affair as a "sinister farce," Mr. X simply affirms that the farce ended well. Conrad's theatrical language undermines the ostensible seriousness of the anarchists' plots and counterplots. They become play-actors in a farce that blinds them to their own insignificance. Deluded by abstract words and habitual gestures, Conrad's revolutionists never exit from their theater of the absurd. In its broadest sense, "The Informer" ridicules the pretense and passion that inform the exultations of human life.

The ironic tale within a tale exposes the anarchists as mediocre actors in a melodrama of comedy and calamity, while the framing narrative makes sport of the fad of aestheticism in everyday life. The narrator, though he professes genteel virtues and lofty ideals, reveals his shallow egotism and materialism as the story progresses. Like one of Du Maurier's chinamaniacs, caricatured so frequently in *Punch,* he sets great store by his "collection of Chinese bronzes and porcelain" (*SS,* 73). Such artifacts function as extensions of the self for individuals

without significant accomplishments.[5] The narrator refers to his collection as "[m]y treasures" which "shall be worth a fortune to my heirs"
(SS, 74). The precautions he takes against the prospect of a fire illustrate
the extent of his dependence on his showpieces. Obsessed with
security, he cannot risk the loss of these rarities. His ego surfaces in his
comment that he hopes he looked intelligent as Mr. X surveyed his
collection. Thus, the two characters share a petty preoccupation with
validating their personal identities through the ownership of fine objects.

Yet the narrator's preconceptions about anarchism impede his
understanding of Mr. X's personality: "I am sure that if such a faith (or
such a fanaticism) once mastered my thoughts I would never be able
to compose myself sufficiently to sleep or eat or perform any of the
routine acts of daily life" (SS, 75). Additionally, he relies on information about Mr. X provided by his friend that seems to conflict drasti-
cally with the cultivated persona he has encountered. This blend of
false pride, romantic preconception, and myopic perception casts
doubt on the narrator's credibility as the central intelligence of the
tale. Moreover, the narrator displays his Casper Milquetoast sensibility
by defining himself as a "quiet and peaceable product of civilization"
who knows "no passion other than the passion for collecting things
which are rare, and must remain exquisite even if approaching the
monstrous. Some Chinese bronzes are monstrously precious" (SS, 76).
This monstrous passion for collecting reverberates with Jamesian lev-
ity, but it also echoes Pater's celebrated conclusion of *The Renais-
sance*.[6] In his portraits of materialistic English collectors who live for
and through their precious artifacts, Conrad trivializes Pater's advice
to sensitive souls to cultivate a passion for what is "rare" and "exquisite." In fact, the narrator actually consciously dehumanizes the phenomenon of Mr. X: "[H]ere I had before me a rare kind of monster. It
is true that this monster was polished and in a sense even exquisite"
(SS, 76). This odd interest in a "polished monster" suggests the narrator's lack of humane feelings because he is so totally obsessed with
his passion for acquisition. This scene calls to mind the narrator's
opening paragraphs, which introduce his nameless friend (perhaps a
fictive replica of Ford Madox Ford[7]), a Parisian collector who "collects
acquaintances. It is delicate work. He brings to it the patience, the
passion, the determination of a true collector of curiosities" (SS, 73).
Pater's exhortation to court the "exquisite passion" of new and delicate impressions is echoed in burlesque in the narrator's friend's
compulsion to collect *objets d'art*.

Rather than fostering "the quickened sense of life" in a "multiplied consciousness," as Pater urged his aesthetic disciples, Conrad's collectors cultivate the pulsating rapture of the auction block. Variations on the word *collect* appear nine times in the first three paragraphs of "The Informer," and in ways that make collecting synonymous with conquest. The narrator's friend, for example, courts new acquaintances like a fin-de-siècle Don Juan: "He observes them, listens to them, penetrates them, measures them, and puts the memory away in the galleries of his mind" (*SS*, 73). Such intimacy masqueraded as style and originality among the *haute bourgeoisie* of the late-Victorian era, and James's fiction, for example, features an abundance of such collectors.

The narrator's smug complacency simply masks his interior nullity. His "whole scheme of life had been based upon a suave and delicate discrimination of social and artistic values" (*SS*, 77). But no such civilized values underlie his egoistic personality. Moreover, Conrad ridicules the narrator's squeamishness when we learn that all forms of violence are as unreal to him as the fantastic creatures of myths and fairy tales. The narrator apologizes for this deficiency in understanding by confessing his "impressionable and imaginative" nature. Yet his cultivation of finer feelings à la Pater actually diminishes his power of discrimination. When meeting Mr. X, he anticipates a wild-eyed fanatic foaming at the mouth, and although disappointed in his preconception, he persists in stereotyping anarchists as incarnations of Satan: "[A]narchists in general were simply inconceivable to me mentally, morally, logically, sentimentally, and even physically" (*SS*, 97). The narrator gasps in wonder at Mr. X's statements, even though he categorically deplores their cynical overtones. As Mr. X begins his interior monologue, the gullible narrator admits he is "all expectation." He marvels at the tale throughout, except for the occasions when he expresses his outraged "sentiment of womanhood." Here, Conrad implies that the narrator's sensitivity is as mawkish as that of female characters in a Victorian melodrama. Toward the end of Mr. X's anecdote, the narrator still takes refuge in his intellectual blindness. In his verbal portrait of a gullible and ignorant sensibility, Conrad borrows a page from James, the master at depicting the social mummery and flummery of the upper classes for its comic effect (see, especially, *The Sacred Fount*).

Mr. X (X for the unknown), exponent of irony, iconoclasm, and Nietzschean nihilism, stands out as the one really remarkable creation in "The Informer." Whatever the historical source for his invention,[8] Mr. X is a bundle of incongruities. An acute chinamaniac who is akin to Du Maurier's caricature Svengali, a resident in London's Nincom-poopiana, he takes center stage as a Pateresque windbag spewing passionate contempt for modern society. The narrator's friend charac-terizes him as "the greatest rebel (*revolte*) of modern times" (*SS*, 73–74). But Mr. X is also "an enlightened connoisseur of bronzes and china" (*SS*, 74). Such a bold contradiction marks only the first stroke of Conrad's portrait of the unknown anarchist. Mr. X's "flaming red revolutionary pamphlets" establish his role as a subterranean Socrates engineering the anarchist movement with the aplomb of a Russian chess master. As "the mysteriously unknown Number One" of revolu-tionists, he inspires secret societies and conspiracies, but his external appearance resembles that of an imperial aristocrat. His "long, Ro-man-nosed countenance" testifies to a "noble family," perhaps an allusion to Prince Peter Kropotkin, the blue-blooded anarchist.

Conrad calls attention to Mr. X's headpiece almost immediately: "In his fur coat and shiny tall hat that terrible man looked fashionable" (*SS*, 74–75). After Mr. X concludes his anecdote, Conrad again focuses on his headgear: "He fitted on his glossy high hat with extreme precision" (*SS*, 101). In "The Partner," "The Secret Sharer," and, most conspicuously, *The Secret Agent*, Conrad invokes absurd humor in his satirical descriptions of hats. Perhaps deriving from Flaubert's ludi-crous depiction of Charles Bovary's fool's cap, or simply a Mad Hatter's madcap sensibility, Conrad's hat trick offers a clue to the eccentric sensibility of the wearer.[9] Thus, thinking caps metamorphose into symbolic headgear, and Mr. X's hat establishes his dubious character.

Dressed at the height of fashion, Mr. X displays "a perfect impas-siveness of expression" (*SS*, 75). The key word *impassiveness* groups Mr. X with the other puppets in Conrad's marionette show. The master anarchist has more refinement and sophistication than the others, yet his dynamic persona depends on his persistent rhetorical displays. Conrad plays on the contrast of inner agitation and outward rigidity as the narrator details Mr. X's "quiet mechanical precision" at the dinner table:

> His head and body above the tablecloth had a rigid immobility. This firebrand, this great agitator, exhibited the least possible amount of warmth and animation. His voice was rasping, cold, and monotonous in a low key. He could not be called a talkative personality; but with his detached calm manner he appeared as ready to keep the conversation going as to drop it at any moment. (*SS*, 76)

Conrad's Mad Hatter of anarchy embodies preposterous contradictions. A revolutionary "firebrand" without "warmth and animation,"
who speaks in a "monotonous" voice with a "detached calm manner," is hardly the image of a man busily shaking the political foundations of Western civilization. Conrad depicts Mr. X as an unmoved
mover, an immobile agitator—a role that ironically parallels Pater's
relationship to late-nineteenth-century aesthetes and Nietzsche's relationship to mid-twentieth-century existentialists. If Peter Kropotkin
serves as the political model for Conrad's mysterious agent provo-
cateur, perhaps Nietzsche embodies most vividly the contrast between outward fragility and inward ferment. By 1905, Nietzsche's
concept of the *Ubermensch* was a popular controversy in intellectual
circles, and Conrad capitalizes on this phenomenon in his contradictory portrait of Mr. X as an underground man who cultivates a passion
for *objets d'art*. In fact, Mr. X informs the narrator that his "writings
were at one time the rage, the fashion—the thing to read with wonder
and horror" (*SS*, 78).[10]

Just as Mr. X ridicules "amateurs of emotion" whose lives consist of
empty "poses and gestures," "The Informer" satirizes political demagogues like Mr. X and effete dilettantes such as the narrator and his
friend, who share the damning trait of self-satisfaction. Mr. X errs in
believing in the existence of "words that have no sham meaning" (*SS*,
78), and Conrad depicts him as a professional parasite gorging himself
on the speeches of demagogues, even though he attempts to distance
himself from the charge of demagoguery: "The demagogue carries the
amateurs of emotion with him. Amateurism . . . is a delightfully easy
way of killing time, and feeding one's own vanity—the silly vanity of
being abreast with the ideas of the day after to-morrow" (*SS*, 78).
Despite his tirade to the contrary, Mr. X falls into the slough of
self-preoccupation. He, too, kills time by amusing himself, to the
dismay of the awestruck narrator. His affectations—verbal and physical, cynical and sophisticated—mark him as the most complex specimen in Conrad's fictional puppet show. Aping the politics of Kropotkin,
the ethics of Nietzsche, and the rhetoric of Pater, Conrad's elegant
anarchist enacts the role of a featured performer in a pessimistic comedy
of manners at the turn of the century. Mr. X could be the protagonist
of *À Rebours* transposed to the stage of *The Importance of Being Earnest*,
or perhaps Dorian Gray amid the extravagant atrocities in Huysmans's
decadent novel *La Bas*.[11] Throughout "The Informer," Conrad travesties the language of the aesthetic movement within the context of
anarchism, ultimately distilling a self-centered vocabulary relating to

no art but the art of the exhibitionist. Both anarchism and aestheticism are variations of narcissism that earn Conrad's everlasting repudiation.

Turning from the closing of this "Ironic Tale" (as "The Informer" is subtitled) to the ending of the multifaceted novel Conrad paradoxically called "A Simple Tale," we can draw out some revealing correspondences between his burlesque of anarchism in the short-story form and his dissection of civilized society in *The Secret Agent*. At the end of "The Informer," Sevrin kills himself as a result of his politico-amorous relationship with Lady Amateur. Similarly, Comrade Ossipon becomes incapable of exploiting his female conquests at the close of *The Secret Agent* because of the "cursed knowledge" of his participation in Winnie Verloc's doom.[12] He even goes so far as to offer to give the Professor the "legacy" he has "inherited" from Verloc. Whereas Sevrin has been victimized by Lady Amateur's gestures, Ossipon has become a victim of his stricken conscience over his victimization of Winnie.

But the most intriguing parallel is found in the disturbing last glimpses of Mr. X and the Professor. After condemning Sevrin's "ardent humanitarianism," Mr. X tells the narrator that one "must be a savage, tyrannical, pitiless, thick-and-thin optimist . . . to make a good social rebel of the extreme type" (*SS*, 101). In like manner, the Professor identifies with the "sound of exploding bombs" and offers a toast "[t]o the destruction of what is . . ." (*SA*, 306). Mr. X expresses contempt for the "[m]ere gestures" of Lady Amateur's class: "That is why their kind is fated to perish" (*SS*, 101). Likewise, the Professor dreams of "a world like shambles" where the weak are utterly annihilated: "Exterminate! Exterminate! That is the only way of progress" (*SA*, 303). And whereas the fastidious Mr. X likes to have his "little joke" with those who take his pontifications in dead earnestness, Conrad has the last laugh in *The Secret Agent* when he exposes the miserable insignificance of the "incorruptible" Professor: the only thing out of keeping with the general poverty of his room is the "enormous iron padlock on the doors of the wall cupboard" where the Professor keeps his explosives (*SA*, 302). Conrad calls attention to the padlock twice in the final chapter, the second time to suggest that only by revisiting this shrine can the Professor obtain relief from the oppressing sight of so many people in the street. The multitude represents flourishing life, even that of Ossipon "marching in the gutter," but the Professor identifies with the extinction of lives, calling death his own weapon. And he can only detonate himself once with the explosive device he keeps in his pocket. Caressing "images of ruin and destruction," the Professor walks out of the last scene in *The Secret Agent* a "frail, insignificant . . . pest" who is both "unsuspected" and powerless (*SA*, 311).[13] Although Conrad allows the Professor to claim he is a "force," we must view him as a pathetic mediocrity, Conrad's personification of self-annihilating solipsism. In *The Secret Agent,* Conrad expands his little joke about anarchism to include all individuals who fool themselves into believing that the will to power confers absolute authority. In reality, it only clears the pathway to self-destruction.

## "Karain"

Because Conrad rarely commits authorial intrusions at crucial points in his fiction, the conspicuous exception in "Karain" substantiates his preoccupation with the reader's response to his art: "We cheered again; and the Malays in the boat stared—very much puzzled and impressed. I wondered what they thought; what [Karain] thought; . . . what the reader thinks?" (*TU*, 52). The question seems partly rhetorical because Conrad frequently manipulates the reader's impressions so that no tenable conclusion can be reached without disregarding or de-emphasizing certain details in the story. At bottom, all rational evaluations prove inconclusive, and his best tales, like existence itself, elude definitive interpretation.

This flair for mystification is reflected in the complex narrative layers of "Karain," and particularly in the final conversation that functions as the story's locking scene. Here the dialogue reveals Conrad's multifaceted artistic strategy, which places the burden of interpretation squarely on the reader. The ostensibly innocuous subtitle of the story ("A Memory") provides a clue to Conrad's method, for the closing conversation between Jackson and the narrator (running at cross-purposes) arises from a random mental association, and the dialogue continues to unfold as if propelled by memory. Conrad delineates the Western tendency to endlessly rehearse past events, which are indelibly stamped on the psyche and continually reinterpreted, subjectively and compulsively. He contrasts the traditional orientation of the Malays with the obsessive egoism governing Western culture. Ultimately, Karain reaches outside his own tradition to lay to rest his psychological phantoms, yet his Western friends persistently befuddle themselves with the ghosts of personal history invoked by their own haunted minds. Existing without a stable sense of tradition, they lack genuine self-reliance and can only deal with the vicissitudes of experience by ransacking their depleted storehouse of anecdotes, platitudes, and exhausted adages that convey the illusion of linear continuity.

Conrad's tale unfolds as a sequence of retrospectives told by an unnamed gunrunner who has returned to Europe. The narrator offers a reminiscence of how he and his cohorts, Hollis and Jackson, smuggled guns to Karain, a native Malay ruler involved in territorial disputes. Although Karain poses as a haughty leader in the light of day, at night he seems beset by paranoia and cannot do without the constant companionship of an old sorcerer. When the gunrunners return for a final sale, they learn of the death of the old wizard. Some days later, Karain boards their ship and confesses that he suffers from remorse. He narrates the story of the betrayal of his friend Pata Matara, whom he had accompanied in pursuit of a Dutchman who had run off with Matara's sister. After many years, they found their quarry, but Karain had become so obsessed with the girl's reputed beauty that he shot Matara before the girl could be killed. Since that day, Matara's phantom has haunted Karain, and only the old wizard's charms could ward off the ghost. Now that the charms are useless, Karain asks the white men to take him to their land of unbelief for protection. Anxious to be rid of Karain, they deliberate, until Hollis decides to give the Malay ruler a potent charm from the West. The talisman, a jubilee sixpence representing Queen Victoria, fascinates Karain, who leaves the ship triumphantly to rejoin his subjects. The Malay rejoicing prompts Conrad's conspicuous authorial intrusion, with its illusion-breaking inquiry concerning the reader's reaction to the resolution.

Although the talisman incident resolves the conflict on a superficial level, Conrad caps his discourse with another recollection. The narrator's chance meeting with Jackson, newly arrived in London, sets the stage for a final, locking scene that could provide a moral judgment on the outcome of the experience. But Conrad thwarts this possibility by failing to provide a univocal assertion to crystallize the significance of the tale. His epilogue begins, innocently enough, with the narrator's interjection "But the memory remains" (*TU*, 53), which functions as a line of demarcation between the main body of the story and its equivocal ending. Then he proceeds to describe the narrator's meeting with Jackson.

Conrad's gunrunners may be in London, but they recall their previous experience clearly. Stopping in front of the store window of a gun shop, Jackson associates the display with the firearms smuggled to Karain: "'The sight of all this made me think of him,' he went on, with his face near the glass . . . and I could see another man, powerful and bearded, peering at him intently from amongst the dark and polished tubes that can cure so many illusions. 'Yes; it made me think of him'" (TU, 53–54; Conrad's ellipsis). The cynical aside about the sure-fire cure for illusions undermines the narrator's fanciful vision of Karain reflected in the glass. For Jackson displays a far greater interest in the Malay chieftain than does the narrator. Jackson, who childishly repeats the phrase "I wonder" and refers to Karain twice as "poor devil," clearly cannot forget the Malay ruler, who was also plagued by phantoms from his past. Unwittingly echoing Conrad's authorial intrusion, Jackson asks the narrator, "What do you think?" (TU, 54). Responding indirectly, the narrator instructs Jackson to look at the restless activity on the street. Conrad converts the commotion of the city's sights and sounds into an ambiance of illusion, vividly described and parceled out into three expository paragraphs that are punctuated repeatedly by Jackson's word "Ye-e-e-s." The elongation of this utterance casts doubt on Jackson's personal epiphany of the compulsive nature of modern life. Moreover, he himself degrades the significance of his insight when he marvels at how unreal the hectic life around him seems in comparison to Karain's melodramatic story. The narrator terminates the inconclusive final scene by parroting his previous assessment of Jackson's maladjustment: "[H]e had been too long away from home" (TU, 56).

Conrad's enigmatic capstone to the story offers no reliable moral judgment on the outcome of the action, since Jackson's awestruck assertions fall flat when closely examined and the wry narrator never fully discloses his true feelings about the episode.[14] Like existence itself, the story of Karain and the gunrunners cannot be reconciled with any conventional formula or systematic frame of reference. But this has not prevented critics from offering codified interpretations of this complex tale, which often minimize the enigmatic closure or else ignore it completely.[15] Significantly, Hollis is not only absent from but also almost irrelevant to the final conversation between Jackson and the narrator. Jackson mentions Hollis once as he attempts to entice the narrator into speculating on "whether the charm worked" for Karain (TU, 54). Not only is Hollis absent from the closing scene, but he does not play a major role in the story, except for his presentation of the charm at the end of chapter 5 and the beginning of chapter 6. Hollis's relative unimportance harmonizes with the slang term hollis, meaning a small pebble.[16] He only springs into action because it would be unwise to take Karain to Europe, and he speculates that the

Malay ruler may go berserk before his people can rise up against him. Hollis's pose as a white witch doctor resonates with hypocrisy, particularly when he laughs at the solution he has quickly devised.

Conrad's joke may extend to the charm itself, which is "fascinating" to Karain and to the gunrunners as well.[17] Hollis, in fact, emphasizes the Queen as a symbol of her country's rapacious and respectable qualities: "She commands a spirit, too—the spirit of her nation; a masterful, conscientious, unscrupulous, unconquerable devil . . . that does a lot of good—incidentally . . . a lot of good . . . at times—" (TU, 49; Conrad's ellipses). The embarrassing pauses in Hollis's declaration reveal his difficulty in defending imperialistic policies. He offers Karain another pretense to replace the defunct charms of the old wizard. But the white men must pretend that the coin has special powers in order to work the magic. Rather than acting as Conrad's moral spokesman, Hollis functions as a younger version of the old wizard. But his sorcery lies not in the token or the words he employs to cast a spell but in human gullibility, the will to believe: "Help me to make him believe—everything's in that" (TU, 50). Karain may be no more ridiculous taking the sixpence into the wilderness than the gunrunners are when they take their European chronometers to another world as they ply their illegal trade.

If Hollis does not qualify as a moral spokesman, does anyone in the story speak for Conrad? The idea of a reliable arbiter of truth is anathema to Conrad's artistic strategy, yet critics have persisted in the search nonetheless.[18] One aspect of the conclusion that requires closer scrutiny is the nature of Jackson's revelation, a personal epiphany that apparently evokes the narrator's apathy. Jackson's childlike sense of wonder in the final conversation is consistent with Conrad's caricature of his romantic sensibility in the middle chapters and offers comic relief from the melodramatic confession of Karain. In the company of the more cerebral narrator and Hollis, Jackson's romantic disposition becomes patently ridiculous. As they pass the time waiting for Karain by playing chess, Jackson strums a guitar and sings Spanish love songs. Although the emphasis on love may prefigure the obsessive passion detailed in Karain's confession, Conrad nevertheless lampoons Jackson's soulful nature. Just before Karain's arrival, Conrad transforms Jackson into a Provençal troubadour, dredging up cultural memories of the courtly love tradition: "Jackson twanged the guitar and gasped out in sighs a mournful dirge about hopeless love and eyes like stars" (TU, 21). Indeed, Conrad plays with this image as he counterpoints Karain's melodramatic confession with farcical depictions of

Jackson. Prior to the beginning of Karain's story, Conrad calls attention to "the long yellow hair of [Jackson's] beard flowing over the strings of the guitar lying on the table" (TU, 26–27). The carefree image of Jackson gives way to Karain's account of an enslavement to obsession. His testimony, a perversion of the romantic yearning for the ideal, prompts Jackson's only major interruption in Karain's narrative, when he accidentally touches the guitar: "A plaintive resonance filled the cabin with confused vibrations and died out slowly" (TU, 35). The "confused vibrations" objectify Jackson's unrest as he listens to the melodramatic confession, a story that (he later admits) seems more real to his romantic sensibility than the mechanized chaos of a London street. In chapter 6, Jackson is the only one who objects to the deception of Karain, complaining that the gift of the sixpence was a cynical gesture. Hollis merely observes that Jackson is "without guile" but "will learn."

Jackson's revelation, then, should be viewed in light of Conrad's burlesque of his romantic attitude. What Jackson sees in the London street, at the narrator's bidding, is a bleak panorama of ruined architecture, blank faces, smoke-filled skies, monstrous vehicles, and other shabby images of despair—all products of human restlessness presented at close quarters. Conrad contrasts the mechanized means of transportation, "queer wreckage adrift upon a river of hats," with the equally mechanical gesture of "a policeman, helmeted and dark, stretching out a rigid arm at the crossing of the streets" (TU, 55). Jackson gazes in wonder at this turbulent scene, his boyish eyes expressing both contempt and amusement. It is scarcely surprising, therefore, that he rejects the nineteenth-century capital of civilized squalor for the romantic memory of a Malay melodrama on a remote tract of land. Switching from the vividly descriptive prose with which he depicts the hectic street life, Conrad delves into abstract rhetoric to convey Jackson's sense of the heart of darkness pulsating within Western culture: "It is there; it pants, it runs, it rolls; it is strong and alive; it would smash you if you didn't look out" (TU, 55). Monotonously repeating the indefinite pronoun, Conrad applies the "beast in the jungle" motif to society at large. Like James, Conrad dwells on appearances solely for the sake of discovering what lies beneath them, if anything. Every London street represents an illusion in progress. Jackson, with his romantic sensibility, recognizes this but cannot free himself from the shackles of memory. Although Conrad may admire the sincerity of the romantic spirit, he never falls into a nostalgic quagmire—at least, not in his fiction.

Conrad's attitude toward the narrator is more difficult to determine, especially in view of the enigmatic epilogue. The terse language
of the narrator's dialogue, juxtaposed with the vividly descriptive
prose passages, makes his responses to Jackson seem patronizing or
supercilious. At times the narrator appears to speak for Conrad, but
more often his comments brand him as an exponent of Western
materialism and hypocrisy. He adopts a neutral stance in a world he
views as a breeding ground for wishful thinkers. Early in chapter 3 he
considers Karain a stereotypical savage—childish, absurd, perhaps
insane, and "racially incapable" of premeditated action. Yet at the
opening of chapter 5 he alters his opinion, praising Karain as a noble
victim of human gullibility and anxiety:

> I thought of his wanderings, of that obscure Odyssey of revenge, of all the
> men that wander amongst illusions; of the illusions as restless as men; of
> the illusions faithful, faithless; of the illusions that give joy, that give sorrow,
> that give pain, that give peace; of the invincible illusions that can make
> life and death appear serene, inspiring, tormented, or ignoble. (*TU,* 40)

The assessment of Karain as an archetypal wanderer does not harmonize with the narrator's more mundane view of him as childishly absurd,
unless this incongruity contributes to Conrad's narrative ambivalence,
which may account for the moral confusion at the close of the tale.
Unlike Marlow, the narrator of "Karain" does not reveal intricate
psychological details about himself through the wisdom of hindsight.
If the narrator's words reveal a personality that is ambiguous at best
and arrogant at worst, his actions demonstrate nothing, literally, for he
never acts throughout the scenario. He praises and condemns, observes and platitudinizes, but he never acts, except in the theatrical
sense of the term when he participates in the charade of duping
Karain into believing in the necromantic charm of the sixpence.

Just as Karain is the dupe of the gunrunners' desperate ruse, so
each Westerner is the dupe of memory. Jackson's state of wonder at
the close of the story corroborates his entrapment in the past. Even
Hollis admits, as he opens his box of memorabilia to locate the sixpence,
that "everyone of us . . . has been haunted by some woman" (*TU,* 47).
Thus, the gunrunners see no great harm in reprogramming Karain's
modus vivendi. Except for Jackson's brief protest, they naturally acqui-
esce in his search for a new illusion. It is the way of the world in the
"unbelieving West," a land haunted by the ghosts of past experiences
and illusions about the future. Significantly, while prefacing his retelling of Karain's confession, the narrator remarks that it is "impossible to

convey the effect of his story. It is undying, it is but a memory, and its vividness cannot be made clear to another mind, any more than the vivid emotions of a dream" (*TU*, 26).

Life, like memory, seems like the dream of an illusion. Most Westerners, Conrad insists, live only vicariously, either in their illusive aspirations or in their memories of a dreamlike past. And though he appears immune to the nostalgia afflicting Jackson in the ambiguous final scene, the narrator discloses his own indulgence in the past throughout the tale, particularly at the outset: "A strange name wakes up memories; the printed words scent the smoky atmosphere of to-day faintly, with the subtle and penetrating perfume as of land breezes breathing through the starlight of bygone nights" (*TU*, 3). Such balmy rhetoric, originating from a former gunrunner who now smuggles memories into the present, testifies to one of Conrad's most enduring themes: our enchantment with the illusions of the past. On a more mundane level, the narrator admits to feeling relief when, in the middle of Karain's confession, he hears the reassuring sound of "the firm, pulsating beat of the two ship's chronometers ticking off steadily the seconds of Greenwich Time" (*TU*, 40). Here the Western concept of fractionalized time, and its attendant temporal fixations, collides with the more natural and fundamental native sense of time. The white men retain their composure in part because they are tethered to machines that steadily measure the passage of time. At the end of the story, Conrad transforms the abstract mechanical pulsations of time into an insidious heartbeat that propels and dominates civilized life. It promotes "progress," it advances "culture," and it "colonizes" the globe.

What dominates Conrad's ending, however, is not the words exchanged between Jackson and the narrator. Less than twenty lines of dialogue make up the conversation that Conrad extends over the last two pages. Jackson struggles to articulate his revelation of the blind, mechanistic thrust of civilization, but he does not comprehend the full cultural implications of his new vision. His passionate repetition of the word *it* illustrates this fragmentary understanding. The narrator remains noncommittal, his complacency more likely showing his arrogance rather than wise passivity. His droll cynicism counterpoints Jackson's emotionally charged declarations, neutralizing the final testimony of the two former shipmates. What dominates the epilogue, therefore, is Conrad's graphic depiction of the London panorama when Jackson and the narrator meet in the Strand. Conrad presents an anatomy of modern urban culture, concretely detailed in the manner of Dickens or Dostoyevsky or Crane's *Maggie*. Significantly, Conrad focuses on vehicles of transportation and communication, instruments of progress that distract our attention from an unmediated perception of life as it is. Thus, he suggests that technological progress has become *our* grand illusion, à la Karain's sixpence. An assortment of children and adults rush pell-mell through the streets, dodging hansoms, omnibuses, and other vehicles in the cluttered thorough-fares. This flurry of activity gives the impression of time marching on, but the "sombre," "resigned" appearance of the physical environment conveys the opposite impression. For behind the facade of progress in Western culture lies a sullen stasis, as society races on a treadmill to oblivion.[19]

Conrad also stresses language as a pernicious diversion that thwarts our attempts to see things as they are. He calls attention to "the gold letters, sprawling over the fronts of houses" (*TU*, 55), the gilded signposts of a broken world dazed into insensibility. Young girls talk vivaciously, workmen are overheard "discussing filthily," and a "line of yellow boards seems endowed with a bizarre animation" (*TU*, 55).[20] Conrad fuses impressions of material advancement and hu-manistic neglect in his depiction of "a ragged old man with a face of despair [who] yelled horribly in the mud the name of a paper" (*TU*, 55). In modern society, human values must yield to massive capitalis-tic enterprises. Small wonder the gunrunners can return to London without compunction from their illegal trade in the Pacific. This final image of despair precedes Jackson's telegraphic articulation of his new insight. Everyone he sees has cultivated the delusions that sup-port the myth of progress, the sole religion endorsed by modern civilization at the turn of the century. For Conrad, every outpost of progress is a distorted looking glass for narcissistic reverie.

The Western psyche lives in the past while life goes on in the present. Modern culture, the expression of Western consciousness, subverts the experience of today by obsessively dwelling on thoughts of yesterday and tomorrow. But yesterday did not happen as we remember it, and the tomorrow we project is only an idealized yesterday. Obsessively attached to the past and future, modern con-sciousness never perceives the fleeting moment for what it is. Conrad exploits this psychological defect throughout "Karain."[21] Using mem-ory as a structuring device, he reverses our expectations by making the most recent memory the most problematical to interpret. Mem-ory, an integral part of the mind's scheme of self-deception, falsifies past experiences and warps anticipations of the future. Moreover,

Conrad turns the myth of the noble savage inside out by endowing Karain with anxieties endemic to the Western sensibility, before dispelling these traumas with cross-cultural hocus-pocus. The ending, rather than resolving the moral question of Hollis's charade, places the talisman incident so far back in the recesses of the memory that it almost loses its central importance. Conrad again reverses our expectations when he makes a romantic buffoon, Jackson, the oracle of his disclosure that the heart of Western civilization is more barbaric and chaotic than any South Sea island. True to the spirit of this ironic discourse, the worldly wise narrator scoffs at a vision more perceptive than his own. The preposterous image of a Malay ruler marching triumphantly back to his people in proud possession of a magical sixpence corresponds to the absurdity of the Westerners' return to England, unaware that their cultural conditioning has spawned all their desires, engendered all their hopes, thought all their thoughts, dreamed all their dreams, and petrified all their memories of a past they never really experienced. The beast in Conrad's jungle is the blind energy of modern materialistic civilization: "[I]t would smash you if you didn't look out" (*TU*, 55).

## "The Partner"

Published roughly eight years after Conrad's last collaboration with Ford, "The Partner" dramatizes another kind of literary cooperation, that of the imaginative artist and the gullible reader.[22] Superficially, Conrad divides his persona into two fictive surrogates: a young writer-narrator in the Jamesian tradition and an old master stevedore who provides the younger man with raw material for a potential story. What emerges from their conversation, however, is not a whale of a tale of high adventure but rather a sporadic debate on the craftsmanship and execution of the art of fiction; this may, in part, account for its almost total neglect by critics and its status as one of Conrad's least-admired works.[23] True, the potboiler plot affords little in terms of entertainment, but this is largely due to Conrad's fragmentation of the crude interior story as a counterpoint to the immaculately polished and scrupulously designed prose format endorsed by the specious writer-narrator. (The notion that Conrad was already declining in artistic ability by the time he wrote "The Partner" cannot fully account for the eccentric quality of this tale.) In sum, Conrad demonstrates that realistic fiction is a contradiction in terms. His exposition of a "silly yarn" in blunt language hints that readers turn to literature not as a way of intensifying their awareness of life but as a way of temporarily avoiding life; the vicarious experience takes them far from mundane actuality. Conrad's reputation as a "romantic" author has no bearing on his artistic creativity except in this regard: he always recognizes the texture of lies in his "romances," no matter how much biographical or historical material he puts into each fiction.[24]

Conrad's tedious and melodramatic interior narrative abounds with convolutions. The narrator, a writer of magazine stories, meets an impressive old ruffian in Westport who scoffs at the "silly yarn" boatmen tell to tourists about the wreck of the *Sagamore*. The writer-narrator, more interested in the old adventurer's mannerisms than in his tale, discusses the process of literary composition with his taciturn drinking partner. Eventually, the conversation prompts the old ruffian to narrate his version of the shipwreck.

The vessel's owners, Captain Harry Dunbar and his brother George, maintain an adequate trade until George enters into partnership with Cloete, a rascal who has recently arrived from America. Dissatisfied with his new investment, Cloete tries to convince George to wreck the ship for the insurance money and then finance the advertisements for a new patent-medicine scheme. George cannot persuade his brother to take a sabbatical away from the ship, and he ultimately rejects Cloete's plan. However, Cloete convinces a lazy "skunk" named Stafford to join the crew of the *Sagamore* as a saboteur. George, after hearing that his naive brother has signed up Stafford for the next voyage, does not take the opportunity to expose Stafford to the Captain. When George and Cloete learn that the ship has been wrecked off Westport, they hurry there hoping that the vessel will sink quickly. Cloete comes aboard the *Sagamore* and encounters Stafford, who has blackmail in mind. He overpowers Stafford and locks him in the cabin. When Stafford, instead of the Captain, mysteriously climbs into the lifeboat, Cloete and the coxswain go back to the cabin to investigate. They find the Captain killed by a bullet through the heart from his own revolver. The coxswain erroneously assumes it a grief-stricken suicide, but Cloete refuses to reveal that Stafford murdered the Captain. Back on shore, the Captain's wife goes mad with grief, Cloete accuses George of indirectly causing his brother's death, and Cloete and Stafford part company in anger. Cloete bemoans the fact that the Captain's unexpected death has deprived him of the chance to make a fortune from the new lumbago pills. Stafford, who initially told Cloete that he shot the Captain (mistaking him for his treacherous "partner"), confesses on his deathbed that he killed the Captain, who surprised him in the act of theft.

The final paragraphs of the tale provide a brief, ironic ending. Conrad's narrator concludes that, since the moral of the story is the old fellow's vindication of the Captain, the discourse does not even deserve a thank-you. But the reasons behind the narrator's rejection expose his naive and diffident nature. Claiming that such an event would not likely occur "in our respectable Channel," he believes the setting of the tale should be transferred to the South Seas in order to be fully accepted by the reading public. The factual basis of the stevedore's tale does not matter to the narrator, who cares more about verisimilitude than he does about actual truth and feels he must pander to the customary expectations of his audience.[25] Such intrigue, he believes, belongs in the barbarous South Seas, far from the respectable, civilized people in England. Even more damning to the narrator's character is his admission that "it would have been too much trouble to cook it for the consumption of magazine readers. So here it is raw, so to speak—just as it was told to me . . ." (WT, 128). Indolence prevents the narrator from garnishing the story for the appetite of his audience. Thus, he implicitly defines realism as whatever readers can swallow. Conrad's gastronomic metaphor serves as a caustic commentary on readers and writers of magazine fiction.[26]

Not possessing the concentration or energy to create a suitable story from the old adventurer's account, the narrator presents the tale "raw"—"but unfortunately robbed of the striking effect of the narrator; the most imposing old ruffian that ever followed the unromantic trade of master stevedore in the port of London" (WT, 128). The key adjective unromantic provides a clue to the contrast of Conrad's internal and external narrators. The writer-narrator clings to the received ideas of conventional fiction, rejecting the "raw" scenario of the "unromantic" stevedore as inapplicable to any preestablished formula. But Conrad consistently rebukes blind obedience to formulaic notions of artistic creativity.[27] In effect, he translates his writer-narrator into an exemplar of the literal-minded reader of his day. The narrator repeatedly interrupts the old ruffian's recital with eureka-like ejaculations: "'Ah!' I cried. 'Now I understand,'" "'By Jove!' I murmured," "'Why!' I cried, 'they missed an immense fortune'" (WT, 102, 116, 126). These utterances prompt only growls of scorn and rage from the stevedore, who may also be expressing the rage of the unfettered artist in Conrad as well.

The narrator's Panglossian insistence on the "respectable Channel" in the final paragraph harkens back to the opening of Conrad's story and casts new light on the narrator's account of his meeting with the "old ruffian." To avoid being thought an idle tippler, he emphasizes that their meeting in "a small respectable smoking-room of a small respectable hotel" accounts for his willingness to cultivate the sailor's acquaintance (*WT*, 89). Cultivating the knack for meeting new people is useful for obtaining ideas for story lines, but the narrator lacks the imagination to make the most of the situation and is distracted by his inability to pigeonhole this new and eccentric phenomenon: "[O]f individuality he had plenty. . . . But he was not easy to classify, . . . I gave him up with the vague definition, 'an imposing old ruffian'" (*WT*, 89–90). Like a young reader entering a library for the first time, he needs to discover which authors belong in which categories. "[O]ppressed by infinite boredom," a cardinal motive for many readers, he searches out the old man once more. Like some readers who exhibit more curiosity about an author's biography than they do about the author's works themselves, the narrator speculates on what forces have contributed to the production of this idiosyncratic specimen of humanity. Once again, the narrator's habits of thought settle on matters of classification. But Conrad recognizes better than most the pernicious effort to compartmentalize life, and he persistently makes sport of the narrator as a mere novice in the field of fiction whose only security lies in mechanically mouthing platitudes, such as "It's said that truth is stranger than fiction" (*WT*, 91).

When the stevedore calls his attention to "a silly lot of rocks" within view, the "writer of stories" immediately transforms his visual perception into a fictionalized verbal painting of the scene. His Pateresque ode to the rocks concludes by transmuting the setting into a two-dimensional pattern of colors on a famous artist's canvas:

> I was looking at them—an acre or more of black dots scattered on the steel-grey shades of the level sea, under the uniform gossamer grey mist with a formless brighter patch in one place—the veiled whiteness of the cliff coming through, like a diffused, mysterious radiance. It was a delicate and wonderful picture, something expressive, suggestive, and desolate, a symphony in grey and black—a Whistler. (*WT*, 91–92)

The rhetorical movement from concrete to abstract images, from the contours of forms to the suggestion of formlessness, punctuated by the direct reference to Whistler's indistinct pictorial style, clearly evokes the "art for art's sake" credo of the British aesthetic movement.

Conrad reinforces his allusion to the aesthetes shortly thereafter when he sets the opening scene of the stevedore's narration in "the Cheshire Cat public house" (*WT*, 93). This phrase functions as a dual reference: first, it names the celebrated feline who directs Alice to the Mad Tea Party in Wonderland; second, and more covertly, it conjures up the Cheshire Cheese tavern, headquarters of the London Rhymer's Club, frequented by Yeats and others who promulgated Pater's aesthetic effusions.[28]

With regard to the aestheticism of Pater and Whistler, Conrad exhibited an approach-avoidance conflict, for he was drawn to the cry of *l'art pour l'art* but repelled by the hedonistic cult of artifice that endorsed and then perverted Pater's epicurean speculations in the decadent nineties. And, although Whistler's *Symphony in Grey and Black* exists solely in Conrad's whimsical imagination, Whistler did title many of his paintings "symphonies" or "nocturnes" of various color combinations. It is even possible that Whistler's works may have served as models or inspirations for Conrad's verbal seascapes and landscapes, not only in this tale but throughout his fiction. Whistler's deliberate attempt to link painting and music would have been intriguing to Conrad, who, in the preface to *The Nigger of the "Narcissus,"* asserts that literary art must "aspire to the plasticity of sculpture, to the colour of painting, and to the magic suggestiveness of music—which is the art of arts" (*NN*, 146) Both Conrad and Whistler subscribed to Walter Pater's 1873 dictum "All art constantly aspires to the condition of music."[29] Whistler's "symphonies" show his effort to transcend form and subject to reach the realm of pure suggestiveness; Conrad's most impressionistic passages display his attempt to accomplish the same feat in fictional prose.[30]

Although expressions like "gossamer grey mist" and "veiled whiteness" recall Whistler's art, and words such as *radiance* and *delicate* echo Pater's aesthetic vocabulary, Conrad actually parodies such effusions in the writer-narrator's patch of purple prose. The stevedore growls out his contempt at this "foolishness." With a salvo of words, the old man (and Conrad) demolishes all artistic fallacies—pathetic, affective, and otherwise. So the lengthy passage on impressionistic rocks can be viewed as a self-parody or as a satire on impressionistic writing in general or, in its largest compass, as an indictment of how fiction turns a naturalistic setting into an attractive tapestry of lies. Yet, despite the narrator's penchant for romanticizing his perceptions, as he listens to the stevedore's tale he always thinks in terms of plausibility, assessing the story's potential credibility in the minds of implied readers. His asides and interjections show that he is assimilating the raw material into the conception of a short story. But at the end of the narration, after his nagging curiosity has been completely satisfied, the narrator suddenly drops the idea of using the material to create a work of fiction. He abandons his collaborator without a word of gratitude.[31] The narrator makes only one positive point throughout the story: he calls our attention to "the striking effect" of the stevedore, an eccentric character who, upon close inspection, may provide a revealing portrait of Conrad himself.

The stevedore's confirmed pessimism mirrors Conrad's fatalistic outlook: "[H]is general contempt for mankind with its activities and moralities was expressed in the rakish set of his big soft hat of black felt with a large rim, which he kept always on his head" (*WT*, 89). The old ruffian's scorn for the short-winded elations of humanity reflects an attitude Conrad often expressed in his letters and fiction. But more significantly, the black felt hat crowning the stevedore's head denotes him as the ironic doppelgänger of the author. Only one year before publishing "The Partner," Conrad had employed a white hat as an emblem of the narrator's "other self" at the conclusion of "The Secret Sharer." Conrad reinforces the arresting image near the midpoint of the stevedore's narration: "The old fellow departed from his impressive immobility to turn his rakishly hatted head and look at me with his old, black, lack-lustre eyes" (*WT*, 116). Whether the stevedore resembles Conrad physically or not matters little; the accentuated hat signals his function in the story as Conrad's "secret sharer," though perhaps in a playful context. Moreover, the words *rakish* and *rakishly* (associated with whoremongering) cast the stevedore in the role of a tale-monger, suggesting how Conrad the artist mined the experiences of Conrad the former mariner to find material for his novels and tales.

The accent on the stevedore's "impressive immobility" stirs recollections of another alter ego, Conrad's most celebrated fictional surrogate, Charlie Marlow: "He was sitting there in absolute immobility, which was really fakir-like and impressive" (*WT*, 90). This "fakir-like" calm recalls Marlow's Buddha postures in *Heart of Darkness*, a work that Conrad evidently had in mind in an earlier comment on the stevedore: "His appearance was that of an old adventurer, retired after many unholy experiences in the darkest parts of the earth" (*WT*, 89). The narrator questions whether the "old adventurer" has ever been outside England, but this does not negate Conrad's evocation of Marlow's journey into the self in the heart of Africa. Obviously, Conrad's tactics are at least partially comedic, for the voyage in "The

Partner" offers a tragic silliness in place of the psychological subtleties in *Heart of Darkness,* but the stevedore-Marlow-Conrad connection cannot be discounted. Time and again, Conrad refers to the old ruffian's "ominous" and "immovable" arm lying on the table. It never moves except when the stevedore tightens his hand to make a fist. If Marlow is an ironic double of Conrad as a young adventurer, the old adventurer in this much later story seems to be an ironic portrait of Conrad as retired mariner, whose storehouse of memories has been ransacked from within by his own artistic impulse. If we accept this premise, it becomes difficult, if not impossible to accept the stevedore's "sally against sea life. Silly sort of life, he called it. No opportunities, no experience, no variety, nothing" (*WT,* 92–93). This blunt catalogue of negations appears totally out of key with Conrad's well-known appreciation of the "solidarity" of sailors and the redeeming aspects of work. Although the stevedore's harangue against life at sea may reinforce the narrator's hunch that the old ruffian had never left England, it may represent the saturnine aspect of Conrad's personality in asserting that few men profit during periods of prolonged isolation at sea.

More importantly, Conrad speaks through the mouthpiece of the "unromantic" stevedore, who opens the story by launching a tirade against the local boatmen for exploiting gullible tourists by lying to them about the wreck of the *Sagamore* (note the possible pun on *saga*). The old ruffian brands their story a "silly yarn" in his first outburst, and he continues to inveigh against the lies of "these silly boatmen" until the last page of Conrad's tale. In between, the stevedore uses his favorite adjectives (*silly, foolish, crazy, mad*) almost compulsively. In a story that focuses on the literary execution of a story, Conrad's choice of words has great significance. Conrad, the inveterate skeptic, views conventional fiction as a contrived lie, a "silly yarn" that only becomes serious in the minds of readers who willingly suspend disbelief, and perhaps common sense. This may explain why "The Partner" totally loses its interest once the stevedore commences his recital, despite the telegraphic shorthand of his narration. Fiction may begin with an invocation to a muse, but this only masks the real magic: the verbal incantation of the spell of wonder. Conrad views the art of fiction as a kind of linguistic snake-charming; its power lies in the talismanic spell it casts over the vicariously involved reader.

The stevedore scoffs at the narrator's remark that most stories begin as anecdotes, or hints for further elaboration. Moreover, the hint the narrator has obtained from the boatmen earns the old ruffian's scorn:

"Damn silly yarn—Hint indeed! . . . A lie!" (WT, 91; Conrad's ellipsis).
Through the stevedore, Conrad implies that fiction starts out as fiction
and undergoes more and more embellishment until it attains an
artificial integrity. (The unity of a story masks the essential disharmo-
nies of life. Fiction depends on patterns, but existence is fundamentally patternless.) Conrad once again resorts to his intrusive hat gambit
to endorse the stevedore's objections to the writer-narrator's pristine
view of artistic creation: "[I]magine this statuesque ruffian enhaloed in
the black rim of his hat, letting all this out as an old dog growls
sometimes, with his head up and staring-away eyes" (WT, 91). Oddly
enough, even the narrator seems to agree with the stevedore, affirming that a false hint may be as sound a foundation for a story as a
truthful anecdote. What really matters to the narrator is the network
of possible connections in a tale. When the stevedore refers to "an
accident," in a different context, the narrator incorporates this idea
into his theoretical system: "[A]n accident has its backward and
forward connections" (WT, 92).

At this point, the stevedore begins to lose interest in the verbal
charades of a writer who aims to please in order to secure the cash
value of his works. But the narrator continues to blather on like a
Jamesian fountainhead: "Sometimes it pays to put in a lot out of one's
head, and sometimes it doesn't. I mean that the story isn't worth it.
Everything's in that" (WT, 92). Everything's in what? And what is
everything? Here Conrad seems to abandon the verbal fencing match
of his interlocutors in favor of linguistic nonsense that one might find
in James's "The Middle Years" or The Sacred Fount. Overall, Conrad
maintains his footing, but on constantly shifting grounds; he contends
that fiction is neither rigid design nor pure accident but somewhere in
between. Like James, he qualifies his statements and immaculately
covers his tracks. The tale within a tale that follows hinges on mistrust,
betrayed loyalties, and bizarre jests. A somber, Poe-like mood dominates the story, which has a disturbing undertone of madness. The
stevedore's melancholy tale, coarsely articulated as it is, does provide
enough raw material for reshaping into something more appealing,
but the narrator lacks the enthusiasm for the task. He shirks the
responsibility yet presents it to the reader nonetheless.

Stripped of its intricate opening and brief conclusion, "The Partner"
could pass for one of Ambrose Bierce's "Negligible Tales." Bierce's
fiction, like Conrad's, dwells on the bitter ironies experienced by
thwarted egos. But in this tale Conrad places the conversation of the
stevedore and the narrator on the same plane as the "tragic" wreck of

the *Sagamore*. Neither event takes firm possession of our sympathies. Convinced that life is one damn thing after another, Conrad remains as detached from the fate of Captain Harry as he is from the petty squabbles of the stevedore and the narrator. By presenting a sentimental discourse reduced to its bare essentials, he mocks the conventional reader's craving for a definitive interpretation. Conrad's endings frequently involve a supposedly objective observer who apparently speaks on behalf of the reader. But this story features a narrator who represents the reader's sensibility from beginning to end. He listens to a "raw" plot and rejects it as inappropriate for a piece of fiction. But the artist makes it his business to see what his audience fails to see. Conrad's task, in his own words, is "to make you see." The "moment of vision" is everything, but of brief duration. Except for the real or imagined revelations in his fiction, Conrad's readers never see behind the veil of words, maya, syntax, or whatever one might call the art of lying for a living. Duped by the wizardly power of the written word, they generally mistake fiction for life, making their home in a web of lies.

## "The Inn of the Two Witches"

Universally damned as a shameless potboiler,[32] even by its own author,[33] "The Inn of the Two Witches" nevertheless casts light on Conrad's skeptical attitude toward narrative in general and the sense of an ending in particular. Critics of this anecdotal tale have documented Conrad's probable debt to Wilkie Collins's "A Terribly Strange Bed"[34] and have commented on the ironic use of the framing narrator to undercut the melodramatic excesses of the interior narrator.[35] However, a careful examination of the framing introduction and the ironic epilogue that bracket the interior narrative reveals Conrad's view of fiction as a tapestry of illusions. The preliminary paragraphs of "The Inn of the Two Witches" function in much the same manner as Hawthorne's sketch "The Custom House" prefaces *The Scarlet Letter*. Just as Hawthorne poses as the editor of a nonexistent manuscript, Conrad's framing narrator plays the role of custodian of some "preserved scraps" of writing. Moreover, Conrad converts the pseudo-editorial introduction into a mockery of fictional conventions. Subtitling his tale "A Find" (an apt touch, considering the derivative nature of the plot), Conrad borrows the necessary ingredients of a gothic tale of terror and prepares the reader for a ratiocinative denouement in the manner of Poe's "The Pit and the Pendulum." But Conrad's epilogue thwarts such an expectation by provoking questions about the nature of the multilayered narrative and providing answers that address only the most superficial issues. Ultimately, he shares Hawthorne's diabolical fascination with the wizard power of language.

Conrad's framing narrator opens the story by describing his "Find" as a "tale, episode, experience—call it how you will . . ." (*WT*, 131). Blurring the boundary between fact and fiction, the narrator asserts the factuality of the tale's content while confirming the artificiality of the form that it takes: "This writing constitutes the Find declared in the sub-title. The title itself is my own contrivance (can't call it invention) and has the merit of veracity" (*WT*, 131–32). Without pausing to discriminate "contrivance" from "invention" or explain how a contrived title "has the merit of veracity," the fictive narrator fabricates an imaginary location for the fictive discovery: "The Find was made in a box of books bought in London, in a street which no longer exists, from a second-hand bookseller in the last stages of decay. As to the books themselves, they were at least twentieth-hand, and on inspection turned out not worth the very small sum of money I disbursed" (*WT*, 132). Not satisfied merely to concoct an imaginary street housing a bookseller on the brink of dissolution, the narrator devalues his purchase, which also contains (at the bottom of the box) the precious Find.[36] When the framing narrator demands the box as well as the books, Conrad adds a Dickensian touch that transports the scene to the Old Curiosity Shop: "The decayed bookseller assented by the careless, tragic gesture of a man already doomed to extinction" (*WT*, 132). Playing on the conventional striving for verisimilitude in the manner of Defoe, Conrad turns the decrepit bookseller into a pathetic caricature, rendering the framing narrator's literary discovery an outrageous fabrication credible only to readers of penny dreadfuls and shilling shockers.

Conrad provides many details concerning the Find but virtually none about the finder, except that the framing narrator has a familiarity with sailing terminology, for a "sea phrase" in the manuscript arrests his "languid attention." Instead, Conrad concentrates on the literary Find, undermining its potential value at every turn. The "dull-faced" manuscript is only a "litter of loose pages," and it reads like "the drone of a monotonous voice" (*WT*, 132). Though the narrator's initial interest stems from the "sea phrase" in the manuscript, only a small portion of the story deals with life at sea. He also discovers, "from internal evidence," that "a good many pages of that relation were missing—perhaps not a great misfortune after all. . . . [A]s I've said, some of his pages (good tough paper too) were missing: gone in covers for jampots or in wadding for the fowling-pieces of his irreverent posterity" (WT, 133).[37] While Conrad teases the reader by keeping the content of the tale a secret, he also makes sport of its value by speculating on the mundane uses to which the missing pages might have been put. Missing, too, is the Spanish inn mentioned in the title, which no longer exists according to the framing narrator. Conrad further complicates the pretense of actuality in his author's note by claiming he had never read Wilkie Collins's "A Terrible Strange Bed" and identifying the germ of his story as a genuine historical incident (WT, xi). But Conrad, who falsified the details of his life on several occasions, has little credence as a reliable authority when offering public pronouncements, particularly in his Jamesian prefaces, written many years after the composition of most of his novels and tales.

The framing narrator also disparages the veracity of Edgar Byrne, who serves as the interior narrator. Byrne makes his "confession" late in life, at the age of sixty. In Conrad's ironic perspective, sixty-year-old Byrne is unable to look back on life with objective detachment, for he remains a perennial dreamer, deluded by the fallacies of hope while young and blinded by nostalgic sentiment when past his prime: "[B]y an amiable attention of Providence, most people at sixty begin to take a romantic view of themselves. Their very failures exhale a charm of peculiar potency. And indeed the hopes of the future are a fine company to live with" (WT, 131). Here Conrad inverts the theme of potentiality that plays such a significant role in "Youth" and Lord Jim, acknowledging the all-too-human tendency to glorify the past and make it a pedestal for future conquests. To Conrad, memories of the past are merely inert shadows, and dreams of the future always lack foundation.

But we can find an untainted note of veracity in the tale, for Conrad does come close to revealing the reason for including an anecdote from Byrne's early youth when the narrator declares that "the romanticism of growing age" encouraged Byrne to relate his adventure for his own satisfaction or to amaze posterity (WT, 131). Here Conrad hints, through the narrative voice, at the possible embroidery of the discourse. And what is his plot except gothic stage managing à la Poe (Byrne's first name is Edgar) and Wilkie Collins? The framing narrator does assert, however, that Byrne's motive was not self-glorification "because the experience was simply that of an abominable fright—terror he calls it. You would have guessed that the relation alluded to in the very first lines was in writing" (WT, 131). The above sentence becomes a hopeless tautology for Conrad never quotes "the very first lines" of Byrne's imaginary manuscript in toto. Instead, he paraphrases the account in bits and pieces that fail to indicate "the relation alluded to" by Byrne, which is also alluded to by the framing narrator.[38] Compared to the *I*-witness accounts that preface "Youth," "Falk," *Heart of Darkness,* and many other narratives that rely on realistic framings, Conrad's verbal tapestry in this case seems ready to unravel at any moment. Thus, to evade the charge of writing a potboiler, Conrad filters the story through the medium of an indifferent witness who responds only to the words he reads. As in "The Partner," the framing narrator actually plays the customary role of the reader in this haunted house of fiction.

Conrad forces us to choose between the nameless narrator and Edgar Byrne, the interior narrative voice, as the more reliable source of information. We cannot place equal faith in both, for the framing narrator disparages Byrne not only as the sixty-year-old teller of the tale but also as the twenty-two-year-old participant in the incident: "Two and twenty is an interesting age in which one is easily reckless and easily frightened; the faculty of reflection being weak and the power of imagination strong" (*WT,* 132). Although the framing narrator demeans Byrne's easily aroused imagination, his own sensibility displays a trace of unbridled curiosity, despite his efforts to conceal it: "'Let's see what it is all about,' I thought, without excitement" (*WT,* 132). Conrad's "Let's see" harkens back to Lewis Carroll's "Let's pretend" premise at the outset of *Through the Looking-Glass.* "Let's pretend" is Alice's favorite expression; she uses it to pass through the mirror and enter a wonderland of imagination. In Conrad's fictive world, the author plays "Let's pretend" and the reader assumes the attitude of "Let's see what it is all about." Thus, the nameless narrator, with his "languid attention," stands for the passive reader of late-Victorian fiction who expects entertainment and symmetry from literature. Like Carroll's Alice and Hawthorne's fictive surrogate in "The Custom House," Conrad's anonymous narrator acknowledges the evocative capacity of language, or the wizard power of words, to use Hawthorne's phrase. Though the framing narrator refers to the "witches" in his title as "merely a conventional expression," he does reserve a place for witchcraft in the modern world:

> Diabolical ingenuity in invention though as old as the world is by no means a lost art. Lost art. Look at the telephones for shattering the little peace of mind given to us in this world, or at the machine guns for letting with dispatch the life out of our bodies. Now-a-days any blear-eyed old witch if only strong enough to turn an insignificant little handle could lay low a hundred young men of twenty in the twinkling of an eye. (*WT,* 133)

Telephones and machine guns are distinctive forms of communication, as well as tokens of materialistic progress, which Byrne should
know from his experience as an officer on board a "sloop-of-war":
"[T]he preserved scraps of his conscientious writing" indicate that his
vessel frequently sent messengers inland to communicate orders to
Spanish patriots (WT, 133–34). Byrne's fragmentary written communication (the tale, referred to as "preserved scraps") is an attempt to
communicate, which engenders the rest of the action of the story.
Likewise, Conrad's fictive explanation of how the nameless narrator
acquired Byrne's manuscript obliquely reflects the processes of fiction-
making; the imaginative act of "Let's pretend" is followed by the
reader's characteristic response, "Let's see."

Actually, the "let's see" element overwhelms the "let's pretend"
impulse in Conrad's derivative gothic thriller. Although the narrator
mocks Byrne's conventional chronological narration, he recreates the
story in the same plodding, routine fashion he deplores, despite its
missing pages and his characterization of the tale as a "litter of loose
pages." The narrator also provides a caveat that exudes the faint odor
of a red herring: "[Y]ou must expect to meet here a certain naiveness
of contrivance and simplicity of aim appertaining to the remote
epoch" (WT, 133).[39] Edgar Byrne's narrative, after establishing a sense
of time and place, offers a "panegyric of a very fine sailor" known as
Cuba Tom, not because he was Cuban but "on account of some
wonderful adventures he had in that island in his young days, adventures which were the favorite subject of the yarns he was in the habit
of spinning to his shipmates of an evening on the forecastle head"
(WT, 134). At this point, the experienced Conradian reader might
expect another layer of narration in which Cuba Tom might play the
Marlovian role of imaginative yarn-spinner, taking charge of relating
the rest of the story. But Conrad declines to play this familiar gambit
and instead makes Cuba Tom a minor character in an inserted tale set
in the old world of the Napoleonic wars.

Manly Cuba Tom, the "professional mentor" of young officer Edgar
Byrne, disembarks with his protégé on a "gloomy autumn morning" to
make a landing at a shallow cove. Tom relies on simple language to
see him through the strange Spanish terrain, an easy chore for a man
who once crossed the island of Cuba on foot with no knowledge of
Spanish. Byrne accompanies Tom only part of the way on the older
man's mission to rendezvous in the mountains with Gonzales, the
local leader who opposes the French. Conrad quickly foreshadows
the disastrous results of Tom's mission: "The officer and the man were

walking now on a thick sodden bed of dead leaves, which the peasants thereabouts accumulate in the streets of their villages to *rot* during the winter for field manure" (*WT,* 136). The bed of dead leaves prefigures the actual bed that later is the cause of Tom's death.

The rest of Byrne's narrative can be summarized briefly. After landing on the Spanish coast and negotiating for a guide at the village wine shop, Byrne sends Tom into the interior, disregarding the warning of a cloaked man with a yellow hat who claims that the guide and shopkeeper are thieves. Initially, Byrne dismisses the warning and returns to his sloop, but he later attempts to overtake Tom and the unscrupulous guide, eventually reaching an inn where Tom had lodged the previous night. Byrne agrees to sleep at the inn, despite the peculiar behavior of the two elderly women who manage the inn (the "witches" mentioned in the title). A fascinating "gipsy girl" shows him to "the archbishop's room," where Byrne spends a harrowing night, haunted by the spectral voice of Tom issuing a warning. Byrne breaks open a locked wardrobe to find Tom's corpse inside. He carries Tom's lifeless body to the bed and later observes the heavy canopy slowly descending upon the mattress. This solves the mystery of Tom's death, but it also deranges Byrne's mind so that he mistakes the arrival of Gonzales and his soldiers the next morning for a French invasion. Assaulting the soldiers with his bare hands, the disoriented Byrne is knocked unconscious.

The gap in the typescript at this point marks the insertion of Conrad's coda, an epilogue of less than two pages, which provides scant information. The moment when Byrne regains consciousness becomes, in the narrator's phrasing, an absurd instance of comic relief: "Here Mr. Byrne describes in detail the skilful manner in which he found his broken head bandaged, informs us that he had lost a great deal of blood, and ascribes the preservation of his sanity to that circumstance" (*WT,* 163). If the bloodletting resulting from Byrne's "broken head" were a certain preventative measure against insanity, the narrator might envy such a fate, for he merely recounts in terse, abbreviated fashion the anticlimactic closing of the tale. Oddly enough, Gonzales, rather than Byrne, acts as the moralizing interpreter of the mysterious events, which he has only partially witnessed: "When asked what had become of the witches, he only pointed his finger silently to the ground, then voiced calmly a moral reflection: 'The passion for gold is pitiless, señor,' he said" (*WT,* 164). And when Byrne feebly inquires from his "improvised litter" about the gipsy girl, Gonzales tells him that she was responsible for setting "that infernal machine" into motion so she could acquire the coat buttons on the uniforms of Tom and Byrne. Edgar Byrne loses his curiosity after his questions elicit Gonzales's indirect admission that his soldiers have killed the three women. Similarly, Byrne remains silent when Gonzales's troops shoot one-eyed Bernardino six times against the wall of his wine shop: "As the shots rang out the rough bier with Tom's body on it went past carried by a bandit-like gang of Spanish patriots down the ravine to the shore, where two boats from the ship were waiting for what was left on earth of her best seaman" (*WT*, 164). The narrator does not pause to consider the ethical value of the four spontaneous executions by the firing squad of a bandit-like gang, but Conrad may be questioning whether these acts of retaliation or punishment are indeed "fitting to the occasion," as Gonzales asserts.

Byrne is too weak throughout the epilogue to do anything but look pale and mourn his dead friend, but Conrad's last description focuses not on Byrne or Tom's corpse or even the trigger-happy Gonzales: "The officer . . . saw on the grey hillside something moving, . . . a little man in a yellow hat mounted on a mule—that mule without which the fate of Tom Corbin would have remained mysterious forever" (*WT*, 165). Why does Conrad single out the yellow-hatted man and his mule for special emphasis in the final lines of the tale? Strictly in terms of the plot, this nameless man had warned Byrne of the possibility of foul play. Conrad associates the warning with his desire to recover his mule, which had been appropriated by Bernardino, the corrupt shopkeeper and *alcalde* (mayor) of the village. The sight of this strange man mounted on his recovered mule indicates that justice has been done, to a certain degree. But on another level of meaning the yellow-hatted man is a personification of disease and instability, an avatar of cosmic entropy, and a highly disturbing and ambiguous image on which to close this melodramatic story of greed and murder.

This eccentric character's first appearance establishes him as an representative of decay, as Conrad immediately identifies him with his omnipresent yellow hat: "Faded and dingy as it was, this covering for his head made him noticeable" (*WT*, 136). Hats and heads are nearly synonymous in Conrad's fiction, and this seriocomic character has headgear to match:

> He was a diminutive person, a mere homunculus, Byrne describes him, in a ridiculously mysterious, yet assertive attitude, a corner of his cloak thrown cavalierly over his left shoulder, muffling his chin and mouth; while the broad-brimmed yellow hat hung on a corner of his square little head. He stood there taking snuff, repeatedly. (*WT*, 137)

This Spanish version of the Mad Hatter (henceforth called the homunculus for brevity's sake) initially recommends Bernardino, his brother-in-law, to the two Englishmen. Later, he revokes his endorsement when he cautions Byrne against leaving Tom in the custody of Bernardino's corrupt guide. This time Conrad presents the homunculus in a more sinister light as a "sprite-like being" with a "predatory nose," a testy disposition, and a "sardonic bitterness" in his speech (*WT*, 140). Yet Conrad undermines this insidious aspect with comic tomfoolery when the homunculus takes "an immense quantity of snuff" from the hollow of his palm.

The word *homunculus* not only describes this eccentric character's diminutive stature but also relates to the germ of suspicion that he spreads to the confounded Edgar Byrne, a germ that engenders intrigue throughout the rest of the discourse. Conrad also depicts the little man as a human chameleon, for he undergoes a series of "rapid changes" in the cameo role he plays. In short, Conrad's enigmatic gnome turns psychological cartwheels, like the Russian harlequin in *Heart of Darkness,* to convince Byrne that Tom is the prey of greedy rascals. Yet Byrne initially interprets the warning as part of the little man's scheme to regain his mule. In response to this rebuff, the homunculus only adds to his own absurd appearance with preposterous gestures: "[T]he diminutive Spaniard, detaching his black glittering eyes from Byrne's face, turned his back on him brusquely with a gesture and a fling of the cloak which somehow expressed contempt, bitterness, and discouragement all at once. He turned away and stood still, his hat aslant, muffled up to the ears" (*WT,* 142). Toying with a Spanish stereotype, Conrad caricatures the homunculus as an absurd puppet in a ludicrous passion play. The idea that this histrionic gnome possesses vital information seems unreasonable. Yet, in a cock-and-bull story such as this, things are seldom what they seem, and, to paraphrase Tertullian's motto, one must believe the absurd *because* it is absurd. Unfortunately for Byrne (and for Tom), such a belief in the implausible comes too late: "A Spanish dwarf trying to beguile an officer of his majesty's navy into stealing a mule for him—that was too funny, too ridiculous, too incredible. Those were the exclamations of the captain. He couldn't get over the grotesqueness of it" (*WT,* 143). What is really grotesque, however, is Conrad's perversion of rational authority. For the captain has less insight into the actual situation than the dwarfish man whose yellow hat implies diseased mentality. *Gnome* itself also signifies an aphorism of truth, and Conrad often pictures truth as an idle, elusive vagrant.

Later, both Byrne and the captain regret not taking the homunculus seriously as their anxiety over Tom's fate intensifies. Yet Byrne secretly returns to the village, in part because he fears meeting his "aggrieved friend in the yellow hat, whose motives were not clear" (*WT,* 144). The homunculus vanishes as Byrne's search for Tom becomes a fruitless quest for certainty. He does not reappear until the final paragraph, when Conrad depicts him as the only satisfied character in the bizarre denouement, an elusive and ridiculous figure shrouded in mystery. By linking Tom's fate to the gnome's mule, Conrad transforms his potboiler into a narrative spun for the reader's idle amusement.

Conrad's unsatisfying coda is also significant because it ignores the supernatural motif announced in the story's title, which is developed only in the middle portion of the narrative. Except for one casual reference (by Gonzales, when addressing Byrne) to "that infernal machine," Conrad abruptly drops all mention of diabolical powers as the epilogue opens, returning Byrne to the world of reason and probability. In fact, the suspicion of witchcraft not only links Byrne to the external narrator and his cynical view of modern witchcraft (i.e., materialistic progress) but also serves as a prolonged transition between the view of the homunculus as a suspicious character and his eventual vindication as a reliable authority. Unlike Wilkie Collins's "A Terribly Strange Bed," Conrad's story includes a host of references to the diabolical spell associated with the lethal bed canopy.[40]

Aside from the ominous foreshadowing, the first hint of suspicion concerning diabolical powers in Byrne's narrative appears in his depiction of "a vile cur" that snarls and then "disappeared so suddenly that he might have been the unclean incarnation of the Evil One" (*WT,* 145). After this "unlucky presage," he describes a barren and desolate landscape reminiscent of Poe's "ghoul-haunted woodland of Weir." The mysterious inn abruptly materializes as a spectral apparition that seems to rise up out of the dark recesses of the night. Forcing his way into the inn and finding a swarthy girl and two old women sitting by the fire, "Byrne thought at once of two witches watching the brewing of some deadly potion" (*WT,* 147). Jumping to a hasty but imaginative conclusion, Byrne automatically converts these personifications of decay and degeneration into supernatural agents akin to the weird sisters in *Macbeth*: "These two unspeakable frights must be . . . affiliated to the devil" (*WT,* 148). When Byrne mentions Tom's name, these human "things without a name" undergo a radical metamorphosis: "An excitement quite fierce in its feebleness possessed them. The doubled-up sorceress flourished aloft her wooden spoon, the puffy monster got off her stool and screeched, stepping from one foot to the other, while the trembling of her head was accelerated to positive vibration" (WT, 149). This bizarre animation, rendered even more absurd by the oxymoron "fierce in its feebleness," colors Byrne's perception of the savagely beautiful "gipsy girl" who lives with the old crones. He considers her a child of Satan nurtured by the "weird harridans for the love of the Devil" (WT, 149–50). Ironically, it is not one of the two witches but the girl who chuckles "impiously" at the mention of the archbishop and gazes at Byrne "so that the red glow of the fire flashed in her black eyes and on her white teeth . . ." (WT, 150–51).

By manufacturing a satanic seduction à la the gothic novelist Matthew ("Monk") Lewis, Conrad mocks the haunted house of the mind as Byrne misconstrues a den of petty thieves as the coven of Mephistopheles. Byrne's rampant imagination does not permit his critical faculty to comprehend the meaning of the "fiendish uproar" that ensues shortly after his arrival. He fails to recognize that the clamorous quarrel between the girl and the "witches" concerns the disposition of his fate. But his paranoid fancy continues to lump these characters together in a diabolical compact: "[H]e saw the two witches 'affiliated to the Devil' and the Satanic girl looking at him in silence" (WT, 151). Byrne takes the phrase "affiliated to the Devil," implanted in his mind by the homunculus, literally. Instead of being on guard against mortal exponents of evil, Byrne suffers psychological paralysis because he dreads the supernatural, to the extent that he imagines his friend calling to him from the realm of shades:

> The world was perfectly dumb. And in this stillness he heard the blood beating in his ears with a confused rushing noise, in which there seemed to be a voice uttering the words: "Mr. Byrne, look out, sir." Tom's voice. He shuddered; for the delusions of the senses of hearing are the most vivid of all, and from their nature have a compelling character. (WT, 152)

By undermining the supernatural warning with Poe-like innuendo, Conrad shifts attention from the actual threat, the bed, to Byrne's haunted mind. In so doing, Conrad casts his lot with the masters of American gothic: Charles Brockden Brown, Hawthorne, Poe, Bierce, and James. Byrne's narrative becomes a vehicle for melodramatic intensities that Conrad subverts through irony: "[I]n the dumb house he heard again the blood pulsating ponderously in his ears, while once more the illusion of Tom's voice speaking earnestly somewhere near by was specially terrifying, because this time he could not make out the words" (WT, 153). Here, as in "The Idiots," one can detect the telltale art of Edgar Allan Poe, but although such gothic elements may seem tangential to Conrad's fiction, they do convey the characteristic Conradian mood of isolation and estrangement, as Byrne feels remote from the rest of mankind.

The discovery of Tom's corpse in the locked wardrobe temporarily halts Byrne's fabrications of supernatural portents, as the young officer attempts to discern the cause of death. He wonders how "those devilish crones" could have killed Tom, leaving no trace of blood anywhere. Finding no marks on the corpse, Byrne concludes that "Tom had died a nameless death, by incomprehensible means" (WT, 158). It would be typical of Conrad's flair for the enigmatic to keep the cause of Tom's death a mystery, but his narrative strategy follows a different direction, toward a mundane and laconic explanation of Byrne's ordeal that reverses our expectation of a diabolical revelation.[41] Instead, Conrad exhausts his supply of infernal rhetoric before his closing scene when Byrne avers that a tongue of flaming terror nearly turned his heart to ashes. Switching from diabolical imagery to Christian allusions, Conrad plays on the gift of tongues (apostolic multilingualism) and the confusion of tongues (Babel's babble) before hinting at the mark of Cain on Tom's forehead. The allusion to Cain and Abel has some validity because Byrne does feel as though he has betrayed his boon companion, but biblical analogy gives way to gothic melodrama as Conrad transforms Byrne's ordeal into a perverse dark night of the soul as he cowers in "expectation of a mysterious and appalling vision" (WT, 160). Instead, Conrad depicts the "appalling vision" of Byrne's psychological palsy:

> he was no longer Edgar Byrne. He was a tortured soul suffering more anguish than any sinner's body had ever suffered from rack or boot. . . . Presently, he thought, the two witches will be coming in, with crutch and stick—horrible, grotesque, monstrous—affiliated to the devil—to put a mark on his forehead, the tiny little bruise of death. And he wouldn't be able to do anything. (WT, 161)

With the graphic depiction of Byrne agonizing on the rack, slightly mitigated by the "tiny little bruise" to be applied by the witches, Conrad offers a melodramatic vision of Byrne's impending victimization. But the protagonist does not succumb to the lethal bed. Paradoxically, Byrne is neither hero nor victim, and Tom is both victim and posthumous hero, since the sound of Tom's voice in Byrne's de-

ranged mind saves the young officer. Moreover, Byrne's consciousness is so disordered that he initially thinks the movement of the bed's
canopy is hallucinatory. When he realizes the bizarre fate he has
escaped—"the devilish artifice of murder" (WT, 162)—Byrne still
exhibits a muddled intellect. Byrne's temporary loss of consciousness
sets the stage for Conrad's matter-of-fact epilogue, in which all references to the supernatural are absent, including the noxious refrain
"affiliated to the devil."[42]

   Thus, Conrad fashions a ghost story that evaporates in the final
pages, but its main interest is the problematical relationship between
the internal and external narrator; also of significance is the taciturn
debunking of the diabolical in the epilogue and the mystifying character of the homunculus (perhaps Conrad's surrogate for the reader),
who attains his desire in the end yet desires only his mule. Whether
Conrad derived the image of a smothering bed from Wilkie Collins or
from an anonymous Spanish anecdote seems less important than
what the story tells us about Conrad's relationship to his fiction and to
his audience. This tale offers one small argument against the reductive
notion that all Conrad wanted was to make the reader "see." Even
more frequently, perhaps, he wanted to pull the wool over the
reader's eyes. Whether one views the final focus on the gnome's mule
as Conrad's self-mocking commentary on his potboiler plot, or
whether one identifies with Byrne or with the external narrator, the
reader feels an undeniable insecurity in reading the story and interpreting its signals. Conrad was right to remain silent about this story:
saying nothing at all saved him from discovering what he was doing in
the act of creation.

# 5

## Despair and Red Herrings

We generally associate a red herring with mysteries that tease our rational sensibilities by diverting us from the truth with false clues. But the same term can also be applied to four of Conrad's most overtly melodramatic short fictions: "The Planter of Malata," "The Idiots," "The Lagoon," and "The Return." These stories are mysteries, after a fashion, that pivot on the artful collision of tone and technique. And even though only "The Lagoon" has found its way into anthologies and earned a place of honor in Conrad's canon, each tale offers perils for readers who take the dramatization of despair at face value.

In truth, Conrad does not wholeheartedly sympathize with any of the major characters in these stories, nor does he provide a firm foundation for readers who vicariously experience the plights of Renouard, Susan Bacadou, Arsat, and Alvan Hervey. In "The Planter of Malata" Renouard is appropriately absent from the final scene, for he only functions as the vehicle for the expression of human follies. In "The Idiots" Susan Bacadou's predicament at the end becomes a kind of trivial afterthought compared to Conrad's undermining of hypocritical institutions and sanctimonious authority in the ironic epilogue. At the close of "The Lagoon," Arsat's adoption of a non-Western perspective becomes problematic as Conrad casts doubt on his attempt to regain his cultural identity. And in "The Return" Hervey's resolute flight from uncertainty at the end of the traumatic locking scene loses its emotional force in light of Conrad's corrosive satire of him and his wife as middle-class nonentities. "The Planter of Malata" and "The Idiots" both end with suicides; "The Lagoon" and "The Return," with symbolic suicides, as Arsat and Alvan Hervey make choices that terminate their former ways of life. Yet, ultimately, these endings subvert the melodramatic content of the stories by ridiculing each protagonist's addiction to illusions. Turning darkest despair into a red herring, Conrad mocks the fixations of belief that goad us into putting our faith in what does not exist.

## "The Planter of Malata"

The few critics who have discussed Conrad's gloomy novella "The Planter of Malata" have illuminated much of his artistic strategy and cultivated valuable literary terrain, yet rarely have they considered the story exclusively on its own terms.[1] Meyer even relates the tale's protagonist to Conrad's retreat from skepticism and introspection after his 1910 breakdown. He calls "The Planter" one of several fictions that tend to "view the world in black and white simplicity, to the end that people are reduced to stereotypes, thoughts to platitudes, and the turmoil of life to a set of easy formulas" (BCM, 222).[2] In particular, these critics fail to take into consideration the peculiarity of Conrad's concluding chapter, which defuses the dramatic power of the tale without diminishing its melodramatic imagery and rhetoric. However, Conrad's twelfth and final "scene" does serve an important function both structurally and thematically. It provides vital evidence of his complex orchestration of the elements of the story, making "The Planter of Malata" simultaneously a parody of the quest for knowledge, a satire on the romantic idealization of womanhood, a burlesque of the estranged loner, and a reductio ad absurdum of the doppelgänger theme.

Conrad's opening chapters feature lengthy discussions between an editor and Geoffrey Renouard, an explorer living in isolation as a silk planter on the island of Malata. Renouard questions the Editor about the Moorsom family, whom he met at a dinner party at the home of the Dunsters. The Editor discloses that Willie Dunster and his father, a retired statesman, have been quietly playing host to Professor Moorsom, his sister Emma, and his daughter Felicia. They constitute a search party intent on finding Felicia's ex-fiancé, Arthur, who left England after being implicated in a financial scandal and has since been vindicated, though the news has not reached him. The Moorsoms hope to exploit Renouard's knowledge of the region to locate Arthur. When they learn that Arthur took an assumed name (Walter) and became Renouard's assistant at Malata, the planter is already too infatuated with Felicia to admit that he buried his new assistant before leaving the island.

Renouard's first impulse is flight, but he allows himself to be coaxed into guiding the search party to Malata in his own ship. Before landing on the island, he resolves to confess the truth, but his attraction to Felicia and his fear that the circumstances of his new assistant's death may be interpreted with suspicion prompt another falsehood. He informs the Moorsoms that Arthur is away on a tour of the islands. After days of agonizing concealment, Renouard takes Felicia to the other side of the island where he points out her ex-fiancé's grave. Immediately he rashly declares his love to Felicia, who is still shocked by the revelation of his deception. He takes her in his arms but instantly loses his resolve. Although Renouard falls to his knees to plead his cause, Felicia coldly rebukes him and walks away. Conrad's penultimate chapter records the withering of Renouard's spirit as his romantic dream vanishes. The Moorsoms leave the island, and the planter dismisses his workers to brood in isolation.

Chapter 12, the final scene (consisting of less than two pages), has significance because of the absence of the title character. In many respects, Conrad's ending subverts the earlier scenes in the novella.[3] The Moorsoms return from Malata and promptly take the mail boat back to Europe, but the Editor becomes intensely curious at the sight of Renouard's schooner lying in port for nearly a month. Taking passage on the ship to Malata, the Editor discovers the island completely abandoned. Assuming that Renouard is dead, the Editor and crew form a search party to find the corpse, hoping to solve the mystery of his disappearance. When they find Renouard's discarded clothing on the beach, the Editor jumps to the conclusion that Renouard accidentally drowned while bathing. But a sailor disputes this because anything within a mile of shore should have been washed out to the reefs. Unwilling to believe that Renouard actually went far enough into the ocean to drown himself, the search party considers his disappearance "inexplicable," and as the Editor takes a last look "at the deserted island," a black cloud "hung listlessly over the high rock on the middle hill; and under the mysterious silence of that shadow Malata lay mournful, with an air of anguish in the wild sunset, as if remembering the heart that was broken there" (WT, 85–86).

At the close of the story, the reader does not wonder what has happened to Renouard but rather why it has happened—why he found it absolutely necessary to swim "beyond the confines of life" with "his eyes fixed on a star" (WT, 85).[4] The mournful closing tableau emphasizes the apparent pathos of Renouard's "broken" heart, as Conrad casts a veil of Victorian sentimentality over the planter's real breakdown, his gradual descent into adolescent romanticism and psychic disintegration.[5] Renouard's downfall is not tragic but pathetic bordering on the absurd. The root causes of Renouard's insane self-destruction are his obsession with Felicia, his prolonged deception of the Moorsoms, and his semiconscious identification with Felicia's dead ex-fiancé. In the final chapter, Conrad turns the tables, substituting Renouard for Arthur as the missing person, for the only way Renouard can displace Felicia's lost love involves making a similar mysterious exit from "the confines of life."

Conrad foreshadows the transformation of Renouard into a ghostly presence as early as the first chapter, when the planter consults the Editor for details about Felicia, hoping that some gossip can "lay [bury] the ghost" of his haunting memories of their meeting.[6] In chapter 3, before he learns that the missing Arthur and his dead assistant Walter are identical, Renouard conjectures that Felicia's ex-fiancé "may be even prospecting at the back of beyond—this very moment" (WT, 24). Conrad extends the posthumous imagery to Renouard's schooner at the outset of chapter 4 in depicting the planter's ship as an eerie corpse. Even as early as chapter 4, the planter senses that he inhabits a twilight zone of spectral dimensions: "[S]everal chairs disposed sociably suggested invisible occupants, a company of conversing shades. Renouard looked towards them with a sort of dread. A most elusive, faint sound of ghostly talk issuing from one of the rooms added to the illusion" (WT, 37). Renouard, "the man of action," seems constantly suspended in a state of hesitation as the embodiment of Conradian immobility, persistently speechless, as if prematurely interred. He clings to the vain hope that Felicia's is strong enough "to drag a man out of his grave" (WT, 40). Here, Renouard (a variation of Reynard) reveals that he is hardly foxlike in his mental capabilities.

At the opening of chapter 6, Conrad foreshadows Renouard's suicide when the spellbound planter recollects the spectacular sight of a waterfall in Menado, which he saw in his adolescence, where a government official leaped to his death because of a painful disease. The still-adolescent Renouard considers himself the victim of a cruel mortal "visitation" comparable to the suicide's torment. Because of the planter's fixation on Felicia, he remains in this pathetic condition for the rest of the story—a "miserable mortal envelope, emptied of everything but hopeless passion . . ." (WT, 44). Thus, Conrad depicts both Renouard and his dream woman as "statuesque . . . in their pallor" (WT, 50), and the ghostly motif becomes even more macabre immediately after Renouard's abortive escape attempt, when he feels "the noose of consequences" tightening around him. At the close of chapter 7, the planter stares up at a funereal sky resembling "an immense black pall." While Renouard prepares to swim from the schooner to the island to pave the way for the Moorsoms' disembarking, his "white torso . . . glimmered, ghostly, in the deep shadows of the deck" (WT, 60). He arrives, naked in the "dead stillness" of the night, at a petrified paradise. When Luiz, Renouard's half-caste foreman, scolds his superior for risking being drowned by making the hazardous swim, Conrad forges the link between the dead assistant and Renouard, the "master" of Malata: "Then you can say of me and Mr. Walter what you like. The dead don't mind" (WT, 62).

Conrad's most conspicuous foreshadowing of Renouard's self-annihilation appears in the final paragraph of chapter 8, when he describes the planter's ontological swim from the island back to the ship in words that he will echo in the last chapter:

> Renouard set his direction by a big star that, dipping on the horizon, seemed to look curiously into his face. On this swim back he felt the mournful fatigue of all that length of the traversed road, which brought him no nearer to his desire. . . . There came a moment when it seemed to him that he must have swum beyond the confines of life. He had a sensation of eternity close at hand, demanding no effort—offering its peace. It was easy to swim like this beyond the confines of life looking at a star. But the thought: "They will think I dared not face them and committed suicide," caused a revolt of his mind which carried him on. He returned . . . with a confused feeling that he had been beyond the confines of life, somewhere near a star, and that it was very quiet there. (WT, 62).

Renouard, the bewildered man of action, rejects the ultimate action that would liberate him from enslavement to a hopeless desire. Yet, in a sense, he has already chosen the path of suicide—the only certain mode of transcending the "confines" of mortal existence. Conrad's myopic protagonist, Arthur's alter ego, does not transcend so much as obliterate the prison house of consciousness in his final decision to "swim beyond the confines of life—with a steady stroke—his eyes fixed on a star" (WT, 85).

In the narrative's last chapters, Conrad associates Renouard's duplicity with the moldering corpse in the shallow grave: "[T]he moral poison of falsehood has such a decomposing power that Renouard felt his old personality turn to dead dust" (WT, 65). Ironically, the buried man's personality seems to live again in the planter, while the living man's personality rapidly decays. When the Professor's sister tells Renouard that meeting Arthur again will be "like seeing a ghost," her comment prompts their discussion of apparitions in general leading to Renouard's assertion that his plantation boys also see ghosts. But, perhaps more significantly, Conrad buries a clue to his artistic strategy in Emma's scatterbrained banter: "'We have a friend, a very famous author—his ghost is a girl. One of my brother's intimates is a very great man of science. He is friendly with a ghost . . . of a girl too,' she added in a voice as if struck for the first time by the coincidence" (WT, 67; Conrad's ellipsis). But this "coincidence" is no accident. Like Hawthorne, Conrad locates the supernatural exclusively in the haunted minds of his characters. Conrad's ghosts are not lost souls but the spirits of lost passions and opportunities. Indeed, he even converts his protagonist into one of the living dead, for while the Moorsoms occupy his plantation house, Renouard leads a posthumous existence, lying sleepless every night on his hammock with his hands folded over on his chest. He stares with "unseeing eyes" at the sunrise that marks another day in his progress toward extinction, as Conrad links him to the fate of the corpse, the island's pathetic secret. (After Renouard's suicide, his corpse becomes Malata's chief mystery.[7]) At the close of chapter 9, the planter promises his foreman, "We shall try to lay that poor ghost" (WT, 68), but by this time Conrad's dual meaning has become easily recognizable: Renouard and Arthur serve as doubles in rigor mortis. On the surface, Renouard's comment conveys to the superstitious native his master's willingness to exorcise the ghost. But, on a deeper level, it signifies his spiritual resignation, an intermittent wish to end the futility of his life.

Nevertheless, Conrad makes sport of the planter's being haunted by the assistant he has recently buried: "[H]e had a disagreeable sense of the dead man's company at his elbow. The ghost! He seemed to be everywhere but in his grave. Could one ever shake him off? he wondered" (WT, 71). While Renouard ruminates, Felicia arrives, her ominous voice, in the midst of the storm, sounding "like a grave song-note" (WT, 72). Conrad's identification of Renouard with Malata, Arthur's burial place, underscores the roles of Renouard and Arthur as alter egos; both are inert, one in life, the other in death. Spiritually dead after telling Felicia of Arthur's death, Renouard identifies with the dead man in the burial mound who has plagued his conscience and haunted his consciousness. The planter, by his own admission, has become a "wraith," an "illusion," for Arthur's passion and disillusionment have become his obsession. Renouard's self-destructive resolve puts Arthur's spirit to rest for a second time: "'Yes,' said Renouard in a lifeless voice. 'He is dead. His very ghost shall be done with presently'" (WT, 79). His insane laughter punctuates the close of chapter 10 as Conrad conflates the ghostly motif with the eclipse of the planter's rationality. As chapter 11 opens, Conrad again juxtaposes Arthur and Renouard, this time asserting that the planter does not ascribe his overwhelming defeat to "that absurd dead man." But Renouard has indeed become an absurd dead man, at least in a spiritual sense. And when the planter promises to haunt Felicia, he merely recapitulates Arthur's life story. Renouard, whose name implies renewal, becomes inextricably entangled with the fate of Arthur on the island "haunted by the ghost of a white man" (WT, 84). Thus, Conrad not only establishes Renouard and Arthur as alter egos but also identifies both white men with the dark, brooding island: "Malata was himself [Renouard]. He and Malata were one" (WT, 58).

While one might attribute this pervasive imagery of ghosts and death to Conrad's foreshadowing of Renouard's suicide, the author identifies Arthur and Renouard throughout the narrative. For example, both characters engage in mysterious conversations with Felicia before they disappear. Arthur, like Renouard, goes to Malata "to be forgotten" by the rest of the world. Even before realizing that Arthur and Walter are one and the same, the planter feels oppressed by the sense of something that he could never undo. Renouard's bizarre dream provides the most conspicuous evidence for the association of the planter with the buried man who has attracted such a distinguished search party: "The lamp, of course, he connected with the search for a man. But on closer examination he perceived that the reflection of himself in the mirror was not really the true Renouard, but somebody else whose face he could not remember" (WT, 32). An absurd Diogenes, he unconsciously confuses the Moorsoms' search for Arthur with his own quest for self-knowledge—a quest that must end in failure once Renouard learns that Felicia is engaged to a dead man. Moreover, the Professor's description of Arthur as "a mere baby" victimized by his "noble confidance" seems appropriate to the planter as well.[8] Conrad resorts to more idiosyncratic rhetoric later in the narrative when the planter ridicules Felicia's rage, employing hyperbolic self-mockery: "Ha! the legendary Renouard of sensitive idiots—the ruthless adventurer—the ogre with a future" (WT, 74). None of these eccentric labels fits the planter, whom Conrad depicts as a hopeless adolescent making childish taunts and threats, as when he informs Felicia that Arthur put "a curse on some woman" before he died and promises to "haunt" her himself. Finally, Conrad links Renouard to Arthur when the planter accuses Felicia of doubting Arthur's "innocence": "And now you will not believe in me—not even in me who must in truth be what I am—even to death" (*WT*, 75).

Renouard's melodramatic identification with Arthur's fate makes him the most extreme example of Conrad's disciples of futility (which include Heyst and Decoud, among others). As a scandal-tainted man of action who seeks refuge from society, he is a parody of the romantic solitary of nineteenth-century fiction, which perhaps includes Lord Jim. Renouard is a "lounging, active man" whose rugged individualism crumbles when he is jolted by sensual desire. At the opening of the novella, the Editor brands the planter's solitude as unhealthy, poisonous, and demoralizing; yet, ironically, Renouard's direct contact with society, specifically with the Moorsoms, catalyzes his self-destruction. His posture as an antisocialite unmoved by sentiment clashes with his role as a foiled Petrarchan lover. The Editor's commentary on Renouard's "sensitive perception" dissolves into groundless flattery once Conrad establishes the planter's misinterpretation of Felicia's initial curiosity at their meeting. Conrad burlesques Renouard's marginal existence with idiosyncratic labels, such as the "sophisticated beggar" tag the Editor attaches to the planter. Entranced by Felicia's form, Renouard contemplates beauty as if he were conducting a scientific experiment, indulging "a meditation on the mechanism of sentiment and the springs of passion" (*WT*, 23). This is his abstract response to falling in love. In the relentless grip of passion, however, he speaks through clenched teeth, gazes at his dream goddess with "boiled eyes," and generally acts like a puppet of sexual desire. Like a trained dog, Renouard submits to the Editor's comic indictment of his misanthropy: "You stand there like a hermit on a seashore growling to yourself" (*WT*, 25). Conrad resorts to some amusing word play at the conclusion of the long conversation at the outset of the story when the planter closes the door of the Editor's office: "[T]he letters of the word PRIVATE like a row of white eyes seemed to stare after his back sinking down the staircase of that temple of publicity" (*WT*, 28). Like Axel Heyst, Renouard has had his privacy invaded by the public world. Yet, unlike Heyst, he is the primary agent of his own undoing.

Conrad depicts the breakdown of Renouard's habitual solitude due to romantic fascination as if it were "the most exquisite torture." Playing upon the notoriety of the planter as a detached man of action, Conrad mocks him with abstractions: "[T]he man of definite conquering tasks,

the familiar of wide horizons, and in his very repose holding aloof
from these agglomerations of units in which one loses one's importance even to oneself" (WT, 35). By placing the planter's secret desire
in a heroic context, Conrad accentuates the mawkish extremes of
Renouard's passion. Devoured by jealousy, Renouard clenches his
teeth in secret and conducts "a sinister watch on his tortures" (WT,
36). Conrad delineates Renouard as a sort of *homo suspensus,* who is
unable to speak and incapable of acting. Ironically, the solitary planter
dreads the departure of the Moorsoms, even though he painfully
recognizes "the absurdity of his emotion." His repressed romantic
impulses boomerang in an extravaganza of masochism as "a self-
inflicted stab" of jealousy pierces him.

In his sterile isolation, Renouard dreams of obtaining Felicia as a
fetching handmaiden to his ambition. Yet his reputation for dauntless-
ness conflicts with his lethargic enslavement to romance: "[T]he young
man, almost ill-famed for his ruthless daring, the inflexible leader of
two tragically successful expeditions, shrank from that act of savage
energy, and began, instead, to hunt for excuses" (WT, 43). The "act of
savage energy" in this case is merely a refusal to become further involved
in the Moorsom search party. Midway through the narrative, Conrad
has reduced his title character to a "mortal envelope" containing
nothing but "hopeless passion" (WT, 44). It becomes impossible to
imagine Renouard carrying off Felicia "into some profound retreat as
in the age of Cavern men" (WT, 45) because Conrad never dramatizes
a scene to substantiate the planter's reputed courage. Furthermore,
Renouard's suppressed passion loses its force when Conrad describes
it in the language of insipid sentiment. Upon discovering that his
"lonely" island will be invaded by the Moorsoms, the reputedly
courageous planter's first impulse is flight, but he soon loses all resolve, bewitched into thinking (like Beckett's psychological paralytics)
that action is pointless: "[T]here was nothing to be done" (WT, 54).

Conrad ridicules Renouard as the most fragile of dreamers, the
most vulnerable of loners. An opportunist as well as a shrinking violet,
the paradoxical planter labors under false hopes as he drifts toward
madness: "With the eyes of a mortal struck by the maddening thun-
derbolt of the gods, Renouard looked up to the sky, an immense black
pall dusted over with gold, on which great shudders seemed to pass
from the breath of life affirming its sway" (WT, 56–57). Blaming his
inadequacies on fate, Renouard absurdly disdains "the breath of life"
and turns self-torment into self-annihilation. But his torment and
eventual destruction are the bizarre result of his psychological inertia.

Arriving at Malata, the planter transmutes Felicia's curiosity about his mysterious island into a coded sexual message: "She had wondered! What about? Malata was himself. He and Malata were one. And she had wondered" (*WT,* 58). This adolescent drivel might be excusable in some of Conrad's characters, but not in the supposedly ruthless Renouard. Yet the passionate planter continues to sow the seeds of significance on barren ground, deluding himself into viewing Felicia as "a shining dream-woman."

Renouard's secret swim to the island in the middle of the night temporarily reestablishes his presumed role as master of all he surveys. Apparently, this ruthless adventurer can only assert his manly nature when no women are in sight; in the presence of femininity he becomes a jellyfish. Despite firm resolves to confess everything, he frantically resorts to fabrications to postpone disclosing the truth. Thus, he fails to play the hero and is unable to lie with conviction. Blinded by his ignorance of women, Renouard has fallen in love with a metaphor, not with a real woman.[9] His excessive praise of her ethereal qualities rings false and bears the stamp of Conrad's scorn.[10] Beginning to crack under pressure, Renouard discovers "the whole extent of his coward-ice." His romantic delirium is rendered in language that suggests Buddha's Fire Sermon: "It seemed to him that he must be on fire, then that he had fallen into a cool whirlpool, a smooth funnel of water swirling about with nauseating rapidity. And then . . . he was walking on the dangerous thin ice of a river, unable to turn back. . . . Suddenly it parted from shore to shore with a loud crack" (*WT,* 71; second ellipsis Conrad's). Renouard awakens with a start from his Petrarchan nightmare of fever and chills, yet his ordeal originates in his own conscious addiction to unfounded dreams of absolute fulfillment.

Conrad resorts to an organic metaphor with an ironic twist just before the confrontation scene when Renouard, after countless post-ponements and prevarications, finally decides to disclose the truth, "feeling suddenly as steady as a rock" (*WT,* 72). But he undermines the planter's rock-like resolve and solidity by focusing on an ominous feature in the topographical surroundings: "Near by, the topmost pinnacle of Malata, resembling the top of a buried tower, rose a rock, weather-worn, grey, weary of watching the monotonous centuries of the Pacific" (*WT,* 73). When the planter informs Felicia that he buried Arthur "[o]n the other side of this rock," Felicia's rage makes little impact on the planter's inanimate facade, which Conrad compares to "the weary rock against which he leaned" (*WT,* 73). Their bitter conversation exhausts his waning vitality. By repressing "the flood of his passion," Renouard becomes devitalized, so that "he felt as one dead speaking" (WT, 77).

Weary of watching himself play the game of blindman's buff with the Moorsoms, Renouard ultimately yields to the Pacific, courting oblivion, his authentic lover. He mocks Felicia's outrage at his ill-timed confession, deprecating himself with preposterous epithets: "Renouard of sensitive idiots—the ruthless adventurer—the ogre with a future" (WT, 74). Then with an assertion of jealous passion Renouard postures as a tragically misunderstood romantic hero: "The flame of her glorious head scorched his face. He flung his hat far away, and his suddenly lowered eyelids brought out startlingly his resemblance to antique bronze, the profile of Pallas, still, austere, bowed a little in the shadow of the rock . . ." (WT, 75). Athena rejected by Medusa? Not quite, but nearly as ludicrous, for Conrad's reference to the "austere" profile of Pallas is totally out of keeping with Renouard's volcanic overflow of lachrymose passions.[11] The Pallas-Renouard analogy is every bit as absurd as the planter's entreaty that Felicia recognize the truth within him, despite his previous litany of falsehoods.

Felicia, although immersed in her own delusions, now realizes the "abominable farce" of Renouard's deceptions and asserts that she, and not the planter of deceptions, stands for truth. Yet Conrad undermines her sincerity by depicting her in an ironic variation of The Thinker's posture: "She sat down on a boulder, rested her chin in her hands, in the pose of simple grief—mourning for herself" (WT, 75). Conrad presents the major characters—Renouard, Felicia, Professor Moorsom, and the Editor—as egoists who cultivate merely the illusion of altruism. Felicia, in particular, clings to a lofty conception of her own destiny, which automatically redeems the mate of her choice: "No word of evil could be whispered of [Arthur] after I had given him my hand" (WT, 76). She speaks with such mesmerizing authority that Renouard is gulled into viewing her as the incarnation of the mystery of the universe: "Renouard meditated, gloomy, as if over some sinister riddle of a beautiful sphinx" (WT, 76). Conrad burlesques the pursuit of ultimate knowledge as a mock-oedipal quest and travesties the relationship of Felicia and Renouard as a romantic sham. In both cases, nothing comes of nothing, as even the planter discovers when he perceives Felicia as an empty Venus: "You are the eternal love itself—only, O Divinity, it isn't your body, it is your soul that is made of foam" (WT, 77). But Renouard, as vacuous as his dream goddess, still kneels before the image of his ludicrous infatuation. They share a common bond, since both remain deluded by their own selfish dreams to the end. The "ghost" that links Renouard to Felicia (Arthur, the dead ex-fiancé) objectifies their life-denying attitudes. She rejects Renouard as a predatory deceiver, convinced that only she can "stand for truth." The planter rejects life itself, believing that Felicia has determined his destiny. Overwhelmed by an irrational sense of defeat, he becomes a terminal case in futility.

The solitary planter withdraws to brood over the loss of Felicia, but what he has actually lost is his capacity to reason. Hermitlike, he watches the eager plantation workers leave the "island haunted by the ghost of a white man" (*WT,* 84). The ghost is now Renouard, who has promised to "haunt" Felicia. By making this empty threat he has already willed himself into extinction. When the Editor lands on "the deserted island" to search for the planter, he confronts a funereal scene that suggests the melodrama of Renouard's final desperate act: "A black cloud hung listlessly over the high rock on the middle hill; and under the mysterious silence of that shadow Malata lay mournful, with an air of anguish in the wild sunset, as if remembering the heart that was broken there" (*WT,* 86). Yet this sentimental claptrap conceals Renouard's real breakdown, his descent into madness based on his myopic idealization of Felicia, his prolonged fraud, and his demented identification with Felicia's dead ex-fiancé. Like the Swede in Crane's "The Blue Hotel," he instigates his own destruction.

Conrad's closing scene also derides the obsession with knowledge that the Professor's search party represents. The "all-knowing Editor," possibly a comic counterpart to Professor Moorsom, "wanted to know more than the rest of the world. From professional incontinence, perhaps, he thirsted for a full cup of harrowing detail" (*WT,* 84). Ironically, he sails to Malata on Renouard's own schooner, and his voyage parallels the planter's vain quest. On the island, the Editor finds evidence of organic chaos, "the plants growing rank and tall on the deserted fields" (*WT,* 85). Conrad depicts this second search party, much like the first expedition to Malata, as an absurd exercise in futility: "For hours the Editor and the schooner's crew, excited by the mystery, roamed over the island shouting Renouard's name; . . . What had happened? . . . It was impossible to tell what had happened" (*WT,* 85; ellipses added). The search party fails to find the dead man, just as the Moorsom expedition failed to bring Arthur back alive, and the "all-knowing Editor" must therefore reconcile himself to a mystery: "Nothing was ever found—and Renouard's disappearance remained in the main inexplicable" (*WT,* 85). Such a failure undermines the Editor's previous boast that "[t]his office is the place where every-thing is known about everybody—including a great deal of nobodies" (WT, 6). Such Jamesian generalities only substantiate the finite quality of human knowledge.

Conrad's mockery of the self-serving, self-congratulatory Editor cannot compare with his character assassination of Professor Moor-som, the reluctant leader of the first search party and "the fashionable philosopher of the age" (WT, 14). When Renouard refers to the Professor as a charlatan in the newspaper office, the Editor mildly disputes the accusation: "Well—no. I should say not. I shouldn't wonder though if most of his writing had been done with his tongue in his cheek. Of course. That's to be expected" (WT, 15). The Editor chiefly admires Moorsom's practical skills in making philosophy "pay." Yet Conrad describes the Professor as living in a meditative limbo, indulg-ing in Schopenhauer-like resignation. Moorsom's habitual investiga-tions and analyses render him "inept for action." He reveals his penchant for misperception when he interprets Renouard's character as detached from strong emotions such as love. The planter, however, views the Professor's lack of sentimentality as characteristic of "the most treacherous of fathers." Moorsom admits to Renouard that he is indeed "a man full of doubts and hesitation" who fears future sur-prises. He also expresses a nihilistic attitude toward his daughter's "sentimental pilgrimage," calling it "nothing but agitation in empty space—to amuse life—a sort of superior debauchery, exciting and fatiguing, meaning nothing, leading nowhere" (WT, 41). Like his daughter, Moorsom claims to possess "an instinct for truth," but, also like Felicia he actually has an instinct for self-delusion. Ironically, he discourses "on the Impermanency of the Measurable" (WT, 45), which aptly describes the tendency of all the major characters to act under the sway of maya (derived from the root ma, meaning to measure, form, or build). Renouard interprets the Professor's words as evidence of "senile excitement" and "intellectual debauchery in the froth of existence! Froth and fraud!" (WT, 45). The "great man," the planter concludes, represents nothing but "the failure of philosophy" to meet humankind's practical needs.

Moorsom's daughter embodies the illusory power of the phenome-nal world. She appears luminously to Renouard "like a magic painting of charm, fascination, and desire, glowing mysteriously on the dark background" (WT, 47). The infatuated planter characteristically yields to absurd longings for Felicia but profoundly distrusts her father, who embodies the spirit of disillusionment. Deluded by his belief that

Felicia represents fate, Renouard abandons the search for truth to
pursue a beautiful illusion. Like the narrator in "A Smile of Fortune,"
he cannot bear the loss of his beatific mirage. During his nocturnal
swim from Malata back to his ship, his star-gazing makes his physical
effort seem eternal, like his fond desire, which is unattainable in this
mundane world:

> Renouard set his direction by a big star that . . . seemed to look curiously
> into his face. On this swim back he felt the mournful fatigue of all that
> length of the traversed road, which brought him no nearer to his desire.
> It was as if his love had sapped the invisible supports of his strength.
> There came a moment when it seemed that he must have swum beyond
> the confines of life. He had a sensation of eternity close at hand,
> demanding no effort—offering its peace. (WT, 62)

Conrad's transcendental rhetoric mocks the puny status of the planter,
who ultimately kills himself over a fairy-tale princess who has no
substance. By making a fetish of this social butterfly in quest of a ghost,
Renouard fails to heed the Professor's warning: "One may meditate
on life endlessly, one may even have a poor opinion of it—but the fact
remains that we have only one life to live. And it is short" (WT, 70).
But the planter dismisses this sentiment as merely another of Moorsom's "confounded platitudes."

After the confrontation scene with Felicia, Renouard finally recognizes his delirious illusion, yet he still commits himself to fatalistic folly:

> [H]e . . . had abandoned himself to a sense of an immense deception
> and the feeling of extreme fatigue. This walk up the hill and down again
> was like the supreme effort of an explorer trying to penetrate the interior
> of an unknown country, the secret of which is too well defended by its
> cruel and barren nature. Decoyed by a mirage, he had gone too far—so
> far that there was no going back. (WT, 79–80)

But Renouard fails to comprehend his own role as a decoy in Felicia's
search for her dead ex-fiancé. The Professor departs like "a banal
tourist" because he has assumed from the start that his daughter's
mission is hopeless. Ultimately, Willie Dunstan's sentimental fabrication of the end of the quest ("how poor Miss Moorsom—the fashionable and clever beauty—found her betrothed in Malata only to see
him die in her arms") makes about as much sense as what actually
happens (WT, 84).

Conrad's story contains all the ingredients of a melodramatic romance: an isolated and alienated adventurer, an idealized statuesque

woman, an archetypal wise old man, and a metaphysical quest for knowledge. But, whether out of dissatisfaction, disinterest, or conscious deliberation, Conrad subverts each of these stock elements and turns his melodramatic plot inside out. He converts the melancholy recluse Renouard into a romantic dupe, voluptuous Felicia into a queen of froth, Moorsom's philosophy into a cultural fad, and the quest for knowledge into a search for the "sinking star" of perennial illusions. Conrad consistently depicts his characters as puppets in a passion play of futility. Taking his hint, perhaps, from Calderón's *La Vida es Sueño* (Life is a Dream), Conrad scorns the fragile susceptibility to illusion innate in human consciousness and the hollow words that trigger mental agitation and emotional outbursts. "The Planter of Malata" is a ghost story with an ironic twist, for the spirit world rests in peace while daylight phantoms run amok. Malata becomes the isle of *mala,* of "dirt, refuse, impurity," in a caustic satire on the inspired frivolities of the human race.

## "The Idiots"

Although Conrad refers to "The Idiots" as "an obviously derivative piece of work" in his 1898 author's note to *Tales of Unrest* (ix), the story cannot be dismissed as merely borrowed melodrama. Conrad's primary concern is not the domestic turmoil involving the parents of four imbecile children but rather the idiotic sensibilities of three successive generations of a family set against a backdrop of widespread political, social, and religious corruption.[12] Like his chief models at the turn of the century—Maupassant, Flaubert, and Zola—Conrad derides the inhumanity of modern institutions, the corruption of their officials, and the foolishness and ignorance of their victims.[13] He crystallizes the multiple meanings of his title in an ironic epilogue that contains abundant sarcasm and only a smattering of consolation. Moreover, Conrad extends his attack on sanctimonious authority to the kingdom of heaven itself.

With regard to the plot of "The Idiots," the story seems melodramatic to the extreme. Passing through Brittany, Conrad's narrator observes the behavior of some retarded children. He makes inquiries and eventually pieces together enough information to relate his own version of their story. The unfortunate children are the offspring of Susan and Jean-Pierre Bacadou, who married with the intention of raising strong sons to tend the farm. As each child proves mentally unsound, Jean-Pierre's frustration leads to verbal and physical abuse of his wife. Provoked into retaliation, Susan stabs him in the neck, flees from the house, and turns to her mother for assistance, but Madame Levaille finds her daughter's act scandalous. Susan flees again. When she hears the voice of a potential rescuer and mistakes it for that of her mortally wounded husband, she panics and leaps into the sea. In a terse epilogue, the narrator reports the recovery of Susan's body and reveals that the Marquis de Chavenes, who is in charge of the agrarian commune, plans to appoint Madame Levaille guardian of the children and administrator of the farm so that the land will not fall into the hands of his political enemies.

Conrad's ironic epilogue broadens the scope of his narrative beyond the limited confines of naturalism by focusing on the lamentable social consequences of the pathetic events rather than their psychological significance. Madame Levaille and the Marquis are temporary survivors of the psychological devastation. Conrad, in fact, establishes a subtle hierarchy of demoralized characters, starting from the lowest order, the "idiots" and their grandparents, and extending to the principal authority figure, the Marquis. The narrator's descriptions and asides offer a caustic commentary on the stultifying effects of the social order in Western culture. By highlighting the idiotic sensibilities of farmers and wedding guests, Jean-Pierre and Susan, Madame Levaille and the Marquis, Conrad broadens the implications of his title and criticizes the very foundations of European civilization, the institutions of marriage, religion, and monarchy.

Conrad associates the narrator's first glimpse of one of the idiots with a grotesque naturalistic depiction of the countryside. The violent sunshine, "clumps of meagre trees," and zigzagging walls give the scene the effect of a clumsy landscape painting. The "undulating surface of the land" features a roadway that looks "like a river of dust crawling out of the hills on its way to the sea" (TU, 56). Conrad frequently uses such fluvial metaphors in the story to prefigure Susan's drowning and dramatize existential instability. The first idiot is a red-faced, disembodied "bullet-head" with "its chin in the dust" (TU, 56–57). His twin bears a resemblance to Hugo's Quasimodo with "his head sunk beneath the shoulders, all hunched up in the flood of heat" (TU, 57). The "flood" and "dust" associated with the introduction of the twins suggest the muddy river that becomes Conrad's paramount motif. His narrator often sees the idiots "drifting . . . according to the inexplicable impulses of their monstrous darkness" (TU, 58). Like her offspring, Susan drifts toward a calamitous fate.

The idiots seem to embody the word *dumbstruck* with their "fascinated" glances "unseeing and unstaring." Conrad relegates the children to the status of animals when the driver informs the narrator that
the four idiots "come home at dusk along with the cattle. . . . It's a
good farm" (*TU,* 58; Conrad's ellipsis). It is a good farm because the
bovine imbeciles are docile; like animals, they roam about the landscape. Conrad at times even demotes them to the level of machines,
as when the narrator remarks that their "voices sounded blank and
cracked like a mechanical imitation of old people's voices" (*TU,* 58).
Linking young and old again, the narrator speculates on the bizarre
image of the "idiot children and the childish grandfather, who sat
grim, angular, and immovable" in the midst of their chaotic home
(*TU,* 64). Conrad's association of the decrepit grandfather with these
odd creatures sarcastically reaffirms the concept of old age as a
second childhood. Moreover, the grandfather's moodiness after the
twins are born also suggests childishness. To avoid hearing the "cack-
ling" of strange women who flock to see the newborn infants, he sits
at the gate "gathered up into a kind of raging concentrated sulkiness"
(*TU,* 61). His aged body, wracked by rheumatism, seems as infirm as
the land itself. After Jean-Pierre assumes control of the farm, "the old
folks felt a shadow—precursor of the grave—fall upon them finally.
The world is to the young" (*TU,* 60).[14] Jean-Pierre's mother also
becomes a target of Conrad's macabre irony, as the narrator describes
her change of address prior to the birth of the twins: "The mother of
Jean-Pierre had gone away to dwell under a heavy stone in the
cemetery . . ." (*TU,* 60). Furthermore, the narrator's chief informer
possesses the same decrepit qualities as the grandparents. He is "an
emaciated and sceptical old fellow" who talks to the narrator "by the
side of a two-wheeled cart loaded with dripping seaweed" (*TU,* 58).
The fluvial reference not only foreshadows Susan's drowning but also
serves as a reminder that although Conrad's tale does not occur in the
South Pacific, it is still a kind of sea yarn that must be examined critically
and not taken at face value.

Conrad's irony extends to solemn rituals as well, such as the
marriage of Susan and Jean-Pierre, which attracts the peasants, who
seem to have stepped out of the pages of *Madame Bovary.* The
wedding guests, who "straggled" to the ceremony, consist of men in
clumsily made jackets and women clad ominously in black. Likewise,
in the epilogue, Susan's body is borne by four men "on the narrow
track of the seaweed carts . . . while several others straggled listlessly
behind" (*TU,* 85). The wedding party is also a "sombre procession"

leading to a lengthy feast that ends with several reputable farmers falling asleep in ditches. Conrad thus suggests that the marriage propels Susan to her own funeral.

Conrad not only identifies farmers in general with the soil, but he also links Jean-Pierre to the land that becomes his obsession. When Jean-Pierre discusses his marriage plans with his father, they converse in a yard "between the outhouses," where "[o]ver the manure heaps floated a mist, opal-tinted and odorous" (*TU*, 59). The implication of future fertility in this passage, along with the reference to "marauding hens" that stop scratching to observe the father and son, offers a portent of the domestic problems that will arise in the marriage. Jean-Pierre's pipe dream of mastery is also rooted to the soil, for he imagines his robust sons reaping the "tribute" of the land. The narrator pauses in his storytelling to wonder what lies at the core of Jean-Pierre's "peasant humanity": "heat, violence, a force mysterious and terrible—or nothing but a clod, a mass fertile and inert, cold and unfeeling, ready to bear a crop of plants that sustain life or give death" (*TU*, 63). Through the narrator's analogy between Jean-Pierre and a clod of earth, Conrad perverts the age-old concept of the Great Chain of Being. He also challenges our traditional position at the midpoint of the chain (as half dust, half deity) when Jean-Pierre muses on "the inferiority of man who passes away before the clod that remains" (*TU*, 71). Lacking the permanence of a clod of earth, we dream of some form of immortality, and in so doing we risk losing our psychological balance. Thus, Conrad underscores the folly of Jean-Pierre's dream of another kind of existence that transcends the present reality. Jean-Pierre falls prey to the delusion of wishing to be "master" of reality, now and in the future. But with only idiotic children to show for his attempts at fertility, he believes that the earth itself denies him happiness and curses him with sterility:

> He looked at the black earth, at the earth mute and promising, at the mysterious earth doing its work of life in death-like stillness under the veiled sorrow of the sky. And it seemed to him that to a man worse than childless there was no promise in the fertility of fields, that from him the earth escaped, defied him, frowned at him like the clouds, sombre and hurried above his head. (*TU*, 70–71).

Jean-Pierre, the human clod, sees the fertile earth as an enemy denying him a symbolic extension of his mortal life. This description fits with Conrad's penchant for animating landscape to express a character's mental state, while at the same time reducing human activity to near physical immobility. When Jean-Pierre is stabbed by Susan, he dies standing still.

Ironically, Jean-Pierre's religious conversion precedes his ultimate disillusionment, dissipation, and death. He decides to convert after his discovery of the twins' idiocy reduces him to psychological paralysis: "[T]he sunk cheeks were like patches of darkness, and his aspect was mournfully stolid, as if he had ruminated with difficulty endless ideas" (*TU,* 63). Hoping to obtain God's blessings, Jean-Pierre converts—a choice that is seen as a political triumph by the priest and the Marquis, who view the conversion of a republican as a step toward greater social stability. But Jean-Pierre's conversion fails to bring positive results, and he turns against his wife and her faith, feeling "like a man who had sold his soul" (*TU,* 67). Jean-Pierre berates Susan for her failure to give birth to normal children. On one occasion, he points out the clock of a church tower, symbolizing Susan's religion, as an empty mask: "[T]he big dial of the clock appeared high in the moonlight like a pallid face without eyes" (*TU,* 68). Jean-Pierre calls Susan's faith a "swindle" in a scene that anticipates the farcical much-ado-about-nothingness in *Waiting for Godot.* On the ride home, he knocks her "into the bottom of the cart, where she crouched, thrown about lamentably by every jolt" (*TU,* 69). The incident recalls their ominous first ride as bride and groom, in which they "were jerked backwards and forwards by the up and down motion of the shafts, in a manner regular and brusque" (*TU,* 60). Here, Conrad's artistry converts the wedding cart into a deterministic wheel of fortune.

Even more ominous is Conrad's lugubrious depiction of the arrival of autumn:

> The clouded sky descended low upon the black contours of the hills; and the dead leaves danced in spiral whirls under naked trees, till the wind, sighing profoundly, laid them to rest in the hollows of bare valleys. . . . [O]ne could see all over the land black denuded boughs, the boughs gnarled and twisted, as if contorted with pain, swaying sadly between the wet clouds and the soaked earth. The clear and gentle streams of summer days rushed discoloured and raging at the stones that barred the way to the sea, with the fury of madness bent upon suicide. . . . [T]he great road to the sands lay between the hills in a dull glitter of empty curves, resembling an unnavigable river of mud. (*TU,* 70)

Conrad uses the pathetic fallacy to exaggerated effect in this passage, but it is more than a random conglomeration of macabre and melodramatic naturalistic images. His sequence of fluvial metaphors culminates in the stark vision of a "river of mud," Conrad's emblem for the stream of time and experience in Western culture. Like Marlow's Thames, it, too, leads to a "heart of darkness." Jean-Pierre, like the gray clouds above him, appears to be "drifting . . . along the very edge of the universe" (*TU,* 70). Like Kurtz, Heyst, Almayer, and other Conradian solitaries, Jean-Pierre allows his obsession with matters beyond the present moment to pave the way for his fall.

Conrad also links Susan's isolation to the organic world, specifically her native territory, "a barren circle of rocks and sands . . ." (*TU,* 61). The "barren circle" corresponds to her repeated failures to give birth to normal children. Conrad compares her wails to the grunts heard in the pigsty, thereby debasing Susan's status as a tragic figure. Conrad's human characters are merely the only members of the animal farm who have the gift of speech.

After Jean-Pierre's murder, Conrad conspicuously alters his focus when Susan abruptly enters her mother's home symbolically tainted—"soaked and muddy." Hearing her pronounce "some incomprehensible words," Madame Levaille fears her daughter has become deranged, as her husband had been in his last years. But Conrad reverses our expectations when the mother, not the daughter, begins to lose her head. Expelled from her mother's house, Susan flees into the night, haunted by a face that appears and reappears, like a diabolical Cheshire Cat, as she runs down the slope. "High sharp rocks" in the water seem to her "like pointed towers of submerged churches" (*TU,* 79), as Conrad subtly indicates that her faith has been drowned in the disillusionments of experience. Rushing past seaweed gatherers, who offer no help, she mistakes a rescuer's cries for her dead husband's voice. Millot, potentially the hero of the story, is both fearless and irreligious—a seemingly minor detail that supports Conrad's attack on institutional Christianity.

Another facet of Conrad's assault on the sacred icons of church and state is revealed in his curious allusions to Poe's poem "The Raven." In the midst of Susan's flight, Conrad repeatedly calls attention to the suggestive name of the vicinity: "Susan met the incoming tide by the Raven islet and stopped. . . . She heard the murmur and felt the cold caress of the sea, and, calmer now, could see the sombre and confused mass of the Raven . . ." (*TU,* 80). Conrad displays his familiarity with the morbidly self-indulgent speaker of Poe's poem at the end of the next paragraph when Susan insistently seems to cry "Nevermore!" while recounting her violent act: "I never saw him fall. Never! Never! . . . Never saw him fall. . . . The old father never turned

his head. . . . Nobody saw him fall. I ran out. . . . Nobody saw" (*TU*,
82; third ellipsis added). Two more references to "The Raven" occur
just before and after Susan's confession. Moreover, a close scrutiny of
the tale reveals a more extensive Poe-like pattern in Conrad's tapestry. The narrator describes Susan's third child as a sequence of negations: "That child, like the other two, never smiled, never stretched its
hands to her, never spoke; never had a glance of recognition for
her . . ." (*TU*, 64). Conrad also connects Susan with another allusion
to Poe's croaking bird when her husband denounces her church:
"'Nobody?' went on Jean-Pierre. 'Nobody there. A swindle of the
crows. That's what this is. Nobody anywhere'" (*TU*, 69). Later, in the
frantic conversation with her mother, Susan echoes Jean-Pierre's irreligious "Nevermore":

> "There's no mercy in heaven—no justice. No! . . . I did not know. . . .
> Do you think I have no heart? Do you think I have never heard people
> jeering at me, pitying me, wondering at me? . . . The mother of
> idiots—that was my nickname! And my children never would know me,
> never speak to me. They would know nothing; neither men—nor God."
> (*TU*, 75; last ellipsis added)

These passages show Conrad appropriating the theme of "The
Raven" (the finality of death despite human yearnings) to bolster his
own view of humankind's cosmic insignificance and the apathetic
remoteness of God, who acts like a sort of absentee landlord. Conrad
dramatizes the dread of awakening to a godless universe as Susan
recalls Jean-Pierre's boast: "There is no God to hold me! Do you
understand, you useless carcase. I will do what I like" (*TU*, 81–82).
Haunted by her husband's expression of the disintegration of all
values, she leaps into the sea. Unaware that aid is at hand, she gives
"one shrill cry for help that seemed to dart upwards . . . straight into
the high and impassive heaven" (*TU*, 84).

In the epilogue, Conrad initially focuses on Madame Levaille's
"dry-eyed" degeneration. She is not so much grief-stricken as dispir-
ited, with her "thick legs" and "old feet" stretched out like those of a
"vanquished warrior" (*TU*, 84). Conrad enhances this impression with
a pun on *sword*, in the image of the dropped weapon, the umbrella,
lying on the "withered sward" (*TU*, 84). However, when the Marquis
passes by, she reverts to her culturally conditioned persona, speaking
to him "dispassionately" and reasonably. Conrad accentuates the
disparity between social classes by contrasting the physical positions
and postures of the two characters in the epilogue: "The Marquis of

Chevanes on horseback, one gloved hand on thigh, looked down at her as she got up laboriously, with groans" (*TU*, 84–85). Madame Levaille shows her defective sensibility in being totally concerned with the social stigma attached to the fact that her dead daughter lies in unconsecrated ground. In response to Madame Levaille's "short shower of tears," the Marquis expresses his sympathy and pronounces the official, falsified account of Susan's death: "I shall speak to the Curé. She was unquestionably insane, and the fall was accidental. Millot says so distinctly. Good day, Madame" (*TU*, 85). In Conrad's epilogue, reason prevails but truth does not. By avoiding a moralistic tone in his narrative voice and concentrating on how life goes on after the death of an individual, Conrad creates an open-ended conclusion that baffles any attempt to impose a conventional frame of reference on the events of the story.

But Conrad does prepare the way for his unresolved denouement in the initial paragraphs of the tale. The narrator, who begins as an active first-person participant and then abruptly fades from the picture, later achieving omniscience in the epilogue, claims he has reconstructed "a tale formidable and simple" but admits that his information comes from "listless answers" to his questions and "indifferent words heard in wayside inns or on the very road those idiots haunted" (*TU*, 58).[15] For him, the story of the idiots represents one of those "disclosures of obscure trials endured by ignorant hearts" (*TU*, 58). What remains obscure, or undisclosed, is the intricacy and intimacy of the conspiratorial nature of institutional authorities.[16] Madame Levaille, a tycoon in miniature, both exploits and is exploited by the Marquis, who receives the good news of the conversion of a political foe from the parish priest, who in turn uses it as an occasion to launch "solemn platitudes about the inscrutable ways of Providence" (*TU*, 64). Church and state, priest and king, owe their power to the will of the masses to consider them agents of divine authority.

But Conrad covertly questions divine judgment and regards modern institutions with skepticism. Moreover, throughout the story, he provides casual hints that heaven itself is untenanted. At the outset, the narrator says the idiots are "a reproach to empty heaven." Later, Jean-Pierre refers to the clock in the church tower as a vacant mask. The "heavens above" Madame Levaille's house, which Conrad describes as "draped in black rags," seem decked out for death (*TU*, 72). To Susan, the high, sharp rocks she passes resemble the "pointed towers of submerged churches" (*TU*, 79). Conrad also depicts the church tower as "a slender and tall pyramid shooting up dark and pointed into the clustered glitter of the stars" (*TU*, 81). The tower is consoling to Susan, yet the comparison of structures built by modern Christians to those built by ancient Egyptians casts a veil of superstition over the religion of the Breton peasants. And finally, pathetically, Susan's last cry ascends "into the high and impassive heaven" (*TU*, 84).

Conrad situates the reference to "impassive heaven" at a crucial point in the narrative, for these are the last words prior to the epilogue, which stands apart from the main body of the tale. In the epilogue, the narrator's point of view seems detached and reportorial, reflecting an almost matter-of-fact tone, in vivid contrast to the emotionally charged rhetoric and patches of purple prose in much of the tale proper.[17] Conrad sets up a collision of word-worlds when he juxtaposes the exposition's concern for the plight of individuals and the terse epilogue's social, institutional orientation. The brief closing scene seems unsatisfactory because it has no explicit message. Its disclosure only reveals the weaknesses of characters in a human zoo. To be sure, Conrad demonstrates his indebtedness to Maupassant, Flaubert, and Zola in this story, but "The Idiots" is more than an "obviously derivative" tale. Conrad's narrative is a satirical fable of Western culture in which medieval feudalism evolves into modern "futilism." On his "animal" farm, God remains an absentee landlord.

## "The Lagoon"

In his Malayan tales, Conrad frequently contrasts Eastern and Western attitudes and usually disparages European culture. He derides Western hypocrisy and rapacity, by-products of modern civilization, and casts a favorable light on the traditional values and instinctive qualities of his fictional South Seas natives. In "The Lagoon," however, Conrad does not draw such a sharp contrast between the white trader and the Malayan warrior.[18] The nameless white man suffers from delusions of self-aggrandizement, but he is not the only character blinded by egoism, for Arsat's confession of how he won Diamelen and ran off with her instead of avenging his brother's death, the pivotal tale within the tale, implies that he, too, is motivated by desire. The lagoon in Conrad's title comes to represent a psychological morass in which the dream of possession leads to a petrification of selfhood.[19] In his struggle to overcome his psychic immobility, Arsat seems to cultivate yet another myopic obsession. He intends to recover his former identity, a pursuit that can only lead to death, either metaphorically or literally. Conrad demonstrates that serenity always lies beyond the reach of those who pursue self-interest or are haunted by the consequences of their previous actions.

The conclusion of the tale is problematical because Conrad presents the perspectives of both the white man and the Malayan without endorsing either viewpoint.[20] To the white man, Arsat's commitment to vengeance seems to be a needless sacrifice. When the Malayan expresses love for his dead brother, the white man answers with a hollow echo of that sentiment: "We all love our brothers" (*TU,* 202). And when Arsat, facing moral solitude, remarks quietly, "I can see nothing," the white man's response is unfeeling: "There is nothing" (*TU,* 203). There is nothing to do, the white man believes, but to go on with the business of living. But Arsat views his situation as a personal crisis; for Diamelen's death marks the end of his enslavement to his obsession and his renewed commitment to his slain brother and his Malayan culture. Still immersed in the darkness of his sensual desire, Arsat can see nothing, but he hopes to find a way back to his former self. This solemn "friend of ghosts," who has been living as an outsider to be with the woman who is sole object of his desire, proclaims his new desire to regain his cultural identity through an act of self-destructive revenge. He vows to negate one betrayal by adding to his original treachery.

After making this vow, Arsat stands "still with unmoved face and stony eyes, staring at the sun" (*TU,* 204). This pose suggests Conrad's general assessment of humanity, civilized or primitive, as capable of progressing only from one form of blindness to another. Furthermore, Conrad accentuates the motif of spiritual myopia in the grim tableau that closes the story: "Arsat had not moved. He stood lonely in the searching sunshine; and he looked beyond the great light of a cloudless day into the darkness of a world of illusions" (*TU,* 204). The white man seems to view Arsat's self-destructive decision as uncivilized, while Arsat himself believes his vow is based on brotherly love. But Conrad complicates this apparent resolution by undermining the perceptions of both Arsat and the white man. They have been blinded by self-interest, and only the Malayan seems to recognize the extent of his own blindness.

Conrad's refusal to name "the white man" throughout the tale suggests that the character represents a cultural stereotype. Arsat has lost his former identity, but the white man has no formal identity at all. The white man functions mainly to give commands, which are wordlessly executed by grunting Malayans who work for him. His canoe brings confusion to a previously undisturbed landscape that is "bewitched into an immobility." Conrad adds another sinister touch by focusing on the carved dragon-head on the prow of the white man's boat, comparing the progress of the vessel to "some slim and amphibious creature leaving the water for its lair in the forest" (*TU*, 188). The white man, spiritually akin to the amphibious dragon, makes an unwarranted intrusion on the silence of the forest. His first command is the only line of dialogue in the initial five hundred words of exposition. Not surprisingly, Conrad depicts the jungle as a postlapsarian, snake-infested paradise: "Here and there, near the glistening blackness of the water, a twisted root of some tall tree showed amongst the tracery of small ferns, black and dull, writhing and motionless, like an arrested snake. . . . Darkness oozed out from between the trees, through the tangled maze of the creepers, . . . darkness scented and poisonous of impenetrable forests" (*TU*, 188–89). The white man's destination, the "marshy bank" of a "stagnant lagoon," would be a perfect lair for a poisonous snake.

Despite years of friendship, the white man has a condescending attitude toward Arsat. Conrad wryly notes that the trader likes the Malayan a little less than he likes his pet dog. To the white man "in the midst of his own pursuits," Arsat is little more than a trained animal who can be useful on occasion. To the Western psyche, caught up in its own endeavors, everything alien to European culture is a curiosity to be either plundered or swept aside. The presence of the white man at Diamelen's deathbed provides the occasion for another of Conrad's ironic asides, a comment on the restlessness of Western culture: "The fear and fascination, the inspiration and the wonder of death— of death near, unavoidable, and unseen, soothed the unrest of his race and stirred the most indistinct, the most intimate of his thoughts" (*TU*, 193). For a Western individual in the nineteenth century, the dread of personal annihilation is the most absorbing thought of all. Nature, itself, also arouses a sense of dread. In contrast to the natives, who have an instinctive rapport with the organic world, the white man can only feel uneasy when confronting the dumb stillness of nature. Conrad juxtaposes the "gnawing suspicion" and the "powerful disturbance" at the root of the white man's being with the profound stillness of the environment. The white trader interprets the organic facade as "the placid and impenetrable mask of an unjustifiable violence" (*TU*, 193). His code of conduct has not prepared him to deal with the incomprehensible. Without his conventional frame of reference, he views the scene as a shadowy land of phantoms struggling to possess vulnerable human hearts.

The white man's subjective vision mirrors his "inextinguishable desires and fears," for the key word in Conrad's sermon on the vanity of human wishes is "possession," the passion for ownership shared by Arsat and the white man. Arsat even hints at this mutual defect when he acknowledges his inability to understand the forces that impel the white man: "[Y]ou went away from my country in the pursuit of your desires, which we, men of the islands, cannot understand . . ." (TU, 194). In narrating his story, Arsat makes a revealing comparison: "We are of a people who take what they want—like you whites" (TU, 196). The white man may appear to lack the blind rapacity of the uninhibited Kurtz, but Conrad groups him with Arsat and his brother as believers in the will to power: "We are men who take what we want and can hold it against many" (TU, 197). Thus, Conrad does not reduce the white man to the neutral role of observer, as some critics claim, but instead employs him as a representative of pernicious colonial influence, which promotes turmoil and unrest, even in peaceful times.

Conrad links the white man to Arsat in yet another revealing way. The lagoon's "weird aspect and ghostly reputation" frighten the polers, who distrust Arsat because he is a stranger and, more importantly, because he has no fear of ghosts (TU, 189). Arsat's disregard for superstition causes the polers to associate him with "unbelievers"— the white men in league with the "Father of Evil," who make "an offensive pretence of disbelief" (TU, 190). Although Arsat does not fear ghosts, he is haunted by remorse, by the bittersweet knowledge that he has attained the object of his desire at the cost of betraying his brother and his Ruler. Furthermore, despite the undeniable melodrama of his subject, Conrad makes sport of the sentimental connotations of the word *heart* throughout the tale. For him, the romantic heart is an excessively glorified incinerator burning with the fires of delusive passion. Here the author seems to have taken to heart the message of Buddha's Fire Sermon, for Arsat suffers from a "burnt-up heart" and announces Diamelen's death by saying, "She burns no more" (TU, 203). Conrad implies that for Arsat and Diamelen intense life means feverish desire. Appropriately, Arsat's passion fades from the scene with "the dying embers of the fire" (TU, 201).

In "The Lagoon," the briefest of his short stories, Conrad chronicles the eclipse of Arsat's passion but not his pride. Employing a technique he also uses in Kurtz's speeches in *Heart of Darkness,* written a few years later, Conrad couches much of Arsat's dialogue in self-referential language. Like Kurtz, Arsat has kicked himself free from the universe and now spouts solipsistic redundancies: "I hear, I see, I wait.

I remember . . ." (TU, 193). Diamelen's death has simply become part of Arsat's "fate," since she functions only as a prized possession in his thinking. Arsat's betrayal of his Ruler and subsequent desertion of his brother are secondary to the ultimate fact in his self-absorbed consciousness: "I had her there! I had her! To get her I would have faced all mankind. But I had her—" (TU, 202). Even when he reports Diamelen's physical condition to the white man, his words reveal his self-preoccupation: "[S]he hears nothing—she hears not me. She sees nothing. She sees not me—me!" (TU, 191). Conrad undercuts the pathos of Arsat's situation at the end by depicting him as a "friend of ghosts," an outsider beyond the pale of human solidarity. Instead of embodying impersonal devotion to discipline, the hallmark of the most positive characters in Conrad's fiction, Arsat's single-minded fixation perverts life.

Conrad's ending, stressing silence and immobility, functions as a summary of the whole story.[21] In fact, the pathetic closing tableau recalls a scene Conrad refers to periodically throughout the tale: Diamelen's deathbed. Diamelen is a pivotal nonparticipant in a story that revolves around her capture and possession. Her qualities imply nonexistence (she is silent, motionless, unseeing, unhearing), because she has been defined by Arsat more as an object than a subject. In her wordlessness and powerlessness, Diamelen shares traits with Kurtz's African mistress and Mrs. Schomberg, among others. She lies on her deathbed as helplessly as when she sat in the canoe during her abduction. In her fever, she hears nothing, except perhaps what the white man fails to hear, as the woods whisper "the wisdom of their immense and lofty indifference" (TU, 194).

Critics have attached significance to the flight of the white eagle following Diamelen's death (TU, 202).[22] To view this as a token of Arsat's redemption would be to misconstrue Conrad's ironic perspective. For just as Arsat's possession of Diamelen is a nonpossession; so, too, his belated commitment to avenge his brother's death is a nonaction, a decision made in a vacuum. Conrad's ending defuses whatever tension has accumulated in the course of Arsat's narrative. The postures Arsat and the white man assume at the close of the story suggest the sentimental attitudes and delusive passions of conventional melodrama, since Conrad covertly sabotages the poignancy of the tableau. In a sense, Arsat exchanges one obsession for another, unmindful of the self-destruction implicit in his conversion to vengeance. The white man, never named and not really dramatically present, leaves the scene of Conrad's drama as powerless a spectator as Diamelen on her deathbed. Unveiling "the dark world of illusions" for an instant, Conrad places the reader in the role of the white man looking back at the wake of his stream of words, looking to find symbols of redemption, looking at a universe of mirrors, and looking for a new obsession to make life meaningful once again.

## "The Return"

A disturbing tale of marital infidelity, "The Return" illuminates one of Conrad's most characteristic endgame stratagems. Unfortunately, critics seldom mention this story except to disparage its shortcomings.[23] Conrad himself prepared the way for this trend by calling "The Return" a "left-handed production" in his author's note to *Tales of Unrest* (x) and referring to it as "odious" and "infernal" in his letters to Edward Garnett shortly after its composition (*CL*, 1:386–88, 391–94). Lawrence Graver considers the story an "example of an artistic road not taken" and "[o]ne of the strangest works in the Conrad canon" (*LG*, 34), largely as a result of the apprentice author's unfamiliarity with the materials of his narrative. But although the tale has more than its share of flaws, it does reveal much about Conrad's attitude toward life and fiction, and the qualified meanings that can be derived from both, as it brings into collision serious epistemological issues and satirical stereotyping.

"The Return" unfolds as a Jamesian discourse involving a case of linguistic "possession" that prevents a husband from reconciling with his wife. Mrs. Alvan Hervey, the only name she has in the story, leaves her husband for another man, only to discover that she cannot go through with her desertion. She returns to her husband, who has just read her farewell note and responds to her sudden reappearance with stunned disbelief. The story's O. Henry ending (the husband abruptly departs) underscores the illusory nature of human knowledge as the opening pages of the final scene emphasize the haunting refrain "impossible to know." Alvan Hervey has just prepared himself to live the rest of his days without his wife, whose love had always seemed assured. Now he finds that he must live with her but without "certitude immaterial and precious" (*TU*, 179), for he believes that he cannot be sure what his wife really thinks or feels. Hervey recognizes that he has been duped by his wife's conventional facade of amiability, and now he must confront a world in which all external signs may be deceptive: "The secret of hearts . . . shall return, veiled forever, to the Inscrutable Creator of good and evil, to the Master of doubts and impulses" (*TU,* 184). The passage echoes an almost identical passage several pages earlier, both of which seem to endorse Descartes' provisional presumption, in his *Meditations,* of God as a divine trickster. Conrad's irony inverts our customary suppositions about the Almighty, making Him not all good but the "Inscrutable Creator of good and evil," not the Master of faith and destiny but "the Master of doubts and impulses" (*TU,* 184). Yet, ultimately, this passage reflects Hervey's inadequacy more than divine limitation.

Toward the end of "The Return" Conrad alters Hervey's mantra from "impossible to know" to "nobody shall know" and "nobody would know" (*TU,* 181, 182). Initially, these phrases pertain to the jolted husband's rationalization that he can still keep secret his wife's temporary desertion. By keeping his doors "impenetrable to the truth," Hervey hopes to avoid the taint of scandal and insure his success in the conformist social world where his "unappeasable ambitions" thrive (*TU,* 180). But Conrad undermines this egocentric dream world by demonstrating the hollowness at its core: "He remembered her smile, her eyes, her voice, her silence, as though he had lost her forever. The years would pass and he would always mistrust her smile, suspect her eyes; he would always misbelieve her voice, he would never have faith in her silence" (*TU,* 183). Wracked by doubt and suspicion, Hervey stares into his wife's unfathomable eyes and sees nothing he can trust. Thus the phrase "nobody would know" attains an additional ironic touch in the penultimate paragraph, when Hervey deserts his wife and appears to become *no body* indeed: "It was as though no sooner gone he had suddenly expired—as though he had died there and his body had vanished on the instant together with his soul" (*TU,* 186). Conrad's three-word last paragraph ("He never returned") gives the story a greater sense of closure than one usually finds in his tales. At this point it seems all too easy to interpret the story as a parable of existential unfathomability,[24] yet Conrad ultimately subverts the protagonist's final disclosure of incertitude by emphasizing the cookie-cutter conformity at the heart of Alvan Hervey's personality.

If we were to consider the ending of "The Return" in isolation from the rest of the text, it would be possible to sympathize with Hervey's estrangement from his wife and from his customary assumptions about human existence. However, Conrad's opening scene mocks his protagonist's claim to individuality.[25] Hervey's "indifferent" face suggests a kinship with a "band of brothers" who are London businessmen who "had all the same stare, concentrated and empty, satisfied and unthinking" (*TU,* 118–19).[26] In addition to ridiculing Hervey's

status in the workaday world, Conrad mocks the protagonist's incapacity to love anyone but himself: "Under the cover of that sacred
and poetical fiction he desired [his wife] masterfully, . . . principally for
the satisfaction of having his own way" (TU, 120). Conrad depicts the
Herveys as emotionless moderns who think in "formulas" and care
only for "profitable facts" (TU, 120). Hervey's scheme of self-aggrandizement depends on the world conforming to his formulaic expectations. Any deviation from the set pattern, such as his wife's desertion,
threatens his psychological stability. Later, in a heated argument with
her, he cries out, "Nothing that outrages the received beliefs can be
right" (TU, 157). Thus, Conrad depicts the Herveys as "a pair of
cautious conspirators in a profitable plot; . . . [t]hey skimmed over the
surface of life . . . like two skilful skaters cutting figures on thick ice . . .
and disdainfully ignoring the hidden stream, the stream restless and
dark; the stream of life, profound and unfrozen" (TU, 123). In language that calls to mind Fitzgerald's equally superficial conspirators in
The Great Gatsby, Daisy and Tom Buchanan, Conrad dramatizes the
vacuous heart of darkness that lies at the core of many conventional
marriages once profit has replaced passion.[27]

But the most damning image of Hervey's moral shallowness and
spiritual blindness is a piece of sculpture that Conrad mentions in the
denouement, which is first described near the outset of the tale: "[A]
marble woman, decently covered . . . with stone draperies, advanced
a row of lifeless toes to the edge of the pedestal, and thrust out blindly
a rigid white arm holding a cluster of lights" (TU, 123). The Herveys
have maintained a decent nonexistence, blinded by their sense of
propriety. In the closing scene, Conrad associates Hervey with darkness and his wife with "a face white as alabaster and perfectly still, like
a woman in a trance" (TU, 170). He specifically compares Mrs.
Hervey to the statue,[28] mocking his protagonist's grand delusion that
he is Pygmalion in total control of Galatea:

> Perhaps her face was rigidly set—but that marmoreal impassiveness,
> that magnificent stolidity, as of a wonderful statue by some great sculptor
> working under the curse of the gods; that imposing, unthinking stillness
> of her features, had till then mirrored for him the tranquil dignity of a
> soul of which he had thought himself—as a matter of course—the
> inexpugnable possessor. (TU, 171)

On one level, Conrad focuses attention on Hervey's appalled
discovery of his marble-perfect wife's capacity for falsehood: "She
looked lies, breathed lies, lived lies—would tell lies—always—to the

end of life! And he would never know what she meant. Never! Never! No one could. Impossible to know" (*TU*, 172). But on a different level Conrad heaps his scorn on the protagonist's naive belief that his wife is as dependable and predictable as a piece of statuary, a prized possession that he can count among his social assets. Hervey is a kind of modern-day counterpart to Browning's Duke of Ferrara, but without the aristocratic lineage or murderous intents. The realization that his wife has a mind of her own forces Hervey to think unfamiliar thoughts that act upon his psyche like a "pestilence," "disintegrating" the very core of his existence. Now the matrimonial roles have been suddenly reversed, and it is Hervey who feels insignificant and powerless. Conrad cleverly contrasts Hervey's old and new perspectives on his wife as his protagonist submits to "the rising tide of impenetrable gloom": "The cluster of lights went out. The girl ascended facing him. Behind her the shadow of a colossal woman danced lightly on the wall" (*TU*, 182). Conrad brackets this revealing passage between two further references to the portentous statue: "[T]he woman of marble, composed and *blind* on the *high pedestal,* seemed to ward off the devouring night with a cluster of lights . . . . [T]he woman of marble, livid and still like a patient phantom, held out in the night a cluster of *extinguished lights*" (*TU*, 182; emphasis added). Here Conrad may be alluding to the traditional masculine tendency to place women on a high pedestal where they can be idealized, admired, and restricted. Once Hervey realizes that his wife has stepped down from the pedestal, and is no longer insulated from life or subject to his control, darkness overwhelms him.[29]

In addition to emphasizing Hervey's psychological blindness, Conrad's tale calls into question his protagonist's reliance on words as a source of security. Peevishly, like a whining child, Hervey responds to his wife's whispered utterance: "Words!": "Words? Yes, words. Words mean something—yes—they do—for all this infernal affectation. They mean something to me—to everybody—to you" (*TU*, 163). Hervey may stamp his foot in irritation, but he cannot stamp out the painful revelation that he has put undue faith in language (specifically, conventional forms of language) to guarantee his stable sense of selfhood.[30] Conrad hints at his protagonist's inability to use words as a shield against chaotic reality in the title of the book of verses written by his wife's lover, "Thorns and Arabesques," and he calls attention to "the contorted gold letters sprawling all over [the cover] in an intricate maze" (*TU*, 179). The mazelike letters objectify the confused labyrinth of Hervey's mind as he tries to rationalize what has become a topsy-turvy world. His wife's return undermines his efforts to take in the terrible import of her farewell note. At one point, Conrad's narrator speculates: "[W]hat did [Hervey] want? The woman—or the certitude immaterial and precious!" (TU, 179). He pursues the "track of the enigma," but ultimately Hervey is exiled from everything he had formerly trusted.[31] Thus, a story that begins with a wife's desertion ends with a husband's desertion, and a closing scene that appears to suggest the basic uncertainty of human existence may actually disclose only the protagonist's folly as a victim of abstract language. The locking scene clashes with the satirical elements in the rest of the text, though at the same time Hervey's exasperated departure crowns his career as a prince of fools.[32]

# 6

## An Accommodation with Chaos

We live in an old chaos of the sun,
Or old dependency of day and night,
Or island solitude, unsponsored, free,
Of that wide water, inescapable.
—Wallace Stevens, "Sunday Morning"

Taken altogether, "Because of the Dollars," "The End of the Tether," and "Il Conde" constitute a kind of tripartite *Tempest*, expressing not Conrad's farewell to the art of fiction but his disdain for the fictionalizing tendencies of ordinary life. In "Dollars," Captain Davidson clings to his naive notion of human goodness, even when he has ample evidence of depravity. In "Tether," Captain Whalley, both physically and morally blind, cannot discern that the fantasy world he has constructed for his daughter's benefit has no reality outside of his own imagination. And in "Il Conde" the title character has built his whole existence on the pretense of being an experienced man of the world; when experience does confront him, in the form of another of Conrad's evil emissaries from the actual world, the Count psychologically implodes. True, the ending of each story resonates with pathos, yet in each case Conrad subverts our natural inclination to sympathize with the defeated protagonist. He mocks those who think they can keep chaos at bay by ordering life according to some logical pattern. Only an individual who acknowledges the rule of happenstance in human existence can escape Conrad's scorn. That individual would implicitly recognize the qualified wisdom of Mr. Stein's dictum in *Lord Jim* that we must immerse ourselves in the destructive element if we hope to preserve ourselves. To pretend that chaos and destruction can be governed in any way, especially linguistically, would be foolhardy. Thus, the pathetic follies of Davidson, Whalley, and the Count document our perennially frustrated attempt to master our fate.

## "Because of the Dollars"

Often dismissed as an inferior, miniature version of *Victory*, and more often totally neglected, "Because of the Dollars" offers one of the most conspicuous examples of Conrad's enigmatic endings. The story features an anonymous narrator who listens to a tale told by an interior narrator, Hollis, who also appears in "Karain." But this characteristically Conradian framework here has a significant twist: the unnamed narrator does not directly comment on Hollis's account at the conclusion. Instead, Conrad plants a seed of doubt when the narrator poses a question that elicits Hollis's final commentary on the nature of the experience. When Hollis ceases his moralizing, Conrad terminates the story, presumably leaving the conventional reader dissatisfied. This ending coincides with Conrad's general tendency of closing his stories in a way that leaves the reader ill at ease, as he noted in his comment on James's fiction. Conrad rarely permits the attentive interpreter of his fiction to gain genuine consolation from a summarizing moral.

In "Because of the Dollars," he takes his skepticism one step further by undercutting the language of fiction, mainly by emphasizing our misguided reliance on labels and epithets, platitudes and clichés. Without these linguistic crutches, individuals can determine relatively little about the outside world; with them, individuals can hide from themselves their lack of understanding (as Ambrose Bierce would put it). Labels and clichés arise from mindless habits of thought, the hasty assumptions and snap judgments that stereotype and fossilize the ever-changing phenomenal world. Language is the supreme fiction, as both Conrad and Stevens recognize, for it imposes an artificial meaning on the mystery of existence. Words codify living experience, converting the flux of organic life into an illusion of stability. Ultimately, we cannot even control the words we use to project the appearance of control.

Conrad's plot resonates with mawkish melodrama.[1] In "a great Eastern port" Hollis points out Captain Davidson as a "really *good* man" to the anonymous narrator. When the narrator requests more specific details, Hollis recounts an anecdote to demonstrate Davidson's good-naturedness. The Davidson episode transpired at a time when the government ordered an exchange of old dollars for new. Davidson's vessel regularly visited isolated outposts, and thus he was required to bring in the old dollars. Unfortunately, Davidson, the man who can apparently do no wrong, spoke out openly about his dollar-laden voyage while gossiping in the tiffin room. At this point Conrad inserts a flashback to a time two years before the exchange of the dollars, when Davidson first discovered that his former acquaintance, Laughing Anne, a reformed "painted woman," was living with Bamtz, a "reformed loafer." Since that time, Davidson has made regular stops at Bamtz's settlement to see Anne and her son, Tony. After the flashback, Hollis takes up the narrative again at the point when Fector, "a professional blackmailer," overhears Davidson's words. Fector passes this information on to two other thugs, Niclaus and a "Frenchman without hands." Together, they plot to steal the dollars from Davidson after taking Bamtz into their confidence.

Later Davidson, his ship loaded with dollars, makes a sentimental decision to visit Anne on his homeward journey. When he arrives at Bamtz's house he finds Anne distracted by her son's illness and the four men talking in a conspiratorial atmosphere. Gradually, Davidson discovers that Anne's anxiety stems not only from Tony's poor health but also from the menace posed by the criminals visiting Bamtz. After telling Davidson of this threat, Anne discloses that she will warn him with her laughter if they decide to attack under the cover of night. Davidson rigs his bunk covers to resemble a sleeping body and waits in hiding with his revolvers. Moments after hearing Anne's "silvery laugh," he sees the thugs board his ship. A brief gunfight ensues, without apparent consequences. When Davidson realizes that the Frenchman is pursuing Anne to punish her for betraying the criminals, the portly Captain leaves his vessel to try to save her. He later finds Anne's lifeless body, her skull crushed by a seven-pound weight she had previously helped to fasten onto one of the Frenchman's arms. Taking Tony back to the ship, Davidson sees the corpse of the Frenchman near the house. The Captain plans to let his wife raise Tony, but she immediately becomes suspicious of Tony's origin and her husband's involvement in the whole affair. When she learns that Tony's mother had been "a vile woman," she accuses Davidson of carrying on a "base intrigue" and eventually deserts him, even after Tony has been sent away "to the White Fathers in Malacca" (*WT*, 210). Davidson, deprived of wife and foster son, becomes a lonely old man.

Conrad's brief coda begins with Hollis's simplistic moral: "This is the story that has spoiled Davidson's smile for him—which perhaps it wouldn't have done so thoroughly had he been less of a good fellow" (*WT*, 210–11). On one level, Hollis's summation has validity. If Davidson had not decided to take care of Anne's son he might still be living in relative harmony with his wife. Certainly he is the well-meaning protagonist of the story, just as Anne is the self-sacrificing martyr, while all the other prominent characters are villains. And Conrad often reveals his pessimistic outlook when dramatizing the futility of good actions in a world of duplicity and deception. But Conrad seldom operates in such a one-dimensional manner, and Hollis's convenient conclusion proves groundless once we consider the author's linguistic strategy throughout the story. Indeed, Conrad employs key epithets to describe his characters with such frequency that he undermines (deliberately, I think) the power of language to portray a personal identity.[2]

Goodness is the most prominent abstraction in the story. Hollis refers to Davidson as a "good man," not only on the first and last pages but on seven other occasions. But when Hollis singles out Davidson to the framing narrator as "a good man . . . I mean a really *good* man," Conrad ridicules this epithet with the narrator's ironic observation: "The 'really *good* man' had a very broad back" (*WT*, 169). Hollis obviously equates goodness with compassion in his superfluous defense of Davidson's character: "[H]e's thoroughly humane . . . I may well call him a *'really* good man'" (*WT*, 171).[3] But Hollis hints at another side of Davidson (or, rather, another way of viewing his natural kindness) in his assertion that "his goodness was of a particularly delicate sort" (*WT*, 190). And although Hollis claims Davidson is not "a soft fool," the ruffians clearly have a different picture of the Captain, viewing him as "an unsuspicious, inoffensive, soft creature" (*WT*, 195). This comment immediately follows Hollis's statement that he knows Davidson as "a man of courage, if ever there was one" (*WT*, 195). Yet the Frenchman sees no sign of bravery in Davidson's "outward placidity," for he considers the Captain a sheep ready for slaughter. Niclaus expresses the same opinion: "He isn't a shooting man" (*WT*, 199). Along similar lines, Anne remembers Davidson's youthful personality as "the quietest of a rather rowdy set" (*WT*, 182). To a certain degree, even Hollis confirms this impression in several of his remarks. While standing guard in his ship at night, Davidson emulates "the stillness of the mouse—a grimly determined mouse. . . .

[H]e was not homicidally inclined" (*WT*, 200, 201). In his closing remarks, Hollis returns to Davidson's placid, nonaggressive manner. Davidson, whether a "good man" or "determined mouse," apparently does not profit from his humanitarian tendencies. His compassion most dramatically manifests itself when he gazes down at Anne's lifeless body, which attests to Davidson's inability to play his heroic role successfully. He feels "morally bound" to Anne's son because of his sense of failure, and this "scrupulous delicacy of feeling" eventually leads to the end of his marriage.

Mrs. Davidson's departure, however, comes as a blessing in disguise, as Conrad insinuates in a montage of conflicting perspectives. Most of Davidson's associates view his wife, who has "a girlish head," a "white, swan-like neck," and a "drooping, innocent profile" (*WT*, 175, 176), as his "heaven-born mate." Mrs. Davidson expresses "wifely anxiety" when her husband embarks on the mission to collect the old dollars. After Davidson had decided to put Tony in his wife's care, he "trusted in the goodness and warmth of her heart, in her woman's natural compassion" (*WT*, 207). Hollis even recalls one of his friends telling him that "[s]he didn't seem to me the sort of woman that would make a fuss about anything" (*WT*, 176). But in this case Hollis simply chimes in with the superficial view of Mrs. Davidson taken by unknowing outsiders.

On a deeper level, Hollis indicates a darker side to her personality, which triggers her self-righteous behavior at the close of the story. While other observers perceive Mrs. Davidson as "a meek, shy little thing," Hollis calls attention to her "convex, obstinate forehead, and her small, pretty, ungenerous mouth" (*WT*, 176). He emphasizes the disparity between appearance and actuality in Mrs. Davidson's personality: "[F]or all her angelic profile, she was a very stupidly obstinate girl" (*WT*, 189). Although Davidson counts on her maternal instincts in making a home for Tony, Hollis paints a portrait of the Captain's wife as cold and self-centered: "[H]er heart was about the size of a parched pea, and had the proportional amount of warmth; and . . . her faculty of compassion was mainly directed to herself" (*WT*, 207–8). Like most of the characters in Conrad's seriocomic scenario, she makes a hasty assumption about human nature when she concludes that Tony is Davidson's child, a possibility that affronts "her most sacred feelings." Mrs. Davidson's "sacred feelings," of course, are indistinguishable from self-centered sentiments. Hollis's final comment on her personality unfolds as a litany of her shortcomings: "A stupid woman with a sense of grievance is worse than an unchained devil. . . . She worked up her sense of her wifely wrongs and of her injured purity . . . her outraged dignity . . . her pure, sensitive, mean little soul" (*WT,* 210).[4]

If Conrad had only illustrated the conflicting perspectives on Davidson and his wife, his tactics would have been remarkably similar to his delineation of Mr. and Mrs. Verloc in *The Secret Agent,* Renouard and Felicia in "The Planter of Malata," and Alvan Hervey and his wife in "The Return." However, his debunking of customary phrases of identification is far more pervasive in "Because of the Dollars." No character seems outside the range of his linguistic deconstruction. For example, the hoodlums plotting against Davidson (roughly corresponding to the three emissaries in *Victory*: Jones, Ricardo, and Pedro) also embody existential incongruities. Fector calls himself a journalist, much in the same way a prostitute might call herself an actress in a police court. At times, "[h]e would also hint that he was a martyr" (*WT,* 186). Hollis calls him "a bright creature" but also "a spare, short, jumpy fellow with a red face and muddy eyes" (*WT,* 185). Later Hollis brands Fector, whose name may be a pun on *malefactor,* as "a professional blackmailer" but not "the bold buccaneer type," for he "had never in his adventurous life used other weapons than slander and lies" (*WT,* 186, 189). Conrad's interior narrator introduces Niclaus as "the fellow with a Tartar mustache and a yellow complexion, like a Mongolian" (*WT,* 186). Almost immediately, Hollis demotes him to the animal kingdom: "One couldn't tell what breed he was" (*WT,* 186).[5] Derogatively, Hollis defines him as "[a] non-descript beggar" who "owned a Malay prau and called himself The Nakhoda, as one would say: The Captain" (*WT,* 186). And when Hollis reintroduces him later in the story, we discover a reference to Niclaus—the white Nakhoda. The "non-descript beggar" *becomes* his self-imposed title, the pretense now masquerading as the reality.

But the most anomalous of these linguistically blurred agents of misfortune is the nameless Frenchman, whom Conrad showers with a host of epithets (e.g., "a maimed Frenchman," "a man without hands," "the huge Frenchman," "that French devil," "the big beast," "the ruffian") without bothering to give him a proper name. He is the ringleader, and Davidson and Laughing Anne speak of him overtly, yet he remains nameless. Moreover, the Frenchman, a powerful, murderous menace, lacks hands. Also incongruously, he formerly kept a tobacco shop. The Frenchman exploits his maimed condition as "a poor, harmless cripple," and kind-hearted Davidson, at the time of the incident, judges him purely by superficial appearances: "[A] man without hands did not strike him as very formidable in any circumstances" (*WT,* 197). Conrad's pun on a handless man not *striking* Davidson is itself striking.

Anne sees through the Frenchman's sham and warns Davidson that he's "a devil," yet she must pretend to be taken in by his sentimental charade and tie the seven-pound weight to the stump on the end of his arm: "A man with an unsuspected power to deal killing blows could take his own part in a sudden scrimmage round a heap of money . . ." (*WT,* 199). The word *unsuspected* provides the key concept in the final pages of Conrad's scenario. The four thugs do not suspect that Davidson has been warned of their plot. Davidson does not suspect that "the maimed Frenchman" has the power to kill Anne, nor does he suspect that one of his stray bullets has killed Anne's murderer. In short, Davidson's goodness creates a psychological blind spot.[6] He is too good to recognize his wife's selfishness or the threat posed by the maimed Frenchman. In keeping with Conrad's pessimistic vision, *goodness* is synonymous with *myopia*. Moreover, Laughing Anne, the reformed prostitute, loses her life in the attempt to save good Captain Davidson. The fates of the two most sympathetic characters in the tale make it obvious why it is improper to speak of heroes or heroines in Conrad's fiction.

The contrasting descriptions of Anne's personality offer another illustration of Conrad's linguistic strategy. Conrad depicts her as "no longer young" one moment and "a haggard, tragically anxious figure" the next (*WT,* 180, 183). Anne is both an "apparition" and a reformed "painted woman" (*WT,* 181, 184). She is a poor woman to Davidson: "'Yes, my poor girl,' he whispered, interpreting her distraction in his own way, though he had nothing precise in his mind" (*WT,* 193). Here Conrad nearly reveals the dynamics of his own artistry, for Davidson, like all the characters in the story, interprets other characters and events subjectively (i.e., according to the clichés and conditioned responses of his culture). In order for these blanket statements to be universally applicable, they must be abstract and stereotypical. Such labels call to mind early twentieth-century literary criticism and its need for heroes and villains and a simple theme involving the battle of good and evil. But Conrad does not endorse such a one-dimensional world-view. Anne cannot be circumscribed by any of the labels affixed to her personality by Hollis, Davidson, or the other characters. To be sure, Conrad persistently identifies Anne with her "pleasant, silvery laugh," yet her laughter becomes a signal of danger for Davidson. Her attire is equally incongruous, for when Davidson first sees Anne outside Bamtz's hut, he registers amazement at finding "this

European woman . . . in a fanciful tea-gown" so deep in the tropics (WT, 181).[7] In fine, she cannot be reduced to the one-dimensionality of a stock character.

But the true laughingstock in Conrad's bizarre melodrama is the farcically named Bamtz, who provides a home for Anne and her son. That home, however, certainly does not resemble the customary domestic refuge, for Bamtz has settled up "some God-forsaken creek," in a "wild place" near an "offensive village mudhole" (WT, 177, 181). Appropriately, a "waste ground" lies in front of Bamtz's hovel: "The house was but a glorified hut on piles, unfenced and lonely" (WT, 191). Bamtz himself is every bit as ridiculous as his name and shanty. Almost from his introduction, his personality seems swallowed up by one of Conrad's comical epithets: "[E]verybody knew what Bamtz was. He was a loafer with a beard. . . . A unique loafer. He made a fine art of it . . ." (WT, 177). Although Hollis later refers to Bamtz as "the reformed loafer," the derisive label adheres to his character, even though he resembles a bookkeeper rather than a pirate. Only the non-English-speaking natives place any credence in Bamtz's "posing mysteriously as a very special trader" (WT, 178).

Like Anne, Bamtz is no longer young, and he maintains a "queer, degraded existence" (WT, 180). Unlike Davidson, Bamtz lacks "moral delicacy," but in the aftermath of the aborted robbery he escapes with impunity, while the Captain saves his dollars at the cost of Anne's life, his marital union, and his little daughter. Though Hollis later calls Bamtz an "ex-vagabond" and "a craven," the most derogatory epithets come from the mouth of the leader of the robbers. While informing Fector and Niclaus of his designs on the dollars, the Frenchman "applied such a contemptuously indecent epithet to Bamtz that when, later, he alluded to him as 'une chiffe' (a mere rag) it sounded quite complimentary" (WT, 188). Conrad reinforces the conversion of this character into an obscene label a bit later when the Frenchman again refers to Bamtz by employing "another awful descriptive epithet quite unfit for repetition" (WT, 188). What Conrad does see fit to repeat, however, is the mindless series of labels and clichés that dominate the superficial perceptions of his characters.[8] From Davidson and Hollis down to Fector and the Frenchman, they all rely on stock phrases and stereotypes to navigate their way through the troubled seas of existence. Although Conrad recognizes life as the unpatterned flux of experience, his characters always frustrate themselves by seeking out a figure in the carpet through some type of formulaic verbalizing.

Conrad's use of the word *good* in the closing scene therefore functions as part of a pervasive ironic pattern of disintegrating rhetoric. Caricaturing the stock characters of popular magazine fiction, he calls attention to the lack of substance of fictional characters in general, who are compositions of mere words. On numerous occasions in his letters Conrad complained of the illusory quality of characters made of words. He may have also learned a lesson in the artistic employment of verbal overkill from Stephen Crane's satirical repetitions throughout his fiction.[9] Such ironic repetitions of clichés and epithets are also evident in James's fiction (e.g., "the man of the world" in "The Pupil" and "a pretty American flirt" in "Daisy Miller"). Both Crane and James (and Conrad perhaps even more so) employ these epithets to deflect perception rather than provide insight into reality. In a more serious context, "The horror!" serves as a final veiling of Kurtz's ultimate realization rather than a precise articulation of the nature of his deathbed revelation. But Conrad's dramatization of Davidson as an unlucky "good fellow" may also hark back to the tradition of the "good man" in eighteenth-century literature. Certainly Fielding represents this tradition, for his *Jonathan Wild* unfolds as an ironic ode to "GREATNESS" in its most sinister connotations. Fielding not only lampoons "the great man" Robert Walpole but also suggests that "the good man" must be satisfied with virtue as its own reward because power and public recognition will always be beyond him. Even more Conradian, to be willfully anachronistic for a moment, is the "Advertisement" prefacing Fielding's novel, which refers to "the black art . . . of deciphering men's meaning when couched in obscure, ambiguous, or allegorical expressions."[10]

Of course, Conrad is more of a kindred spirit to Crane and James than to Fielding. Yet he suggests another dimension in his final paragraph that contains a caustic irony more typical of Fielding's novels than the works of his American contemporaries. When the framing narrator asks what has happened to Tony, Hollis's response reveals that the extended anecdote has artistic symmetry as well as a fabricated moral: "Oh! That's the finishing touch! . . . Tony has grown into a fine youth—but there you are! He wants to be a priest; his one dream is to be a missionary" (*WT*, 211). To Hollis, Tony's spiritual calling is the crowning detail of the story. Tony, the offspring of a reformed harlot, will follow in his martyred mother's footsteps by becoming a missionary. Yet the Jamesian phrase "there you are" signals the inadequacy of Hollis's comprehension, which becomes more apparent in his last glimpse of Davidson: "So Laughing Anne's boy will lead a saintly life in China somewhere; he may even become a martyr; but poor Davidson is left out in the cold. He will have to go downhill without a single human affection near him because of those old dollars" (*WT*, 211). Hollis's conclusion seems myopic for several reasons. First, Davidson's lack of caution in spreading word of carrying the dollars, rather than the dollars themselves, actually led to the calamity at Bamtz's wharf. Second, when last seen in "Karain," Hollis was congratulating himself for passing off a Queen Victoria medal as a magic talisman to placate a troubled Malay chieftain. (This transaction does not add to his stature as a spokesman for Conrad.) Third, Hollis implicitly devalues the potential worth of Tony's missionary activities by lamenting that Anne's son, Davidson's last "human affection," will be far away from the lonely Captain.

While one might argue that Davidson is better off living alone than in the company of his mistrusting wife, for the moment let us leave Davidson "out in the cold" to pursue the implications of Hollis's casual remark that Tony "will lead a saintly life in China somewhere" (*WT*, 211). Conrad's choice of China is intriguing for two reasons. First, consider the one-sentence penultimate paragraph leading into Hollis's conclusion: "He [Hollis] counted carefully the change handed him by the Chinaman waiter, and raised his head" (*WT*, 211). In this brief passage Conrad foreshadows Tony's Chinese destination but also implies Hollis's preoccupation with money. Second, the two closing references to China bring the story full circle, taking us back to the friendship of Davidson and the Chinese shipowner, a relationship built on mutual trust. The shipowner, derisively labeled "the old mandarin" by Hollis, ordered a new vessel for Davidson shortly before his own death. The *Sissie*—Glasgow that Davidson brought to Bamtz's wharf was an earlier, smaller version of the ship of the same name that he now commands. Hollis, "a firm believer in the final value of shades" (*WT*, 170), considers the purchase of a new ship for Davidson a sentimental gesture designed to comfort the poor Captain. So Tony goes to China to preach the Gospel and Davidson acquires a new ship from his Chinese benefactor. Considered strictly in terms of profit and loss, Davidson has gained a new, larger vessel and no longer has to deal with his self-centered wife. In spiritual terms, he can take pride in Tony's missionary work. So what has spoiled his smile? Loneliness, as Hollis imagines? Or Davidson's semiconscious aware-ness of his own inadequacies? In any case, the dollars only provided the material means for his bungled mission.

Conrad refrains from commenting on the significance of Davidson's experience through the framing narrator. Yet the narrator's inquiry
about Tony's eventual fate probes the future, whereas Hollis's answer
looks back to the melancholy past. Conrad fully realized that human
beings attempt to explain the present in terms of a subjective past and
a nonexistent future. The past always glows with nostalgic significance, and the future seems to promise much more gratification than
the present moment provides. So individuals consistently minimize
the importance of the present, tainted as it is by the "malady of the
quotidian," to use Eliot's words. Resorting to the language of labels
and clichés also assists in evading the present. "Davidson the *really*
good man" is an encapsulation without real meaning and rightly
belongs with other misleading Conradian signifiers such as "Heyst the
Hermit" (in *Victory*), "the Great Personage" (in *The Secret Agent*), "one
of us" (in *Lord Jim*), and "The horror!" (in *Heart of Darkness*). Conrad
acutely felt the implications of the simple fact that fiction is fundamentally nothing but words, and words are everything and nothing in the
modern world. Anticipating the literature of silence, made popular by
Samuel Beckett, Conrad creates a disintegrating rhetoric in "Because
of the Dollars" to dramatize the bankruptcy of ordinary language.
Words are nothing but counters, whether in a literary masterpiece or
in a shameless potboiler, a term often applied to the ironically titled
"Because of the Dollars." The great literary artists project illusions that
transform words into multifaceted mirrors reflecting the manifold
illusions of life.

It is nearly impossible to discuss "Because of the Dollars" without
referring to *Victory*, its pessimistic touchstone, particularly because of
Davidson's appearance in both and their similar endings. "Dollars"
and *Victory* both conclude with the death of a self-sacrificing woman
and Davidson's ill-fated efforts to do the right thing. Although the final
chapter of *Victory* is an epilogue of little more than four pages recounting Davidson's interview with "an Excellency," Conrad's ending
really commences with the sudden and surprising appearance of the
well-meaning Captain at Lena's deathbed near the midpoint of the
penultimate chapter of the novel. The shock of Davidson's unexpected
arrival may be an artistic flaw, as Albert Guerard insists,[11] yet he plays
an important role in relating the final incidents of Heyst's story.

As in "Dollars," Conrad undermines the Captain's good intentions
at the end of the narrative. In his conversation with the Excellency,
Davidson relates how Mrs. Schomberg had warned him of the danger
facing Heyst after she overheard her husband talking to two rascals

who asked about the location of Heyst's island. Impressed by Mrs. Schomberg's agitation, Davidson nevertheless "confessed that while going back, he began to have his doubts as to there being anything in it" (V, 409). He also admits that when he arrived at Diamond Bay in quiet darkness he was reluctant to go ashore at once because he was fearful of intruding on the privacy of Heyst and Lena. He only goes ashore when he sees a clear sign of something wrong: "a big white boat, adrift with the dead body of a very hairy man inside, bumping against the bows of his steamer" (V, 409). Davidson's characteristic delicacy comes into play once more, after Lena's death, when he leaves Heyst alone to mourn her passing and returns to his ship. Although he has departed at Heyst's insistence, he notes that this seemed agreeable because "I didn't want to intrude on his grief" (V, 410). The interval allows Heyst to set fire to his bungalow, immolating both himself and the dead body of Lena. And although Davidson attempts to console himself that "fire purifies everything," Conrad's last glimpse of the well-meaning Captain shows a man wiping the perspiration off his forehead and murmuring his final word—"Nothing!"—"with placid sadness" (V, 410, 412). Davidson's good intentions have come to nothing because he could not play the roles of hero and decent man simultaneously.

Just as Conrad associates Davidson's temperament with placidity in the last chapter of *Victory*, he links the remorseful Captain to "placid" eyes and a "scrupulous delicacy of feeling" in "Dollars" (WT, 210). But even more significant is the effect that finding Anne's dead body has on Davidson, an effect that corresponds to his regret for the loss of Heyst and Lena: "Davidson . . . was overcome by remorse. She had died for him. His manhood was as if stunned. For the first time he had felt afraid" (WT, 205). Shortly thereafter, in an image reminiscent of Kurtz's feeble attempt to escape from Marlow's steamer, Conrad graphically depicts "Davidson crawling away on all fours from the murdered woman—Davidson unmanned and crushed by the idea that she had died for him in a sense" (WT, 205). The key term here is "unmanned," which harks back to the notion of the Captain's "stunned" manhood. Anne died to preserve his life, and this paramount impression prompts Davidson to take her son into his own home. Thus Anne saves him, ultimately, to lead a life of loneliness and isolation. Moreover, his solitary existence is burdened with a lingering sense of guilt, which the Captain first feels when he, alone, carries out the burial of Anne at sea:

[W]hile he was rendering these last services to the dead, the desolation of that life and the atrocious wretchedness of its end cried aloud to his compassion, whispered to him in tones of self-reproach.

He ought to have handled the warning she had given him in another way. He was convinced now that a simple display of watchfulness would have been enough to restrain that vile and cowardly crew. But the fact was that he had not quite believed that anything would be attempted. (WT, 207)

Davidson not only blames himself for Anne's death but also internalizes her desolate life and brutal murder. His self-reproach, as in the case of his doubts about Mrs. Schomberg's warning, hinges on his reluctance to acknowledge evil in the world. And so he ends up as "poor, good Davidson," in both the novel and the short story, unable to prevent harm to those he likes and inadvertently fragmenting his family by taking in Anne's son. Conrad converts Anne's characteristic laugh into a fatal sound and Davidson's trust in his wife's "natural compassion" into a "fatal move."[12] Clearly goodness can only be an absolute in a perfect world.

Davidson's rescue of Tony corresponds, to some extent, with Heyst's rescue of Lena from Zangiacomo's clutches early in Victory. That rescue likewise leads to a fatal denouement, almost as if Conrad designed both novel and short story to corroborate the old adage "The road to hell is paved with good intentions." Notwithstanding the view of many critics that Victory ends with the moral triumph of Lena, the novel is both a repudiation of nihilism and Conrad's most nihilistic work. The note to the first edition, in fact, teases us with the affirming-annihilating polarity of the book when Conrad declares that the last word he wrote for the novel was "the single word of the title" (V, vii). Here Conrad implicitly juxtaposes the title Victory with the emphatic last word of the narrative, Davidson's "Nothing!"[13] Since the novel ends with the suicide of Heyst, whom Lena has saved at the cost of her own life, can it really be a moral victory? True, Conrad does equate Heyst's characteristic detachment from the external world with a spiritual slumber, yet when he awakens he perishes, like Eliot's Prufrock drowning at the sound of human voices when he arises from sleeping. If Heyst does attain an epiphany about himself, Conrad sums it up craftily when the former grandstanding philosopher tells Lena, "I have been a disarmed man all my life as I see it now" (V, 404).[14]

Conrad's ambivalent attitude toward nihilism can even be found in the most romantic assertion in Victory: "Ah, Davidson, woe to the man whose heart has not learned while young to hope, to love—and to put its trust in life" (*V,* 410). We might be inclined to take such a statement at face value, as many critics have, if it were a passage from Keats's letters or from Coleridge's "This Lime Tree Bower My Prison," but in its context it can be read in two contradictory ways. First, it can be read as a rejection of the elder Heyst's pessimistic indoctrination of his son and, second, as a pessimistic insinuation that hoping, loving, and trusting are the province of the young, who eventually must see their illusions shattered by the calamities of adulthood. As a partial corrective to the first interpretation, consider Conrad's earlier observation that before Heyst met Lena "he had been used to think clearly and sometimes even profoundly, seeing life outside the flattering optical delusion of everlasting hope, of conventional self-deceptions, of an ever-expected happiness" (*V,* 82). Conrad recognized too well that the only thing that is ever everlasting in the human puppet show is maya. Five chapters from the end of the novel, Heyst tells Ricardo that a menacing cloud overhead may be "nothing in the end . . ." (*V,* 374). Nothing does seem to prevail in the end, for Heyst and Lena and the three emissaries from the so-called real world all die, and Davidson tells the Excellency, with more than a touch of futility in his voice: "There was nothing to be done there" (*V,* 412). Conrad's "nothing to be done" echoes in the absurd conversations of Beckett's tramps in *Waiting for Godot,* for both Conrad and Beckett recognized that those who act understand the world only dimly.

## "The End of the Tether"

As in the case of "Typhoon," interpretations of "The End of the Tether" generally pivot on the question of the Captain's culpability. Early reviewers found tragic dignity and even grandeur in the fate of Captain Whalley.[15] Yet, more than a half century after the publication of Conrad's novella, critics have discounted the poignant and touching aspects of the tale in favor of more incisive analyses of Whalley's psychological defects and spiritual myopia.[16] These critics offer valuable insights into the Captain's moral dereliction, yet this does not entirely invalidate the poignancy of Whalley's demise. Indeed, a careful inspection of Conrad's closing pages reveals that opposing elements are held in balance; sentimental and ironic implications are locked in a dynamic tension. For Conrad's text prohibits us from arriving at a definitive conclusion about Whalley's character, which is as self-contradictory as Captain MacWhirr's identity in "Typhoon."

Human personality, as in "The Secret Sharer," remains enigmatic and unknowable.

In the three conversations preceding the epilogue (between Van Wyck and Sterne, Van Wyck and the lawyer, and the lawyer and the bank manager), Conrad weaves an intricate web of rumors, half-truths, clichés, lies, and platitudes that bears scant relation to what happened on board the *Sofala* and fails to illuminate the character of Captain Whalley. Both Sterne and Van Wyck elect to conceal their knowledge of Whalley's blindness, the former suppressing evidence in a court of inquiry and the latter remaining circumspect in confidential talks. In this fashion, Conrad arranges his ironic epilogue, which details Ivy's reception of her father's posthumous letter. He focuses on the drab domesticity of Ivy's home, where her invalid husband remains out of sight, cloaked in rugs. Ivy has "no presentiment of evil" when she tears open the envelope addressed in the lawyer's handwriting. She reads the lawyer's cliché-riddled announcement that her father "is no more." Retaining her composure, Ivy tears open her father's envelope to snatch out the enclosure. The tone of Whalley's last message is pontificating yet also touching: "I am writing this while I am able yet to write legibly. I am trying hard to save for you all the money that is left; I have only kept it to serve you better. It is yours. It shall not be lost; it shall not be touched. . . . I must come to you. I must see you once more" (*Y,* 338). Though he expresses the pride of an Old Testament Jehovah, Whalley does gain sympathy with his dying wish. Ironically, the old Captain writes that God has forgotten him, yet he asks Ivy to praise God in her prayers, since the Almighty has finally ended her father's miserable life. His daughter, however, never reads beyond the first sentence of the third paragraph. Ivy remains strangely impassive: "Her eyes were dry: no cry of sorrow or whisper of thanks went up to heaven from her lips. Life had been too hard, for all the efforts of his love. It had silenced her emotions" (*Y,* 338–39). Yet in a vision she seems to see her "august and tender" father's return. There is no denying the pathos of Conrad's epilogue, as Ivy places Whalley's letter next to her heart and "remains motionless," thinking of her father. But Conrad's final lines are open to divergent interpretations: "There had been whole days when she had not thought of him at all—had no time. But she had loved him, she felt she had loved him after all" (*Y,* 339). Taken at face value, these last words crown the poignancy of the epilogue. But given the hints of Ivy's apathy in the passage, one must question the depth and sincerity of Ivy's sentimental reverie, for she may have only *felt* "she had loved him after all."

The subtle undertone of qualification at the end of the novella calls into question the relationship of Whalley and his daughter. Just as the patriarchal Captain puts blind faith in providence to assist his financial endeavors, he places blind trust in Ivy's love for him and in his power to "save" her from ruin through his earnings. Likewise, Ivy has blind faith in her father's eternal generosity, so much so that she imagines his safe return after reading of his death. Typically, Conrad divests both of these deluded believers of all certitude, for their faith exists in a vacuum. Whalley's solitary death by water corresponds to Ivy's spiritual isolation in the "southern hemisphere." To Conrad, every individual is an island with only tenuous lines of communication to the outside world. Ivy's failure to see her dead father as he really is and Whalley's failure to perceive what lies before his sightless eyes underscore Conrad's view of the pointlessness of transcendent belief. Whalley, Ivy, and even Van Wyck discover that strategies of evasion offer no solution to the problem of finitude. Everyone lives in the shadow of eventual extinction—"in the midst of life, we are in death" (Y, 271).

Conrad hints at the inadequate relationship of father and daughter as early as the first chapter, when Whalley regrets giving Ivy permission to marry the man she unluckily chose. As the lengthy flashback begins, the Captain stares at photographs of Ivy, her husband, and her two children "set in black frames"—an ominous image present every day at his table. Ivy, in the Captain's eyes, was meant to cling to him:

> He had named her Ivy because of the sound of the word, and obscurely fascinated by a vague association of ideas. She had twined herself tightly round his heart, and he intended her to cling close to her father as to a tower of strength; forgetting while she was little, that in the nature of things she would probably elect to cling to someone else. (Y, 174)

Whalley's overwhelming devotion to his daughter persists even after she leaves for Australia with her "poor stick" of a husband, whose "studied civility" earns the Captain's disfavor. Learning that Ivy's husband is now an invalid, Whalley takes pride in thinking that his daughter will cling to him forever. But Conrad implies that their relationship hinges on the old Captain's perpetual generosity and the gratification of Ivy's needs without a word of gratitude to her provider. Whalley never informs her of his problems, and he would have been "shocked" if Ivy ever thanked him for his generosity to her. When words of gratitude might produce shock, the relationship is unbalanced indeed. Conrad depicts a one-way love between father and daughter, who trust each other perfectly yet almost never see each other. What does shock Whalley, however, is the idea of Ivy using his two hundred pounds to open a boarding-house, which the Captain associates with disrepute and "rapacious" landladies. The objection to Ivy's choice of vocation arises from the Captain's "aristocratic heart of hearts." He views her decision as an indictment of his capacity to support her on a permanent basis, which is an insult to his titanic pride in his God-given vitality.

Facing an empty, lonely life, Whalley does consider taking all his savings and throwing himself on his daughter's doorstep, but he rejects this impulse as a surrender to enervation. Conrad implies that the Captain cannot rejoin his daughter because he defines his role in her life as her provider, not as her dependent. The pathos of his downfall and death, therefore, arises from his pride. The Captain cannot be honest and humble with the one individual who loves him, or so he thinks. Conrad also depicts their relationship as tainted by emphasizing the role of money, not love, in their attachment. Whalley considers his last five hundred pounds as "Ivy's money—invested in her father" (Y, 211).

As his final voyage nears its end, he reminisces about his dead wife and distant daughter. His wish to see Ivy once more is revealing: "He had been starved of love too long. He imagined her tenderness" (Y, 328). "Imagined" indeed, for Conrad provides no evidence of Ivy's previous tenderness, gratitude, or devotion to her father. Whalley may venerate his daughter simply because he thinks she resembles his dead wife. Significantly, during the crisis that precedes the ship's collision, Whalley sees only the illusion of his daughter: "In this passage of inexpressible anguish he saw her face—the face of a young girl—with an amazing strength of illusion. No, he must not give himself away after having gone so far for her sake" (Y, 329). The Captain's reluctance to yield to his infirmity stems from his fixation on an irretrievable past, on the illusion of his married daughter as "a young girl" who needs his protection. Like many of Conrad's deluded protagonists, Whalley evokes sympathy throughout his self-destructive course of action, especially when he refuses to abandon the sinking ship in the misguided belief that he is sacrificing everything for the love of Ivy. But this self-sacrificing impulse does not exonerate him from the folly of attempting to perpetuate the myth of his past achievements as "dare-devil Harry Whalley."

Conrad considerably diminishes the poignancy of Whalley's symbolic resurrection in the epilogue by undermining the Captain's character throughout the novella. He exposes Whalley's pride, particularly in connection with the fame the Captain acquired as an explorer of the South Pacific, even though his early experiences are ancient history to younger sailors. Like Tennyson's Ulysses, Whalley finds shore life tedious and desires "the illusion of affairs," not to seek a newer world but to hold fast to the comfort of his old world and preserve "the continuity of his life." Despite his religious conviction and his senti-mental attitude toward Ivy, Whalley displays a predisposition to he-donism and materialism; he takes great satisfaction in his possessions, his reputation, and his love for Ivy. After "the great failure" consumes his accumulated wealth, Whalley suddenly finds that his comforting old world has "departed," and he feels estranged from the modern age of steamers geared to a "time-table of appointed routes."

At this point, Conrad shifts the tone radically to depict the Captain as a biblical patriarch, "a lonely figure walking purposefully, with a great white beard like a pilgrim . . ." (Y, 181). Conrad calls into question Whalley's purposes from this point until the end of the tale. The Captain's unwise purposes spring from his "truly aristocratic temperament," which partially derives from his memory of his father, Colonel Whalley, who lived on "very slender means besides his pension, but with distinguished connections" (Y, 181). Captain Whal-ley accumulates the fortune his well-connected father never earned, yet after his financial ruin nothing but his aristocratic manner remains. He may still assume the "grand air" of an old admiral, but he is now "lost like a straw in the eddy of a brook amongst the swarm of brown and yellow humanity . . ." (Y, 182). Living a kind of posthumous existence, Whalley takes refuge in his sense of perpetual physical vitality: "Once rather proud of his great bodily strength, and even of his personal appearance, conscious of his worth, and firm in his rectitude, there had remained to him, like the heritage of departed prosperity, the bearing of a man who had proved himself fit in every sort of way for the life of his choice" (Y, 187). Lacking the security of financial resources, Whalley overvalues the power of his physical health to ward off the inevitable encroachments of time. He makes every effort to talk himself out of the belief that he is now "obsolete." But he can't avoid wallowing in nostalgia, and the "mental backwash" sweeps him toward the fallacy of hope. Thus, Whalley's pathetic downfall is a direct result of his decision "in the prime of life . . . to serve no one but his own auspicious Fortune" (Y, 197). Like Almayer, Willems, Lord Jim, Kurtz, and the young Marlow, he casts his fate with the shifting winds of destiny.

Whalley enters a world of hazard when he steps on board the *Sofala* to strike a deal with Massy, the ship's owner. Conrad prefigures the Captain's blindness in his depiction of the "beshrouded" vessel in the harbor. Even the canal water that Whalley crosses in making his decision has turned to pitch in the twilight. Equally ominous is the description of Whalley's return, which implies a drastic metamorphosis of his psyche: "The lofty vaults of the avenues were black—all black overhead—and the porcelain globes on the lamp-posts resembled egg-shaped pearls, gigantic and luminous, displayed in a row whose farther end seemed to sink in the distance . . ." (Y, 213). Ultimately, Whalley and the *Sofala* also "sink in the distance"—a fate hinted at by the Captain's first impression of the funereal vessel: "A laid-up steamer was a dead thing . . . as cold and still and pulseless as a corpse" (Y, 214). These ominous foreshadowings precede Whalley's succession of white lies, which he rationalizes as necessary compromises of his dignity for Ivy's sake. Concern for his daughter's welfare thus becomes a camouflage for his unwillingness to acknowledge the natural limitations of old age.

As Whalley becomes further enmeshed in a network of deceptions and self-delusions, Conrad notes that a shadow marches with the Captain, "slanting on his left hand—which in the East is a presage of evil" (Y, 215). Though Conrad depicts the sinister force as external to Whalley, the root cause of the calamity that befalls him is the Captain's hankering for command. Sterne, the mate, after deducing Whalley's blindness, mistakes the old man's indomitable will for a motive he can more readily comprehend, "the reckless perversity of avarice" (Y, 254). Whalley relives his dare-devil youth in what might be called his second childhood. But in Sterne's prejudicial view the Captain's fraud amounts to an attempt to swindle "God Almighty Himself." Whalley's "superb confidence" in his strength prompts him to take God's approval of his actions for granted: "In the midst of life we are in death, but he trusted his Maker with a still greater fearlessness—his Maker who knew his thoughts, his human affections, and his motives. His creator knew what use he was making of his health—how much he wanted it" (Y, 271). With God as a spiritual confidante, how can the Captain possibly go wrong?

Whalley's pride in his divinely endowed vitality suggests an arrogant hubris that Conrad mitigates somewhat in the poignancy of the epilogue.[17] Yet Whalley's avowal that his course of action is endorsed by God seems a minor misdeed in comparison to the base motives of the characters who surround him: the lottery-crazed Massy, the would-be usurper Sterne, the dipsomaniacal Jack, and perhaps even the antisocial Van Wyck. But Whalley misperceives their intentions, just as he misperceives his own triumph as a sacrifice for Ivy: "Captain Whalley was gazing fixedly with a rapt expression, as though he had seen his Creator's favorable decree written in mysterious characters on the wall" (Y, 291–92). To be sure, the handwriting is on the wall, but Whalley fails to decipher it long before he becomes literally blind. Only to Van Wyck, who heaps lavish praise on the Captain, does Whalley confess that his deception has recklessly endangered the ship. His conscience perverted by pride, Whalley permits self-deception to lead to outright fraud. Convinced that he does not deserve blindness and still wishing to help Ivy, he tries to deceive everyone on board, ultimately with calamitous results. Conrad's analogy of Whalley and Samson breaks down, however, for the Captain brings destruction upon himself but allows Massy, his chief enemy, to prosper from the catastrophe. Lacking the tragic nobility of Samson or Lear, Whalley now feels estranged from God, or at least from his own concept of a beneficent Creator.

Blind chance, not providence, seems to rule in Conrad's world. Earlier in the narrative, while the Captain converses with Eliott, another captain, Conrad depicts the cathedral as inaccessible: "The sacred edifice, standing in solemn isolation . . . presented a closed Gothic portal to the light and glory of the west" (Y, 198). Religion offers scant consolation to Whalley, except when he links his own stubborn resolve to God's will. Conrad makes another religious reference later in the novella when the old Captain leaves Van Wyck's house, after confessing his blindness, like "a presumptuous Titan" cast down "from his heaven" (Y, 305). The analogy is valid from one perspective but bogus from another. Like the mythical titans, Whalley revolts against an immortal decree, his failing eyesight, and suffers a fate similar to their imprisonment in the dark dungeon of Tartarus with the children of Night. But unlike Chronos and his siblings, the patriarchal Captain does not stand on an equal footing with God, though he myopically perceives his role as that of an instrument of divine will. Moreover, Conrad employs these biblical and mythological allusions to emphasize the Captain's perceptual uncertainty, a reflection of the modern individual's search for substance in a world of dissolving shadows:

> A great incertitude enveloped him. The horizon was gone; the sky mingled darkly with the sea. . . . And a frightful doubt of the reality of what he could see made even the remnant of sight that remained to him an added

torment, a pitfall always open for his miserable pretence. . . . The hand
of God was upon him, but it could not tear him away from his child.
And, as if in a nightmare of humiliation, every featureless man seemed
an enemy. (Y, 303)

Conrad often juxtaposes Whalley's spiritual bankruptcy with Massy's
"passion" for games of chance. Both characters place their trust in
invisible authorities, Whalley hoping that God will condone his "passion of paternity" and Massy dreaming of a system that will accurately
predict the winning lottery number. So while the Captain sits alone
after having fallen into the abyss, Massy searches for the lucky number
that will gratify his fierce passion for success. Conrad fills his initial
chapter with talismanic incantations of the mystical number three
(sacred to myths, magic, and Christian tradition) and accentuates
Massy's mania for numbers in the final chapters, converting the
"highway of the Far East" into a "monotonous huckster's round" for a
pathetic ship of fools (Y, 166). The Captain foolishly clings to the past
while Massy foolishly dreams of an opulent future.

Whalley's physical blindness forces him to confront his fallacious
hopes, which he had never recognized because of his moral blindness:

> [E]very moment brought home to Captain Whalley's heart the humili-
> ation of his falsehood. He had drifted into it from paternal love, from
> incredulity, from boundless trust in divine justice meted out to man's
> feelings on this earth. . . . He had caught at every hope; and when the
> evidence of his misfortune was stronger than hope, he tried not to
> believe the manifest thing.
>     In vain. In the steadily darkening universe a sinister clearness fell
> upon his ideas. In the illuminating moments of suffering he saw life,
> men, all things, the whole earth with all her burden of created nature,
> as he had never seen them before. (Y, 324)

Conrad offers no dark night of the soul leading to enlightenment, for
the ultimate "illumination" is a revelation of emptiness, not transcendence. Whalley's obstinate attachment to the imagined sources of his
security—his unfailing strength, the eternal love of Ivy, his permanent
status as provider—eventually plunges him into moral anarchy and
linguistic skepticism: "The punishment was too great for a little presumption, for a little pride. And at last he came to cling to his
deception with a fierce determination to carry it out to the end, . . .
Did words mean anything? Whence did the gift of speech come?" (Y,
324–25). Words now seem to mean nothing because Whalley has
embraced illusions as the source of order in his life. The Captain, who

in his dare-devil youth charted voyages into unknown seas, finishes his seafaring career as a figurehead on a "monotonous huckster's round." His pathetic self-deception ends when Massy's treacherous deception leads the ship to catastrophe. When these deceptions collide, Whalley experiences the "horror of incertitude" that has been shadowing him since he first stepped on board the *Sofala*. Despite the threat Whalley makes to Massy that justice must be done, the old Captain never takes advantage of his new illumination, preferring to cling to his delusion that he can still be a provider to Ivy, even in death. Thoughts of his daughter drag him down to his doom as surely as the iron pieces, evidence of Massy's treachery, that Whalley puts in his pockets to insure his drowning.

Throughout the story, Conrad intersperses pessimistic assessments of human nature to distract our attention from the defects in Whalley's character. The Captain's naive refrain—"And the world is not bad"—resounds with irony in light of the vulgarity of the men he commands. Whalley is unable to comprehend the ulterior meaning of Elliott's probing question: "Aren't you a bit tired by this time of the whole show?" (Y, 201). Conrad implies that Whalley's advanced age should cue the old Captain to renounce his addiction to the sea. Of course, Elliott is unaware of the circumstances provoking Whalley's search for employment. Like the protagonists of *Tales of Unrest*, Whalley's predicament is largely a matter of self-victimization. Conrad suggests this in a seriocomic vignette at the close of chapter 7, when he speculates on the impression the restless crew of the *Sofala* would make on an average native:

> [P]erhaps a youth fresh from a forest village, would stand motionless in the shadows of the deck listening to the endless drunken gabble. His heart would be thumping with breathless awe of white men: the arbitrary and obstinate men who pursue inflexibly their incomprehensible purposes— beings with weird intonations in the voice, moved by unaccountable feelings, actuated by inscrutable motives. (Y, 224)

The "incomprehensible purposes," "unaccountable feelings," and "inscrutable motives" of westerners are scarcely more understandable to the main characters of Conrad's story than they are to the hypothetical islander standing beyond the pale of European civilization.

Obsessed with the passage of time, Whalley, the titular leader of a ship of fools, shares Massy's pride and disillusionment. Even though Massy has lost "the vanity of possession," he fears losing a position that is no longer worth having, because it would lead to a "material" embarrassment. Just as Massy wishes to own a ship solely to enjoy the status of ownership, so the Captain wishes to remain in command despite his diminishing capabilities. The patriarchal blind man sub-scribes to a Rousseau-like view of mankind that Conrad could never endorse: "Whalley believed a disposition for good existed in every man, even if the world were not a very happy place as a whole. In the wisdom of men he had not so much confidence" (Y, 289). In contrast, Van Wyck's "sheer disgust" of what the world calls progress is more in keeping with Conrad's outlook. By allying himself with the dictates of providence, Whalley cultivates the illusion that his will transcends the fallible wisdom of humanity, and he drowns in the quixotic dream that he can permanently master his fate.

## "Il Conde"

A deceptively simple narrative that looks back to James's "The Beast in the Jungle" and forward to Thomas Mann's "Death in Venice," Conrad's "Il Conde" has been the focus of sporadic critical contro-versy.[18] The diversity of critical interpretations of the tale testifies to the intriguing complexities of a potboiler reputedly knocked off in a mere ten days. In this study, I will not attempt to reconcile these divergent interpretations but, rather, show how Conrad's opening and closing scenes mirror one another to expose the derelict sensibility of the Count. For the title character's ostensibly sentimental portrait, like that of Captain Davidson and Captain Whalley, obscures a more cynical portrait that Conrad paints beneath the surface of the narra-tive. All three protagonists, though men of the world, lack the inner resources to deal with their unique predicaments and thus fail to reconcile themselves to the chaos of experience. The Count's failure, like Whalley's, is a fatal mistake, resulting in his voluntary annihilation.

At the outset of the tale, an unidentified narrator relates his first meeting with an aged aristocrat, also nameless, who is courteously referred to as *Il Conde* by all the servants in Naples. The narrator stresses the Count's idealism, naiveté, and well-ordered lifestyle. Re-siding in Naples provides leisure and amusement for the Count, but, more importantly, it offers him the only hospitable climate for his rheumatic ailments. The narrator never learns the name or nationality of the distinguished aristocrat, though he does know that the Count thrives on a modest fortune not of his own making. When the narrator returns to Naples after ten days at the bedside of a sick friend, he finds the Count crestfallen and desperate. The old man relates the story of an "abominable adventure" that transpired in the narrator's absence. While walking up and down a "somber" alley in the *Villa Nazionale* during an outdoor concert, the Count was robbed at knifepoint by a young Italian *Cavaliere,* who abruptly vanished, angry at the small booty obtained from his victim. Taking advantage of a twenty-franc piece he had withheld from the robber, the Count attempts to satisfy his hunger at the Café Umberto. But there he once again meets the *Cavaliere,* who insults the old man for holding back the money and vows revenge. When the Count learns from Pasquale, the obsequious cigarette vendor, that the robber is a Camorra, a member of a Neapolitan secret society known for blackmail and robbery, the Count dismisses the possibility that Pasquale may be fabricating the notion and decides to leave the country as a result of this singular "outrage" to his dignity.

Conrad's ending commences as the Count finishes telling his story. Though the narrator shares the Count's sense of outrage, he still views the old man's reaction to the incident as excessive. *Il Conde* has made his choice; he has decided to cease to be, for in choosing self-exile from Naples he consciously dooms himself. Apparently only death can alleviate his sense of permanent disgrace. In the closing scene, the narrator watches the Count board the train carrying him homeward to almost certain annihilation.[19] The aged aristocrat is literally faithful to the Neapolitan adage "'See Naples and then die.' *Vedi Napoli e poi mori*" (*SS,* 289). Superficially, the narrator's final farewell to the Count is a poignant salute to a pathetic figure bent on self-destruction: "I raised my hat with the solemn feeling of paying the last tribute of respect to a funeral *cortège. Il Conde's* profile, much aged already, glided away from me in stony immobility, behind the lighted pane of glass—*Vedi Napoli e poi mori!*" (*SS,* 289). So much for Conrad's situational pathos, but what are we to make of the deeper significance of this funereal locking scene? Would Conrad scoff at favorable evaluations of the Count's character, as he did when he read the sentimental critical assessments of Captain Whalley in "The End of the Tether"? To grapple with these questions we must examine the structure of this anecdotal tale, particularly the harmonious interplay of the opening and closing scenes. A careful scrutiny of the beginning and the ending of Conrad's story casts light on what transpires in between and illuminates the faulty sensibility of the outwardly cultivated title character.

The Count's "stony immobility" in the final scene calls to mind Conrad's emphasis on "the celebrated Resting Hermes" at the outset of the story (*SS,* 269). This sculptural allusion is intriguing (literally

Hermes means "he of the stone heap") since Hermes traditionally is associated with mobility as the guide of souls to the underworld and as the patron god of travelers and thieves. Conrad links the posture of the sculpted Hermes to the Count's conventional responses to the elegance of the statue (see Carter, 58). In so doing, he implicitly identifies Il Conde with the sculpture that miraculously survived the devastation of "Herculaneum and Pompeii: that marvelous legacy of antique art whose delicate perfection has been preserved for us by the catastrophic fury of a volcano" (SS, 269). Conrad's emphasis on the statue's amazing preservation assumes greater significance when viewed in the context of Egyptian mythology, which associated Hermes with Thoth, god of letters and knowledge, and later transfigured this deity into Hermes Trismegistus (Hermes Thrice Great), the god of magic and alchemy. Thus the story's opening scene, prefaced by the epigraph Conrad reiterates at the end, "Vedi Napoli e poi mori" (SS, 269, 289), becomes a lesson in cultural anthropology, for the Count embodies the fragile symmetry of classical art.

Yet in one crucial respect the analogy breaks down. Conrad does not endow Il Conde with Hermes' role as giver of fertility.[20] Furthermore, although Conrad associates the Count with classical antiquity, he underscores the old nobleman's intense sense of foreboding as he looks at the aggressive faces of imperialistic Rome in the Museo: "[H]e had expressed his dislike of the busts and statues of the Roman emperors in the gallery of marbles: their faces were too vigorous, too pronounced for him . . ." (SS, 270). So the elderly aristocrat fears aggression yet is identified with the artifacts of ancient creativity, ironically preserved for posterity by volcanic forces of destruction. Unlike Resting Hermes, however, Conrad's "fairly intelligent man of the world" disintegrates when threatened by a hostile force. The Count assumes the downcast posture of defeat when the narrator meets him in the dining room after the robbery has transpired: "Instead of sitting erect, gazing all round with alert urbanity, he drooped over his plate" (SS, 274). And instead of emulating Mercury in repose, the devastated Count, who chooses exile, personifies civilization in full rout.

The young Cavaliere also unconsciously apes the pose of Resting Hermes. Midway in the narrative, he sits with "his head drooping on his breast. He never stirred, as though he had fallen asleep there, but . . . [h]e sat leaning forward. His elbows were propped on his knees, and his hands were rolling a cigarette. He never looked up from that occupation" (SS, 279). Like Hermes, he is an exponent of life and death, as his resemblance to sculptured marble implies when he becomes "the man on the garden seat, still leaning forward with his elbows on his knees. It was a dejected pose. In the semi-obscurity of the alley his high shirt collar and his cuffs made small patches of vivid whiteness" (*SS*, 279). After the initial disappearance of the robber, the Count collapses into another of his unconscious imitations of the statue: "He sat all in a heap, panting with the shock of the reaction" (*SS*, 283). Later that evening, in the Café Umberto, the Count again sees the robber sitting alone at a table: "The smooth olive cheeks, the red lips, the little jet-black mustache turned up gallantly, the fine black eyes a little heavy and shaded by long eyelashes, that peculiar expression of cruel discontent to be seen only in the busts of some Roman emperors—it was he, no doubt at all. But that was a type" (*SS*, 285–86). In linking the Count and the *Cavaliere* to the statue of Hermes, Conrad objectifies the opposing poles of ancient Roman culture. The discontented young thug embodies the avarice and rapacity of the Roman Empire on the rise. The Count, conversely, personifies the decadent mood of Imperial Rome during its decline, when it wallowed in smug self-indulgence.[21] Time and again, Conrad associates the elderly aristocrat with the faded grandeur of classical Rome, for the Count

> had tried various climates, . . . but the only one which suited him was the climate of the gulf of Naples. The ancient Romans, who, he pointed out to me, were men expert in the art of living, knew very well what they were doing when they built their villas on these shores. . . . They came down to this seaside in search of health, bringing with them their trains of mimes and flute-players to amuse their leisure. (*SS*, 270–71)

The Count's indulgence in relaxation and amusement imitates the frivolity of Roman hedonism: "A little amusement, as he said, is necessary for health. Mimes and flute-players, in fact. But unlike the magnates of ancient Rome, he had no affairs of the city to call him away from these moderate delights. He had no affairs at all" (*SS*, 271–72).

Conrad's description suggests much more than simply a picture of a retired gentleman with no pressing distractions. The "mimes and flute-players" associated with ancient Roman diversions and the delights of modern Naples suggest that the Count is leading a sham existence, for later Conrad links the Count's narration of his "abominable adventure" to the performance of miming: "[T]he Count . . . acted the whole thing in pantomime. . . . [H]e went through all the motions of reaching into his inside breast pocket, taking out a pocket-book, and handing it over" (SS, 282). As background music to the robbery, Conrad provides "the sweet thrilling of flutes and clarinets" (SS, 282). When the robber demands the Count's watch, the aged aristocrat acts out "the dumb show of pulling out his watch" (282). The Count conveys his refusal to part with his rings when he "repro-duced the gesture" of resignation that frustrated the robber into a premature departure. Moreover, the "tremendous crash" of the con-cert band's finale suggests the fall of the Roman Empire and its decadent civilization. The Count's "pantomimic rendering" of the robbery fits perfectly with the dissonant sounds of a concert set in the ruins of a transcontinental empire. Furthermore, after relating his story, the Count, trembling, falls back in his seat, in a grotesque parody of the Resting Hermes. Conrad's locking scene sets the stage for the aristocrat's exile from the mild Mediterranean to the harsh climate of Northern Europe. The "*train de luxe* of the International Sleeping Car Company" is a fitting site for the last pantomime of the Count, whose fossilization into "stony immobility" at the end was preordained at the beginning (SS, 289). This ancient gentleman appar-ently has been spiritually asleep his whole life.

The narrator views the self-exiled Count's train as a "funeral *cortège*," and funereal images recur throughout the story. At the outset the narrator speculates that *Il Conde* "never had any grave affairs to attend to in his life" (SS, 272). Even the lush garden where the robbery occurs suggests the oblivion of a tomblike enclosure: "This magic spot, behind the black trunks of trees and masses of inky foliage, breathed out sweet sounds mingled with bursts of brassy roar, sudden clashes of metal, and grave, vibrating thuds" (SS, 277). Such ominous sounds call to mind Matthew Arnold's "darkling plain" where "ignorant armies clash by night," and indeed Conrad does describe the concert as a chaos of noise, occasionally harmonious but more often dominated by the "disorderly murmur" of voices and shuffling feet. He also includes a Dantesque depiction of the sophisticated crowd: "Hun-dreds more sat on chairs in more or less concentric circles, receiving unflinchingly the great waves of sonority that ebbed out into the darkness" (SS, 277). This count of dubious morality stares at the crowd with "tranquil enjoyment," but he also seeks the "promise of solitude" where "the sound of the orchestra became distinctly deadened" (SS, 278). Whether the Count had hoped to lure the young thief into a homosexual encounter at the concert or whether Conrad is merely underscoring *Il Conde's* willful entry into the world of hazard, the aged aristocrat surely courts death at close quarters.

After the robbery, the Count catches sight of a streetcar that suggests a coffin of massive proportions: "A tramcar resembling a long glass box wherein people sat with their heads strongly lighted, ran along swiftly within sixty yards of the spot where he had been robbed" (*SS,* 284). This passage calls to mind Marlow's vision of the heart of darkness, but it also reinforces the perennial wisdom of the biblical adage "In the midst of life we are in death," which Conrad cites in "The End of the Tether." Following his tramcar ride to the Café Umberto, *Il Conde* confronts the *Cavaliere* for the second time, and the young man's attire (all in black, except for a "dark green bow tie") reinforces the complementary associations of death and life in the myth of Hermes. The *"train de luxe* of the International Sleeping Car Company," the luxurious flute-train of antiquity transformed into a modern funeral train, looms as the ultimate emblem of death, for the train accelerates the Count's progress toward extinction, a path he has been following for most of the tale: "He had seen it with startling thoroughness—and now he was going to his grave" (*SS,* 289).

In the closing scene Conrad stresses the self-destructive nature of the Count's decision. *Il Conde's* decision is not a spur of the moment whim; he makes his choice after spending a week in bed: "His delicate conception of his dignity was defiled by a degrading experience. He couldn't stand that. No Japanese gentleman, outraged in his exaggerated sense of honor, could have gone about his preparations for *Hara-kiri* with greater resolution. To go home really amounted to suicide for the poor Count" (*SS,* 288). Concluding, after long deliberation, that only death can amend his sense of private yet permanent disgrace, "the poor Count" forfeits his claim to our wholehearted sympathy by his extreme sensitivity. (Note that Conrad subtitled the story "A Pathetic Tale," which suggests that we should be wary of viewing the Count as a tragic victim.) If, however, the reason for his departure had been mainly fear, *Il Conde* would deserve at least some pity, for the young thug does threaten him with revenge. The reference to hara-kiri authenticates the Count's self-destructive urge, and Conrad makes a similar reference earlier in the narrative, when *Il Conde* pantomimes the story of his holdup at knifepoint: "He put the tip of his finger on a spot close under his breastbone, the very spot of the human body where a Japanese gentleman begins the operations of the *Hara-kiri,* which is a form of suicide following upon dishonor, upon an intolerable outrage to the delicacy of one's feelings" (*SS,*

279–80). Hara-kiri is an honorable suicide performed by someone who wishes to avoid disgrace. Paradoxically, it offers an escape from responsibilities but also demands great fortitude. Conrad's allusion seems appropriate, but how would news of the robbery bring disgrace upon the victim, unless, as Hughes and Steinmann have argued, the Count deliberately conceals his homosexual involvement from the narrator? To explore this question we must return to the closing scene.

In the ending, Conrad places an intriguing commentary between two references to the familiar Neapolitan adage. A close examination of this brief passage reveals one of Conrad's most characteristic themes, Western egocentrism: "'See Naples and then die.' *Vedi Napoli e poi mori*. It is a saying of excessive vanity, and everything excessive was abhorrent to the nice moderation of the poor Count. Yet, as I was seeing him off at the railway station, I thought he was behaving with singular fidelity to its conceited spirit. *Vedi Napoli!*" (*SS*, 289). By juxtaposing the "excessive vanity" of the adage with the "nice moderation" of the Count and then commenting on his "singular fidelity" to its "conceited spirit," Conrad undermines *Il Conde's* claim to authentic nobility.[22] The word *nice* is particularly ironic because it is so vacuous. In the scene in which the Count relates the story of his robbery, the narrator cites the old man's politeness and empathy: "He was very nice about my friend. Indeed, he was always nice, with the niceness of people whose hearts are genuinely humane" (*SS*, 274). Perhaps even more significantly, after the Count tells the story of his "abominable adventure," the narrator recognizes some of what lies behind *Il Conde's* sense of outrage: "He was shocked at being the selected victim, not of robbery so much as contempt. His tranquility had been wantonly desecrated. His lifelong, kindly nicety of outlook had been defaced" (*SS*, 284). The character who never earned the fortune that made his life luxurious also never stands up to the thing that threatens it. Unlike the sentimental narrator, Conrad puts the elderly "man of moderate feelings" on trial and finds him wanting.

Like Axel Heyst, the Count hopes to retire from any contact with evil in the world. But, unlike Marlow in the Congo, *Il Conde* does not recognize that human beings have merely a *choice* of nightmares. Compelled to choose between burning and rotting, he persists in his preference for a middle road that does not exist in a world of risk and contingency. Unlike Arsat in "The Lagoon," the Count dooms himself not by responding to the dictates of his cultural identity, but by overreacting to a danger that has no place in his dream world of relaxed retirement from the vicissitudes of life. Unlike the rapacious

Roman conquerors and the decadent Roman magnates, the Count takes pride in his excessive moderation as a guide to the conduct of life. But no middle way exists for an individual who rejects the world as it is. As Conrad remarked in *A Personal Record,* one must, if circumstances dictate, eat dog to survive. Depicting a Darwinian world of struggle, change, and survival of the fittest, Conrad illustrates the pathetic demise of those who are most effete. He finds scant virtue in the dismal spectacles of the blind Captain Whalley and the fastidious Count vainly attempting to keep chaos at bay. As Marlow's Mr. Stein might put it, to avoid immersion in the destructive element of life means ceasing to want to live. Thus, the vehicle speeding the fastidious Count to his doom is appropriately a plush, amply cushioned coffin.

[W]e knew we were fated, before the ebb began to run, to hear about one of Marlow's inconclusive experiences.

—Conrad, *Heart of Darkness*

If you want a happy ending, that depends, of course, on where you stop your story.

—Orson Welles, *The Big Brass Ring*

That no doubt is how the story ought to end, with . . . everything picked up into some radiant bland ambiguous higher significance, in calm of mind, all passion spent. However life, unlike art, has an irritating way of bumping and limping on, undoing conversions, casting doubt on solutions, and generally illustrating the impossibility of living happily or virtuously ever after; . . . I might take this opportunity to tie up a few loose ends, only of course loose ends can never be properly tied, one is always producing new ones. Time, like the sea, unties all knots. Judgments on people are never final, they emerge from summings up which at once suggest the need of a reconsideration. Human arrangements are nothing but loose ends and hazy reckoning, whatever art may otherwise pretend in order to console us.

—Iris Murdoch, postscript to *The Sea, The Sea*

# Coda

## Conrad's Inscrutable Sense
## of an Ending

Before physicist Werner Heisenberg patented one of the most famous catch phrases of the modern age in the context of quantum mechanics, Conrad, in the twilight of the nineteenth century, discovered the "uncertainty principle" with regard to human existence. As Jonathan Rose has observed, Joseph Conrad was more preoccupied with "the intellectual disintegration of the late nineteenth century" than any of his English contemporaries.[1] Rose argues that for a time Conrad descended into nihilism, overwhelmed by a vision of nothingness and the futility of all human action.[2] But does this temporary (or, more likely, periodic) nihilistic tendency make Conrad a nihilist? This has been a hotly debated topic in critical circles ever since J. Hillis Miller raised the specter of nihilism in his essay on Conrad's philosophical pessimism.[3] Although E. M. Forster had alluded to Conrad's alleged lack of a "creed" nearly three decades prior to Miller's study,[4] the image of Conrad as a poet of metaphysical darkness conflicts with many scholars' notion of an author who affirmed his belief in "a few simple ideas" such as fidelity and solidarity.

Actually, rather than branding Conrad's fiction nihilistic, Miller views his works as exploring nihilism and endeavoring to transcend the relativity and uncertainty of the phenomenal world:

> The aim of all Conrad's fiction is to destroy in the reader his bondage to illusion, and to give him a glimpse of the truth, however dark and

disquieting that truth may be. His work might be called an effort of demystification. It attempts to rescue man from his alienation. His problem in reaching his goal is double: to lift the veil of illusion, and to make the truth appear. (*Poets of Reality,* 18–19)

Yet what if Conrad's "truth" affirms that all we ever know is illusory? Modern individuals, in order to conceal or ignore the unknowability of existence, have imposed identifying labels on the chaos surrounding them and persistently mistake the labels for reality. Conrad's fiction, Miller asserts, dramatizes the radical disjunction between word and thing, name and phenomenon, underscoring the arbitrary relationship between the spectator and the world (47). Miller emphasizes that linguistic skepticism plays a significant role in Conrad's art of disillusionment:

Words, the medium of fiction, are a fabrication of man's intellect. They are part of the human lie. One way to define the darkness is to say that it is incompatible with language. . . . Words are a sign of man's imprisonment within illusions, but the language of fiction is the substance of a story which has no existence outside words. (36–37)

It may seem paradoxical that a writer such as Conrad, who composed more than twenty volumes of fiction, had such profound doubts about the efficacy of language. Yet I contend that the authentic nihilist would never bother to write at all, out of the conviction that all words are equally meaningless. No creative writer can be an authentic nihilist, for verbal expression is an act of affirmation, even if couched in pessimistic rhetoric.

A number of important critics have followed Miller's lead in exploring the dark side of Conrad's fiction,[5] but an especially compelling argument is offered by C. B. Cox, who views Conrad as rejecting the notion of absolute truth in favor of a relativistic perspective. Cox sees Conrad as rebelling against the Victorian presupposition that the mind can master reality, for he knew too well the inherent limitations of rationality and the incomprehensibility of experience.[6] If mental constructs are merely consoling illusions, then the universe must be absurd and meaningless (*Joseph Conrad,* 10). Placing Conrad's confrontation with nothingness in the context of the post-Darwinian pessimism that pervaded late-Victorian culture, Cox maintains that what makes Conrad distinctively modern in his response to the disintegration of values is his dedication to creating art out of incertitude (17). Conrad brings his own sense of disillusionment to the creation of literary art and prevents his readers "from resting at ease in illusion": "In Conrad's greatest works there is no conclusive resolution of meanings" (12). Out of this profound sense of pessimism, Cox asserts, Conrad fashioned an art of paradox, giving form and meaning to fiction that mirrors the formlessness and meaninglessness of life (11). Conrad frequently leads up to what could be a satisfactory resolution of a moral predicament only to frustrate the reader's expectation of an appropriate conclusion (172). Conrad's relativism defines reality in terms of what it is *not*: "Conrad does not believe that the human mind can uncover absolute truth; instead we can only substitute an ability to describe objectively the veil of appearance" (173). Nevertheless, Cox emphasizes that Conrad staunchly resists the seductions of nihilism, striving instead to affirm something in the face of nothing. Ultimately, Conrad elects to affirm humane values.

Conrad's celebrated mission to make the reader "see" also needs amplification in equally elementary terms. Conrad wanted to recreate what he himself saw, the *appearances* of his own experience, both as a participant and as a detached observer. But when he packaged his memories and recollections in language, he found that he had merely created illusory narratives. Having nothing but appearances with which to work, he nevertheless felt compelled to penetrate the veil of existential illusion with a linguistic illusion. In so doing, he became an ironic cultural historian of our belief that we can master reality. At bottom, what Conrad makes his reader see, in the words of Winnie Verloc, is that "life doesn't stand much looking into" after all (*SA*, xiii).

This bewildering blend of linguistic and epistemological skepticism can be especially discerned in a letter (14 December 1897) to R. B. Cunninghame Graham, in which Conrad responds sarcastically to the idea that Singleton, in The Nigger of the *"Narcissus,"* needs an education:

> Would you seriously . . . cultivate in that man the power to think. Then he would become conscious—and much smaller—and very unhappy. Now he is simple and great like an elemental force. Nothing can touch him but the curse of decay—the eternal decree that will extinguish the sun, the stars one by one, and in another instant shall spread a frozen darkness over the whole universe. Nothing else can touch him—he does not think.
>
> Would you seriously wish to tell such a man: "Know thyself." Understand that thou art nothing, less than a shadow, more insignificant than a drop of water in the ocean, more fleeting than the illusion of a dream. Would you? (*CL*, 1:423)

In addition to mocking the Socratic motto long cherished by Western rationalists, Conrad ridicules thought itself, ironically suggesting that human greatness resides in simple awareness. For self-knowledge leads to the paralyzing realization that each of us is "the illusion of a dream."[7] In another letter to Cunninghame Graham (31 January 1898), Conrad unleashes a tirade on the curse of human consciousness:

> Egoism is good, and altruism is good, and fidelity to nature would be the best of all, and systems could be built, and rules could be made—if we could only get rid of consciousness. What makes mankind tragic is not that they are the victims of nature, it is that they are conscious of it. To be part of the animal kingdom under the conditions of this earth is very well—but as soon as you know of your slavery the pain, the anger, the strife—the tragedy begins. We can't return to nature, since we can't change our place in it. Our refuge is in stupidity, in drunkeness [sic] of all kinds, in lies, in beliefs, in murder, thieving, reforming—in negation, in contempt—each man according to the promptings of his particular devil. There is no morality, no knowledge and no hope; there is only the consciousness of ourselves which drives us about a world that whether seen in a convex or a concave mirror is always but a vain and floating appearance. (CL, 2:30)

Identifying self-consciousness as a tragic form of slavery, Conrad views the modern individual as trapped in an unnatural world of shifting illusions, with no hope for refuge or even stability. And yet, as Conrad himself recognized, "one becomes useful only by recognizing the extent of the individual's insignificance within the arrangement of the universe" (quoted in *FRK*, 319).

In my prelude, I considered Conrad's fiction in the context of his multilingualism, his linguistic skepticism, and his suspicion concerning meaning in fiction. Now I want to consider his work as a whole with respect to the problem of narrative closure, which became a prominent and even controversial topic in literary criticism with the publication of Frank Kermode's pioneering study.[8] Kermode was not the first commentator on the subject, but he was the first to place literary endings in a broader context where literature and life overlap and myths and fictions serve as necessary illusions. In so doing, he attempts "to relate the theory of literary fictions to the theory of fictions in general . . ." (*Sense of an Ending*, 36). Endings fascinate us, Kermode maintains, because we are insatiably future-oriented: we need to know our relation to the beginning and the end at every moment (52). We need fictions to serve as illusions of order to keep chaos at bay. Moreover, our fictions must become more complex to address the increasing complexity of the world itself (67). In the modern age,

Kermode asserts, novels have become our necessary fictions, our chief source of spiritual consolation (128). And the novel must constantly reshape itself to preserve its consoling function in a rapidly changing world. Modern fictions must reflect the essence of life as patternless and mutable, and the imaginative novelist must take into account the contingencies of existence. Thus, patterns must give way to dissonance, or else the novelist falsifies reality (130). Although fictions may offer another kind of truth, Kermode contends that they must always deceive in order to fulfill their function: "The novel . . . has to lie. Words, thoughts, patterns of word and thought, are enemies of truth, if you identify that with what may be had by phenomenological reductions" (140). We turn to fictions repeatedly, hoping to find the "supreme fiction," which cannot exist, for we cannot exist in our world as "connoisseurs of chaos" (155, 164).

Nearly a decade before the publication of Kermode's study, Robert M. Adams speculated that irresolution can provide a satisfactory conclusion, in opposition to the traditional view of closure as the resolution of symbolic action.[9] Adams defines "open form" as including a major unresolved conflict that the literary artist brings into prominent display (*Strains of Discord,* 13). Challenging the traditional view of inconclusive endings as flawed artistry, Adams concludes that "openness" conveys an incongruity or disparity that is part and parcel of an artist's whole vision of life (207). In contrast to the resolution of conflict that closes a thematically unified work of art, the open form involves balancing contradictory elements (209). Thus, rather than imposing a simplified resolution of the action, the open form balances the irreconcilable complexities to bring art closer to life. Alan Friedman argues that the course of modern literature has been a gradual movement away from the closed form and toward open form.[10] He affirms that traditional literary form, with a few notable exceptions, resolves or closes off both action and theme at the end of a work. Defining a "closed novel" as a fiction that finally contains its "underlying ethical form" and an "open novel" as one that does not contain its ethical form, Friedman maintains that traditional novels enclose experience at their conclusions (*Turn of the Novel,* 16–17). In the fiction of Hardy and Conrad, Friedman detects the beginning of the shift away from closed form, preparing the way for a modern literature in which "[e]ndlessness has become an end in itself" (27–30).[11]

Offering a different perspective on the evolving form of the novel, Bernard Bergonzi asserts that "[t]he novel is concerned, above all, . . . with imposing a beginning, a middle, and an end on the flux of experience. . . ."[12] But despite this Aristotelian context, Bergonzi insists that the novel is anything but a "literary pigeon-hole" (*Situation of the Novel,* 15). He laments that

> discussion of the novel has become inevitably historicist and teleological; the early masters of the novel are seen as imperfectly pointing towards the later achievement of Flaubert and Turgenev and James. Such a teleology may be one more example of the novel's seemingly inevitable involvement with "ends"; it is very much part of the critical attitude that we associate with James and Conrad and Ford Madox Ford, and which has evolved into an academic critical orthodoxy in England and America. . . . (17)

Bergonzi takes issue with the historical view of the novel's evolution, citing the diversity of experimentation and innovation in eighteenth-century fiction, as opposed to the stagnant realism of nineteenth-century fiction. Cervantes, Fielding, and Sterne display "a comparable uncertainty about the nature of the form and its power to convey reality" which calls to mind the "epistemological skepticism" of modern novelists from Conrad to Robbe-Grillet (189). He also notes the "spectacular advance" of the modern novel from 1890 to 1930 when compared to the static inventiveness of the four decades after 1930 (19–20). The problem with the nineteenth-century novel, according to Bergonzi, is that it took itself too seriously and became trapped within its formal structures.[13] Bergonzi rightly contends that although the narrative strategies of the twentieth-century novel seem a necessary departure from nineteenth-century conventions, that departure is very much in the spirit of early novelists such as Defoe and Sterne.

The British novelist and critic David Lodge pinpoints the changing attitude toward language as contributing to the development of modernist techniques and constituting a major point of departure from the conventional forms of realistic fiction. He observes that there is a reality outside the bounds of language, but we have no means other than language by which we can describe it.[14] This problematical situation underscores the fact that realism cannot convey our sense of an increasingly complex reality (*Novelist at the Crossroads,* 33). In his explanation of the artistic shift from closed form to open endings, Lodge states that "historical changes in literary fictions correspond to historical changes in *knowledge*" (46). What curbs these changes, however, is the "conservative influence" of the audience, which resists anything more radical than gradual alteration in forms (46).

Lodge's compatriot, Malcolm Bradbury, accepts the view that "[t]raditional fiction is bankrupt," for he believes that the nineteenth-century notion of copying the external world no longer holds true as the basis for fiction.[15] Because of the modern awareness of "the contingency of fiction," its status as a verbal construct, the old conventions of narrative have lost their value (*Possibilities*, 6). Realism has been revealed as merely the pretense of an objective perspective. Unlike other forms of narrative, Bradbury insists, the novel makes what is not verifiable appear real (23). Although he identifies Sterne and Fielding as major innovators of fiction, Bradbury maintains that most of the technical breakthroughs leading to the opening of novelistic form took place just prior to the First World War (85). Attributing this shift in fictional form to the artistry of Conrad, Ford, James, Lawrence, Joyce, Woolf, and Forster, Bradbury sees the modern novel becoming even more concerned with epistemology than in previous ages: "[I]t is a mode of inquiry into the knowable, analogous in its empirical modes and methods to other forms of written inquiry" (11). Because the novel offers an empirical mode of understanding, Bradbury sees the modern novel as dramatizing the failures of traditional realism; it also documents "a deep cultural failure in communal language" (21). It is but a short step from the observation of the failure of language to the observation that all discourse is fictive, for all forms of communication partake of fictionality, to a certain degree (21). Therefore, modern readers view novels essentially as "verbal constructs" and language as the primary "order-making" system (8, 9). Language has been unmasked as sheer artifice, useful though it is in the practical matters of day-to-day living.

Critics who wish to view twentieth-century fiction as a major point of departure treat open-endedness as a radical alteration of literary form; critics who wish to see twentieth-century fiction as a continuation of traditional narrative treat open-endedness as a modification of the convention of closure. One of these latter critics, David H. Richter, opposes the glorification of open form, with its characteristic open ending.[16] On the one hand, he argues that many eighteenth-century novels feature endings that could be called "open" (*Fable's End*, 3). On the other, he finds many innovative modern novels (e.g., *A Portrait of the Artist as a Young Man* and *To the Lighthouse*) not as open-ended as some commentators believe (8). Richter also argues that aesthetically satisfying open endings represent a form of closure (4). Thus, he views twentieth-century fiction as still bound to Aristotle's tripartite division of literary art into beginning, middle, and end.

In vivid contrast to Richter, Alan Warren Friedman maintains that the term *modern* pertains not to a specific time frame or literary movement but to fiction that is open, indeterminate, and self-conscious.[17] Although Friedman's study of "multivalence" generally concerns modern multivolume narratives, he also elaborates on the multiple perspectives and reflexivity that typify novels since the era of Flaubert and James.[18] Obviously, Friedman is dealing with variations on the theme of ambivalence; he disparages "univalent" fiction, characterized by authorial intrusion and a clear-cut narrative stance, describes "ambivalent" narrative as fiction with two perspectives that produces moral confusion, and upholds "multivalent" art as transcendent because it engenders a multitude of possible perspectives (*Multivalence*, 3). Not surprisingly, he contends that most twentieth-century novels are multivalent, for they dramatize multiple, conflicting perspectives and rarely indicate the author's moral standpoint (x). These multivalent works exhibit two primary characteristics: "(1) a self-conscious awareness of itself as artifact, . . . and (2) a counterpointing of conflicting ethical stances" (25). Furthermore, Friedman argues that multivalent narratives deal with the elusiveness of truth and the illusory quality of absolute moral standpoints (14). Absolute ethical perspectives are limited epistemological viewpoints, which the multivalent novelist mocks via "deliberate counterpointing" of "opposing moral stands" (4). Because reality is bewilderingly amorphous and no moral perspective is absolutely valid, the reader must participate in the creative process to keep the irreconcilable opposites in a state of dynamic tension (27).

Friedman also indicates how the modern sense of an ending has become congenitally pluralistic as a result of the opening up of literary form:

> The genre is further complicated by the multiple possibilities for resolving the moral conflicts that arise. The simplest (and least "modern") is to appoint a definitive moral spokesman. . . . More problematical approaches deploy participant narrators . . . offering their only partially acceptable attempts at resolutions, or ironic commentators . . . offering theirs. Or else a confused protagonist/narrator will wind up mired deeper in confusion than ever . . . or actually attain something resembling a moral resolution . . . though only a temporary and partial one because it remains in flux. Or such works may reflect a stripping away, a negating of the central perspective, and an affirming (if at all) only by implication . . . or their partially self-validating resolutions may remain counterpoised against each other, none of them ever simply acceptable or rejectable. . . . (*Multivalence*, 26–27)

By cataloging the variations of prominent endings, Friedman has documented the organic relationship between the complexities of modern literature and the confusions of modern existence. His listing of "problematical approaches" to narrative resolution mirrors the various artistic strategies employed by Conrad in the stories I have already discussed. No matter whether the narrator is participant or protagonist or remains outside the confines of the action, Conrad refuses to validate any resolution of the conflict. Even though a locking scene may seem conclusive in isolation from the rest of the narrative, considered as a whole the narrative does not wholeheartedly affirm a particular final perspective.

D. A. Miller takes a more radical antiteleological stand in his approach to closure than the most avant-garde postmodernist.[19] Yet he asserts that even in the traditional novel of the nineteenth century one can find "self-betraying contradictions" in the sense of an ending (*Narrative and Its Discontents,* 281). In Miller's view, endings repress narrative flow rather than crown the novel's achievement. He puts aside matters of closed artistic form and the randomness of life to concentrate on "the principles of production and the claims of closure to a resolved meaning" (xi). Miller offers a concrete definition of *closure,* but he devaluates its importance, emphasizing "the *functions* of an ending: to justify the cessation of narrative and to complete the meaning of what has gone before" (xi). He argues that closure never governs the meaning of a narrative, via "end-determination"; "novels do not 'build' toward closure" but reach their terminus almost as if the ending were a "wholly arbitrary imposition" (xiii–xiv). Miller also maintains that closure actually suppresses the narrative, rather than putting it at rest, and thus the association of "closural disclosures" and artistic truth is fallacious (97–98). To Miller, genuine closure remains in the realm of the impossible, so the narrative often seems suspended (xi). All closure is artificial since the narrative cannot produce the terms that would insure its arrest: "These must be imported from elsewhere, from a world untouched by the conditions of narratability. Yet as soon as such a world is invoked in the novels—its appearance is necessarily brief—its authority is put into doubt by the system of narrative itself" (266–67). Closure may imply resolution, but it never completely resolves narrative conflicts, so it remains a pretense (267).

In modern literature every telling has a tailing, to borrow Joyce's words, and Miller contends that every ending is "a retrospective illusion" that organizes the narrative material "into a meaningful pattern. Indeed, twentieth-century narrative theory usually assumes that *telos* produces the meaningfulness of narrative in the first place" (241–42). Thus, the emphasis of twentieth-century narrative method on "the priority of ending, or narrative closure," seems an unfounded assumption (xiii). Miller issues a warning against all criticism that isolates closure from the rest of the artistic product:

> Once the ending is enshrined as an all-embracing cause in which the elements of a narrative find their ultimate justification, it is difficult for analysis to assert anything short of total coherence. One is barred even from suspecting possible discontinuities between closure and the narrative movement preceding it, not to mention possible contradictions and ambiguities within closure itself. (xiii)

Miller's stress on "discontinuities" and his caution regarding a teleological reading of narrative have a special pertinence with regard to Conrad's fiction, which not only tends to subvert final disclosures but also to mock the goal-orientation of the Western psyche. I consider Conrad's art nonteleological rather than antiteleological because his fiction does not invalidate endings but rather holds endings and the narratives that lead up to them in dynamic tension. Marlow's lie to the Intended, his ode to the East in "Youth," and the captain's new self-confidence at the end of "The Secret Sharer" are all vital elements in the narrative. But none of these endings should be taken at face value or as Conrad's final judgment on the action.

Even though the specious distinction between closed and open form has finally been abandoned, endings are still a problematical issue in critical circles, and several scholarly journals have devoted special issues to the topic of closure.[20] Peter Brooks, in his rehabilitation of the disparaged concept of plot, has stressed narrative endings as an important ingredient in determining the meaning of literary works.[21] In his scrutiny of modernist and postmodernist literature, Brooks finds that closure has become the Godot of narrative. Waiting for the end has become the new conventional ending.[22] Brooks considers the diminishing of the narrative ending a conclusive device in the context of the increasing fragmentation, self-reflexive ironies, arbitrariness, and playfulness of the post-Flaubertian modern novel (*Reading for the Plot,* 317). All these narrational developments have only increased the burden that falls to the reader of twentieth-century literature. Complicated endings may baffle or disappoint readers, who must retrace the narrative from the end backward in order to construct meaning (323). Perhaps this is what Conrad really meant when he said that he wanted to "make" the reader "see"—to compel the reader to shoulder the burden of interpretation and understanding. (Conrad was but one of several major modern authors who resorted to narrative ambiguity, suggesting one kind of ending while hinting at another.) But the conventional late-Victorian reader of fiction surely was not prepared to play such a role. The modern reader, on the other hand, can no longer remain a passive receiver of the author's message, for the signal has been scrambled and must be unscrambled before it can be comprehended. Indeed, the process of scrambling and unscrambling may be what we now mean by "reading," if we accept that "the medium is the message." The reader must read from beginning to end and then retrace the author's steps from end to beginning. Conrad's endings are not all red herrings, but neither are they definitive, which is one reason why meticulous rereading is essential in coming to grips with the issues embedded in his fiction.

Conrad's short fiction frustrates the Western reader's efforts to reach a comfortable conclusion, and yet his stories address multitudes of such readers. Thus, he often provides counterfeit endings that seem to offer a consoling and satisfying denouement while nevertheless conflicting with other elements in the discourse. The endings of "The Secret Sharer," "Typhoon," "The Return," "The Partner," "The Idi-ots," and "Il Conde" exhibit this bogus quality. But in other tales he seems more concerned with inverting or reversing the main thrust of the narrative and offers a conclusion that runs contrary to the reader's expectations, as in "Falk," "Youth," *Heart of Darkness,* "A Smile of Fortune," "The Planter of Malata," and "Because of the Dollars." Writers of Conrad's era and readers of our era would respond to the conflicting perspectives, not to the tempting illusion of a univocal summation. On other occasions, his stories close in an enigmatic or ironic fashion, often with two irreconcilable perspectives held in dynamic tension, as in *The Shadow Line,* "An Outpost of Progress," "The Informer," "Karain," "The Inn of the Two Witches," "The Lagoon," and "The End of the Tether." But it would be a mistake to apply these distinctions rigidly. If Conrad's sense of an ending is "inscrutable," it is not because we fail to fathom his meaning but because he provides multiple meanings through the strategic employment of his closing scenes and epilogues. In a sense, Conrad is his own deconstructionist, and his fiction celebrates indeterminacy.

In this study I have analyzed in detail nineteen of Conrad's best or most problematical short fictions, but his other tales deserve a brief mention here. Three tales feature rather conventional epilogues. "An Anarchist" wallows in pathos and despair, with only one striking element in its ending: a rather cryptic Hawthornesque statement affirming that anarchists have warm hearts and weak heads.[23] Another tale of endured suffering, "Prince Roman" has at least one note of irony embedded in its sentimentality. Although the Prince returns from exile to become a valuable member of his community, his daughter and son-in-law consider him a "poor judge of men": "They think that I let myself be guided too much by mere sentiment" (*TH,* 55). "The Tale" has an epilogue that returns to the point of departure in the narrative, as the commanding officer reveals to his lover that he was the man who sent the Northman and his ship to their doom in the story he has related to her. The epilogue concludes on a strong note of moral indeterminacy, yet it is tarnished by the woman's stock sentimental response.[24] Two stories display a kind of bland circularity in their conclusions. "Gaspar Ruiz," the stuff of popular magazine fiction, stresses melodrama and sentimentality in the symbolic reincarnation of Gaspar in his daughter, Erminia.[25] "The Brute" is an anecdotal potboiler that opens and closes with the narrator's smile and glance at "Miss Blank," the barmaid.

The other stories all make use of closing scenes but not successfully enough to merit being called locking scenes, in the sense of *Heart of Darkness* and "The Secret Sharer." "The Black Mate" (Conrad's first tale, though published almost two decades after its original composition) emphasizes deception throughout the narrative and features a surprise ending. Bunter has been dyeing his hair black, but now his wife's legacy makes his charade unnecessary. Its final scene focuses on Bunter's superstitious Captain, who has devils on the brain, according to his sister (*TH,* 120). The melodramatic conclusion of "Tomorrow" anticipates the "madness and despair" refrain of *The Secret Agent* in depicting Bessie Carvil's victimization by the three men in her life. In the closing scene, Conrad portrays Bessie as a latter-day tenant of Dante's inferno, where hope is another word for madness.[26] The implausibly happy closing scene of "The Duel" partly reconciles the tension of the plot yet does contain one significant irony: Feraud persists in his animosity toward D'Hubert and nostalgically recollects the old days of the Napoleonic wars, never realizing that D'Hubert is now supporting him financially. In "Freya of the Seven Isles," the closing conversation between the narrator and "old Nelson (or Nielsen)" comes close to being an authentic locking scene, but it has minimal dramatic impact. Nelson seems "senile and childish at the same time" (*TLS,* 233), but ironically he keeps telling the narrator that Freya was too "sensible" to have really loved Jasper. Yet the narrator views Freya, like Bessie Carvil, as "vanquished in her struggle with three men's absurdities" (*TLS,* 238). When he finally tells Nelson that she died for love, the self-deluded old man can only sob in despair, "And I thought that she was so sensible" (*TLS*, 238).[27] Finally, the closing scene in "The Warrior's Soul" employs a poignant but pathetic tableau as Tomassov silently contemplates the body of DeCastel, whom he has killed as a way of discharging his debt to the French officer. Although Conrad emphasizes Tomassov's "warrior" soul and his exile after the killing, DeCastel, before he is shot, calls Tomassov a "milksop." This tale inspired Conrad's revealing statement in a letter to Pinker: "The story I believe is quite sufficiently developed for Mag[azine] Pub[lication]. I'll work on it for book form" (cited in *LG*, 166). Conrad's comment may suggest only that he was apologizing for the mediocrity of "The Warrior's Soul," but it may also show that Conrad viewed magazine stories as a quick way to put bread on his table, to be followed by more painstaking artistic editing when assembling the magazine pieces for publication in book form.

The conclusion to the partly autobiographical "Amy Foster" deserves a bit more commentary, for it offers not only a poignant account of Amy's abandonment of Yanko and his death but also an ironic perspective on divergent human responses to cultural differences. Doctor Kennedy, who narrates the last few pages of the story, rightly expresses concern for his fatal patient, Yanko, whom he describes as "a wild creature under the net . . . a bird caught in a snare" (*T*, 141). At this point Yanko is once again speaking English after raving in his own language during his fever, but his wife is no longer there to hear his desperate communication, and he dies with the English word "merciful" on his lips. The exile had hoped to establish a new life in England, but he becomes trapped in the net of an alien culture, the snare of a foreign language. While Kennedy feels empathy for Yanko, Amy Foster's father, whom the doctor meets at the end of the story, interprets Yanko's demise as a blessing in disguise—a callous view shared by Amy herself, who never speaks of the husband by whom she conceived a child. Like Gaspar Ruiz, Yanko seems reincarnated in his offspring, for Johnny has affinities with his dead father: his frightened "big black eyes" display "his fluttered air of a bird in a snare" (*T*, 142). Although Johnny is Yanko's namesake, he is known as "Amy Foster's boy." Yanko lives on through Amy's son, yet she has exiled the memory of her husband from her conscience: "[H]is memory seems to have vanished from her dull brain as a shadow passes away upon a white screen" (*T*, 142). Conrad ends his tale by juxtaposing Kennedy's appreciation of Yanko's loneliness and despair with Amy's passionate maternal tenderness in ministering to her son. In this

narrative one can detect Conrad's own ambivalence about his departure from Poland as a youth and his establishment in England as a
novelist writing in a language other than his native tongue.

It is difficult to summarize Conrad's narrative endgames definitively, since my analysis has cast doubt on the validity of any conclusion articulated through the imperfect medium of language. Because
I have argued that Conrad recognized that language is "a wilderness
of words," it would be insincere to build here a cozy log cabin of
semantic certainty. Furthermore, although the study of narrative has
made a significant contribution to the study of fiction by distinguishing
between story and discourse, Conrad's novels and tales, particularly
those with subversive endings, demonstrate that discourse, rather than
imposing meaning on the events narrated, can only express a fictive
meaning. Conrad sensed not only that language is unable to encompass or interpret experience but also that language only interprets
itself. Words have no real referents outside the wilderness of words.
Linguistic skepticism was much in the air among intellectuals of
Conrad's time, but readers continued to cling to the shelter of language and to yearn for fiction that would provide vicarious pleasures
and tidy conclusions reinforcing the platitudes of the day. Ultimately,
Conrad found himself writing for two audiences: the convention-bound
reading public and innovative fellow authors such as Crane, James,
and Ford, who viewed definitive endings as an artificial imposition on
the ceaseless flux of human existence.[28] In Conrad's best tales, he
satisfies both audiences. A former colleague once told me that although his students enjoy reading and discussing literature they nevertheless wish that the answers were printed in the back of the book,
as in a mathematics text. The endings of Conrad's short stories do not
provide such definitive answers, and his steadfast refusal to endorse
"a few simple ideas" in his epilogues and locking scenes coincides
with our late-twentieth-century preoccupation with incertitude and
instability, making Joseph Conrad, Poland's English genius, our contemporary.

# Notes

## Prelude

### The Language of Fiction and the Fiction of Language

1. Words such as *wonder, illusion, enchantment, ghostly, shadowy, magic,* and *spell* reverberate throughout his novels and tales.

2. Ford Madox Ford, whose recollections are not always reliable, testified to Conrad's love-hate relationship with the English language. See, in particular, his *Joseph Conrad: A Personal Remembrance* (London: Duckworth, 1924), 214–15, and *Return to Yesterday* (New York and London: Liveright, 1932), 216–17, 282–88. In the last twenty years critics have made up for the initial lack of emphasis on Conrad's attitude toward language.

3. As Frederick R. Karl has pointed out, Conrad's use of a multitude of narrators, outside observers, letters, diaries, journals, and other means of reporting events in his fiction testifies to his imaginative attempt to understand and recapture the past (*FRK,* 458).

4. As Jeremy Hawthorn, *Joseph Conrad: Language and Fictional Self-Consciousness* (Lincoln: University of Nebraska Press, 1979), has noted: "General questions about the relationship between thought and language, about the difference between writing and speech, about the oddity of language constituting both a means to communication and also the medium of knowledge, these perhaps all occur more readily to the polyglot, and certainly can be found congealed into the substance of Conrad's fiction. They lead on, almost inevitably, to a curiosity about fiction, about . . . what novels are and what they do. . . . " (xi).

5. Ian Watt notes that Conrad's frequent use of the word *illusion* testifies to his "philosophical skepticism" (*IW,* 248). Indeed, two of his earliest stories, "The Lagoon" and "Youth," end with the word *illusions.*

6. For valuable insights into Conrad's complex cultural background (in addition to *FRK,* 7–121, and *ZN,* 3–38, the best biographical sources), see *IW,* 1–33, and Brian Spittles, *Joseph Conrad—Text and Context: Writers in Their Time Series* (New York: St. Martin's, 1992), 1–28.

7. Conrad noted in a letter to Edward Garnett (20 January 1900) that his father specialized in Oriental studies and philology at St. Petersburg University but left without a degree (*CL,* 2:246).

8. With regard to Conrad's multilingual background, Karl observes: "Such awareness of the limits of languages and their cross-fertilization was excellent preparation for a man who would create a distinctive cadence and rhythm in English, as different from the practices of his predecessors as Joyce's and Woolf's were from theirs" (*FRK,* 91).

9. Bernard C. Meyer makes an interesting point with regard to Conrad's adoption of English: "That in the telling of his tales Conrad confined himself to an alien tongue is not surprising in view of his recurring quest for a new

identity. . . . [T]he English language served an important and probably indispensable function in Conrad's writing, for it aided him in placing a psychological distance between the dramas of his fictional world and their origins within the memories and experiences of his unhappy past" (*BCM*, 359).

10. Zdzisław Najder casts doubt on Conrad's public pronouncements on his choice of language: "It is true that his English was not a matter of 'adoption' but simply a result of partly accidental turns his life had taken. Nevertheless, Conrad wished to infuse his life, and particularly the public aspect of it that he regarded as most precious—his works of fiction—with the sense of an overriding purposefulness; he did not want the tricky problem of language . . . to appear to have been determined by external circumstances" (*ZN*, 115–17). See also *FRK*, 191, and *ZN*, 222–23, 231.

11. See *IW*, 186, for an interesting commentary on Conrad's attitude toward "the quasi-magical power of words."

12. In "The Gift of Tongues: The Languages of Joseph Conrad," *Conradiana* 15 (1983): 83–109, Martin S. Ray contends that Conrad's polyglot background made him aware of language as a provisional representation of reality. This contradicts Flaubert's reliance on *le mot juste,* to which Conrad gave lip service, perhaps hoping to deny his recognition of the true nature of language (101).

13. Although I find none of the explanations for Conrad's decision to write in English absolutely compelling, Karl makes a good point in emphasizing that Conrad's long service on British ships and his need to master English for his maritime examinations may have had a continuing effect in his writing career (*FRK*, 191). Najder likewise stresses the "external circumstances" that led to Conrad's adoption of English, but he also notes that English seems to have a rich vocabulary when compared to the Polish language (*ZN*, 115–17).

14. Werner Senn, *Conrad's Narrative Voice* (Bern: Francke Verlag, 1980), even argues that Conrad was attracted to English because the "very indirectness of expression, through the polysemy and varied connnotations of English words, offered both a challenge and a unique opportunity to his unique talent" (17).

15. Ray, "Language and Silence in the Novels of Joseph Conrad," *Conradiana* 16 (1984): 19–40, makes a similar point in distinguishing between the requirements of language in Conrad's two professions. To a sailor language is a precise instrument, whereas to an artist language offers a way of capturing "the fleeting and evanescent impressions of an imaginatively apprehended reality" (28).

16. Even toward the end of his life, in his preface to *The Shorter Tales of Joseph Conrad* (Garden City, N.Y.: Doubleday, Page, 1924), he maintained that his stories are the result of "much conscious thought bearing not only on the problems of their style but upon their relation to life as I have known it, and on the nature of my reactions to the particular instances as well as to the general tenor of my personal experience" (vi).

17. Senn argues that Conrad's technique paradoxically strives for both "evocation and evasion" (*Conrad's Narrative Voice*, 10).

18. Hawthorn affirms that "few writers are more conscious than Conrad that a word is only a word, and can be trusted, distrusted, falsified, denied, amplified, and corrected. . . . For Conrad the sign, and particularly the word, is a fascinating and complex thing, and the relationship between sign and referent engages his almost obsessive attention. . . . In the course of his investigation into the nature of the sign Conrad asks questions not only about language, but about that professional use of language which constitutes fiction (*Joseph Conrad,* 5, 6).

19. Although the theoretical statements in Conrad's correspondence are more spontaneous than his deliberate affirmations in his other published writings, such as his prefaces, one could argue that they do offer insight into the mind of a literary artist in the throes of creation, unlike the declarations of an author surveying his work in retrospect. (Consider the distancing factor in James's prefaces, for example.)

20. The male protagonist of "The Return" personifies this tendency when he becomes virtually a linguistic puppet: "The sound of that sentence evidently possessed some magical power, because, as soon as he had spoken, he felt wonderfully at ease; . . . [h]e watched the effect of his words. . . . He listened to himself with solemn emotion. It seemed to him that the room, that every word and every gesture had the importance of events preordained from the beginning of all things, and summing up in their finality the whole purpose of creation" (*TU,* 149–50).

21. At the close of *An Outcast of the Islands*, Willems experiences a revelation of the futility of words. But the truth, at least in his case, does not set him free. Instead, it fetters him to an all-pervasive sense of emptiness: "Speech, action, anger, forgiveness, all appeared to him alike useless and vain, appeared to him unsatisfactory, not worth the effort of hand or brain that was needed to give them effect. . . . The breath of his words, of the very words he spoke, fanned the spark of divine folly in his breast . . ." (*OI,* 272, 273). Conrad's association of language and breath is not a frivolous linkage, since our word *spirit* derives from a root word meaning "wind." Therefore, words are inspiriting in a dual sense; when an individual is deprived of a cherished verbal illusion the result is spiritual deflation, as in the case of Willems.

22. The epithets applied to Heyst in *Victory* serve a similar purpose, undermining the convenient compartmentalization of the phenomenal world.

23. In *The Rhetoric of Joseph Conrad* (Amherst, Mass.: Amherst College Press, 1960), one of the significant early studies of Conrad's attitude toward language, James L. Guetti Jr. has argued that Conrad envisioned an unbridgeable chasm between experience and linguistic expression. And if experience cannot be communicated in meaningful terms, then truth always remains inexpressible. Guetti concludes that "[t]he world of Conrad's rhetoric is a world that in its uncertainty seems between the experiences and the meaning of life. . . ." (47). Even more pointedly, William W. Bonney declares that "Conrad's texts . . . invite interpretation at the same time they discredit it, while concommitantly admitting nevertheless that the discredited activity is

inevitable. Interpretation, like all perception, involves the sporadic, alogical displacement of one word by another under the reigning illusion that the whole process involves the rational, purposeful substitution of equals for equals, opposites for opposites" (*WWB*, 199). Along similar lines, Senn argues that Conrad employs a radical "logoskepticism" that emphasizes semantic ambiguity and incertitude to suggest the futility of authentic communication. Furthermore, Senn affirms that Conrad's linguistic skepticism prompted him to manipulate "semantic indeterminacy" in order "to evoke that sense of bafflement that stimulates active, imaginative inquiry and interpretation but also discourages all hope of ultimate and complete success" (*Conrad's Narrative Voice*, 35). Ray observes that Conrad was frustrated in his Flaubertian quest for *le mot juste* by his consciousness of the arbitrariness of language ("Gift of Tongues," 101). He also affirms that the amorphous quality of language in general contributed to the undermining of Conrad's confidence in his writing, just as his decision to write in English made him aware of the duplicity of any particular language (98).

24. G. Jean-Aubrey, *Joseph Conrad: Life and Letters* (Garden City, N.Y.: Doubleday, Page, 1927), 2:288.

25. Moreover, Hawthorn argues that Conrad's distrust of language prompted his skeptical scrutiny of the function and value of not only language but also fiction, which is, of course, entirely made up of duplicitous words (*Joseph Conrad*, 2). Hawthorn finds a conspicuous semantic ambiguity in early works such as *Lord Jim* and *Heart of Darkness* "culminating in the most self-conscious of Conrad's novels, *Under Western Eyes*," in which Conrad examines the language of fiction for what it purports to express as well as for what it fails to express, and he concludes that "in grappling with these questions Conrad is also grappling directly with the usefulness and morality of fiction itself, with, in short, the worth of his second vocation" (103). Hawthorn claims that ultimately Conrad's fiction calls into question the very nature of self-consciousness.

26. In a revealing letter to the *New York Times "Saturday Review"* (2 August 1901), the still-evolving artist gave vent to a miniature manifesto on the state of fiction at the turn of the century:

> [I]n the sphere of an art dealing with a subject matter whose origin and end are alike unknown there is no possible conclusion. The only indisputable truth in life is our ignorance. Besides this there is nothing evident, nothing absolute, nothing uncontradicted; there is no principle, no instinct, no impulse that can stand alone at the beginning of things and look confidently to the end. . . .
>
> The only legitimate basis of creative work lies in the ourageous recognition of all the irreconcilable antagonisms that make our life so enigmatic, so burdensome, so fascinating, so dangerous—so full of hope. They exist! And this is the only fundamental truth of fiction. (*CL*, 2:348–49)

27. "On Truth and Lie in an Extra-Moral Sense," in *The Portable Nietzsche*, trans. Walter Kaufmann (New York: Viking, 1968), 42–47. In a letter to Helen Sanderson (22 July 1899) Conrad evinces his awareness of the German philosopher and iconoclast when he refers to the "mad individualism of Nietsche" (*CL*, 2:188).

28. See, in particular, George J. Worth, "Conrad's Debt to Maupassant in the Preface to *The Nigger of the 'Narcissus,'*" *Journal of English and Germanic Philology* 54 (1955): 700–704; Paul Kirschner, *Conrad: The Psychologist as Artist* (Edinburgh: Oliver and Boyd, 1968): 191–229; and Yves Hervouet, "Conrad and Maupassant: An Investigation into Conrad's Creative Process," *Conradiana* 14 (1982): 83–111.

29. See especially Elsa Nettels, *James and Conrad* (Athens: University of Georgia Press, 1977).

30. James almost seems to echo Conrad's remarks in his preface to *Roderick Hudson* in *The Art of the Novel* (New York: Scribner, 1962): "Really, universally, relations stop nowhere, and the exquisite problem of the artist is eternally but to draw, by a geometry of his own, the circle within which they shall happily *appear* to do so. He is in the perpetual predicament that the continuity of things is the whole matter, for him, of comedy and tragedy; that this continuity is never, by the space of an instant or an inch, broken, and that, to do anything at all, he has at once intensely to consult and intensely to ignore it" (5).

31. To give but a few examples: "Daisy Miller" concludes with the revelation of Daisy's primal innocence, but the source of this revelation is Giovanelli, whose veracity is hardly irrefutable. The closing scene in *The American* offers one of James's earliest renunciation tableaux, yet Christopher Newman's sudden glance at the letter being consumed by the fire calls into question his status as a really "good man" who cannot ruin the Bellegardes. *The Bostonians* also ends on an ambivalent note as Verena professes her happiness despite the tears she sheds and James's narrator ominously predicts that her marriage to Ransom will occasion more weeping in the years to come. *The Turn of the Screw*, of course, offers James's most illustrious example of an ambiguous denouement, for critics are still trying to determine not only whether the ghosts exist outside the governess's mind but also whether Miles actually dies at the end. In the final scene of *The Sacred Fount*, the narrator's fabricated theories concerning human psychology collapse like a house of cards when Mrs. Briss tells him he is "crazy." "The Jolly Corner" also subverts the action of the story when Alice assures Bryden that the phantom he has encountered bears no relation to his excessively introverted personality. Yet the evidence in the story points to Bryden's psychological double as an embodiment of his own egocentrism.

32. Once again, a few examples must suffice: "The Bride Comes to Yellow Sky," with its surprising, ironic conclusion (almost in the manner of O. Henry), inverts the reader's conventional expectation when the Wild-Western shootout never materializes and the purported desperado walks off into the sunset without firing a shot at the lawman he has threatened to kill. Along

similar lines, but in a more serious context, "The Open Boat" juxtaposes the dramatic rescue on shore with the lamentable spectacle of the drowned oiler, who had heroically volunteered to take extra turns at the oars. Crane further undermines the saving of the other desperate men by referring to the "sinister hospitality" of the land, suggesting that their extermination has not been canceled but merely postponed. "The Monster" presents an even more jaundiced view of human existence in its final chapter as the aptly named Grace cries over the fifteen empty cups at the tea party no one attended. Crane uses the racial prejudice of the townspeople as the foundation for his indictment of institutional Christianity and hypocritical Western culture. Likewise, the conclusion of *Maggie: A Girl of the Streets* mocks the facade of Christian piety that conceals a self-serving egocentrism when Mary Johnson tearfully announces her forgiveness of the dead daughter she had scorned throughout her life. But the most intriguing of Crane's ironic endgames appears in "The Blue Hotel," a story that provides its own critical commentary in the form of a conversation between the cowboy and the easterner in a retrospective epilogue. The easterner's hyperbolic rationalization of their mutual complicity in the death of the Swede prompts the cowboy's simplistic protestation of innocence, but neither character has clear insight into the forces that determined the Swede's murder. In this, as in so many of Crane's (and Conrad's) stories, we are risking deception by accepting the point of view of any single character. Conrad was indeed correct in calling Crane a "slippery" artist.

33. With regard to both life and literature, Conrad affirmed that he had remained steadfast to a personal "view that rejects all formulas, dogmas and principles of other people's making. These are only a web of illusions" (quoted in *FRK*, 363).

34. In reference to what he calls the Conradian "technique of evocation and evasion," Albert Guerard, *Conrad the Novelist* (Cambridge: Harvard University Press, 1958), notes that Conrad resorted to a wide variety of artistic strategies as a "conscious and deliberate means of controlling the reader's responses, of manipulating his feelings. And this is what sets Conrad apart from any earlier English novelist: his creation of conflict in the reader, and his fine control of that conflict" (59). In *The Deceptive Text: An Introduction to Covert Plots* (Sussex: Harvester, 1984), Cedric Watts uses the term "Janiform" to describe novels such as *Heart of Darkness,* which feature a conclusion that only accentuates the problems of the narrative "and turns us back, searching more anxiously into the novel's meaning" (14). He argues that modern fiction offers structures that challenge linearity in order to dramatize "a kind of epistemological and moral schizophrenia" (15). Watts sees Conrad's fiction in this light, and I tend to concur.

35. Speaking of Ford's charge that the endings of some of Conrad's best novels seem contrived and unimpressive because they display "an artistic reversal of their earlier parts," Karl contends that "[a]brupt endings or summary conclusions characterize many of [Conrad's] novels, or else the pacing of the later sections follows a different time sequencing from what the reader

had been prepared for in earlier parts" (*FRK*, 557). While the pressures of serialization may have played a role in the formulation of Conrad's endings and these endings do not seem to provide a satisfactory denouement from an ordinary reader's viewpoint, I believe that Conrad was deliberately challenging the whole notion of conventional closure in his novels and short fiction. He was too much of an iconoclast to adopt any narrative formula.

36. Barbara Hernstein Smith, *Poetic Closure: A Study of How Poems End* (Chicago: University of Chicago Press, 1968).

37. In this same context, Smith states that closure "announces and justifies the absence of further development; it reinforces the feeling of finality, completion, and composure which we value in all works of art; and it gives ultimate unity and coherence to the reader's experience of the poem by providing a point from which all the preceding elements may be viewed comprehensively and their relations grasped as part of a significant design" (*Poetic Closure*, 36).

38. Smith adds that "when universals and absolutes (words such as 'all,' 'none,' 'only,' and 'always') occur in assertions, they are themselves the expressions of the speaker's inability or refusal to qualify. And we may add superlatives to this category, for they have the same expressive effect. To speak of what is 'highest,' 'last,' 'best,' or 'most' is, of course, also to assert extremities, absolutes, and ultimates. All such nonqualifying words and phrases tend to have closural effects when they occur as terminal features in an utterance or poem, for they not only reinforce our sense of the speaker's conviction but are themselves expressions of comprehensiveness, climax, or finality" (*Poetic Closure*, 183).

39. She concludes that "[w]here conviction is seen as self-delusion and all last words are lies, the only resolution may be in the affirmation of irresolution, and conclusiveness may be seen as not only less honest but *less stable* than inconclusiveness" (*Poetic Closure*, 240–41).

40. Marianna Torgovnick, *Closure in the Novel* (Princeton, N.J.: Princeton University Press, 1985).

41. Among the novels Torgovnick links to the epilogue device are *Tom Jones, Jane Eyre, Wuthering Heights, Vanity Fair, Madame Bovary, Middlemarch, War and Peace, The Way of All Flesh, Women in Love, Light in August,* and *The Sound and the Fury.*

42. She notes that "A circular ending may suggest growth and change in a character . . . or it may show stagnation or stasis in a character. . . . It may return to the novel's initial themes in order to resolve them . . . to repeat them . . . or to reaffirm an ambivalence developed throughout the novel . . ." (*Closure in the Novel*, 199).

43. In *The Turn of the Novel* (New York: Oxford University Press, 1966), Alan Friedman charts the course of modern literature as a gradual movement away from the closed form and toward open form. He argues that traditional literary form, with a few notable exceptions, resolved or closed off both action and themes at the end of a work (xv). Defining a "closed novel" as a work that contains its "underlying ethical form" and an "open novel" as a

work that does not contain its ethical form, Friedman maintains that traditional novels enclose experience at their conclusions (16–17). In the fiction of Hardy and Conrad, Friedman sees the beginning of the shift away from closed form, preparing the way for a modern literature in which "[e]ndlessness has become an end in itself" (27–30).

44. In *Conrad's Endings: A Study of the Five Major Novels* (Ann Arbor: University of Michigan Press, 1984), Davidson argues that "each of his novels achieves a characteristically Conradian sense of an ending by incorporating into its conclusion the very impossibility of conclusion that necessarily compromises the task of writing an ending or of writing definitively about one" (5).

45. For example, Jeremy Hawthorn, *Joseph Conrad: Narrative Technique and Ideological Commitment* (London: Edward Arnold, 1990), devotes three of his ten chapters to Conrad's shorter works (*Heart of Darkness*, "An Outpost of Progress," and "The Tale"), although he does refer to a few other stories in passing.

## 1: First Command

1. The tale has been institutionalized as a seminal work in the doppelgänger tradition, which includes Poe's "William Wilson," Dostoevsky's *The Double*, Wilde's *The Picture of Dorian Gray*, and Stevenson's *Doctor Jekyll and Mr. Hyde*. Conrad made this categorization inevitable with his incremental repetition of phrases such as "my double," "my other self," "my secret self," "the secret sharer," and "my second self," which appear on more than thirty occasions in the story. For an insightful commentary on Conrad's exploration of the self in this story and related fiction, see, in particular, chapter 1 ("The Journey Within") of Albert Guerard's *Conrad the Novelist* (1–59) and Meyer's chapter on "The Secret Sharers" in *BCM* (154–67).

2. See, in particular, Carl Benson, "Conrad's Two Stories of Initiation," *PMLA* 69 (1954): 46–56; Louis H. Leiter, "Echo Structures: Conrad's 'The Secret Sharer,'" *Twentieth Century Literature* 5 (1960): 159–75; Charles G. Hoffmann, "Point of View in 'The Secret Sharer,'" *College English* 23 (1962): 651–54; Robert A. Day, "The Rebirth of Leggatt," *Literature and Psychology* 13 (1963): 74–81; Daniel Curley, "The Writer and the Use of Material: The Case of 'The Secret Sharer,'" *Modern Fiction Studies* 13 (1967): 179–94; Gloria R. Dussinger, "'The Secret Sharer': Conrad's Psychological Study," *Texas Studies in Language and Literature* 10 (1969): 559–608; Mary-Lou Schenck, "Seamanship in Conrad's 'The Secret Sharer,'" *Criticism* 15 (1973): 1–15; H. M. Daleski, *Joseph Conrad: The Way of Dispossession* (New York: Holmes and Meier, 1976), 171–83; Terry Otten, "The Fall and After in 'The Secret Sharer,'" *Southern Humanities Review* 12 (1978): 221–30; and Joan E. Steiner, "Conrad's 'The Secret Sharer': Complexities of the Doubling Relationship," *Conradiana* 12 (1980): 173–86.

3. See, for example, Porter Williams Jr., "The Matter of Conscience in Conrad's 'The Secret Sharer,'" *PMLA* 79 (1964): 626–30; J. D. O'Hara, "Unlearned Lessons in 'The Secret Sharer,'" *College English* 26 (1965):

444–50; Robert D. Wyatt, "Joseph Conrad's 'The Secret Sharer': Point of View and Mistaken Identities," *Conradiana* 5 (1973), 12–26; Frank B. Evans, "The Nautical Metaphor in 'The Secret Sharer,'" *Conradiana* 7 (1975): 3–16; and David Eggenschwiler, "Narcissus in 'The Secret Sharer': A Secondary Point of View," *Conradiana* 11 (1979): 23–40.

4. The discovery of the floating hat is a weakness in the story, according to Daleski, "for it makes [the narrator's] achievement of knowledge too much a matter of chance—and turns the highest kind of seamanship into a tightrope of contingency" (*Joseph Conrad,* 183). He does suggest, however, that the hat represents the narrator's pity for Leggatt, which ultimately saves the novice captain.

5. Daleski atttributes the "moral blurring" of the captain's sense of duty to "Conrad's preoccupation with the psychological aspects of his story, the preoccupation clearly revealing itself in the title of the story and the numerous references in the tale itself to second selves and doubles. His concern, indeed, is with the coexistence in the individual psyche of radically opposed qualities" (*Joseph Conrad,* 174).

6. Jakob Lothe, *Conrad's Narrative Method* (Oxford: Clarendon, 1989), also sees the closing scene as part of the "circular movement" of the story and adds that "[t]he ending of 'The Secret Sharer' places a renewed emphasis on the importance of the visual" with regard to the hat and the looming mass of Koh-ring (64). He contends that the suspense of the final scene distracts us from a full realization of the serious moral problem of the captain's dereliction of his duties in order to save Leggatt (65). Thus, the moral ambiguity of the narrative remains unresolved.

7. Norman Sherry, *Conrad's Eastern World* (Cambridge: Cambridge University Press, 1966), notes that the *Paknam* was a ship commanded by Captain Joshua Lingard, an exponent of European dominion in the Orient (116–17).

8. Symbolicaly, the pagoda (a Far Eastern version of the Buddhist Stupa, or ceremonial burial mound) projects the transiency and uncertainty of existence and consecrates the wisdom of Buddha as the sole means of deliverance from the beguilements of time. Conrad refers to the Paknam pagoda frequently in his three tales of first command: "Falk," "The Secret Sharer," and *The Shadow Line*.

9. Guerard points out that "in Jungian psychology a hat, in dreams, represents the personality, which can be transferred symbolically to another" (*Conrad the Novelist,* 25).

10. Leggatt, like Jim, is a parson's son who dreads the thought of his father learning of his disgrace. The narrator's reminding of Leggatt that "[w]e are not living in a boy's adventure tale" (*TLS,* 131) calls to mind Jim's adolescent romantic dreams of adventure both before and during his first voyage. And just as Jim protests against the idea that his desertion of the *Patna* could be fairly judged by a rational court of inquiry, Leggatt also questions the validity of any supposedly impartial jury: "What can they know whether I am guilty or not—or of *what* I am guilty either? That's my affair" (*TLS,* 131–32).

Leggatt thanks the narrator for his compassion and empathy in language echoing Jim's similar gratitude to Marlow: "It's a great satisfaction to have got somebody to understand. You seem to have been there on purpose. . . . It's very wonderful" (*TLS*, 132). Wonderful, indeed, for to Marlow Jim is "one of us," and to the narrator of "The Secret Sharer" Leggatt seems his "own reflection" (*TLS*, 101). Small wonder, then, that the captain risks everything to assist the fugitive's escape from arrest on the charge of manslaughter, just as Marlow makes every effort to find Jim a position far away from gossip about the *Patna* incident.

11. Conrad also links Jim's desertion of the *Patna* to the dark cloud of unknowing that approaches the ship just before the catastrophe. He uses a similar dark cloud for much the same purpose in *The Shadow Line* and likewise Koh-ring as an omen of the captain's disastrous course in "The Secret Sharer."

12. Conrad delights in playing games with hats and heads. He uses incongruous hats as emblems of absurd anarchic sensibilities in *The Secret Agent*, a cartwheel hat to objectify the harlequin's manic-depressive temperment in *Heart of Darkness*, and the "rakkishly hatted head" of the "old ruffian" as an index of a yarn-spinner's crochety personality in "The Partner." For a discussion of Conrad's playful use of hats, see William Bysshe Stein, "*The Secret Agent*: The Agon(ie)s of the Word," *boundary 2* 6 (Winter 1978): 521–40.

13. For example, Lawrence Graver calls "Falk" a "curious" tale that "lacks the suggestiveness of stories like 'Heart of Darkness' and 'The Shadow-Line' with which it has so much in common" (*LG*, 104). Karl sees at the story's core a simple contrast of Hermann's "bourgeoise reactions" and Falk's "primitive hungers. A potentially large theme, it is dissipated in the conclusion to the cannibalistic episode . . . in which the taboo of eating man's flesh never achieves the intensity [Conrad] is striving for" (*FRK*, 513).

14. Stanton de Voren Hoffman, in *Comedy and Form in the Fiction of Joseph Conrad* (The Hague: Mouton, 1969), considers "Falk" a burlesque comedy that "is anti-problem, anti-experience, anti-initiation, the reflection of a strong and frequently unchecked nihilism" (112). See also Edward Said, *Joseph Conrad and the Fiction of Autobiography* (Cambridge: Harvard University Press, 1966), 104–14; Daniel R. Schwarz, "The Significance of the Narrator in Conrad's 'Falk: A Reminiscence,'" *Tennessee Studies in Literature* 16 (1971): 103–10; Joel R. Kehler, "The Centrality of the Narrator in Conrad's 'Falk,'" *Conradiana* 6 (1974), 19–30; Deirdre David, "Selfhood and Language in 'The Return' and 'Falk,'" *Conradiana* 8 (1974): 137–47; and *WWB*, 19–21.

15. David, Bonney, Kehler, and Schwarz emphasize the tension between civilization and atavism, but Bonney goes a step further in contending that Falk never really transcends civilization, and therefore the narrator's optimistic conclusion is ironic (*WWB*, 19). David is at the opposite extreme in her contention that "Falk is permitted to live happily ever after with the girl of his choice. In short, 'Falk' is a fairy tale" ("Selfhood and Language," 137). This

runs counter to the rather gloomy view of the married couple at the beginning of the story, which must be contrasted with the more affirmative view of Falk and his beloved at the end. Walter E. Anderson, "'Falk': Conrad's Tale of Evolution," *Studies in Short Fiction* 25 (1988), 101–8, goes to the utmost extreme, however, contending that the Hermann family is distant from the "corrupt world," for they "embody civic virtues so long taken for granted that nearly all notions of our remote beginnings on this planet have been relegated to their collective unconscious" (104). This view does not take into account Hermann's regarding his niece as extra baggage on the voyage back to Europe.

16. In addition to David, Webster, Bonney, and Kehler, see also Bruce Johnson, *Conrad's Models of Mind* (Minneapolis: University of Minnesota Press, 1971), 52–53, 130–35; Paul Kirschner, *Conrad: The Psychologist as Artist,* 267–69; and Tony Tanner, "'Gnawed Bones' and 'Artless Tales'—Eating and Narrative in Conrad," in *Joseph Conrad: A Commemoration,* ed. Norman Sherry (London: Macmillan, 1976), 17–36. All of the above discuss "Falk" as a dramatization of Schopenhauer's will to live.

17. Stephen K. Land, *Conrad and the Paradox of Plot* (London: Macmillan, 1984), misses this point entirely, largely because he focuses on the title character and ignores the role of the narrator when he says that "Falk" features "one of Conrad's rare happy endings" (97).

18. J. S. Farmer and W. E. Henley, *Slang and Its Analogues* (1890–1904; reprint, New York: Arno, 1970), 7:76.

19. Both Schwarz ("Significance of the Narrator)" and Kehler ("Centrality of the Narrator") focus on the problematical nature of the narrator. David ("Selfhood and Language"), in stark contrast, mostly ignores the narrator's role in the story.

20. Kehler argues that the narrator's appreciation of the physical attractions of Hermann's niece borders on "potential for lechery" ("Centrality of the Narrator," 27).

21. In *Thorns and Arabesques*, William W. Bonney argues that the pagoda represents an authority superior to that of Falk or the narrator, namely, the metaphysical concept of Annihilation, which is the final measure of human experience (*WWB,* 19–21). But Bruce Johnson, "Conrad's 'Falk': Manuscript and Meaning," *Modern Language Quarterly* 26 (1965): 267–84, contends that the pagoda references do not constitute an endorsement of Buddhism.

22. For similar views of the story as a drama of initiation, see also Benson, "Conrad's Two Stories of Initiation," 46–56; Jerome Zuckerman, "The Architecture of *The Shadow-Line,*" *Conradiana* 3 (1971–72): 87–92; Daniel R. Schwarz, "Achieving Self-Command: Theme and Value in Conrad's *The Shadow-Line,*" *Renascence* 29 (Spring 1977): 131–41; and Jeremy Hawthorn, introduction to *The Shadow-Line* (Oxford and New York: Oxford University Press, 1985), vii–xxv. Ian Watt takes a more philosophical view of the narrator's "moral initiation" in "Story and Idea in Conrad's 'The Shadow-Line,'" *Critical Quarterly* 2 (1960): 133–48.

23. Said argues that the narrator's ordeal teaches him the real meaning of being himself: "to cross the line of shadowy, unrealized ambitions into a sort

of restricted, terrible reality . . . that always falls short of those ambitions" (*Joseph Conrad*, 186).

24. Hawthorn briefly touches upon Conrad's use of divinity figures (Introduction, xiii–xix) and sees Ransome as Christlike—an interpretation that adds to the irony of his parting ways with the narrator at the end of the tale. He also associates Burns with hell, though the mate lacks the satanic implications of a Kurtz (xv).

25. Speaking of the "mutability and indeterminacy" of Conrad's central metaphor, Watt observes that "[a] shadow-line is not a definite boundary that one crosses consciously, whether in space, like a line of longitude, or in time: Conrad isn't dealing with the rather obvious temporal indicators of adulthood . . . yet although it is mysterious and elusive, projected almost at random through the chance collisions of the individual with his endlessly varying environment, it has a compelling universality" ("Story and Idea," 137). J. Bakker, "Crossing the Shadow-Line," *Dutch Quarterly Review of Anglo American Letters* 5 (1975): 195–205, asserts that Conrad's metaphor "not only indicates the transitory stage between youth and maturity, but on a deeper symbolic level also signifies the shadowy stage of the primordial struggle of being over non-being" (203).

26. Though Ransome's departure at the end of *The Shadow Line* does not have the same impact as Scratchy Wilson's refusal to shoot Potter in Crane's "The Bride Comes to Yellow Sky" or compare to the simultaneous redemption and extinction of little Miles in James's *The Turn of the Screw*, it does function in a similar way to surprise us, until we reread the narrative once again and realize that Conrad has prepared this moment well in advance.

27. Said interprets Ransome's departure as a reminder to the narrator "of the spiritual compromise that each man must unashamedly make with his life" (*Joseph Conrad*, 194). In contrast, Land claims that "[t]he Captain's reluctant parting with Ransome is significant of his own conquest of the impulse to withdraw fearfully from life" (*Conrad and the Paradox of Plot*, 217).

28. According to Watt, the narrator achieves only a "severely qualified victory": "There is no heroic finality; and in the narrator's last interview with Giles we can find no warrant for believing that the shadow-line is crossed once and forever: we are never . . . in the clear; nor are the forces of inertia ever wholly vanquished" ("Story and Idea," 145–46).

29. Defending himself against the charge of supernaturalism in *The Shadow Line*, Conrad in his author's note stated that "[t]he world of the living contains enough marvels and mysteries as it is; marvels and mysteries acting upon our emotions and intelligence in ways so inexplicable that it would almost seems to justify the conception of life as an enchanted state" (vii).

30. The chief steward's plaintive "Oh, dear! Oh, dear!" echoes the White Rabbit's "Oh dear! I shall be too late!" in *Alice in Wonderland*. Furthermore, the steward's room contains "piles of cardboard boxes" suggestive of Carroll's preposterous compartmentalizations and the White Knight's invention of a bottomless box. At times, the steward adopts the pose of Humpty-Dumpty, spewing "nonsense" with only "the top of his head" visible. And in a scene

that mimics the illogicality of the Mad Tea Party, he expresses "dismay" at the narrator's request for accomodations, even though "there were plenty of vacant rooms" (SL, 10). The narrator most resembles the enchanted Alice during his interview in Captain Ellis's office when he says, "I felt a heaviness of limbs as if they had grown bigger since I had sat down on that chair" (SL, 32). His statement calls to mind Alice's many physical alterations in Wonderland.

31. Bakker comments that in the final conversation with Captain Giles, "the narrator's initial feeling of being different and superior, the kind of feeling not unusual for a man who has gone through a major emotional upheaval, is adequately toned down by the older man's mature skepticism" ("Crossing the Shadow-Line," 205). Contrarily, Land maintains that the conversation demonstrates that "the [narrator] has abandoned his initial pose of inexplicable detachment and has engaged himself fully in the demands of his calling. . . . [H]e triumphs in the end, presumably because . . . he finally abandons his withdrawal from the world and resumes his career in the mainstream of life" (Conrad and the Paradox of Plot, 218). I tend to concur with Bakker's view.

32. Conrad once wrote Cunninghame Graham (14 January 1898) that "salvation lies in being illogical" (CL, 2:17).

33. Zuckerman acknowledges Ransome's status as "the perfect sailor," yet he notes that Conrad's emphasis on his weak heart suggests human limitation and imperfection, and thus Ransome serves as a more complex role model for the narrator than many critics have recognized ("Architecture of The Shadow-Line," 91).

34. Paradoxically, or perhaps self-contradictorily, Hawthorn argues that The Shadow Line shows "the inescapable limitations of any human attempt to control human destiny" and yet suggests that "mankind must not rely on magic or benevolent gods, but must act as if we have the key to our own fate" (Introduction, xviii). I contend that Conrad iconoclastically strips away all vestiges of higher authority—superstition, religion, science, and even Emersonian self-reliance—in divesting the narrator of all spiritual consolations on his voyage across the shadow line.

35. Speaking of the narrator's plunge to "the lowest possible level of self-esteem" during the voyage, Benson views the narrative as charting the transition from egocentrism to a compassionate recognition of the importance of human solidarity: "The resolution is accomplished by the captain's acceptance of his role in the human society, a society forever characterized by evils and weaknesses as well as by ideals. Indeed, in Conrad's world spiritual strength is conditioned by and can grow only from the acknowledgement of the pervasiveness of human frailty and evil" ("Conrad's Two Stories of Initiation," 52).

## 2: The Clash of Nebulous Ideas

1. For arguments in favor of Marlow's maturation, see N. V. M. Gonzales, "Time as Sovereign: A Reading of Joseph Conrad's 'Youth,'" Literary

*Apprentice* 17 (1954), 106–22; J. Oates Smith, "The Existential Comedy of Conrad's 'Youth,'" *Renascence* 16 (1963), 22–28; V. J. Emmett Jr., "'Youth': Its Place in Conrad's *Oevre*," *Connecticut Review* 4 (1970), 49–58; and Paul Bruss, *Conrad's Early Sea Fiction* (Lewisburg, Pa.: Bucknell University Press, 1979), 58–69. For negative assessments of Marlow's actions and opinions, see Walter F. Wright, *Romance and Tragedy in Joseph Conrad* (Lincoln: University of Nebraska Press, 1949), 9–12; Murray Krieger, "Conrad's 'Youth': A Naive Opening to Art and Life," *College English* 20 (1959), 275–80; John Howard Wills, "A Neglected Masterpiece: Conrad's 'Youth,'" *Texas Studies in Literature and Language* 4 (1962), 591–601; John Crawford, "Another Look at 'Youth,'" *Research Studies* 37 (1969), 154–56; James W. Mathews, "Ironic Symbolism in Conrad's 'Youth,'" *Studies in Short Fiction*, 2 (1972), 117–23; and John Howard Weston, "'Youth': Conrad's Irony and Time's Darkness," *Studies in Short Fiction* 11 (1974), 399–407.

2. Mathews calls attention to Conrad's framework, which "creates a deceptive contrast between two perspectives" and does not render meaning directly ("Ironic Symblism," 117). Moreover, he maintains that the narrative implies "the inefficacy of the Christian religion in developing man's self-knowledge" (119). Krieger explores Conrad's tactical irresolution, but from the standpoint of artistic form. In his view, Conrad aims for a meaning that must remain ineffable. Thus, there can be no triumphant conclusion that would substantiate a simple code but only a dilemma that resonates with indefiniteness and irresolution ("Conrad's 'Youth,'" 278).

3. See Leo Gurko, *Joseph Conrad: Giant in Exile* (New York: Macmillan, 1962), 79–82.

4. Oddly enough, Conrad employs this image in a serious context in a letter to Edward Garnett (23–24 March 1896): "If we are 'ever becoming—never being' then I would be a fool if I tried to become this thing rather than that; for I know well that I never will be anything. I would rather grasp the solid satisfaction of my wrong-headedness and shake my fist at the idiotic mystery of Heaven" (*CL,* 1:268).

5. For an analysis of Conrad's biblical allusions in the tale, see Lloyd S. Thomas, "Conrad's 'Jury Rig' Use of the Bible in 'Youth,'" *Studies in Short Fiction* 17 (1980), 79–82.

6. Buddhists consider watchfulness and alertness among the supreme virtues. See, for example, the Dhammapada, chapters 2, 13, and 21.

7. In a letter to E. L. Sanderson (12 October 1899), Conrad writes: "I am incorrigible; I will always look to another day to bring something something [sic] good, something one would like to share with a friend—something—if only a fortunate thought. But the days bring nothing at all—and thus they go by empty-handed—till the last day of all. I am always looking forward to some date to some event: when I finish this; before I begin that other thing—and there never seems to be any breathing time, not because I do much but because the toil is great" (*CL,* 2:203–4).

8. A letter to Marguerite Poradowska (20 July? 1894 ) offers another example of Conrad's own concern with the irretrievable past: "I well under-

stand this yearning for the past which vanishes little by little, marking its route in tombs and regrets. Only that goes on forever. . . . Man must drag the ball and chain of his individuality to the very end. It is the [price] one pays for the infernal and divine privilege of thought; consequently, it is only the elect who are convicts in this life—the glorious company of those who understand and who lament but who tread the earth amid a multitude of ghosts with maniacal gestures, with idiotic grimaces" (*CL,* 1:162–63; translated from the French by Karl and Davies).

9. William W. Bonney argues that the central word *youth* fragments the notion of a continuum of potential human growth, and therefore Marlow can only react cynically at the thought of a temporal period that has been annihilated by the flux of time itself (*WWB,* 25).

10. Jocelyn Baines details Conrad's familiarity with Flaubert's works in *Joseph Conrad: A Critical Biography* (New York: McGraw-Hill, 1960), 145–48, although never specifically mentioning *Bouvard et Pecuchet.*

11. A. T. Tolley, "Conrad's Favorite Story," *Studies in Short Fiction* 3 (1966), 314–20, observes that "[o]ne of the chief points of the story is the vulnerability of apparently well-established patterns of thought and behavior" (317).

12. Although I dispute his notion that the narrator is "the major figure of the tale," Daniel R. Schwarz, *Conrad:* Almayer's Folly *to* Under Western Eyes (Ithaca, N.Y.: Cornell University Press, 1980), is correct in his assessment that Kayerts and Carlier "can only function within highly organised bureaucratic structures in which individuality has lost its meaning" (26).

13. Jacob Lothe argues that "[n]ot only is the reader's first impression strongly dependent on the pointed ending; rereading 'An Outpost of Progress' we find that much in its main textual body is oriented towards the ending and takes on additional meaning if read in the light of it" (*Conrad's Narrative Method,* 46). He is not very specific about this additional meaning, although he does note that "the deterioration and downfall of Kayerts and Carlier are strongly connected with their trade duties and the setting in which they are placed by trade" (53). Land views the final scene as an abbreviated "version of the usual Conradian ending, in which a figure from the hero's former world arrives to pass (in this case merely to witness) judgment" (*Conrad and the Paradox of Plot,* 41). Conrad's work, however, resists such formulaic interpretations.

14. In "A Textual History of Conrad's 'An Outpost of Progress,'" *Conradiana* 9 (1979): 143–63, Robert W. Hobson points out that Conrad capitalizes "Director" consistently in the autograph manuscript, even though there is some inconsistency in the book version of the story (156).

15. Referring to "Kayerts's pose in death," Katharine Rising, "The Complex Death of Kayerts," *Conradiana* 23 (1991): 157–69, says that "Conrad has made him a perverse Christ, a victim less than submissive to his god, the long-awaited director. Godot arrives, but too late" (163).

16. Lawrence Graver makes this point when he notes the similarity of Kayerts and Carlier and Flaubert's Bouvard and Pecuchet (*LG,* 11).

17. This passage calls to mind the final scene in "Karain," in which Jackson marvels at the unreality of the bustling activity on the hectic city's streets. The compulsive actions of these urban dwellers strikes Jackson (and Conrad) as fundamentally illusory (*TU*, 54–55).

18. Ian Watt presents a cogent discussion of Conrad's distrust of abstract language in relation to the locking scene involving Marlow and the Intended (*IW*, 244–46).

19. I take issue with H. M. Daleski, who contends that Conrad "bungled" the final scene and did not adequately prepare for it: "Marlow's lie . . . obstinately remains an ordinary white lie" (*Joseph Conrad*, 75).

20. The meaning of Marlow's lie, and indeed of his entire narrative, particularly with regard to the function of language, has become a popular topic in Conrad studies. See, for example, Jerome Meckier, "The Truth about Marlow," *Studies in Short Fiction* 19 (1982): 373–79; Henry Staten, "Conrad's Mortal Word," *Critical Inquiry* 12 (1986): 720–40; Nina Pelikan Straus, "The Exclusion of the Intended from Secret Sharing in Conrad's *Heart of Darkness*," *Novel* 20 (1987): 123–37; Fred L. Milne, "Marlow's Lie and the Intended: Civilization as the Lie in *Heart of Darkness*," *Arizona Quarterly* 44 (1988): 106–12; Thomas Loe, "*Heart of Darkness* and the Form of the Short Novel," *Conradiana* 20 (1988): 33–44; and Eric Trethewey, "Language, Experience, and Selfhood in Conrad's *Heart of Darkness*," *Southern Humanities Review* 22 (1988): 101–11.

21. See Lee M. Whitehead, "The Active Voice and the Passive Eye: *Heart of Darkness* and Nietzsche's *The Birth of Tragedy*," *Conradiana* 7 (1975): 121–35. Eloise Knapp Hay, *The Political Novels of Joseph Conrad: A Critical Study* (Chicago and London: University of Chicago Press, 1963), points out that Conrad is indebted to Nietzsche for one major theme in *Heart of Darkness*: "that civilization depends for its conquest of the earth on a combination of lies and forgetfulness" (153).

22. Friedrich Nietzsche, "On the Prejudices of Philosophers," in *Beyond Good and Evil*, trans. Walter Kauffmann (New York: Random House, 1966), 9–32.

23. See, in particular, George Butte, "What Silenus Knew: Conrad's Uneasy Debt to Nietzsche," *Comparative Literature* 41 (1989): 155–69.

24. Watt notes that the "gap between the verbal sign and its meaning" is obtrusive in modern literature and that a characteristic of modern literature is its separation of the presentation of events and the reader's need to see "larger connecting meanings" in them (*IW*, 197). Nowhere are these gaps more obtrusive than in *Heart of Darkness*, which emphasizes the absence of those "larger connecting meanings."

25. Djuna Barnes, *Nightwood* (New York: New Directions, 1937), 129, 136.

26. In connection with Kurtz's celebrated final cry, I think it is essential to consider Conrad's quasi-nihilistic response to Cunninghame Graham, in his letter of 15 June 1898, concerning imperialism in Africa. The whole passage is in French, the language of the Belgian agents in the Congo (translated by Frederick R. Karl): "There are no converts to ideas of honour, justice, pity,

freedom. There are only people who, without knowledge, understanding, or feeling, drive themselves into a frenzy with words, repeat them, shout them out, imagine they believe in them—without believing in anything but profit, personal advantage, satisfied vanity. And words fly away, and nothing remains, do you understand? Absolutely nothing, oh foolish man! Nothing. A moment, a wink of the eye and nothing remains—only a drop of mud, cold mud, dead mud cast into black space, rolling around an extinguished sun. Nothing. Neither thought, nor sound, nor soul. Nothing" (CL, 2:70). No more eloquent exegesis of "The Horror! The horror!" could be imagined.

27. Hay makes a sound point when she asserts "that the male world of civilized Europe no less than the woman's world is entirely 'out of it.' The house of the Intended in the final scene . . . is a good image for the 'house' of all Europe" (Political Novels of Joseph Conrad, 151). Similarly, C. B. Cox, Joseph Conrad: The Modern Imagination (London: Dent, 1974), defends the artistic merit of the confrontation scene by saying that Marlow's lie is appropriate because the Intended is as hypocritical as the European civilization that nurtured her. She has transformed Kurtz into a false ideal through her devotion, and "this self-deception is a psychological necessity for her" (58).

28. Bruce Henricksen, Nomadic Voices: Conrad and the Subject of Narrative (Urbana and Chicago: University of Illinois Press, 1992), argues that "Kurtz is not a character in the traditional sense" (66). For Marlow constructs Kurtz's identity out of fragments of information, the opinions of others, and a brief encounter with a dying man in the wilderness. Thus, he "is lent a bogus or tentative selfhood in Marlow's enunciations" (66).

29. In his illuminating chapter on Heart of Darkness ("An Unreadable Report") in Reading for the Plot: Design and Intention in Narrative (New York: Random House, 1985), 238–63, Peter Brooks correctly points out that "[t]o present 'the Horror!' as articulation of that wisdom lying in wait at the end of the tale, at journey's end and life's end, is to make a mockery of storytelling and ethics, or to gull one's listeners—as Marlow himself seems to realize when he finds that he cannot repeat Kurtz's last words to the Intended, but must rather cover them up by a conventional ending. . . ." (250).

30. I have discussed this topic at some length in "'Dead in the Centre': Conrad's Confrontation with Nothingness," Studies in the Humanities 5 (1976): 38–43.

31. Mark A. Wollaeger, Joseph Conrad and the Fictions of Skepticism (Stanford, Calif.: Stanford University Press, 1990), aptly notes that "[a]lthough Marlow's lie to the Intended imposes the false closure of popular romance on a radically inconclusive story . . . the act of narration that constitutes the greatest part of the novella issues as a response to the lie he once told. Retelling his story within Kurtz's, Marlow rescues what meaning he can from the corruption of Kurtz's idealism" (76).

32. In "Lying as Dying in Heart of Darkness," PMLA 95 (1980): 319–31, Garrett Stewart observes that "Marlow realizes the double nature of language, its power to illuminate and ennoble but also to corrupt, and he imagines Kurtz as a disembodied annunciation of this very duality" (321). Stewart also

notes that the awkward namelessness of Kurtz's fiancée focuses attention on her epithet ("the Intended"), which "seems to incarnate in her all the original Kurtz's best blind intentions, [and] admits her even more readily than otherwise into the sphere of his searing universal revelation: . . . A lie that would liquidate the tragedy, Marlow's fib exposes the lie of idealism that generates it" (326). George E. Montag, "Marlow Tells the Truth: The Nature of Evil in *Heart of Darkness*," *Conradiana* 3 (1971–72): 93–97, and James Ellis, "Kurtz's Voice: The Intended as 'The Horror!'" *English Literature in Transition* 19 (1976): 105–10, both identify Kurtz's fiancée as representative of his unfulfilled ambitions and of his horrified reaction to that realization.

33. In contrast, Juliet McLauchlan, "The 'Value' and 'Significance' of *Heart of Darkness*," *Conradiana* 15 (1983): 3–21, links the superimposed image of Kurtz on his Intended to the "undoubted" moral victory resulting from Kurtz's struggle with himself and condemnation of his actions (10). She calls this image the "moral center" of the novella, but this familiar, upbeat interpretation hinges on a literal acceptance of Marlow's favorable interpretation of Kurtz's alleged final words. McLauchlan's reading is weakened, however, by her blanket generalization that there is "no inherent falsity in words. Falsity supervenes only when words are not realized in appropriate action" (17).

34. According to Henricksen, "[s]ince Kurtz's history remains a matter of speculation, it is impossible to know and evaluate him with the kind of narrative knowledge that questions of identity and selfhood normally require. . . . Kurtz is curiously without a story that we can know with any certainty" ("Nomadic Voices," 54).

35. William Bysshe Stein emphasizes Marlow's journey toward selflessness in three articles dealing with Conrad's oriental affinities: "The Lotus Posture and *Heart of Darkness*," *Modern Fiction Studies* 2 (1956–57): 167–70; "Buddhism and *The Heart of Darkness*," *The Western Humanities Review* 2 (1957): 281–85; and "*The Heart of Darkness*: A Bodhisattva Scenario," *Orient/ West Magazine* 9 (1964): 39–52.

36. Stewart contends that Marlow's final words ("too dark—too dark altogether") apply not only to the Intended but to himself as well, and thus he represses "the tragic truth" of Kurtz's end so that he may return to civilization ("Lying as Dying," 328). If so, then this repression conflicts with the final image of Marlow as a compassionate occidental Buddha, supposing, of course, that the Eastern idol image is legitimate and not a parody.

37. Ian Watt says that "Conrad uses Marlow to give his tale neither the full close of the plot of earlier fiction, nor James's more limited completeness in the formal structure, but a radical and continuing exposure to the incompleteness of experience and the impossibility of fully understanding it" (*IW*, 208). See also *IW*, 241–53, and James L. Guetti, *The Limits of Metaphor: A Study of Melville, Conrad, and Faulkner* (Ithaca, N.Y.: Cornell University Press, 1967), 46–68.

38. According to Werner Senn, in *Heart of Darkness* "[t]raits, impressions, even 'facts,' are vague, deceptive, ambiguous or contradictory, the 'qualitative aspect of things' resists identification, and we are left with a world of

objects that cannot be properly perceived and identified, let alone understood, and which therefore remain 'impenetrable,' and any experience of them, however intense, 'unspeakable.' Yet with singular persistence and devotion (not to say compulsion), Marlow attempts to interpret the diffuse and inexplicable, always aware of the fact that, as J. Hillis Miller ("Joseph Conrad") says, sense impressions 'are no more ultimate reality than their interpretation into meanings and objects'" (*Conrad's Narrative Voice,* 23). Along similar lines, Cox comments that Conrad deliberately creates a narrative that calls "attention to its own inadequacies" (*Joseph Conrad,* 49).

39. Brooks dubs Conrad's masterpiece "a detective story gone modernist: a tale of inconclusive solutions to crimes of problematic status. In its representation of an effort to reach endings that would retrospectively illuminate beginnings and middles, it pursues a reflection on the formal limits of narrative, but within a frame of discourse that appears to subvert finalities of form" ("Reading for the Plot," 238).

40. Two oft-quoted oriental adages are worth mentioning here: "The man who claims to know, knows nothing; the man who claims nothing, knows" and "He who knows does not speak; he who speaks does not know." Conrad, and no doubt the Buddha-like Marlow, would concur.

41. Wollaeger seems to ignore the external narrator's final words when he observes that "[t]he novella ends inconclusively by returning us to the narrative frame and the impossibility of knowing whether any of Marlow's immediate listeners learned anything from the story, let alone understood what Conrad called its 'secondary notions'" (74). In fact, he questions whether Marlow himself completely understands "the significance of his own narration" (*Joseph Conrad and the Fictions of Skepticism,* 77).

42. Throughout *Heart of Darkness* Conrad persistently defines whatever reality lies behind the phenomenal world in terms of what it is not. He defines reality by negation, by denial of any convenient formula on which to base one's approach to life.

43. Henricksen comments that "Conrad intentionally foregrounds not only the tension between narrator and story but that between narrator and audience, revealing a pragmatics by which the reader must always impose his or her own metanarratives and interpretative strategies in an attempt to wrest meaning from a text that always warns us of the arbitrariness of interpretation" (*Nomadic Voices,* 69).

## 3: Homo Ludicrous

1. One notable exception is Stanton de Voren Hoffman's *Comedy and Form in the Fiction of Joseph Conrad* (The Hague: Mouton, 1969).

2. Conrad's interpretation of Shaw's satiric barbs as insulting is excerpted from H. G. Wells's autobiography as cited in Baines, *Joseph Conrad,* 234.

3. Paul Kirschner, "Conrad and Maupassant: Moral Solitude and 'A Smile of Fortune,'" *Review of English Literature* 8 (1966): 62–77. Kirschner concludes that "Conrad and Maupassant were deeply united in their tormenting

sense of human isolation. This feeling was genuine and personal in Conrad; but Maupassant provided him with a precedent and a model of literary expression . . . " (77).

4. William Lafferty, "Conrad's 'A Smile of Fortune': The Moral Threat of Commerce," *Conradiana* 7 (1975): 63–74, primarily focuses on the narrator's conflict regarding his commercial and noncommercial self.

5. Jerome Zuckerman, "'A Smile of Fortune': Conrad's Interesting Failure," *Studies in Short Fiction* 1 (1964): 99–102, likens the narrator's failure in love to his failure to command, arguing that the themes of love and rule counterpoint and also reinforce each other. Zuckerman also distinguishes "Fortune" from "Conrad's other late works about captains, where self-knowledge brings the poise and assurance necessary for success" (102).

6. Bonney offers another possible interpretation of the name by etymologizing *Jacobus* as the "Old Pretender" (*WWB*, 72).

7. Cedric Watts, "The Narrative Enigma of Conrad's 'A Smile of Fortune,'" *Conradiana* 17 (1985): 131–36, ironically asserts that "[t]he central image of the tale is that of the lush, perfumed flower-garden; but from the transaction in the walled garden results a cargo of rank, decaying potatoes" (133).

8. Daniel R. Schwarz, *Conrad: The Later Fiction* (London: Macmillan, 1982), views the tale as "a dramatic monologue in which the speaker's tormented conscience gradually reveals a far different version of events from that he believes he is telling, despite his conscious and semiconscious efforts to evade the implications of his relationship with Alice" (10).

9. According to Meyer, the story unfolds as "a fantasy designed to convert humiliation and defeat into bittersweet success, from which the author might retire with honor" (*BCM*, 77).

10. Jacobs's *The Skipper's Wooing* (1896) features a similar exposition in theme and treatment.

11. Details such as this have led Meyer to speculate that Conrad projected his own characteristic aloofness upon the outcast girl (*BCM*, 84). The male-female role reversals of the narrator and Alice seem to substantiate this interpretation.

12. In contrast to Alice's childish outlook, Conrad views civilization as corrupt not because of occasional outbreaks of violence but because "petty larceny," propaganda, and duplicity have become the order of the day. No wonder he empathizes with so many secret sharers in his fiction—outcasts, hermits, outlaws, and solitaries of one sort or another.

13. Bonney notes how Conrad's "rhetorical ambiguities" intermingle "eros and mammon. The very title contains the word 'fortune,' which can denote material wealth as well as, more generally, a chance occurrence, and which is personified mythically by the frustratingly detached goddess Fortuna. A 'smile of fortune' takes place when prosperity and chance are uniquely and fortuitously combined, and an indifferent cosmos appears to reflect and fulfill human needs, as in this tale Fortuna's fatal femininity responds affectionately

with a bag of loot. These ambiguities stand remote from an ideal love relationship" (*WWB*, 75).

14. The heart of the story, according to Leo Gurko, is the narrator's adverse reaction to Alice's rejection of his passion. Emotionally shattered, "he replaces his sexual disappointment with a sudden lust for money, and when this fails to fill his psychic emptiness, resigns his command and returns to Europe" (*Joseph Conrad,* 209). But Conrad never firmly establishes Alice's rejection. Instead, he makes the crucial scene ambiguous. The narrator never knows whether Alice caught sight of her father entering the room before she broke away from his embrace. He also never learns why she did not return at his call or why she came back much later.

15. Graver's estimate reflects the perspective he established in an earlier analysis, "'Typhoon': A Profusion of Similes," *College English* 24 (1962): 62–64: "[I]n 'Typhoon' Conrad is not at all concerned with the shadowy or elliptical nature of truth. On the contrary: he is interested primarily in the triumph of a naive, unimaginative hero; and in this story, reality is concrete, open to empirical analysis" (62). For another positive appraisal of MacWhirr's conduct, see T. A. Birrell, "The Simplicity of *Typhoon*: Conrad, Flaubert, and Others," *Dutch Quarterly Review of Anglo-American Letters* 10 (1980): 272–95.

16. Although he calls "Typhoon" one of Conrad's better works of fiction, Guerard considers its "preoccupations . . . nearly all on the surface" and thus the story requires "no elaborate interpreting" (*Conrad the Novelist,* 294).

17. See, for example, John Howard Wills, "Conrad's 'Typhoon': A Triumph of Organic Art," *North Dakota Quarterly* 30 (1962): 62–70; Paul S. Bruss, "'Typhoon': The Initiation of Jukes," *Conradiana* 5 (1973): 46–55; Christof Wegelin, "MacWhirr and the Testimony of the Human Voice," *Conradiana* 7 (1975): 45–50; and *WWB*, 31–50. Most of these critics insist that to gain a better understanding of Conrad's characterization of MacWhirr we need to take into consideration his effect on Jukes, who is also an important focal point in the narrative. Interestingly, Karl views MacWhirr as a simple character who must make complicated decisions: "He embodies a view of life which has within it all the complexities we associate with a more sophisticated individual; what is involved is his resolve, and that, in turn, is connected to his ability to enter into the workings of nature" (*FRK,* 506).

18. Najder cites "Typhoon" as an example of Conrad's earlier works, which apply an "ironic question mark" at the end, "even when the hero managed to overcome all obstacles" (*ZN,* 361).

19. Wegelin maintains that Conrad's presentation of MacWhirr as both hero and fool underscores the "author's devotion to the multiplicity of truth" ("MacWhirr," 49).

20. Joseph Kolupke, "Elephants, Empires, and Blind Men: A Reading of the Figurative Language in Conrad's 'Typhoon,'" *Conradiana* 20 (1988): 71–85, remarks that "Jukes's final condescending judgment of MacWhirr as a 'stupid man' represents a considerable weakness of character on his part—it is as if the truth he discovered in the moment of crisis has been replaced by his former glib notions, a blindness more reprehensible in the light of his new

stock of experience. We are left to conclude that he still does not know MacWhirr" (78).

21. Lothe calls attention to these letters, but only to assert that they provide "personal perspectives on the events related by the authorial narrator" and a "variant on the authorial narrative" (*Conrad's Narrative Method,* 105). He also comments on the significance of the fact that the story ends with Jukes's letter but does not really spell out the significance (104). Bonney notes that "[t]hese epistles prove to be a significant key to the main characters' respective psychic capacities and susceptibilities" (*WWB,* 38).

22. For example, he never adequately prepares for the typhoon because he thinks of it as a bit of "dirty weather," and he remains attached to this innocuous but misleading label until he is surprised by the storm's ferocity and begins to fear that the ship will sink.

23. Of course, these names were also in currency during Conrad's years in the South Pacific (see Sherry, *Conrad's Eastern World,* 26, 238, 270).

24. Land refers to Conrad's creation of MacWhirr as "caricature rather than portraiture" and notes that "his combination of utter simplicity with spectacular competence is generally unconvincing" (*Conrad and the Paradox of Plot,* 92).

25. Wollaeger observes that the story "finally draws back from its tentative assertion of MacWhirr's value by closing with Jukes's unflatteringly ironic letter at the captain's expense. . . . While the irony denies MacWhirr the unequivocal status of hero, the narrative clearly imbues him with the power to counter Jukes's potential loss of self, and the comedy restrains the more introspective meditations on identity found in *Lord Jim*" (*Joseph Conrad and the Fictions of Skepticism,* 124). Schwarz goes even further in qualifying the assertions that Jukes makes in his letter. He underscores Conrad's declaration that the letter is "calculated" to convey the impression that Jukes showed a "light-hearted, indomitable resolution" during the ordeal: "The contents of his letter undercut the perspicacity of his grudging and condescending final statement. . . . Clearly, Jukes does not experience a major character transformation . . ." (*Conrad: Almayer's Folly to Under Western Eyes,* 118).

26. I tend to disagree with Daleski, who argues that Jukes undergoes an initiation into a new understanding of himself as a result of his experience with MacWhirr during the typhoon (*Joseph Conrad,* 112).

27. Bruss, "'Typhoon': The Initiation of Jukes," argues that Jukes does mature in the course of the voyage, whereas Eberhard Greim, "Rhetoric and Reality in Conrad's 'Typhoon,'" *Conradiana* 24 (1992): 21–32, views the story as dramatizing the "failed initiation" of Jukes: "[H]is final verdict, which sounds as if the Captain had succeeded in spite of himself, is both comical and deplorable in its obstinacy . . ." (30).

28. Prior to the storm, MacWhirr objected to Jukes's reference to the Chinese as "passengers." In his one-dimensional, literalistic mind, all passengers must be white. Furthermore, he calls Jukes's suggestion to take the steamship off course and avoid the typhoon a "mad" scheme just "to make the Chinamen comfortable" (*T,* 31). During the crisis, the sailors totally forget

about the Chinese below deck, except for MacWhirr, whose sole concern is to preserve order above and below deck. When Jukes returns to the Captain to explain how the coolies have been organized by the crew, MacWhirr cuts him short with the catch phrase, "Had to do what's fair" (*T*, 82). Despite Jukes's suspicion that the Chinese will eventually cut the sailors' throats, MacWhirr stands his ground on questionable morality: "Had to do what's fair, for all—they are only Chinamen. Give them the same chance with ourselves—hang it all" (*T*, 88).

29. David Daiches, *The Novel and the Modern World* (Chicago: University of Chicago Press, 1939), has argued that Conrad is merely interested in creating moods and atmosphere in connection with the typhoon, and therefore a depiction of the second phase of the storm would be redundant (63). But this is hardly a convincing argument. More recently, Lothe has argued that Conrad omitted a second description of the gale because "it would not have added substantially to the very effective first one but would instead, unavoidably, have seemed anticlimactic" (*Conrad's Narrative Method*, 115). Experienced mariners would no doubt testify that the second onslaught of a hurricane—its backside, so to speak—is anything but anticlimactic in its fury.

30. Over the last decade or so, critics have begun to examine the problematic role of language in this narrative. Charles I. Schuster, "Comedy and the Limits of Language in Conrad's 'Typhoon,'" *Conradiana* 16 (1984): 55–71, sees Conrad's characterization of MacWhirr and Jukes as a way of focusing attention "on the inadequacies of written language and its imaginative uses. For although Conrad endorses the view that language is essential to a definition of humanity, he limits that endorsement to everyday oral usage: conversation, talk, command. Written forms—letters and books and narrative accounts especially—are called into question. Both the literalist MacWhirr and the imaginative Jukes undercut the possibility of story-telling as a meaningful activity in its root sense, that is, as an activity which is 'meaning full'" (65). Sooyoung Chon, "'Typhoon': Silver Dollars and Stars," *Conradiana* 22 (1990): 25–43, does not agree that "Typhoon" subverts the possibility of story-telling but does affirm that it questions the capacity of language to encompass all aspects of reality, especially in view of the fragmentary perceptions conveyed in the three letters at the end of the story: "The three inept letters may prove the inadequacy of traditional monologic narratives to 'recover the actual event,' but this does not necessarily invalidate story-telling itself" (26).

31. Early in the tale, Conrad suggests that the mechanization of shipping has produced hellish consequences, such as the smokestack emitting "an infernal sort of cloud, smelling of sulphur" (*T*, 21). And Conrad later personifies the engine as an iron mouth fed by mute, atavistic sailors like the "donkeyman" (*T*, 71).

32. Bonney even argues that MacWhirr's crisis "evolves as an obvious meteorological analogue of his psychic incapacity" (*WWB*, 36).

33. As Sooyoung Chon observes, "MacWhirr only believes in the denotational and pragmatic use of language. For him, language is a tool absolutely

chained to reality and facts. His linguistic habit favors such primary features of language as names that retain the strongest of the links between the linguistic order and the order of reality" ("'Typhoon': Silver Dollars and Stars," 28).

34. See John Vernon, *The Garden and the Map: Schizophrenia in Modern Literature* (Urbana: University of Illinois Press, 1973), particularly his cogent analysis of the psychological and geographical implications of *Heart of Darkness* (28–38).

35. Though MacWhirr cuts a foolish figure in the game of tag with his shoes, Conrad adds yet another note of derision to his portrait of an incompetent when the Captain goes "through all the movements of a woman putting on her bonnet before a glass" (*T*, 36). Considering MacWhirr's unfulfilling marriage, such an ironic role-reversal seems apropos.

# 4: On the Brink of a Disclosure

1. See Diana Culbertson, "'The Informer' as Conrad's Little Joke," *Studies in Short Fiction* 2 (1974): 430–33.

2. It is almost impossible to think of the Professor without recalling the notorious Unabomber, who allegedly used the pseudonym "Conrad" when checking into hotels prior to mailing his bombs in California.

3. The historical source for Mr. X's anecdote is found in Ford's story of the Rossetti family's involvement with anarchist publications (see *FRK*, 588).

4. Schwarz observes that "'The Informer' depends upon a narrator who does not understand either the implications of his encounter with the anarchist, Mr. X, or Mr. X's motives for telling his tale of anarchists. The reader shares X's joke at the expense of the narrator, at the same time that Conrad invites the reader to watch the narrator condemn himself out of his own mouth" (*Conrad: Almayer's Folly to Under Western Eyes*, 185–86). Sevrin's last words call to mind Prince Roman's admission at his trial that he had participated in the national uprising "from conviction," when he could have blamed his actions on his grief over the death of his wife. Yet the Prince's conviction of the rightness of his course of action did not prevent him from enlisting in the revolt under an assumed name, to protect his family and perhaps to minimize publicity about his decision to join the nationalist cause. But Conrad does not seem to accentuate this disparity as much as one might expect. (Conviction, of course, plays a vital role in *Under Western Eyes*, in which Razumov encounters many men and women professing anarchist convictions that run counter to what he pretends to be. Ultimately, he meets his fate at the hands of a double agent who ironically punishes Razumov for his betrayal of a cause that neither one ever believed in.)

5. See Allan Hepburn, "Collectors in Conrad's 'The Informer,'" *Studies in Short Fiction* 29 (1992): 103–12.

6. Conrad the literary theoretician had earlier pillaged the ideas and language of Pater's essay "Style" for his own artistic manifesto, as laid out in the preface to *The Nigger of the "Narcissus."*

gospel of Mrs Eddy. And it is perfectly capable from the height of its secular stability to look down upon the artist as a mere windlestraw!" (CL, 4:285).

27. For example, in a letter to William Blackwood (22 August 1899), Conrad states: "The question of art is so endless, so involved and so obscure that one is tempted to turn one's face resolutely away from it. I've certainly an idea—apart from the idea and the subject of the story—which guides me in my writing, but I would be hard put to it if requested to give it out in the shape of a fixed formula" (CL, 2:194).

28. In The Secret Agent, a novel of disguised dandyism, Conrad overtly refers to "the little parlour of the Cheshire Cheese" (SA, 231).

29. "The School of Giorgione," in Selected Writings of Walter Pater, ed. Harold Bloom (New York: New American Library, 1974), 55.

30. In an undated letter to Edward Thomas, Conrad noted that Pater's writing style far outshines his own: "For the man was a stylist first and last—and I am a vagabond and a stranger in the language. . . . I am now passing through a phase of acute sensitivity as to my own style. It seems the most impossible jargon having the mere merit of being bizarre (if that's a merit) and all your dearest fellows appreciation of it a most amiable, a most precious (to me) form of lunacy" (cited in FRK, 691).

31. "The Partner" has a supremely ironic title, for all partnerships in the tale involve treachery: George betrays Harry, Cloete betrays George, Stafford betrays Cloete, and the writer-narrator betrays his drinking partner, the stevedore. Conrad adds one more irony by alluding to the parable of the Good Samaritan at the close of the stevedore's account, thus underscoring the futility of trust in the modern world.

32. Lawrence Graver, for example, calls the story one of Conrad's "least demanding works," one of his "simple pieces of no narrative complexity . . ." (LG, 94). He also refers to the tale derisively as a "dismal fabrication" (LG, 198). Najder calls it "probably the most trivial of [Conrad's] short stories" (ZN, 383), and Karl "one of his worst stories" (FRK, 726).

33. Jessie Conrad, Joseph Conrad as I Knew Him (Garden City, New York: Doubleday, 1926), lumps "The Inn of the Two Witches" with "stories Conrad could never find a good word for" (119).

34. See Paul Franklin Baum, "A Source," Modern Language Notes 33 (1918): 312–14.

35. Barbara H. Solomon, "Conrad's Narrative Material in 'The Inn of the Two Witches,'" Conradiana 7 (1975): 75–82. Solomon concludes that Conrad adapted his source material to his characteristic manner in order to (1) depict a "strained mental state" caused by an event rather than focusing on the event itself; (2) distance the reader from the story and its internal narrator; and (3) ironically subvert the testimony of the internal narrator by means of the framing narrator's detached commentary (80–81).

36. Conrad's persistent capitalization of the word find evokes an aura of immortality, one of the stock conventions of fictionizing, implying that the story will long outlast the physical circumstances that produced it.

37. This passage calls to mind not only the opening chapters of Melville's *Redburn* but also chapter 45 of *White-Jacket,* which comically describes "Publishing Poetry in a Man-of-war" via cannonading. Conrad, of course, always claimed to dislike Melville's sea fiction.

38. Conrad's penchant for mystification only partially explains this puzzle. If his preliminary remarks constitute a hoax in the pseudo-erudite tradition of Defoe and Poe, he must want to distance himself from duped readers (or else share a wry smile with the perceptive members of his audience at the expense of readers who accept his words without question).

39. If the phrase "naiveness of contrivance" is insufficiently oxymoronic, then consider the word *simplicity* in light of Conrad's ironic subtitle for *The Secret Agent:* "A Simple Tale."

40. Conrad could have been telling the truth when he denied knowledge of Collins's tale, for the two stories share relatively little in common aside from the focal point on the lethal bed. The ex-soldier who leads Collins's narrator to the bedroom is in the habit of taking snuff, like Conrad's homunculus. Like the homunculus, the ex-soldier has a dual persona. First he warns against potential thieves lying in wait for the narrator on his way home. Then he coaxes the narrator into drinking champagne and drugged coffee before ushering him into the bedroom. Like the homunculus, too, the ex-soldier is not what he seems, since he was really dismissed from the Grand Army because of idleness, though he poses as having been brave. Conrad also may have been fascinated by Collins's emphasis on the "spellbound" and immobilized narrator, who barely escapes death.

41. If Conrad has been slavishly imitating Poe or Collins, then he certainly deviates from their methods at the end. His epilogue lacks Poe's climactic melodrama as well as Collins's full disclosure and wrapping up of all loose ends.

42. Conrad's subtle use of supernatural allusion is exemplified in his use of images related to iron. The most conspicuous example occurs in Conrad's description of Byrne's inventory of the archbishop's bedroom prior to the discovery of Tom's body: "The window was shuttered and barred with an iron bar. . . . [H]e went to the door to examine the fastenings. They consisted of two enormous iron bolts sliding into holes made in the wall" (*WT,* 155). The use of iron as a protective device is not unusual. In Wilkie Collins's tale, "The Terribly Strange Bed," an iron case conceals the screw that manipulates the bed's canopy, a device constructed by "infernal ingenuity." But Conrad also employs references to iron to reinforce the diabolical undertones of his story. For iron weapons and implements have long been associated with magic and the supernatural. Joseph Campbell, *Occidental Mythology* (New York: Penguin, 1964), notes that the early Iron Age (900–400 B.C.) "was characterized at the outset by a gradual introduction of iron tools among bronze, fashioned by a class of itinerant smiths, who in later mythic lore appear as dangerous wizards . . . " (291). It is not surprising that Conrad would exploit this association in his fiction. What is surprising, however, is his subtle artistic touch in this gothic melodrama. Conrad's references to iron occur only in Byrne's internal narrative, not in the framing narrator's introduc-

tory remarks or to the epilogue. Significantly, Conrad employs these references exclusively in connection with the journey to the inn and never in connection with the homunculus. Conrad's first and final references—"that iron-bound shore" and "an iron-bound coast" (*WT*, 135, 157)—frame the motif within the context of Byrne's search for Tom. Moreover, he associates the motif with the witches' cauldron in *Macbeth*: "The sorceress with the spoon ceased stirring the mess in the iron pot, the very trembling of the other's head stopped for the space of a breath" (*WT*, 148). Conrad also links the motif to the gipsy girl who escorts Byrne "upstairs carrying an iron lamp from the naked flame of which ascended a thin thread of smoke" (*WT*, 152). Since Conrad associates Byrne's ordeal with fire and brimstone, the presence of the lamp in the bedroom throughout the night enhances the supernatural atmosphere of the scene.

## 5: Despair and Red Herrings

1. Bruce Johnson, *Conrad's Models of Mind*, 177–204, deals with the story in relation to *Victory* and *The Rescue*. Joel R. Kehler, "'The Planter of Malata': Renouard's Sinking Star of Knowledge," *Conradiana* 8 (1976): 148–62, views "Planter" as a quasi-allegorical quest for knowledge in a world in which truth is unattainable. Owen Knowles, "Conrad and Mérimée: The Legend of Venus in 'The Planter of Malata,'" *Conradiana* 11 (1979): 177–84, denigrates the tale as an interesting and problematical failure, yet he demonstrates the influence of Mérimée and also documents the parallel scenario in the working notes for a play (never written) by Conrad and Crane, *The Predecessor*, concocted by Conrad's would-be collaborator, Stephen Crane. In contrast to the above, Juliet McLauchlan, "Conrad's Heart of Emptiness: 'The Planter of Malata,'" *Conradiana* 18 (1986): 180–92, does discuss the novella on its own terms and attempts to rehabilitate its lackluster reputation as a miniature version of *Victory*. But she ignores the comic dimensions of the story by investing Renouard's and Felicia's shallowness and the planter's illusory enchantment with greater meaning than the text warrants. "The Planter of Malata" lacks the psychological and metaphysical profundity of *Heart of Darkness*, and we must focus instead on the novella's burlesque overtones, which ultimately clash with the melodrama of the final chapter.

2. Meyer is correct in calling characters such as Renouard "two-dimensional caricatures resembling personages in fairy tales or characters in a morality play" (*BCM*, 233). But he does not entertain the notion that Conrad may have used the planter to serve a satirical purpose.

3. McLauchlan finds the last paragraph especially "jarring" in its excessive sentimentality ("Conrad's Heart of Emptiness," 178 n.11), yet Conrad's final words turn pathos into bathos, particularly when we realize that our last impression of Malata is provided by the sensationalizing viewpoint of the Editor, who may be already making up the headline for his exclusive report on the island mystery.

4. Acknowledging the novella's vacillation "between psychological study and allegorical romance," Schwarz rightly notes that Renouard's mind and motives remain obscure (*Conrad: The Later Fiction,* 29, 32). We are never sure if Conrad wants us to sympathize with the planter or reject his self-deceptive conduct.

5. Knowles notes that Conrad depicts a "psychological breakdown in Renouard" ("Conrad and Mérimée," 182), but he does not elaborate on this observation.

6. Paul L. Wiley, *Conrad's Measure of Man* (Madison: University of Wisconsin Press, 1954), views the planter as "symbolic of Western man in his last hour," his impulse to action arrested by his inability to resist devitalizing sensual infatuation (160). Yet, except for the labels ascribed to Renouard, nothing about him seems remotely martial or heroic, contrary to Wiley's perspective.

7. Although McLauchlan calls Renouard's decision to kill himself "inevitable," given the destructive "power of illusions" ("Conrad's Heart of Emptiness," 180), the planter's suicide seems absurd in the context of Conrad's lampoon of Renouard as the solitary nonconformist. Indeed, the planter conforms to the most banal traits of the popular romantic hero.

8. The reduction of Arthur to the status of "a mere baby" could be a sly allusion to Stephen Crane's phrase "the mere boy," which is rife in his fiction. Since Crane and Conrad once contemplated collaborating on this story, it would not be far-fetched to suspect that Crane had a role in the creation of Renouard.

9. Admittedly, Conrad occasionally lapses into Victorian sentimentality in his fiction (as in his depiction of Heyst's affected fondness for Lena in *Victory*), yet in this story the excesses of self-indulgence seem more appropriate to the title character, rather than the detached author who guides the protagonist to an absurd annihilation.

10. Karl views Renouard and Heyst as suicides "who fail their women in one way or another" (*FRK,* 751).

11. We should also not overlook the seemingly casual gesture of Renouard tossing his hat away, for in Conrad's fiction the loss of a hat often corresponds to the abandonment of rationality, as it does, for example, in *Lord Jim* and "The Secret Sharer."

12. The story continues to be read as a Conradian battle of the sexes, although Ruth L. Nadelhaft, *Joseph Conrad* (Atlantic Highlands, N.J.: Humanities Press International, 1991), has recently argued that the tale does not express Conrad's fear of and hostility toward women but shows "compassion and empathy" for the confining roles that women have been traditionally forced to play. As in the case of Hemingway's fiction, feminist scholars seem determined to rehabilitate Conrad's attitude toward women. And they may be right. Perhaps we should take Conrad at his word when he says, "Men are always cowards. . . . I think it is only women who have true courage" (quoted in *FRK,* 343).

13. See Milton Chaikin, "Zola and Conrad's 'The Idiots,'" *Studies in Philology* 52 (1955): 502–7.

14. Note, however, that Conrad's scenario undermines this platitude, since the young characters in the story fall victim to either idiocy or a violent death.

15. Edward Said correctly notes that "the content of the tale, for all its sensational operatics, still seems somewhat 'obscure' to the traveler. Between the recollecting narrator and the actual tale there is a barrier that is eternally closed. . . . [T]his hedge of mystery . . . becomes an important fact in the story" (*Joseph Conrad and the Fiction of Autobiography,* 88).

16. Hugh Epstein, "'Where He Is Not Wanted': Impression and Articulation in 'The Idiots' and 'Amy Foster,'" *Conradiana* 23 (1991): 217–32, suggests that Conrad's narrative strategy involves the disclosure of a "dark hinterland" that lies beyond the pale of the phenomenal world; yet "The Idiots" fails "to narrate the disclosure," and thus Conrad does not provide the reader's imagination with enough evocative material to formulate that disclosure (222).

17. Responding to Guerard's charge that Conrad lost control near the end of the story, Schwarz, "Moral Bankruptcy in Ploumar Parish: A Study of Conrad's 'The Idiots,'" *Conradiana* 1 (1969): 113–16, takes note of the appropriateness of the melodramatic elements prior to Susan's death: "That Conrad has control and knows what he is doing is indicated when he returns to the ironic point of view to show Madame Levaille bemoaning *her* misfortune in order to clinch the Marquis' sympathies and be awarded the Bacadou land. . . . What does go *somewhat*—but not disastrously—wrong is that the narrator's abrupt switch, from cold and ironic understatement to an almost gothic rendering of alien man set against the primitive elements, is *tonally* incongruous" (116). But tonal incongruity, I believe, lies at the heart of Conrad's artistic strategy.

18. Schwarz argues that the story demonstrates that natives are not inferior and that the essential elements of human existence are the same: "[D]espite differences in customs and the level of civilisation, mankind shares basic goals and dreams" (*Conrad: Almayer's Folly to Under Western Eyes,* 28).

19. Michael A. Lucas, "Styles in 'An Outpost of Progress' and 'The Lagoon,'" *Conradiana* 21 (1989): 203–20, argues that Arsat's guilt "points to the futility and insignificance of human endeavor . . ." (216).

20. Wollaeger states that the story does not resolve the question of belief regarding Diamelen's death. "The narrative simply stops with a perfunctory reference to 'a world of illusions,' but neither the narrator nor Conrad decides which world is illusory—Arsat's or the white man's" (40).

21. In this regard, Conrad anticipates Beckett, whose works typify the literature of silence and immobility. Both Conrad and Beckett seem to have been moving toward a literary art founded on the assumption that there is nothing to be said and nothing to be done. Captain Davidson, at the close of *Victory,* might concur.

22. See, in particular, Guy Owen, "Conrad's 'The Lagoon,'" *The Explicator* 18 (May 1960): Item no. 47, and George Walton Williams, "Conrad's 'The Lagoon,'" *The Explicator* 23 (September 1964): Item no. 1. From the mid-1950s to the mid-1960s *The Explicator* served as a valuable forum for critical discussions of the significance of the ending of "The Lagoon."

23. The most extreme condemnation comes from Guerard, who calls the tale "Conrad's worst story of any length, and one of the worst ever written by a great novelist" (*Conrad the Novelist*, 96).

24. See, for example, Dale Kramer, "Conrad's Experiments with Language and Narrative in 'The Return,'" *Studies in Short Fiction* 25 (1988): 1–11, which emphasizes the tragic implications of Hervey's final realization but neglects the satirical elements that lead up to the locking scene.

25. Wollaeger largely ignores the satirical dimension in his treatment of the story as a Schopenhauer-infused psychodrama in which Hervey experiences two epistemological epiphanies that may reflect Conrad's own anxieties about marriage (*Joseph Conrad and the Fictions of Skepticism*, 51–56).

26. Moreover, Conrad fashions a fine symmetry by introducing Hervey via the "slamming of carriage doors" and announcing his exit with the thunderous sound of "a door slammed heavily" (*TU*, 118, 186).

27. David refers to "self-conscious performance" and the "repressive mechanisms of middle-class culture" as the two major concerns of "The Return" ("Selfhood and Language," 138).

28. Nadelhaft sees "the vividly described light fixture" as corresponding to the imprisonment of Mrs. Hervey's marriage (*Joseph Conrad*, 70).

29. I do not claim that Conrad aspired to advance the cause of feminism, but "The Return" can be read as both a sympathetic treatment of the male perspective and also an indictment of that limited point of view. In her feminist analysis of the story, Nadelhaft treats the story as a dramatization of the modern "tendency to avoid serious intimacy" and focuses on Mrs. Hervey's point of view, even though Conrad tells the tale from Alvan Hervey's perspective (*Joseph Conrad*, 69–77). Nadelhaft perhaps goes a bit too far in attempting to rebut the interpretation of "The Return" as a reflection of "Conrad's own anxieties about marriage" (73) when she claims that the final confrontation of the Herveys "presents both the capacity and the willingness of [Conrad's] women characters to be engaged with the world in a powerful and authentic way" (72). If anything, the final glimpse of Mrs. Hervey is that of a defeated individual who resigns herself to resuming her former role after finding herself unable, or unwilling, to change her situation.

30. David affirms that Hervey "uses language to assert himself in the act of assertion. . . . [I]n showing how a loquacious member of the bourgeoisie like Hervey uses language for concealment, Conrad's story dramatizes the ways that the words a bourgeois culture has at its disposal conceal essential emotion" ("Selfhood and Language," 141).

31. Nadelhaft maintains that Hervey's departure at the end of the story suggests that "a newly honest relationship is so perilous that a husband must leave rather than become engaged in such a project" (*Joseph Conrad*, 74). Hervey's desertion expresses his fear that every woman conceals information "about the darkness at the heart of the universe. . . . What Hervey wants, what Conrad suggests *men* want, from women, is relief from the uncertainty of the world, from uncertainty itself. What women want, the wife suggests—Conrad suggests—is *themselves*" (76).

32. David declares that Hervey's exit at the end of "The Return" does not resolve "the conflicts of self-consciousness and language," for Conrad shows Hervey "almost ridiculously self-satisfied with his possession of a new moral truth. The ending confirms . . . he is really no different at the end of his fictional experience from the way he had been at the beginning" ("Selfhood and Language," 142). While I dispute David's claim that Conrad sustains the "caustic tone" of the story in the locking scene, I agree with her contention that Hervey remains myopic from first to last.

## 6: An Accommodation with Chaos

1. Conrad even converted "Because of the Dollars" into a two-act play called *Laughing Anne* in the hope of exploiting its high-strung emotionality.

2. In literary art, repetition can reinforce meaning through occasional reiteration or it can subvert meaning through persistent reiteration. Conrad's repetitions in "Because of the Dollars" are not incremental (augmenting the already established meaning) but detrimental (subverting the established meaning), and perhaps intended to make fun of the escape-seeking readers of magazine fiction.

3. Hollis's insistent reiterations of this innocuous phrase suggest a defensive posture, and, indeed, each character in the story views Davidson from a different perspective. To Hollis, he is not only a "*really* good man" but also "poor Davidson" and even "the remorseful Davidson." To the framing narrator, Davidson is "a seaman" and a "sympathetic stout man." He is the "same good Davy" to Laughing Anne (*WT,* 182) and "a man that could do no wrong" (*WT,* 173) to the Chinese owner of Davidson's ship, the idiosyncratically named "*Sissie*—Glasgow." Furthermore, Hollis elaborates on the Oriental owner's partiality toward his occidental Captain: "[Y]ou couldn't tell if it was Davidson who belonged to the Chinaman or the Chinaman who belonged to Davidson" (*WT,* 170). Hollis even refers to the owner as "Davidson's Chinaman," reversing their roles. We learn little about Davidson, whom Hollis buries under a mass of boy-scout abstractions (e.g., "Davidsonian kindness," "moral excellence," "sensitive humanity").

4. One might consider the trashing of Mrs. Davidson's "angelic profile" as part and parcel of Conrad's alleged misogyny, and there may be some validity in this view, but her two-sided personality harmonizes with the pattern of incongruous characterization throughout the story.

5. This statement calls to mind Ricardo's persistent rhetorical questions in *Victory,* for example, "What do you think a fellow is?—a reptile?" (*V,* 300).

6. Schwarz, commenting on Hollis's overzealous praise of Davidson's "moral excellence," views the story as a lesson by which the good Captain learns about "the existence of human malice" (*Conrad: The Later Fiction,* 28–29).

7. Conrad apparently thought well enough of the epithet "Laughing Anne" to use it as the title of the stage version of "Because of the Dollars." I

suspect that the tragic or pathetic death of someone linked to mirth appealed to his sense of life's futility.

8. In the first three chapters of *Victory*, Conrad refers to Heyst in the following playful epithets to dramatize the various perspectives on his protagonist: "Heyst the Hermit," "Enchanted Heyst," "Hard Facts," "Heyst the Spider," "Naive Heyst," and "Heyst the Enemy."

9. For instance, Crane repeats the phrase "the mere boy" in chapter 14 of *Maggie: A Girl of the Streets* fourteen times, converting what is ostensibly a serious scene into a farcical episode.

10. Henry Fielding, *The Life of Mr. Jonathan Wild the Great* (New York: New American Library, 1961), xix. See, in particular, book 1, chapters 1, 6, 8, 11, 14; book 2, chapters 2, 5, 7–9; book 3, chapters 2–5, 9; book 4, chapters 4, 12, 14.

11. Guerard has nothing but scorn for *Victory*'s conclusion. He finds Davidson's sudden appearance improbable and unwarranted, and he believes that the omniscient narrator could have depicted the holocaust as effectively (*Conrad the Novelist*, 274).

12. Davidson's delicacy plays a part in his wife's growing suspicions about Tony. He initially decides to conceal the facts concerning his rescue of the orphaned boy out of his desire to not make his wife more anxious while he was away from home.

13. Arnold E. Davidson considers Captain Davidson's "Nothing!" an example of Conrad's delayed decoding. The word means one thing to the Captain, but Conrad forces us to comprehend its larger implication in the silence that follows the last word of the novel (*Conrad's Endings*, 101).

14. Heyst's sense of being "disarmed" as he speaks to the mortally wounded Lena corresponds with Davidson's sense of being "unmanned" at the sight of Anne's corpse. In each case, the woman has heroically sacrificed herself for a man who proves not entirely worthy.

15. Conrad was so exasperated by reviewers who emphasized Captain Whalley's poignancy that he wrote Edward Garnett (22 December 1902): "Touching, tender, noble, moving. . . . Let us spit!" (*CL*, 2:468; Conrad's ellipsis). But many contemporary critics still find the Captain's actions admirable in general. For example, Land calls Whalley's selfless motives "pure and worthy" and his objective "ideal" (*Conrad and the Paradox of Plot*, 100, 101). For Land, the Captain "is a man of unusual ability marked out for destruction for a single misuse of his talent" (102).

16. The Captain's vitality, according to William T. Moynihan, "Conrad's 'The End of the Tether': A New Reading," *Modern Fiction Studies* 4 (1958): 173–77, pertains only to physical strength, not spiritual energy; when age and blindness rob Whalley of his strength, he falls, as hollow as Kurtz and without the majesty of Lear (174). Lawrence Graver, "Critical Confusion and Conrad's 'The End of the Tether,'" *Modern Fiction Studies* 9 (1963–64): 390–93, amplifies Moynihan's view, arguing that Whalley has tenacity and that one can sympathize with his predicament, "but that in no way excuses his lapse into duplicity and cowardice, even if such deception had been originally

prompted by love" (392). Sanford Pinsker, "'The End of the Tether': Conrad's Death of a Sailsman," *Conradiana* 3 (1971–72): 74–76, sees Whalley as a sort of Lord Jim in reverse, clinging "to a past that is every bit as romantic as the one to which Jim aspires—and every bit as fatal" (75). Likewise, Said contends that "[t]he central tension of the story is the connection of Whalley's increasing blindness to his increasing sense of honor and fidelity; the blinder he becomes, the more he clings to an outmoded code of action" (*Joseph Conrad and the Fiction of Autobiography*, 116). Attributing Whalley's failure to his blind faith in divine providence, Gloria L. Young, "Chance and the Absurd in Conrad's 'The End of the Tether' and 'Freya of the Seven Isles,'" *Conradiana* 7 (1975): 253–61, views the Captain's death in a larger context: "[M]an's mythologies, having no relevance to reality, betray him"; believing in a divinely ordered world, Whalley actually lives in "a world of flux and chance" (254). Along similar lines, Daniel R. Schwarz, "A Lonely Figure Walking Purposefully: The Significance of Captain Whalley in Conrad's 'The End of the Tether,'" *Conradiana* 7 (1975): 165–73, contends that "Whalley's hubris is paradoxically in his faith, in his belief that he lives in space imbued with Divine blessing because God endorses his motives and works His will through him" (169); finally, Paul S. Bruss, "'The End of the Tether': Teleological Diminishing in Conrad's Early Metaphor of Navigation," *Studies in Short Fiction* 13 (1976): 311–20, views the Captain's blindness as "a metaphor for Whalley's, or even Western man's, spiritual decline" (319).

17. As Pinsker has noted, Whalley's pride calls to mind Willy Loman's similar delusion (see "'The End of the Tether': Conrad's Death of a Sailsman").

18. In his pioneering essay, "Adam, Axel, and 'Il Conde,'" *Modern Fiction Studies* 1 (1955): 22–25, John Howard Wills discusses the story as a dual allegory of the "Fall or Expulsion from Eden" and "the Ivory Tower myth of the *fin-de-siècle*." In his view the Count loses his innocence when forced to confront the "animality" of existence and becomes radically estranged from his illusory life of painless amusement. John V. Hagopian, "The Pathos of 'Il Conde,'" *Studies in Short Fiction* 3 (1965): 31–38, disputes Wills's allegorical reading and views the Count as "only an upper class J. Alfred Prufrock" who becomes "a pathetic victim" when assaulted by the vigor and vitality he dreads (33). He also emphasizes the narrator's role in providing "an ironic commentary on the decay of the aristocracy and the vulnerability of innocence" (32). Lawrence Graver endorses Hagopian's argument, branding the story as "one of the most artful of Conrad's potboilers" (*LG*, 144). Taking Hagopian's emphasis on the narrator one step farther, Daniel R. Schwarz, "The Self-Deceiving Narrator of Conrad's 'Il Conde,'" *Studies in Short Fiction* 6 (1969): 187–93, questions the objectivity of the teller of the tale, who empathizes with the Count, with whom he has much in common. According to Schwarz, the narrator is narrow, limited, and even imperceptive (187–88). Like the Count, the narrator is an "overcivilized aesthete" haunted by "repressed instincts and passions" (190). Moreover, the Camorra who robs the Count and terrorizes him into fleeing Naples objectifies the suppressed self beneath the veneer of cultivated values (191). But the "unreliable narrator,"

Schwarz contends, never recognizes the Camorra as the Count's alter ego, nor does he realize that he and the Count are secret sharers of the same conventional sensibility (193). Along similar lines, Ernest Carter, "Classical Allusion as the Clue to Meaning in Conrad's 'Il Conde,'" *Conradiana* 3 (1971–72): 55–62, argues that Conrad's story dramatizes the Count's "self-judgment and self-punishment." Carter believes that Conrad foreshadows the Count's meeting with the Camorra in the opening scene, in which the narrator and the Count admire the statue of the Resting Hermes. The ancient Greek god's association with thievery and music has ironic repercussions in the robbery scene near the concert, where the Count loses his illusory contentment and discovers his invalid existence. Finally, in essays published in the same issue of *Conradiana* 7 (1975): Douglas A. Hughes, "Conrad's 'Il Conde': A Deucedly Queer Story," 17–25, and Theo Steinmann, "Il Conde's Uncensored Story," 83–86, cogently analyze the Count's version of the robbery as a distortion of the truth, fabricated by the self-censoring Count to conceal his homosexual involvement with the Camorra.

19. Meyer makes the intriguing assertion that the central action of "Il Conde" is an inversion of that in *The Secret Agent* (*BCM*, 196). Instead of an older man inadvertently leading a youth to his death, a young man condemns an elderly man to his doom.

20. As Carter points out, "The Count understands nothing of the powerful forces of fertility and death the statue symbolized for the classical world; for him it represents simply the 'delicate perfection' of art, it has nothing to do with life" ("Classical Allusion as the Clue to Meaning in Conrad's 'Il Conde,'" 58).

21. As Romanian philosopher E. M. Cioran has said in *The Temptation to Exist* (New York: Quadrangle Books, 1968), "A civilization exists and asserts itself only by acts of provocation. Once it begins to calm down, it crumbles. Its culminating moments are its formidable ones, during which, far from husbanding its forces, it squanders them" (50).

22. *Conde*, meaning "count," "earl," or "chief of gypsies" in Spanish, ramifies linguistically into the Italian *condottiere* ("leader of a band of mercenaries"), the French *condamne* ("condemned person" or "convict"), and the English *conduct* and *conductor*, derived from the Latin *conductus* ("escort") and *conducere* ("to bring together"). This sort of etymologizing, whether conscious or not on Conrad's part, illuminates the classical allusions to the myth of Hermes, god of travelers and guide of souls to the underworld. It also casts an ironic light on the robbery, which occurs at an outdoor *concert* (from the Italian *concerto*, derived from *concertare*, "to be in accord"). Conrad may also be engaging in word play, deliberately or unconsciously, in prefixing the Italian word *il* ("the") to the Spanish word *conde*, implying a spiritual illness at the root of the Count's eccentric sensibility. Conrad claimed in his author's note to *A Set of Six* that he had merely misspelled the title of his story, though he does not indicate whether he misspelled the article or the noun.

# Coda

## Conrad's Inscrutable Sense of an Ending

1. *The Edwardian Temperament: 1895–1919* (Athens: Ohio University Press, 1986), 49.

2. For a more optimistic assessment of Conrad's response to late-Victorian nihilism, see John A. Lester Jr., *Journey Through Despair: 1880–1914* (Princeton, N.J.: Princeton University Press, 1968), 186–90.

3. J. Hillis Miller, "Joseph Conrad," in *Poets of Reality: Six Twentieth Century Writers* (Cambridge: Harvard University Press, 1965), 13–67.

4. See E. M. Forster, "Joseph Conrad: A Note," *Abinger Harvest* (New York: Harcourt Brace Jovanovich, 1936), 136–41. This brief essay has given us the oft-quoted observation that "the secret casket of [Conrad's] genius contains a vapour rather than a jewel" (138). But Forster is referring more to the essays in *Notes on Life and Letters* than to Conrad's fiction as a whole.

5. See, in particular, Royal Roussel, *The Metaphysics of Darkness* (Baltimore: Johns Hopkins University Press, 1971); Leon F. Seltzer, *The Vision of Melville and Conrad: A Comparative Study* (Athens: Ohio University Press, 1970); Cedric Watts, *A Preface to Conrad* (London and New York: Longman, 1982); and R. A. Gekoski, *Conrad: The Moral World of the Novelist* (New York: Barnes and Noble, 1978).

6. Cox, *Joseph Conrad*, 9, 11.

7. As Mark Twain's mysterious stranger tells Theodore: "[Y]ou are but a *thought*—a vagrant thought, a useless thought, a homeless thought, wandering forlorn among the empty eternities!" See "The Mysterious Stranger," in *The Mysterious Stranger and Other Stories* (New York: New American Library, 1962), 253.

8. Frank Kermode, *The Sense of an Ending: Studies in the Theory of Fiction* (London: Oxford University Press, 1967).

9. Robert M. Adams, *Strains of Discord: Studies in Literary Openness* (Ithaca, N.Y.: Cornell University Press, 1958).

10. Alan Warren Friedman, *The Turn of the Novel* (New York: Oxford University Press, 1966), xv.

11. Friedman's study of the evolution of the modern novel substantiates a point made by Mark Schorer in his essay "Technique as Discovery," in Philip Stevick, ed., *The Theory of the Novel* (New York: Free Press, 1967): "Under the 'immense artistic preoccupations' of James and Conrad and Joyce, the form of the novel changed, and with the technical change, analogous changes took place in substance, in point of view, in the whole conception of fiction. And the final lesson of the modern novel is that technique is not the secondary thing that it seemed to Wells, some external machination, a mechanical affair, but a deep and primary operation; not only that technique *contains* intellectual and moral implications, but that it discovers them" (72). Schorer credits the technique of modern fiction with totally assimilating

the complexity of modern consciousness and penetrating "the depths of our bewilderment" (83).

12. Bernard Bergonzi, *The Situation of the Novel* (London: Macmillan, 1970), 13.

13. Bergonzi also notes that "[t]he author became less of a presence, . . . and dwindled to a voice, a commentator obtruding from time to time through the chinks of an increasingly autonomous narrative, to offer reflections or speculations on the action. It was inevitable that with the advent of a consciously dramatic and personal form of the novel, this remnant of the authorial presence would be swept away. The principles . . . of Flaubert and James, of Conrad and Ford and Joyce, banished the obtrusive narrator, and stressed the ideal of the novel as a self-contained, self-sufficient work of art, whose creator would be conspicuously absent" (Ibid., 190).

14. David Lodge, *The Novelist at the Crossroads and Other Essays on Fiction and Criticism* (Ithaca, N.Y.: Cornell University Press, 1971), 60.

15. Malcolm Bradbury, *Possibilities: Essays on the State of the Novel* (London: Oxford University Press, 1973), 27, 7.

16. David H. Richter, *Fable's End: Completeness and Closure in Rhetorical Fiction* (Chicago: University of Chicago Press, 1974), 6.

17. Alan Warren Friedman, *Multivalence: The Moral Quality of Form in the Modern Novel* (Baton Rouge: Louisiana State University Press, 1978), 16.

18. Friedman speaks of a "double self-consciousness" in modern "multivalent" fiction that displays narrative reflexivity and a self-dramatized narrator (Ibid., 2).

19. D. A. Miller, *Narrative and Its Discontents: Problems of Closure in the Traditional Novel* (Princeton, N.J.: Princeton University Press, 1981).

20. See, in particular, *Nineteenth-Century Fiction* 33, no. 1 (1978), *Critical Inquiry* 7, no. 1 (1980) and 7, no. 4 (1981), and *Yale French Studies,* no. 67 (New Haven, Conn.: Yale University Press, 1984).

21. See Brooks, *Reading for the Plot,* especially the concluding chapter, "Endgames and the Study of Plot," 313–23.

22. According to Brooks, "[e]nds, it seems, have become difficult to achieve. In their absence, or their permanent deferral, one is condemned to playing: to concocting endgames, playing in anticipation of a terminal structuring moment of revelation that never comes, creating the space of an as-if, a fiction of finality. There is a wait for an end that never achieves satisfaction. When ending comes, it is more in the nature of stalemate than victory. . . . Our most sophisticated literature understands endings to be artificial, arbitrary, minor rather than major chords, casual and textual rather than cosmic and definitive. Yet they take place: if there is no spectacular denouement, no distribution of awards and punishments, no tie-up, through marriages and death, of all the characters' lives, there is a textual finis—we have no more pages to read" (Ibid., 313–14).

23. "[T]he bitterest contradictions and the deadliest conflicts are carried on in every individual breast capable of feeling and passion" (*SS*, 161).

24. The narrator admits that even though he gave the Northman the wrong course as a test to see whether he was telling the truth, "it proves nothing. . . . I believe—no, I don't believe. I don't know. At the time I was certain. . . . I don't know whether I have done stern retribution—or murder; . . . I don't know. I shall never know" (TH, 80). But this ironic realization is partly muted when the woman throws her arms around the narrator's neck: "She knew his passion for truth" (TH, 81). Conrad's final paragraph partly regains the intense incertitude: "'I shall never know,' he repeated, sternly, disengaged himself, pressed her hands to his lips, and went out" (TH, 81). For an extended treatment of "The Tale" as a dramatization of epistemological uncertainty, see Lothe, Conrad's Narrative Method, 72–86. Lothe convincingly relates the narrative complexity of the text and the emphasis on incertitude in the ending to Conrad's pervasive skepticism, but the closing scene of "The Tale" still comes across as fairly typical late-Victorian melodrama. Lothe acknowledges the melodramatic elements yet argues, as I have regarding many of the stories discussed in this study, that these elements contribute to the creation of "a modernist text offering conflicting interpretive possibilities" (86).

25. Lawrence Graver notes that this is one of Conrad's rare uses of a Maupassantian surprise ending, but, unlike its employment in "An Outpost of Progress," the resulting effect is not shocking but "crudely sentimental": "Instead of providing his story with 'a sting in its tail,' Conrad ends with a gentle touch of benevolence" (LG, 128).

26. Graver rightly states that "[t]he final pages of 'Tomorrow,' in which Conrad tries to convince the reader of [Bessie's] misery, are among the most discomforting examples of his 'adjectival insistence' . . . " (LG, 111).

27. In response to the Century's rejection of "Freya," Conrad wrote Garnett (4 August 1911): "As to faking a 'sunny' ending to my story I would see all the American Magazines and all the american (sic) Editors damned in heaps before lifting my pen for that task" (CL, 4:469. But Garnett did write Conrad's literary agent, Pinker, that he had detected "a certain weakness in the manipulation of the tragedy at the close" (CL, 4:470).

28. Najder cites the letter to Arthur T. Quiller-Couch (23 December 1897) in which Conrad affirms that as the solitary author writes "he thinks only of a small knot of men—three or four perhaps—the only ones who matter" as evidence that Conrad wrote for an elite readership (ZN, 217).

# Works Cited

Adams, Robert M. *Strains of Discord: Studies in Literary Openness*. Ithaca, N.Y.: Cornell University Press, 1958.

Anderson, Walter E. "'Falk': Conrad's Tale of Evolution." *Studies in Short Fiction* 25 (1988): 101–8.

Baines, Jocelyn. *Joseph Conrad: A Critical Biography*. New York: McGraw-Hill, 1960.

Bakker, J. "Crossing the Shadow-Line." *Dutch Quarterly Review of Anglo-American Letters* 5 (1975): 195–205.

Barnes, Djuna. *Nightwood*. New York: New Directions, 1937.

Baum, Paul Franklin. "A Source." *Modern Language Notes* 33 (1918), 312–14.

Benson, Carl. "Conrad's Two Stories of Initiation." *PMLA* 69 (1954): 46–56.

Bergonzi, Bernard. *The Situation of the Novel*. London: Macmillan, 1970.

Billy, Ted. "'Dead in the Centre': Conrad's Confrontation with Nothingness." *Studies in the Humanities* 5 (1976): 38–43.

Birrell, T. A. "The Simplicity of *Typhoon*: Conrad, Flaubert, and Others," *Dutch Quarterly Review of Anglo-American Letters* 10 (1980): 272–95.

Bonney, William W. *Thorns and Arabesques: Contexts for Conrad's Fiction*. Baltimore: Johns Hopkins University Press, 1980.

Borges, Jorge Luis. "The Analytical Language of John Wilkins," *Other Inquisitions: 1937–1952*. Translated by Ruth L. C. Simms. Austin: University of Texas Press, 1965.

Bradbury, Malcolm. *Possibilities: Essays on the State of the Novel*. London: Oxford University Press, 1973.

Brooks, Peter. *Reading for the Plot: Design and Intention in Narrative*. New York: Random House, 1985.

Bruss, Paul S. "'Typhoon': The Initiation of Jukes," *Conradiana* 5 (1973): 46–55.

———. "'The End of the Tether': Teleological Diminishing in Conrad's Early Metaphor of Navigation." *Studies in Short Fiction* 13 (1976): 311–20.

———. *Conrad's Early Sea Fiction*. Lewisburg, Pa.: Bucknell University Press, 1979.

Butte, George. "What Silenus Knew: Conrad's Uneasy Debt to Nietzsche." *Comparative Literature* 41 (1989): 155–69.

Campbell, Joseph. *Occidental Mythology*. New York: Penguin, 1964.

Carter, Ernest. "Classical Allusion as the Clue to Meaning in Conrad's 'Il Conde.'" *Conradiana* 3 (1971–72): 55–62.

Chaikin, Milton. "Zola and Conrad's 'The Idiots.'" *Studies in Philology* 52 (1955): 502–7.

Chon, Sooyoung. "'Typhoon': Silver Dollars and Stars." *Conradiana* 22 (1990): 25–43.

Cioran, E. M. *The Temptation to Exist*. Translated by Richard Howard. New York: Quadrangle, 1968.

Conrad, Jessie. *Joseph Conrad as I Knew Him*. Garden City, N.Y.: Doubleday, 1926.

Conrad, Joseph. *The Complete Works of Joseph Conrad*. 24 vols. Canterbury Edition. Garden City, N.Y.: Doubleday, Page, 1924.

———. Preface to *The Shorter Tales of Joseph Conrad*. Garden City, N.Y.: Doubleday, Page, 1924.

Cox, C. B. *Joseph Conrad: The Modern Imagination*. London: Dent, 1974.

Crawford, John. "Another Look at 'Youth.'" *Research Studies* 37 (1969): 154–56.

Culbertson, Diana. "'The Informer' as Conrad's Little Joke." *Studies in Short Fiction* 2, 4 (1974): 430–33.

Curley, Daniel. "The Writer and the Use of Material: The Case of 'The Secret Sharer.'" *Modern Fiction Studies* 13 (1967): 179–94.

Daiches, David. *The Novel and the Modern World*. Chicago: University of Chicago Press, 1939.

Daleski, H. M. *Joseph Conrad: The Way of Dispossession*. New York: Holmes and Meier, 1976.

David, Deirdre. "Selfhood and Language in 'The Return' and 'Falk.'" *Conradiana* 8 (1974): 137–47.

Davidson, Arnold E. *Conrad's Endings: A Study of the Five Major Novels*. Ann Arbor: University of Michigan Press, 1984.

Day, Robert A. "The Rebirth of Legatt." *Literature and Psychology* 13 (1963): 74–81.

Dussinger, Gloria R. "'The Secret Sharer': Conrad's Psychological Study." *Texas Studies in Language and Literature* 10 (1969): 559–608.

Eggenschwiler, David. "Narcissus in 'The Secret Sharer': A Secondary Point of View." *Conradiana* 11 (1979): 23–40.

Ellis, James. "Kurtz's Voice: The Intended as 'The Horror!'" *English Literature in Transition* 19 (1976): 105–10.

Emmett Jr., V. J. "'Youth': Its Place in Conrad's Oevre." *Connecticut Review* 4 (1970): 49–58.

Epstein, Hugh. "'Where He Is Not Wanted': Impression and Articulation in 'The Idiots' and 'Amy Foster.'" *Conradiana* 23 (1991): 217–32.

Evans, Frank B. "The Nautical Metaphor in 'The Secret Sharer.'" *Conradiana* 7 (1975): 3–16.

Farmer, J. S., and W. E. Henley. *Slang and Its Analogues*. New York: Arno, 1970.

Fielding, Henry. *The Life of Mr. Jonathan Wild the Great*. New York: New American Library, 1961.

Ford, Ford Madox. *Joseph Conrad: A Personal Remembrance*. London: Duckworth, 1924.

———. *Return to Yesterday*. New York, London: Liveright, 1932.

Forster, E. M. "Joseph Conrad: A Note." In *Abinger Harvest*. New York: Harcourt Brace Jovanovich, 1936.

Fowles, John. *The Magus*. New York: Dell, 1965.

Friedman, Alan. *The Turn of the Novel*. New York: Oxford University Press, 1966.

Friedman, Alan Warren. *Multivalence: The Moral Quality of Form in the Modern Novel.* Baton Rouge: Louisiana State University Press, 1978.

Gekoski, R. A. *Conrad: The Moral World of the Novelist.* New York: Barnes and Noble, 1978.

Gonzales, N. V. M. "Time as Sovereign: A Reading of Joseph Conrad's 'Youth.'" *Literary Apprentice* 17 (1954): 106–22.

Graver, Lawrence. "'Typhoon': A Profusion of Similes." *College English* 24 (1962): 62–64.

———. "Critical Confusion and Conrad's 'The End of the Tether.'" *Modern Fiction Studies* 9 (1963–64): 390–93.

———. *Conrad's Short Fiction.* Berkeley and Los Angeles: University of California Press, 1969.

Greim, Eberhard. "Rhetoric and Reality in Conrad's 'Typhoon.'" *Conradiana* 24 (1992): 21–32.

Guerard, Albert. *Conrad the Novelist.* Cambridge: Harvard University Press, 1958.

Guetti Jr., James L. *The Rhetoric of Joseph Conrad.* Amherst, Mass.: Amherst College Press, 1960.

———. *The Limits of Metaphor: A Study of Melville, Conrad, and Faulkner.* Ithaca, N.Y.: Cornell University Press, 1967.

Gurko, Leo. *Joseph Conrad: Giant in Exile.* New York: Macmillan, 1962.

Hagopian, John V. "The Pathos of 'Il Conde.'" *Studies in Short Fiction* 3 (1965): 31–38.

Hawthorn, Jeremy. *Joseph Conrad: Language and Fictional Self-Consciousness.* Lincoln: University of Nebraska Press, 1979.

———. Introduction to *The Shadow-Line.* Oxford World's Classics Edition. Oxford and New York: Oxford University Press, 1985.

———. *Joseph Conrad: Narrative Technique and Ideological Commitment.* London: Edward Arnold, 1990.

Hay, Eloise Knapp. *The Political Novels of Joseph Conrad: A Critical Study.* Chicago and London: University of Chicago Press, 1963.

Henricksen, Bruce. *Nomadic Voices: Conrad and the Subject of Narrative.* Urbana and Chicago: University of Illinois Press, 1992.

Hepburn, Allan. "Collectors in Conrad's 'The Informer.'" *Studies in Short Fiction* 29 (1992): 103–12.

Herbert, Wray C. "Conrad's Psychic Landscape: The Mythic Element in 'Karain,'" *Conradiana* 8 (1976): 225–32.

Hervouet, Yves. "Conrad and Maupassant: An Investigation into Conrad's Creative Process." *Conradiana* 14 (1982): 83–111.

Hobson, Robert W. "A Textual History of Conrad's 'An Outpost of Progress,'" *Conradiana* 9 (1979): 143–63.

Hoffman, Stanton de Voren. *Comedy and Form in the Fiction of Joseph Conrad.* The Hague: Mouton, 1969.

Hoffmann, Charles G. "Point of View in 'The Secret Sharer.'" *College English* 23 (1962): 651–54.

Hughes, Douglas A. "Conrad's 'Il Conde': A Deucedly Queer Story." *Conradiana* 7 (1975): 17–25.

James, Henry. *The Art of the Novel*. New York: Scribner, 1962.

Jean-Aubry, G. *Joseph Conrad: Life and Letters*, Two Volumes. Garden City, N.Y.: Doubleday, Page, 1927.

Johnson, Bruce. "Conrad's 'Karain' and *Lord Jim*," *Modern Language Quarterly* 24, no. 1 (1963): 13–20.

———. "Conrad's 'Falk': Manuscript and Meaning." *Modern Language Quarterly* 26 (1965): 267–84.

———. *Conrad's Models of Mind*. Minneapolis: University of Minnesota Press, 1971: 177–204.

Karl, Frederick R. *Joseph Conrad: The Three Lives*. New York: Farrar, Straus and Giroux, 1979.

Karl, Frederick R., and Laurence Davies, eds. *The Collected Letters of Joseph Conrad*. 4 vols. Cambridge: Cambridge University Press, 1983–90.

Kehler, Joel R. "The Centrality of the Narrator in Conrad's 'Falk'" *Conradiana* 6 (1974): 19–30.

———. "'The Planter of Malata': Renouard's Sinking Star of Knowledge," *Conradiana* 8 (1976): 148–62.

Kermode, Frank. *The Sense of an Ending: Studies in the Theory of Fiction*. London: Oxford University Press, 1967.

Kirschner, Paul. "Conrad and Maupassant: Moral Solitude and 'A Smile of Fortune.'" *Review of English Literature* 8 (1966): 62–77.

———. *Conrad: The Psychologist as Artist*. Edinburgh: Oliver and Boyd, 1968.

Knowles, Owen. "Conrad and Mérimée: The Legend of Venus in 'The Planter of Malata.'" *Conradiana* 11 (1979): 177–84.

Kolupke, Joseph. "Elephants, Empires, and Blind Men: A Reading of the Figurative Language in Conrad's 'Typhoon.'" *Conradiana* 20 (1988): 71–85.

Kramer, Dale. "Conrad's Experiments with Language and Narrative in 'The Return.'" *Studies in Short Fiction* 25 (1988): 1–11.

Krieger, Murray. "Conrad's 'Youth': A Naive Opening to Art and Life." *College English* 20 (1959): 275–80.

Lafferty, William. "Conrad's 'A Smile of Fortune': The Moral Threat of Commerce." *Conradiana*, 7 (1975): 63–74.

Land, Stephen K. *Conrad and the Paradox of Plot*. London: Macmillan, 1984.

Leiter, Louis H. "Echo Structures: Conrad's 'The Secret Sharer.'" *Twentieth-Century Literature* 5 (1960): 159–75.

Lester, John A., Jr. *Journey Through Despair: 1880–1914*. Princeton, N.J.: Princeton University Press, 1968.

Lodge, David. *The Novelist at the Crossroads and Other Essays on Fiction and Criticism*. Ithaca, N.Y.: Cornell University Press, 1971.

Loe, Thomas. "*Heart of Darkness* and the Form of the Short Novel." *Conradiana* 20 (1988): 33–44.

Lothe, Jakob. *Conrad's Narrative Method*. Oxford: Clarendon, 1989.

Lucas, Michael A. "Styles in 'An Outpost of Progress' and 'The Lagoon.'"
    *Conradiana* 21 (1989): 203–20.
Mathews, James W. "Ironic Symbolism in Conrad's 'Youth.'" *Studies in Short
    Fiction* 2 (1972): 117–23.
Maupassant, Guy de. *Pierre and Jean*. Translated by Leonard Tancock. Har-
    mondsworth, England: Penguin, 1979.
McLauchlan, Juliet. "The 'Value' and 'Significance' of *Heart of Darkness*."
    *Conradiana* 15 (1983): 3–21.
———. "Conrad's Heart of Emptiness: 'The Planter of Malata.'" *Conradiana*
    18 (1986): 180–92.
Meckier, Jerome. "The Truth about Marlow." *Studies in Short Fiction* 19
    (1982): 373–79.
Meyer, Bernard C. *Joseph Conrad: A Psychoanalytic Biography*. Princeton,
    N.J.: Princeton University Press, 1967.
Miller, D. A. *Narrative and Its Discontents: Problems of Closure in the Tradi-
    tional Novel*. Princeton, N.J.: Princeton University Press, 1981.
Miller, J. Hillis. "Joseph Conrad." *Poets of Reality: Six Twentieth Century
    Writers*. Cambridge: Harvard University Press, 1965: 13–67.
Milne, Fred L. "Marlow's Lie and the Intended: Civilization as the Lie in *Heart
    of Darkness*." *Arizona Quarterly* 44 (1988): 106–12.
Montag, George E. "Marlow Tells the Truth: The Nature of Evil in *Heart of
    Darkness*." *Conradiana* 3 (1971–72): 93–97.
Moynihan, William T. "Conrad's 'The End of the Tether': A New Reading."
    *Modern Fiction Studies* 4 (1958): 173–77.
Murdoch, Iris. *The Sea, The Sea*. New York: Penguin, 1978.
Nadelhaft, Ruth L. *Joseph Conrad*. Atlantic Highlands, N.J.: Humanities Press
    International, 1991.
Najder, Zdzisław. *Joseph Conrad: A Chronicle*. New Brunswick, N.J.: Rutgers
    University Press, 1983.
Nettels, Elsa. *James and Conrad*. Athens: University of Georgia Press, 1977.
Nietzsche, Friedrich. "On the Prejudices of Philosophers." In *Beyond Good
    and Evil*, translated by Walter Kauffmann, 9–32. New York: Ran-
    dom House, 1966.
———. "On Truth and Lie in an Extra-Moral Sense." In *The Portable Nietzsche*,
    translated by Walter Kaufmann, 42–47. New York: Viking, 1968.
O'Hara, J. D. "Unlearned Lessons in 'The Secret Sharer,'" *College English* 26
    (1965): 444–50.
Otten, Terry. "The Fall and After in 'The Secret Sharer.'" *Southern Humanities
    Review* 12 (1978): 221–30.
Owen, Guy. "Conrad's 'The Lagoon.'" *The Explicator* 18 (May 1960): Item
    no. 47.
Pater, Walter. *Selected Writings of Walter Pater*. Edited by Harold Bloom.
    New York: New American Library, 1974.
Pinsker, Sanford. "'The End of the Tether': Conrad's Death of a Sailsman."
    *Conradiana* 3 (1971–72): 74–76.

Poe, Edgar Allan. "The Philosophy of Composition." In *Essays and Reviews,*
    13–25. New York: Library of America, 1984.
Ray, Martin S. "The Gift of Tongues: The Languages of Joseph Conrad."
    *Conradiana* 15 (1983): 83–109.
———. "Language and Silence in the Novels of Joseph Conrad." *Conradiana*
    16 (1984): 19–40.
Richter, David H. *Fable's End: Completeness and Closure in Rhetorical Fiction.*
    Chicago: University of Chicago Press, 1974.
Rising, Katharine. "The Complex Death of Kayerts." *Conradiana* 23 (1991):
    157–69.
Rose, Jonathan. *The Edwardian Temperament: 1895–1919.* Athens: Ohio Uni-
    versity Press, 1986.
Roussel, Royal. *The Metaphysics of Darkness.* Baltimore: Johns Hopkins Uni-
    versity Press, 1971.
Said, Edward W. *Joseph Conrad and the Fiction of Autobiography.* Cam-
    bridge: Harvard University Press, 1966.
Schenck, Mary-Lou. "Seamanship in Conrad's 'The Secret Sharer.'" *Criticism*
    15 (1973): 1–15.
Schorer, Mark. "Technique as Discovery." In *The Theory of the Novel,* edited
    by Philip Stevick. New York: Free Press, 1967.
Schuster, Charles I. "Comedy and the Limits of Language in Conrad's 'Ty-
    phoon.'" *Conradiana* 16 (1984): 55–71.
Schwarz, Daniel R. "The Self-Deceiving Narrator of Conrad's 'Il Conde.'"
    *Studies in Short Fiction* 6 (1969): 187–93.
———. "Moral Bankruptcy in Ploumar Parish: A Study of Conrad's 'The
    Idiots.'" *Conradiana* 1 (1969): 113–16.
———. "The Significance of the Narrator in Conrad's 'Falk: A Reminis-
    cence.'" *Tennessee Studies in Literature* 16 (1971): 103–10.
———. "'A Lonely Figure Walking Purposefully: The Significance of Captain
    Whalley in Conrad's 'The End of the Tether.'" *Conradiana* 7 (1975):
    165–73.
———. "Achieving Self-Command: Theme and Value in Conrad's *The
    Shadow-Line.*" *Renascence* 29 (1977): 131–41.
———. *Conrad:* Almayer's Folly *to* Under Western Eyes. Ithaca, N.Y.: Cornell
    University Press, 1980.
———. *Conrad: The Later Fiction.* London: Macmillan, 1982.
Seltzer, Leon F. *The Vision of Melville and Conrad: A Comparative Study.*
    Athens: Ohio University Press, 1970.
Senn, Werner. *Conrad's Narrative Voice.* Bern: Francke Verlag, 1980.
Sherry, Norman. *Conrad's Eastern World.* Cambridge: Cambridge University
    Press, 1966.
Smith, Barbara Hernstein. *Poetic Closure: A Study of How Poems End.* Chi-
    cago: University of Chicago Press, 1968.
Smith, J. Oates. "The Existential Comedy of Conrad's 'Youth.'" *Renascence*
    16 (1963): 22–28.

Solomon, Barbara H. "Conrad's Narrative Material in 'The Inn of the Two Witches.'" *Conradiana* 7 (1975): 75–82.

Spittles, Brian. *Joseph Conrad: Text and Context*. Writers in Their Time Series. New York: St. Martin's Press, 1992.

Staten, Henry. "Conrad's Mortal Word." *Critical Inquiry* 12 (1986): 720–40.

Stein, William Bysshe. "The Lotus Posture and *Heart of Darkness*." *Modern Fiction Studies* 2 (1956–57): 167–70.

———. "Buddhism and *The Heart of Darkness*." *The Western Humanities Review* 2 (1957): 281–85.

———. "*The Heart of Darkness*: A Bodhisattva Scenario." *Orient/West Magazine* 9 (1964): 39–52.

———. "Conrad's East: Time, History, Action, and Maya." *Texas Studies in Literature and Language* 7 (1965): 265–83.

———. "The Eastern Matrix of Conrad's Art." *Conradiana* 1 (1969): 1–14.

———. "*The Secret Agent*: The Agon(ie)s of the Word." *boundary 2* 6 (1978): 521–40.

Steiner, Joan E. "Conrad's 'The Secret Sharer': Complexities of the Doubling Relationship." *Conradiana* 12 (1980): 173–86.

Steinmann, Theo. "Il Conde's Uncensored Story." *Conradiana* 7 (1975): 83–86.

Stevens, Wallace. "Sunday Morning." In *The Collected Poems of Wallace Stevens*. New York: Random House, 1954.

Stewart, Garrett. "Lying as Dying in *Heart of Darkness*." *PMLA* 95 (1980): 319–31.

Straus, Nina Pelikan. "The Exclusion of the Intended from Secret Sharing in Conrad's *Heart of Darkness*." *Novel* 20 (1987): 123–37.

Tanner, Tony. "'Gnawed Bones' and 'Artless Tales'—Eating and Narrative in Conrad." In *Joseph Conrad: A Commemoration*, edited by Norman Sherry, 17–36. London: Macmillan, 1976.

Tolley, A. T. "Conrad's Favorite Story." *Studies in Short Fiction* 3 (1966): 314–20.

Thomas, Lloyd S. "Conrad's 'Jury Rig' Use of the Bible in 'Youth.'" *Studies in Short Fiction* 17 (1980): 79–82.

Torgovnick, Marianna. *Closure in the Novel*. Princeton, N.J.: Princeton University Press, 1981.

Trethewey, Eric. "Language, Experience, and Selfhood in Conrad's *Heart of Darkness*." *Southern Humanities Review* 22 (1988): 101–11.

Twain, Mark. *The Mysterious Stranger and Other Stories*. New York: New American Library, 1962.

Vernon, John. *The Garden and the Map: Schizophrenia in Modern Literature*. Urbana: University of Illinois Press, 1973.

Walton, James. "Mr. X's 'Little Joke': The Design of Conrad's 'The Informer.'" *Studies in Short Fiction* 4 (1967): 322–33.

Watt, Ian. "Story and Idea in Conrad's *The Shadow-Line*." *Critical Quarterly* 2 (1960): 133–48.

———. *Conrad in the Nineteenth Century*. Berkeley and Los Angeles: University of California Press, 1979.

Watts, Cedric. *A Preface to Conrad*. London and New York: Longman, 1982.
————. *The Deceptive Text: An Introduction to Covert Plots*. Brighton, England: Harvester, 1984.
————. "The Narrative Enigma of Conrad's 'A Smile of Fortune.'" *Conradiana* 17 (1985): 131–36.
Wegelin, Christof. "MacWhirr and the Testimony of the Human Voice." *Conradiana* 7 (1975): 45–50.
Welles, Orson (with Oja Kodar). *The Big Brass Ring*. Santa Barbara, Calif.: Santa Teresa Press, 1987.
Weston, John Howard. "'Youth': Conrad's Irony and Time's Darkness." *Studies in Short Fiction* 11 (1974): 399–407.
Whitehead, Lee M. "The Active Voice and the Passive Eye: *Heart of Darkness* and Nietzsche's *The Birth of Tragedy*." *Conradiana* 7 (1975): 121–35.
Wiley, Paul L. *Conrad's Measure of Man*. Madison: University of Wisconsin Press, 1954.
Williams, George Walton. "Conrad's 'The Lagoon.'" *The Explicator* 23 (September 1964): Item no. 1.
Williams Jr., Porter. "The Matter of Conscience in Conrad's 'The Secret Sharer.'" *PMLA* 79 (1964): 626–30.
Wills, John Howard. "Adam, Axel, and 'Il Conde.'" *Modern Fiction Studies* 1 (1955): 22–25.
————. "Conrad's *Typhoon*: A Triumph of Organic Art." *North Dakota Quarterly* 30 (1962): 62–70.
————. "A Neglected Masterpiece: Conrad's 'Youth.'" *Texas Studies in Literature and Language* 4 (1962): 591–601.
Wollaeger, Mark A. *Joseph Conrad and the Fictions of Skepticism*. Stanford, Calif.: Stanford University Press, 1990.
Worth, George J. "Conrad's Debt to Maupassant in the Preface to *The Nigger of the 'Narcissus*,'" *Journal of English and Germanic Philology* 54 (1955): 700–704.
Wright, Walter F. *Romance and Tragedy in Joseph Conrad*. Lincoln: University of Nebraska Press, 1949.
Wyatt, Robert D. "Joseph Conrad's 'The Secret Sharer': Point of View and Mistaken Identities." *Conradiana* 5 (1973): 12–26.
Young, Gloria L. "Chance and the Absurd in Conrad's 'The End of the Tether' and 'Freya of the Seven Isles.'" *Conradiana* 7 (1975): 253–61.
Zuckerman, Jerome. "'A Smile of Fortune': Conrad's Interesting Failure." *Studies in Short Fiction* 1 (1964): 99–102.
————. "The Architecture of *The Shadow-Line*." *Conradiana* 3 (1971–72): 87–92.

# Index